Economic Growth and Environmental Sustainability

D1493718

A key area of public policy is the question of how, and how much, to protect the environment. At the heart of this is the twenty-year-old heated debate over the nature of the relationship between economic growth and environmental sustainability. Is environmental sustainability compatible with indefinite economic growth? Is environmentally sustainable economic growth, or 'green growth', a contradiction in terms?

This volume approaches this central problem by drawing on the theoretical resources of environmental and natural resource economics. Avoiding the confusion that often surrounds these issues the author provides rigorous and detailed expositions of the concept of sustainability, the Commoner-Ehrlich Equation, the Environmental Kuznets Curve, integrated environmental and economic accounting, the economics of climate change and environmental taxation. Individual chapters are organised as self-contained, state-of-the-art expositions of the core issues of environmental economics, with extensive cross-referencing from one chapter to another, in order to guide the student and policy maker through these complex problems.

Paul Ekins breaks new ground in defining the conditions of compatibility between economic growth and environmental sustainability, and provides measures and criteria by which the environmental sustainability of economic growth, as it occurs in the real world, may be judged. It is argued that 'green growth' is not only theoretically possible but economically achievable and the author shows what environmental and economic policies are required to bring this about. Finding the political will to implement these policies is the challenge at the heart of sustainable development.

Economic Growth and Environmental Sustainability will be welcomed by students of and researchers in environmental economics and environmental studies, as well as all interested policy makers.

Paul Ekins is Reader in Environmental Policy in the Department of Environmental Studies, Keele University and a Programme Director of the sustainable development charity Forum for the Future, directing its Sustainable Economy Programme. He is the author of numerous books, including *A New World Order* (1992) and editor, with M. Max-Neef, of *Real-Life Economics* (1992). In 1994 he received the United Nations Environmental Programme Global 500 Award 'for outstanding environmental achievement'.

Economic Growth and Environmental Sustainability

The prospects for green growth

Paul Ekins

London and New York

First published 2000 by Routledge
11 New Fetter Lane, London EC4P 4EE

Simultaneously published in the USA and Canada
by Routledge
29 West 35th Street, New York, NY 10001

Routledge is an imprint of the Taylor & Francis Group

Typeset in Baskerville by The Florence Group, Stoodleigh, Devon
Printed and bound in Great Britain by Biddles Ltd, Guildford and King's Lynn

British Library Cataloguing in Publication Data
A catalogue record for this book is available from the British Library

Library of Congress Cataloging in Publication Data
Ekins, Paul.
  Economic growth and environmental sustainability: the prospects
  for green growth / Paul Ekins.
    p.   cm.
  Includes bibliographical references.
  1. Sustainable development. 2. Economic development –
  Environmental aspects. I. Title.
  HD75.6.E36   1999
  338.9–dc21   99–12976
                  CIP

ISBN 0–415–17332–9 (hbk)
ISBN 0–415–17333–7 (pbk)

Contents

List of figures   vi
List of tables   vii
Preface and acknowledgements   ix

1 Introduction   1

2 Perceptions of environmental scarcity   23

3 Wealth creation: distinguishing between production, welfare, growth and development   51

4 The concept of environmental sustainability   70

5 Accounting for production and the environment   115

6 Population, affluence, technology and environmental impacts   154

7 Review and critique of the Environmental Kuznets Curve hypothesis   182

8 The dividends from environmental taxation   215

9 Decision making and the costs related to climate change   242

10 Sustainability and sulphur emissions: the case of the UK, 1970–2010   283

11 Conclusions   316

Bibliography   327
Index   353

Figures

1.1	World carbon emissions from fossil fuel burning, 1950–94	10
2.1	External costs of pollution and a Pigouvian tax	27
3.1	A three-factor model of the creation of wealth and utility	51
3.2	Stocks, flows and welfare in the process of production	53
4.1	Setting a sustainable level for an environmental function	83
4.2	Mapping processes of unsustainability	85
4.3	Production, consumption and environmental impacts of and in country N	88
4.4	The role of ecological capital in production and welfare creation	98
4.5	A framework for sustainability indicators	107
5.1	Flows of money as they are entered into the national accounts	118
5.2	Development of environmental capacity in period t	131
6.1	Benefits and costs of environmental policies	164
7.1	Possible shapes of environment–income relationships	186
7.2	Relationship between income and environmental performance for twenty-two OECD countries	198
7.3	Income/population distribution and EKC turning points	209
8.1	Optimal environmental taxation with no abatement	215
8.2	Optimal environmental taxation with abatement	217
8.3	The effect of wage subsidies on unemployment	221
9.1	US GDP loss projections, average of all EMF models	262
9.2	Possible paths for energy and economic efficiency	272
9.3	Consumption per capita under a base scenario and four scenarios of control of global warming	281
10.1	UK SO_2 emissions, 1970–95	284
10.2	SO_2 emissions by fuel use, 1970–95	284
10.3	SO_2 emissions by fuel user, 1970–95	285

Tables

1.1 Symptoms of environmental unsustainability and their causes 7

1.2 Greenhouse gases and their contribution to the anthropogenic greenhouse effect 9

1.3 Moderate, severe and extreme land degradation by region 17

1.4 World production, reserves and R/P ratios for various minerals at various dates 20

3.1 Has the UK become more 'developed' from 1961–91? 62

4.1 Types of sustainability and their interactions 71

4.2 Calculations of global environmental space and necessary reductions from four European studies 91

4.3 Alternative classifications of environmental media and themes 109

4.4 Classification of environmental themes based on environmental functions 110

4.5 Implications of environmental sustainability principles 111

5.1 Schema for an environmental balance sheet 130

5.2 Environmental distances and methods of valuation 133

5.3 Matrix for the construction of the Sustainability Gap 145

6.1 Relative pollution (or damage) intensities of polluting or low-polluting practices 167

7.1 Environment–income relationships for different indicators from different studies 188

7.2 Income and environmental performance 199

7.3 Growth of GDP, energy and fertiliser use, various emissions and municipal waste 202

7.4 Emissions of four pollutants in 2050 209

7.A1 Econometric relationships between income and various environmental indicators 211

8.1 Changes in environmental pressures between 1990 and 2010 across themes 233

8.2	Total taxes as per cent of end-user price of petrol (households)	238
8.3	Some environmental taxes in some OECD countries	239
9.1	Estimates of annual damage and adaptation costs from global warming incurred by the US economy and the global economy	248
9.2	Damage due to doubling of atmospheric CO_2 equivalents for different regions	249
9.3	Sectoral competitiveness effects for a carbon and energy tax	265
9.4	Export share of various UK sectors as a percentage of total UK exports in 1989	267
10.1	Sectoral value-added, energy use, SO_2 emissions and related intensities	290
10.2	Factors contributing to SO_2 reductions	295
10.3	The effect of structural change on SO_2 reductions	298
10.4	Some estimates of damage costs from sulphur emissions	301
10.5	Marginal and average costs of SO_2 abatement from 1980 levels	304
10.6	SO_2 emissions from large combustion plants and the LCPD limits	307
10.7	Total SO_2 emissions and the SSP limits	308
10.8	SO_2 emissions from power stations and the HMIP limits	309

Preface and acknowledgements

This book is the outcome of work that has been carried out since 1990. Its foundation is my Ph.D. thesis, which was successfully completed at the end of 1996. Early versions of several of the chapters have also been published in various books and journals, as listed at the end of these Acknowledgements. However, all the chapters have been updated since their publication, and many of them have been substantially revised to take account of new external developments or the evolution of my thinking. The major conclusions of the work remain unchanged by these revisions, which have mainly served, I hope, to clarify the arguments, but there have also been one or two changes of emphasis. An example is the increased weight now given in Chapter 8 to the arguments that express scepticism over the likelihood that environmental taxation will yield a substantial increase in output as well as environmental improvement.

The central focus of the book is the relationship between environmental sustainability and economic growth, and the prospects of achieving environmentally sustainable economic growth, the 'green growth' of the book's sub-title. However, to do this theme justice I have had to range widely through many issues in environmental and resource economics and beyond. Therefore a number of the chapters may be read as more or less self-contained, detailed expositions of the state-of-the-art in some of these issues. These include the concept of sustainability (Chapter 4), integrated environmental and economic accounting (Chapter 5), the Commoner-Ehrlich equation ($I = PCT$, Chapter 6), the Environmental Kuznets Curve (Chapter 7), the dividends from environmental taxation (Chapter 8), the economics of climate change (Chapter 9) and the economics of reducing UK sulphur emissions (Chapter 10). However, I have also tried to give extensive cross-references from one chapter to another, in order to develop the argument as a whole and show how these individual issues are related to it.

Because the book originated as a Ph.D. thesis, there are a number of places where treatment of the issues becomes quite technical. I decided against removing, or oversimplifying, these, partly so that the book can be used with relatively advanced students at universities, but also because the general reader can safely skip the more technical sections without imperilling their ability to grasp the book's essential arguments and conclusions. I hope, though, that in all cases where a more technical treatment has been used, its study will yield a deeper understanding than would have been possible without it.

Grateful thanks are due to Ron Smith at Birkbeck College, London, for his helpful advice as supervisor of the thesis on which this book is based; to John Proops at Keele University, for his comments on an early draft of the thesis; and to Terry Barker of Cambridge Econometrics and the University of Cambridge, to whom I owe a special intellectual debt. Other people whose work has inspired me, as will become apparent from the book itself, include Roefie Hueting, Herman Daly, David Pearce, Kerry Turner, Rudolph de Groot and many others. Many thanks to all of them. Thanks are also due to Michael Jacobs, Sandrine Simon and Stefan Speck, for many stimulating discussions during our joint work, which is reflected in the book as referenced below. Similar thanks are due to co-members of the so-called Nairobi Group which produced the UNEP Manual on environmental accounting referenced under Chapter 5 below. Of course, I remain responsible for any errors of fact or interpretation which may remain, and which will hopefully be corrected as the fascinating issue at the book's heart, the growth/environment relationship, continues to unfold.

Paul Ekins
Keele and London
January 1999

The references of the early previously published versions of this work are as follows:

Chapters 1, 6

Ekins, P. and Jacobs, M. 1995 'Environmental Sustainability and the Growth of GDP: Conditions for Compatibility' in Bhaskar, V. and Glyn, A. Eds *The North, the South and the Environment*, Earthscan, London, pp.9–46.

Chapter 2

Ekins, P. 1993 'Limits to Growth and Sustainable Development: Grappling with Ecological Realities', *Ecological Economics*, Vol. 8 No. 3 (December), pp.269–88.
Ekins, P. 1996 'Economics, Environment and Resources' in Warner, M. Ed. *International Encyclopedia of Business and Management*, Routledge, London, pp.1253–68.

Chapter 3

Ekins, P. 1992 'A Four-Capital Model of Wealth Creation' in Ekins, P. and Max-Neef, M. Eds *Real-Life Economics: Understanding Wealth Creation*, Routledge, London/New York, pp.147–55.

Chapter 4

Ekins, P. 1994 'The Environmental Sustainability of Economic Processes: a Framework for Analysis' in Van den Bergh, J. and Van der Straaten, J. Eds *Concepts, Methods and Policy for Sustainable Development: Critiques and New Approaches*, Island Press, Washington, DC, pp.25–55.

Ekins, P. 1995 'Economic Policy for Environmental Sustainability' in Crouch, C. and Marquand, D. Eds *Re-inventing Collective Action: From the Global to the Local*, Book Special Issue of *Political Quarterly*, pp.33–53.

Ekins, P. 1997 'Sustainability as the Basis of Environmental Policy' in Dragun, A.K. and Jakobsson, K.M. Eds *Sustainability and Global Environmental Policy: New Perspectives*, Edward Elgar, Cheltenham, pp.33–61.

Chapters 4, 5

Ekins, P. and Simon, S. 1998 'Determining the Sustainability Gap: National Accounting for Environmental Sustainability', Office for National Statistics, London, pp.147–67.

Chapter 5

Ekins, P. 1995 'Failures of the System of the National Accounts' in Van Dieren, W. Ed. *Taking Nature into Account*, report to the Club of Rome, Copernicus/ Springer Verlag, New York, chap. 5, pp.60–81.

UNEP (United Nations Environment Programme) 1999 (forthcoming) *Integrated Environmental and Economic Accounting: an Operational Manual*, UNEP, Geneva.

Chapter 7

Ekins, P. 1997 'The Kuznets Curve for the Environment and Economic Growth: Examining the Evidence', *Environment and Planning A*, Vol. 29, pp.805–30.

Chapter 8

Ekins, P. 1997 'On the Dividends from Environmental Taxation' in O'Riordan, T. Ed. *Ecotaxation*, Earthscan, London, pp.125–62.

Chapter 9

Ekins, P. 1995 'Rethinking the Costs Related to Global Warming: a Survey of the Issues', *Environmental and Resource Economics*, Vol. 6 No. 3 (October), pp.231–77.

Ekins, P. 1996 'Economic Implications and Decision-Making in the Face of Global Warming', *International Environmental Affairs*, Vol. 8 No. 3, pp.227–42.

Ekins, P. and Speck, S. 1998 'The Impacts of Environmental Policy on Competitiveness: Theory and Evidence' in Barker, T. and Köhler, J. *International Competitiveness and Environmental Policies*, Edward Elgar, Cheltenham, pp.33–69.

1 Introduction

1.1 OUTLINE OF THE BOOK

This book is an investigation of the relationship between environmental sustainability, economic growth and human welfare, with an emphasis on the first two. This relationship is an important one. Certainly economic growth remains perhaps the prime objective of economic policy. Certainly too environmental sustainability has over the last ten years climbed high up the public agenda. Whether these two public objectives are in fact compatible or not is of critical concern. Indeed, for some economists, 'the link between sustainable resource use and growth is, perhaps, the key economic question' (Goldin and Winters 1995: 2).

The link is also a much studied one. The literature on economic growth and the environment is huge, as the very partial bibliography for this book indicates. Yet the widest disagreement about the relationship remains. Common (1995: 112ff.) notes a difference of opinion between (some) economists and (some) biologists on this issue. But there are just as significant disagreements between economists. Thus Goldin and Winters (1995: 14) conclude that 'economic growth and development are perfectly consistent with environmental protection', while for Daly (1990: 1), 'sustainable growth is an oxymoron'.

Common (1995: 45) asks the question 'Which view is correct?' and immediately answers it: 'No-one really knows. Reasonable people may reasonably differ on the question.'

This book will arrive at a somewhat different conclusion. It will show that the views in question are both correct in that they are consistent with the assumptions on which they are based. This shifts the question to: what are their assumptions? and which assumptions are correct? The book identifies the assumptions and explores their theoretical and practical implications. It makes some assumptions of its own in order to arrive at an operational definition of sustainability. It identifies the conditions for economic growth to be compatible with environmental sustainability. It examines the evidence of the link between economic performance and different environmental impacts. It finds that actually the relationship between economic growth and environmental sustainability, in general and across different environmental dimensions, can be characterised in some detail, and broad conclusions that are useful for policy makers can be drawn.

The book proceeds from the hypothesis, evidence for which is presented later in this chapter, that environmental resources are not currently being used sustainably. This has resulted in political commitments to achieve sustainable development and a need to know what impacts, if any, moves towards sustainable development will have on economic growth.

Chapter 2 is an historical survey of previous approaches to the use and potential scarcity of environmental resources, from Malthus and the classical economists, through the evolution of environmental and resource economics, to the empirical work of Barnett and Morse, the 'Limits to Growth' debate and the emergence and dominance of the concept of sustainable development. From the environmental and resource economics literature it clearly emerges that economic optimality and unsustainability can be compatible. Sustainability therefore need not result from the pursuit of optimality. This suggests that, if sustainable development is the objective of environmental policy, sustainability will have to be explicitly pursued in its own terms.

In the third chapter a conceptual model is developed which identifies the contribution of the environment to the economic process, and that of both the environment and the economic process to human welfare. The model diagrammatically links a production function and a utility function in a way that is implicit in much of the literature but has not been explicitly described in this way before. It is intended that the model be a realistic description of the underlying phenomena, so that it purposely retains elements that are intractable to formal analysis and avoids simplifying assumptions, so that it is not developed mathematically. However, the model provides the underpinning conceptual basis for the chapters that follow. It is initially used to distinguish between different kinds of growth, failure to do which has resulted in much of the confusion in the literature. It is then used to relate these kinds of growth to the concepts of development and human welfare.

Chapter 4 both defines and elaborates on the concept of environmental sustainability as it relates to economic processes. It sets out a framework of analysis that defines the concept and makes it operational, by postulating a set of principles of environmental sustainability. Various ways of characterising the sustainable use of non-renewable resources are treated mathematically and compared, such that the characteristics relate to the distinction between weak and strong sustainability which is often drawn in the literature. Environmental sustainability emerges from the analysis in this chapter as an overarching concept within which environmental policy can be coherently and consistently organised.

Whether economic growth and environmental sustainability are compatible is then at least partly dependent on how economic growth is measured.

Substantial efforts have now been invested in exploring how to adjust the national accounts for environmental impacts. Insofar as these adjustments are made, accounting for economic activity will better reflect the environmental contribution to it, and economic growth will be more closely related to a real increase in wealth creation. Chapter 5 explores how the national accounts might incorporate the environmental dimension, and suggests how the disagreement in the literature as to how defensive expenditures should be treated in the national accounts might be resolved. It further concludes that, although the concept of sustainable national income has played an important intellectual role in providing a rationale for adjusting the national accounts for environmental effects, it cannot be derived from simple subtractions from GNP, as has sometimes been proposed. However, this chapter derives a new indicator, here called the 'sustainability gap', which is a monetary indicator, based on current prices, of the gap between current and sustainable use of the environment.

Reconciling economic growth with environmental sustainability will require the reduction of the environmental impacts of current activity to sustainable levels and then their maintenance at these levels while incomes continue to grow. The technological change required to achieve this is explored through a numerical simulation using the Commoner-Ehrlich equation, $I = PCT$, which indicates a necessary reduction in T, the overall environmental impact per unit of consumption, of up to 90 per cent over fifty years if sustainability and income growth are to be attained. Various relationships between P, C and T are possible, which may make such a reduction more or less difficult. Reducing T without constraining growth in C can be achieved only through costless technical change or the correction of government or market failures. Evidence is presented which suggests that there are a surprisingly large number of opportunities for such change and such corrections.

Recent work has shown that, beyond a certain level of income, some aspects of environmental quality improve with further economic growth, a relationship that has been called an Environmental Kuznets Curve. It has been suggested that this may be a general characteristic of the growth/environment relationship. However, Chapter 7's examination of the evidence leads to several rather different conclusions. First, the studies' empirical results, taken as a whole, show a number of contradictions, and in some of the studies the underlying econometrics is weak. Second, the level of income in poor countries is such that, even if their environmental quality were to improve once the hypothesised incomes had been attained, the environmental damage caused in attaining this level would be very great, and much would be irreversible, with unpredictable but possibly very serious results. Third, with regard to high income countries, there is no evidence that their environment overall is improving. Indeed, an aggregate environmental dataset for these countries weakly suggests the contrary, while the datasets of the OECD and European Commission suggest this rather more strongly. The analysis in this chapter shows that the comforting hypothesis of an Environmental Kuznets Curve, which in its strongest version suggests that all that is required for growth-sustainability compatibility is the achievement of a certain income level, must be rejected.

Chapter 8 explores the hypothesis that a possible source of current inefficiency which may allow a win-win outcome for growth and the environment is the taxation system. The double dividend hypothesis suggests that shifting taxation onto the use of environmental resources from other factors of production may improve environmental quality and increase economic efficiency by reducing tax distortions. The chapter shows how this is theoretically plausible, though still controversial. Modelling suggests that any positive effects on output from a tax shift are likely to be small at best. The impact on employment could be more significant. However, the principal benefit of environmental taxation will be environmental improvement, and this should remain its primary objective.

The following two chapters apply the insights of the earlier work to two environmental problems of considerable policy concern, to see whether it is likely that environmental sustainability with regard to these problems can be achieved without constraining economic growth. Chapter 9 explores the issue of reducing carbon emissions in order to mitigate climate change. Much of the modelling literature suggests that the substantial reductions that are required for climate stability will incur substantial costs. However, expressing these costs as a reduction in the growth rate shows them actually to be rather small. In addition, the chapter identifies a number of reasons why they may also have been overestimated. When the secondary benefits of reducing carbon emissions are also taken into account, a significant reduction in carbon emissions appears possible at zero net cost. Beyond that, the cost of stabilising atmospheric concentrations of greenhouse gases depends largely on the development of non-carbon energy technologies.

The second case study in Chapter 10 looks at the UK emissions of sulphur dioxide and measures that have been taken to control them, most recently the limits of the Second Sulphur Protocol (SSP) and national limits on sulphur emissions from the power generation sector. The limits are explicitly based on the sustainability principle of the critical load. The possible evolution of sulphur emissions in the UK is analysed, and the costs estimated of applying the SSP and national constraints. Somewhat surprisingly, it emerges that the very substantial reductions in UK sulphur emissions mandated by these constraints are unlikely to be costly and will not have an appreciable macroeconomic effect.

Overall this book attempts to resolve the controversy that continues to permeate the issue of the growth-environment relationship. It maps out the conditions for compatibility for economic growth and environmental sustainability, refuting those who have declared sustainable economic growth to be an oxymoron. It also shows that such conditions have never yet been achieved by an industrial economy, and are stringently binding on future economic performance, refuting the proposition that environmental sustainability will be a more or less inevitable outcome from economic growth. The analysis and case studies suggest that sustainable economic growth is not only theoretically possible, but technologically feasible and economically achievable. But it requires determined, long-term policy commitment, and fundamental changes in consumer lifestyles and preferences. The major uncertainty is now whether the political commitment, and the willingness to embrace the necessary preference and lifestyle changes, will be forthcoming.

1.2 ENVIRONMENTAL UNSUSTAINABILITY

1.2.1 Unsustainability: some conclusions

In the twenty years 1972–92, between the UN Conference on the Environment in Stockholm and that on Environment and Development (UNCED) in Rio de Janeiro, scientific opinion gradually hardened that the damage being inflicted by human activities on the natural environment renders those activities unsustainable. It has become accepted that the activities cannot be projected to continue into the future either because they will have destroyed the environmental conditions necessary for that continuation, or because their environmental effects will cause massive, unacceptable damage to human health and disruption of human ways of life.

This is not the place for a detailed review of the evidence that has led to the scientific consensus, but the now perceived seriousness of the problem can be illustrated by a number of quotations of the conclusions of bodies which have conducted such a review. Thus the Business Council for Sustainable Development stated in its report to UNCED: 'We cannot continue in our present methods of using energy, managing forests, farming, protecting plant and animal species, managing urban growth and producing industrial goods' (Schmidheiny 1992: 5). The Brundtland Report, which initiated the process which led to UNCED, had formulated its perception of unsustainability in terms of a threat to survival: 'There are thresholds which cannot be crossed without endangering the basic integrity of the system. Today we are close to many of these thresholds; we must be ever mindful of the risk of endangering the survival of life on earth' (WCED 1987: 32–3).

The World Resources Institute (WRI), in collaboration with both the Development and Environment Programmes of the United Nations, concluded, on the basis of one of the world's most extensive environmental databases, that: 'The world is not now headed toward a sustainable future, but rather toward a variety of potential human and environmental disasters' (WRI 1992: 2). The World Bank, envisaging a 3.5 times increase in world economic output by 2030, acknowledged that: 'If environmental pollution and degradation were to rise in step with such a rise in output, the result would be appalling environmental pollution and damage' (World Bank 1992: 9). The Fifth Action Programme of the European Community acknowledges that 'many current forms of activity and development are not environmentally sustainable' (CEC 1992a: 4), as indicated by 'a slow but relentless deterioration of the environment of the Community, notwithstanding the measures taken over the last two decades' (CEC 1992b: 3).

In its annual *State of the World* reports, the Worldwatch Institute has documented current environmental damage, concluding in 1993:

> The environmentally destructive activities of recent decades are now showing up in reduced productivity of croplands, forests, grasslands and fisheries; in the mounting cleanup costs of toxic waste sites; in rising health care costs for cancer, birth defects, allergies, emphysema, asthma and other respiratory diseases; and in the spread of hunger.
>
> (Brown *et al.* 1993: 4–5)

These trends mean: 'If we fail to convert our self-destructing economy into one that is environmentally sustainable, future generations will be overwhelmed by environmental degradation and social disintegration' (ibid.: 21).

Little wonder, therefore, that in 1992 two of the world's most prestigious scientific institutions saw fit to issue a joint statement of warning:

> Unrestrained resource consumption for energy production and other uses ... could lead to catastrophic outcomes for the global environment. Some of the environmental changes may produce irreversible damage to the earth's capacity to sustain life. ... The future of our planet is in the balance.
>
> (RS and NAS 1992: 2, 4)

1.2.2 Unsustainability: the symptoms

The concept of sustainability will be discussed and amplified further in Chapter 4. For the present, an environmentally unsustainable activity is simply taken to be one which cannot be projected to continue into the future, because of its negative effect either on the environment or on the human condition of which it is a part. The main symptoms of unsustainability, with their principal causative agents and the geographical level to which they mainly apply, can be simply grouped as in Table 1.1. This grouping is similar, but not identical, to that in OECD (1994a: 12), which separates eutrophication out from toxic contamination, groups traffic with urban air pollution under 'urban environmental quality', and, most interestingly, ignores the depletion of non-renewable resources altogether, although it includes energy supply under 'General Indicators'. This seems

Table 1.1 Symptoms of environmental unsustainability and their causes

Problem	Principal agents
Pollution	
Greenhouse effect/climate change (global)	Emissions of CO_2, N_2O, CH_4, CFCs (and HFCs), O_3 (low level), PFCs, SF_6
Ozone depletion (global)	Emissions of CFCs
Acidification (continental)	Emissions of SO_2, NO_x, NH_3, O_3 (low level)
Toxic contamination (continental)	SO_2, NO_x, O_3, particulates, heavy metals, hydrocarbons, carbon monoxide, agrochemicals, organo-chlorides, eutrophiers, radiation, noise
Renewable resource depletion	
Species extinction (global)	Land use changes (e.g. development, deforestation), population pressure, unsustainable harvest (e.g. overgrazing, poaching), climate change, ozone depletion (in future)
Deforestation (global, regional)	Land use changes, population pressure, unsustainable harvest (e.g. hardwoods), climate change (in future)
Land degradation/loss of soil fertility ((bio)regional, national)	Population pressure, unsustainable agriculture, urbanisation, development, climate change (in future)
Fishery destruction (regional, national)	Overfishing, destructive technologies, pollution, habitat destruction
Water depletion ((bio)regional, national)	Unsustainable use, climate change (in future)
Landscape loss	Land use changes (e.g. development), changes in agriculture, population pressure
Non-renewable resource depletion	
Depletion of various resources	Extraction and use of fossil fuels, minerals
Other environmental problems	
Congestion (national)	Waste-disposal, traffic

something of an omission. Another similar list is found in Holmberg and Karlsson (1995: 98), with the addition of 'the introduction of new and strange organisms'.

From an inspection of Table 1.1, two immediate observations can be made about the symptoms of unsustainability. The first is the extent to which the problems are interlinked. The second is the fact that the most important problems are those of pollution and depletion of renewable resources.

1.2.3 Unsustainability: the evidence

Any survey of the evidence for environmental unsustainability which is serving only as an introduction is bound to be partial and simplified. At best, it can give a quantitative indication of the most important trends and processes and act as a preliminary overview, from which a more detailed exploration of the literature can be undertaken if desired. This survey draws heavily on a number of compendia of information, including the biannual *World Resources*, produced by the World Resources Institute in collaboration with UNDP and UNEP, the annual *State of the World* reports published by the Worldwatch Institute, which are in turn compiled from a wide range of primary datasets and research reports and, for European data, the encyclopaedic *Dobris Assessment* (EEA 1995). It should be emphasised that uncertainty is a characteristic of much of the data, especially with reference to processes of global environmental change, which means that the results of environmental unsustainability could be more or less serious than is currently believed likely to be the case.

Climate change

The greenhouse effect is a universally accepted phenomenon whereby certain gases (most importantly water vapour and carbon dioxide, CO_2) in the earth's atmosphere are more transparent to the short-wave radiation from the sun than to the long-wave reradiation from the earth's surface. Thus the atmosphere traps solar radiation in a similar manner to a greenhouse. Without the greenhouse effect the earth's average surface temperature would be $-18°C$ rather than $+15°C$ (Cline 1992: 15).

Human activities, especially economic activities, are adding significantly to the atmosphere's greenhouse gases, by the emission most importantly of CO_2 from the burning of fossil fuels and deforestation, but also of chlorofluorocarbons, methane, nitrous oxide and other gases. This has led to scientific speculation about an anthropogenic greenhouse effect which could lead to further warming of the earth's average surface temperature, and which perhaps has already done so, and to climate change.

Carbon dioxide levels in the atmosphere have risen about 25 per cent since pre-industrial times due to human activities; the concentration of methane has more than doubled from pre-industrial levels. The different warming potentials of different gases are commonly converted to 'carbon dioxide equivalents', and a benchmark for the assessment of anthropogenic global warming is often taken as the doubling of these CO_2-equivalents over pre-industrial levels. On current trends this is expected to be reached in the second half of the next century.

Table 1.2 gives some estimates of the contributions to global warming of the various greenhouse gases (GGs) and the reductions in GG emissions that are thought necessary to stabilise their atmospheric concentrations.

Table 1.2 Greenhouse gases and their contribution to the anthropogenic greenhouse effect

Greenhouse gas	Main anthropogenic sources[a]
Carbon dioxide (CO_2)	Fossil fuel burning (77%), deforestation (23%)
Chlorofluorocarbons (CFCs)	Various industrial uses
Related gases (HFCs, HCFCs)	(e.g. refrigerators)
Methane (CH_4)	Rice paddies, livestock digestion, gas leakage
Nitrous oxide (N_2O)	Biomass and fossil fuel burning, fertiliser use, land use changes
Other[b]	Fossil fuel burning

	Warming potential ($CO_2 = 1$)[c]	% contribution to greenhouse effect[d] 1980–90	1990+	Rate of growth, 1992, %[e]	IPCC rec. reduction, %[f]
CO_2	1	55	61	0.5	> 60
CFCs etc.	7,300[g]	24	11.5	4	75–85[g]
CH_4	21	15	15	0.9	15–20
N_2O	290	6	4	0.25	70–80
Other[b]	40[h]	—	8.5	n.a	—

Notes:
a *Source:* Leggett (1990: 17)
b Principally tropospheric ozone, O_3, formed by NO_x and CO emissions
c *Source:* Houghton *et al.* (1990: 60), 100-year integration time
d *Source:* Houghton *et al.* (1990: xx, xxi). The 1990+ column is the GG's relative contribution over 100 years from 1990
e *Source:* WRI (1992: 205)
f *Source:* Houghton *et al.* (1990: xviii)
g For CFC-12, the major CFC contributor to global warming
h For tropospheric ozone

Figure 1.1 shows the growth of emissions of carbon dioxide from fossil fuel burning since 1950, with 1995 emissions being the highest ever. So were 1995 global average temperatures. The three hottest years since record-keeping began in 1866 have all occurred in the 1990s (Brown, Flavin and Kane 1996: 66).

The effects of failing to halt global warming are still highly uncertain. Possible negative effects include the extinction of species that fail either to migrate or adapt to changed climatic conditions; loss of agricultural productivity where weather patterns become hotter, drier or more erratic than is agriculturally desirable; sea-level rise with inundation of coastal zones; a greater frequency of extreme weather conditions; and an increase in vector-borne diseases. The possible benefits of global warming are enhanced agricultural productivity in some mid- and high-latitude areas; and greater comfort with reduced heating costs in presently colder areas, which might offset somewhat the greater discomfort of higher temperatures in presently hotter areas.

Over the past 100 years global sea-level has risen by 10–25cm, with the likelihood that this is related to the simultaneous rise in global

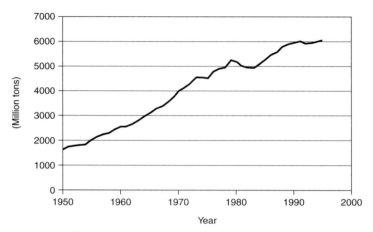

Figure 1.1 World carbon emissions from fossil fuel burning, 1950–94
Source: Brown, Flavin and Kane (1996: 65)

temperatures of 0.3–0.6°C (Houghton *et al.* 1996: 26, 29, 30). A sea-level
rise of 1 metre, at the top of the Intergovernmental Panel on Climate
Change (IPCC) range of possibilities for the next century (ibid.: 41), could
displace populations, destroy low-lying urban infrastructure, inundate
arable lands, contaminate fresh-water supplies, and alter coastlines. The
impacts could be disastrous. For example, the flooding of the deltas of
Egypt and Bangladesh would deprive the former of 15 per cent of its
arable land and the latter of 14 per cent of its net cropped area (Woodwell
1990: 128). Worldwide, hundreds of millions of people could be displaced.

The IPCC's most recent estimate of global warming is 0.9–3.5°C by 2100
relative to 1990: 'the average rate of warming would probably be greater
than any seen in the last 10,000 years' (Houghton *et al.* 1996: 39–40). Cline
(1991) extended the trends of the IPCC 1990 report, projecting a mean
global warming of about 10°C over 250–300 years. Such an increase could
multiply by several times IPCC estimates of damage, e.g. a sea-level rise of
4 metres would seem likely (Cline 1991: 915).

As shown in Table 1.2, GG emissions derive mainly from the burning
of fossil fuels, deforestation and various agricultural practices. While a
majority of the world's climate scientists, as represented by the IPCC,
consider that 'the balance of evidence suggests that there is a discernible
human influence on climate change' (Houghton *et al.* 1996: 39–40), there
continue to be sceptics over both the science and the likelihood of significant damage from climate change (see, for example, Beckerman 1991;
A. Solow 1991; ESEF 1996).

Broome (1992: 16) observes: 'Human-induced global warming, then,
could possibly start a chain of events that could lead to the extinction of
civilization or even of humanity. This is a remote possibility, but it exists.'

Thus the global warming issue in its scope and uncertainties exemplifies many of the common characteristics of the modern environmental problematique and is the subject of detailed discussion in Chapter 9.

Ozone depletion

Production of CFCs peaked in 1988 and had fallen by 77 per cent by 1994 (Brown *et al.* 1996: 14). The terms of the Montreal Protocol, most recently revised in December 1995, provide for the production of CFCs to have been phased out in industrial countries by 1996 and in developing countries ten years later, with other ozone-depleters being subject to different timetables of control. However, it will be 2005 before stratospheric levels of chlorine, which is what damages the ozone layer, start to decline. Until then they will continue to increase, both because of the quantities of CFCs already produced that are not yet in the lower atmosphere and, once there, the length of time (ten to fifteen years) it takes for them to reach the upper atmosphere (Meadows *et al.* 1992: 148). Even if all governments comply with the Montreal Protocol, full recovery of the ozone layer is not expected until about 2100 (WRI 1996: 316).

The 3 per cent loss of ozone noted in 1991 over the US and other temperate countries could cause as many as 12 million extra skin cancers in the US alone (WRI 1992: 200). Another 3 per cent depletion, expected by the year 2000 (ibid.: 200), could cause a further 9–18 per cent increase in such cancers (Meadows *et al.* 1992: 145). Measurements over Antarctica in September 1991 indicated a 50–60 per cent ozone loss (WRI 1992: 200).

Probably more important than its effects on human health are the impacts of ozone depletion on ecosystems. For example, marine phytoplankton produce as much biomass as all terrestrial ecosystems combined and are at the base of the marine food chain. Increased UV-B radiation reduces phytoplankton productivity, which was 6–12 per cent lower than usual inside and outside the Antarctic ozone-hole region in the spring of 1990. One estimate suggests that a 16 per cent reduction in ozone concentration may lead to a 5 per cent reduction in phytoplankton and a 6–9 per cent reduction in fish stocks. A 10 per cent reduction in marine phytoplankton would reduce the annual oceanic uptake of CO_2 by 5 gigatonnes of carbon, about as much as is released annually through the combustion of fossil fuels (EEA 1995: 526).

Ozone depletion in the upper atmosphere causes cooling, which offsets some of the greenhouse effect (Houghton *et al.* 1996: 20). This effect will start to diminish once the stratosphere starts to recover during the next century.

Acid deposition

The principal effects of the deposition of acid atmospheric pollutants are the acidification of soils and water, and damage to forests, crops and buildings, and to human health (see p. 301). Water acidification results in a decline of fish and other aquatic life, which is now pronounced in several countries: more than 20 per cent of Sweden's 85,000 medium and large lakes are acidified, with 4,000 having suffered major biological damage. The number of highly acidified lakes in New York's Adirondack mountains grew from 4 to 51 per cent between the 1930s and 1970s. Of the affected lakes, 90 per cent had lost all their fish (McCormick 1989: 37). From 1940–75 1,750 out of 5,000 lakes in southern Norway became completely devoid of fish because of acidification, with another 900 lakes being seriously affected. In the mid-1990s a survey of 13,600 fish stocks in southern Norway revealed that 2,600 had become extinct and 3,000 had reduced their number of individuals (EEA 1995: 98).

Symptoms of forest decline grew fast during the 1980s: by 1986 87 per cent of West Germany's firs were damaged, two-thirds of them seriously (McCormick 1989: 30). A study in 1990 concluded that 75 per cent of Europe's forests were suffering damaging levels of sulphur deposition, and 60 per cent of them were enduring nitrogen deposition above their critical loads (WRI 1992: 198). Fifty-four per cent of Czech forests have suffered irreversible damage (EEA 1995: 561). Although overall acid emissions in Western Europe have fallen sharply in the 1990s, more than a quarter of Germany's trees, 55 per cent of Poland's trees and 28 per cent of Norway's trees still suffer from more than 25 per cent defoliation because of acidification (Brown, Flavin and Kane 1996: 70). In Europe as a whole 24 per cent of trees had defoliation greater than 25 per cent in 1992, up 2 per cent from the year before (EEA 1995: 560). Most recently it has been reported that evidence is growing 'that damage to ecosystems from acid deposition may be more fundamental and long-lasting than was first believed' (WRI 1998: 182).

In addition to damage to ecosystems, damage to crops and buildings from acid deposition is thought to be economically substantial, although there is considerable uncertainty over the actual figures. Damage estimates include $31 billion in 1983 to US wheat, corn, soybeans and peanuts; $500 million in eleven European countries in 1981 (McCormick 1989: 40–1); and the cost to Europe of corrosion of buildings has been estimated by the UN Economic Commission for Europe as $1.3–6.5 billion per annum (cited in McCormick 1989: 48).

Trends for global emissions of the principal acid gases, sulphur dioxide and nitrogen oxide, are difficult to assess. In OECD countries sulphur dioxide emissions fell by 25 per cent over the 1980s and by 38 per cent between 1970 and the late 1980s, even while GDP grew by 30 per cent over the 1980s, and 77 per cent from 1970. By 1993 SO_2 emissions were down by 32 per cent from 1980 levels (OECD 1995a: 19–23). However, nitrogen oxide emissions grew by 12 per cent from 1970–87, largely because road traffic grew by 93 per cent, faster than GDP (OECD 1991b: 21, 23, 53, 61). By 1993 OECD NO_x emissions were at practically the same level as in 1980 (OECD 1995a: 24–8).

The USSR and countries of Eastern Europe all had higher per capita sulphur emissions in 1989 than in Western Europe and North America (WRI 1992: 64), though the restructuring of and, in some cases, reduction in economic activity since then will have reduced these in some countries. Nitrogen dioxide emissions, on the other hand, are more similar between the West and former Communist countries, reflecting the former's far higher rate of car ownership and use. While lack of data prevents any clear quantitative assessment of Third World trends in this area, it is clear that air pollution in rapidly industrialising countries is increasingly damaging both the environment and human health. Already in the late 1980s China had the third highest emissions of SO_2 in the world (McCormick 1989: 197). These grew by 20 per cent between 1989 and 1993, leaving China with ambient concentrations of SO_2 that are among the highest in the world (WRI 1998: 117). On these trends acid depositions there may one day exceed those experienced in Eastern and Central Europe, where both acid rain levels and forest damage were acute in the 1980s.

Toxic pollution

There are many pollutants which are injurious to health and only the briefest account of their scope and effects can be given here. The great majority of these pollutants are the products of industrial development, but two significant exceptions are pollution by sewage and from indoor fires. Indoor pollution, from cooking or heating by burning wood, straw or dung, adversely affects 400–700 million people and contributes to acute respiratory infections that kill up to 4 million children annually, permanently damaging the health of many more, children and adults (World Bank 1992: 52). Sewage is the major cause of water contamination worldwide, with 1.7 billion people still not having access to adequate sanitation, a number that grew by 70 million during the 1980s. Sewage treatment is rarer still: in developing countries over 95 per cent is untreated before being discharged into surface waters (WRI 1992: 167). Universal access to clean water and adequate sanitation would cut the incidence of Third World country disease dramatically: per year, 2 million fewer child deaths from diarrhoea, and 200 million episodes of the illness; 300 million fewer people with roundworm; 150 million fewer with schistosomiasis (World Bank 1992: 49). Needless to say, growing water scarcity (see pp. 17–18) and pollution from other sources are making access to clean water and adequate sanitation more difficult to provide.

Pollutants from industrialisation are seriously degrading the quality of air, water and soils. Outdoor air pollution has three principal man-made sources – domestic energy use, vehicular emissions and industrial production – all of which increase with economic growth unless they are abated. The World Bank notes:

If the projected growth in demand for vehicular transport and electricity were to be met with the technologies currently in use, emissions
of the main pollutants deriving from these sources would increase five-
fold and elevenfold, respectively, by about 2030. Yet in the mid-1980s
more that 1.3 billion people, mainly in the Third World, already lived
in cities with air which did not meet WHO standards for SPM
(suspended particulate matter), causing an estimate 300,000–700,000
premature deaths.

(World Bank 1992: 52)

Lead is the other major pollutant in Third World cities, principally from
car exhausts. Over half the newborns in Mexico City have blood lead
levels high enough to impair their development (WRI 1992: 51), while in
Bangkok children have lost an average of four IQ points or more by age
7 because of lead pollution (World Bank 1992: 53). In China studies have
found that as many as 50 per cent of children have unacceptably high
blood lead levels (WRI 1998: 59). How bad such situations can become
is illustrated by Katowice in Poland, where lead levels in soil reach about
fifty times the permitted level. One study showed the difference in IQ
between children with high and low blood lead levels to be 13 points, and
indicated other profound health differences (WRI 1992: 62).

Central and Eastern Europe provide many examples of the damage
uncontrolled industrialism can cause. Among 'serious environmental health
hazards', WRI lists:

high levels of sulphur dioxide, oxides of nitrogen, lead and other
hazardous chemicals in the ambient air . . .; contamination of groundwater and soil by nitrogenous fertilizers, pesticides and toxic metals;
contamination of rivers by sewage and industrial waste; and a variety
of chemical, physical, biological and psychosocial health hazards in
the workplace.

(WRI 1992: 62)

In assessing the results of such a situation in Russia, the head of the
Russian Academy of Medical Sciences shocked the world with his frank-
ness: 'We have already doomed ourselves for the next 25 years.' Eleven
per cent of Russian infants suffer from birth defects. 'With half of the
drinking water and a tenth of the food supply contaminated, 55% of school
age children suffer health problems' (Brown *et al.* 1993: 10).

Although in OECD countries the health impacts of pollution are much
less severe, they can still be substantial. A 1998 report for the UK
Government found that three pollutants that contributed to poor air quality in UK cities (particulates, SO_2 and ozone) were responsible for 24,000
premature deaths a year (DOH 1998). On a per capita basis, 'the OECD
countries are overwhelmingly the world's major polluters, both within their

own borders and in their contribution to global environmental degradation' (WRI 1992: 18). Their 16 per cent of the world's population consumed 43 per cent of 1989's global production of fossil fuels, most of its production of metals and well over a proportionate share of industrial materials and forest products. Per capita consumption of resources in OECD countries is often several times the global average. For example, OECD countries account for 78 per cent of all road vehicles (OECD 1991a: 13). Because resources from economic activity eventually become wastes, the pollution emanating from these countries should come as no surprise: 40 per cent of global sulphur dioxide and 54 per cent of nitrogen oxides emissions; 68 per cent of industrial wastes by weight; 38 per cent of global potential warming impact from emissions of greenhouse gases (WRI 1992: 17). Chemicals represent a particular challenge. Around 100,000 different chemicals are in commercial production, with 200–300 new ones entering the market each year. According to EEA (1995: 591): 'Adequate toxicological and ecotoxicological data have been produced for only a very small fraction of the chemicals, and data on environmental pathways and ecotoxicological effects are even more sparse.' Despite long-standing and well-developed systems of waste management, in OECD countries 'industrial residues – acidic materials, heavy metals, and toxic chemicals – degrade soils, damage plants, and endanger food supplies' (WRI 1992: 18).

Species extinction

Norman Myers wrote in 1986:

> When we consider just the numbers involved, let alone the compressed time-frame of the episode, . . . we may suppose we are on the verge of one of the greatest extinction episodes to occur during the four billion years since the start of evolution. . . . The extinction spasm pending may well rank as the greatest impoverishment of Earth's species since the first flickerings of life.
>
> (Myers 1986: 4)

Yet, as the World Bank notes: 'The complex web of interactions that sustains the vitality of ecosystems can unravel even if only a small number of key species disappear' (World Bank 1992: 59). On no issue of unsustainability is human ignorance so profound as in its understanding of biodiversity. Identified species are fewer than 1.5 million, but over 30 million, of which over 90 per cent are insects, are thought to exist (ibid.: 60). At such levels of ignorance, figures of extinction rates are little more than informed speculation. Harvard biologist Edward O. Wilson puts the minimum loss of invertebrate species at 50,000 per year (Brown *et al.* 1992: 9). More certain is that the tropical forests, covering 6–7 per cent of the Earth's land surface, contain 50–90 per cent of all species. Myers places nearly 40 per cent of all species in the forests of Latin America outside Amazonia and those of Africa outside the Zaire basin (Myers 1986: 12), most of which look likely to disappear by the early years of the next century. The World Conservation Union considers that 34 per cent of the world's fish species are threatened with extinction (WRI 1998: 190). The Dobris Report on the European environment classifies as 'threatened' 42 per cent of Europe's mammal species, 45 per cent of its reptiles, 30 per cent of its amphibians and 52 per cent of its freshwater fish (EEA 1995: 222 (Table 9.10)). 'All the evidence points to the inescapable fact that the extent and quality of remaining natural ecosystems is in decline and that in certain cases this decline is accelerating' (ibid.: 220). Myers writes: 'We are unconsciously conducting a superscale experiment with Earth's biotas' (1986: 2). Unfortunately it is an experiment conducted in almost total ignorance, and which can never be repeated.

Deforestation

It is estimated that the Earth's forest cover is now only just over half what it was in pre-agricultural times, but the amount of undisturbed, primary forest in relatively large ecosystems is only about a fifth of the original amount (WRI 1998: 187). Europe has practically no original forests; the US outside Alaska has only 5 per cent of its original forests (Brown *et al.* 1991: 74). The large expanses of remaining primary temperate forests in Canada and the former Soviet Union, saved so far by their remoteness, are now also being felled, with Canada losing 200,000 ha p.a. (Brown *et al.* 1993: 6).

In tropical countries only half the original area of forests remains, and over half of this has already been logged or degraded in some way (Brown *et al.* 1991: 74). Moreover, the rate of tropical deforestation accelerated markedly during the 1980s, reaching 17 million ha p.a. in 1991, compared to 11.3 million ha in the early 1980s, an increase of 50 per cent (WRI 1992: 118). Some countries' deforestation has proceeded even faster than this. Thus Indonesia's rate has quadrupled since 1970, now destroying 1 million ha annually. Thailand's forest cover between 1961 and 1988 shrank from 55 per cent to 28 per cent (ibid.: 47). In 1990–5 deforestation in developing countries averaged 13.7 million ha p.a. (WRI 1998: 185).

Land degradation

In the past forty-five years 'about 11% of the Earth's vegetated soils have become degraded to the point that their original biotic functions are damaged and reclamation may be costly or, in some cases, impossible' (WRI 1992: 111). In total, by 1990 poor agricultural practices had contributed to the degradation of 562 million ha, about 38 per cent of cropland worldwide, with an additional 5–6 million ha lost each year to severe soil

Table 1.3 Moderate, severe and extreme land degradation by region

	Degraded area (DA) *(million hectares)*	*DA as per cent of* *vegetated land*
World	*1215.4*	*10.5*
Europe	158.3	16.7
Africa	320.6	14.4
Asia	452.5	12.0
Oceania	6.2	0.8
North America	78.7	0.4
Central America & Mexico	60.9	24.1
South America	138.5	8.0

Source: WRI (1992: 112)

degradation since then (WRI 1998: 156–7). Nearly 500 billion tons of topsoil have been lost since 1972 (Brown *et al.* 1993: 4), a process that continues at a rate of 24 billion tons a year (ibid.: 12). Table 1.3 shows how 'moderate, severe and extreme' land degradation affects different regions. EEA (1995: 152) classifies 'major soil threats' (with the percentage of European land area affected in brackets) as water erosion (115 million ha, or 12 per cent), wind erosion (4 per cent), acidification (9 per cent), pesticides (19 per cent), nitrates and phosphates (18 per cent), soil compaction (4 per cent), organic matter loss (0.3 per cent), salinisation (0.4 per cent) and waterlogging (0.1 per cent). Forty-four per cent of Spain's land area is affected by some kind of erosion. The activities principally leading to land degradation are deforestation, overgrazing and agriculture.

Water depletion

The most obvious reason for water scarcity, of course, is drought: about 80 arid and semi-arid countries with some 40 per cent of the world's population experience periodic droughts (WRI 1992: 160). Increasingly, however, rising levels of water use are threatening water scarcity. Global water use has risen by a factor of three, or by 50 per cent per capita, since 1950 (Brown *et al.* 1993: 22): 69 per cent of this is used for agriculture, 23 per cent for industry and 8 per cent for domestic uses. By the year 2025 water withdrawals for irrigation are expected to increase by 50–100 per cent and for industry by 100 per cent (WRI 1998: 189). Domestic use is also projected to rise sharply. Globally, water abstraction is currently increasing at a rate of 4–8 per cent per year (EEA 1995: 319). Such increases can only serve to exacerbate already severe trends in some places of falling water tables, depleted groundwater resources and inadequate supplies.

Thus in Beijing water tables have been falling 1–2 metres per year and a third of the wells have run dry, yet its total water demand in the year

2000 is projected to outstrip its current supply by 70 per cent (Brown *et al.* 1993: 26). The countries of the Middle East and North Africa face a situation of particular difficulty. Nearly all available supplies are being used, yet populations in some of the countries are projected to double over twenty-five years. The potential conflict in the situation is obvious, especially where water resources are shared. For example, 86 per cent of Egypt's water comes from the Nile, most of the waters of which originate in eight countries upstream. In Europe, over one-third of countries have 'low, very low or extremely low' water availability, and twenty countries receive a high proportion of their water from transboundary rivers (EEA 1995: 58, 60).

Water withdrawn for industrial and domestic uses is largely returned to surface water systems after use, but often in a polluted condition, where it can degrade the water resource for other users or damage the environment.

Fish depletion

In 1990 the total global fish catch declined for the first time in thirteen years. In 1989 the global fish catch had reached 100 million tonnes, but failed to reach that level in any of the subsequent three years (Brown *et al.* 1995: 33). By 1989 all the oceanic fisheries were being fished at or beyond their limit, with thirteen of the fifteen largest in decline (Brown *et al.* 1996: 4). The recovery of the fish catch to 101 million tonnes in 1993 and 1994 was largely due to an increasing contribution from aquaculture, but continuing population growth has meant that the global per capita fish catch has fallen from 19.4 to 18.0kg per person from 1988–94. Since 1977 30 per cent of US fish stocks have declined (WRI 1992: 179). In July 1992 Canada reacted to dwindling catches off Nova Scotia and Labrador by banning all cod and haddock fishing in the area for two years, at a cost of $400 million in unemployment compensation and retraining (Brown *et al.* 1993: 8). In the UK in 1996 for nearly half the stocks fished 'the spawning population was estimated to be at a level where there is a risk of stock collapse' (DETR 1997: 111).

Perhaps even more threatening to fish stocks in the long term than over-fishing is the ongoing pollution and destruction of coastal habitats where 90 per cent by weight of the world marine catch reproduces. Wetlands, mangroves and salt marshes are being rapidly cleared for urban, industrial and recreational uses: tropical countries have lost over 50 per cent of their mangroves and the US 50 per cent of its wetlands (WRI 1992: 177). Most of the world's sewage still flows untreated into coastal waters (ibid.: 176), its pollution augmented by a variety of toxic chemicals, and further pollution from rivers. Thus a 1991 survey of eighty-five coastal watersheds in the US found that upstream sources, including agricultural and urban run-off, accounted for about 70 per cent of the nitrogen and 60 per cent of the phosphorus in the estuaries studied (ibid.: 182). Such pollution can cause algal blooms, which have been reported from coastal areas around the world, and which can lead to mass kills of fish; or it can cut harvests, as in the US's Chesapeake Bay, which produced only one-eighth the oyster catch of a century ago (Brown *et al.* 1993: 8); or it can render fish unfit for human consumption. These trends augur very badly for the future of tropical developing countries, many with fast-growing populations, 60 per cent of whom currently rely on fish for 40 per cent or more of their protein.

Non-renewable resource depletion

The depletion of non-renewable resources (e.g. minerals, fossil fuels) which caused much of the anxiety about unsustainability in the 1970s (see, for example, Meadows *et al.* 1972), and which appears to be an unsustainable activity by definition, has declined dramatically in perceived importance. Despite growing fossil fuel use, proven reserves of fossil fuels are higher now than they have ever been: over 1 trillion barrels of oil, compared to about 650 million in 1971; 140 trillion cubic metres of natural gas, compared to 50 in 1971; and 1 trillion tonnes of coal (1971 figure not given in source). New discoveries and more efficient use of, and substitution away from, non-renewable resources has tended to keep constant, or even lengthen, the 'lifetime' of the reserves at current rates of use (defined as the known reserves/annual production, or R/P, ratio). The 1996 R/P ratios (where R is reserves, P is production) were 41 (31), 62 (38) and 224 (2300) for oil, natural gas and coal respectively (all data from BP 1997: 8, 24, 30). The figures in brackets are the 'lifetimes' of the fuels that were forecast in *Limits to Growth* (Meadows *et al.* 1974: 56, 58) back in the 1970s. There is no reason to think that ultimately recoverable reserves will not be much higher than today's estimates. For example, for oil some estimates put this figure at over 2 trillion barrels (WRI 1996: 277).

Similarly Table 1.4 shows the R/P ratio for seven minerals in 1970, 1988 and 1990, using three different sources of data. Although several of the 1990 R/P figures seem quite short periods of time, they are little changed from the 1970 figures. Some, indeed, have increased. Only lead and nickel appear to have become substantially more scarce, but the 1970 R/P ratio for nickel must be suspect, as it indicates a reserve level of the resource which must have been revised substantially downwards given the 1990 R/P ratio and interim production. The World Bank 500 year R/P ratio for zinc must be accounted doubtful in view of the other sources' estimates.

In one sense, any level of use of non-renewable resources is unsustainable, and, of course, new discoveries and the emergence of substitutes cannot be guaranteed. But the time-scales involved in this depletion now seem much less pressing than for pollution and the depletion of renewable resources. However, notwithstanding these favourable trends, fossil

Table 1.4 World production, reserves and R/P ratios for various minerals at various dates

Minerals	World production (million metric tons)		R/P ratios years[a]			Reserves ratio[b]
	1970[c]	1990[d]	1970[c]	1988[e]	1990[d]	
Copper	8.56	8.81	36	32	36	1.04
Aluminium	75[f]	109	100	1000	200	3.73[g]
Lead	3.5	3.37	26	12	21	0.77
Mercury	8.7[f]	5.8	13	—	22	—
Nickel	0.81[f]	0.94	150	59	52	0.72[g]
Tin	0.25	0.22	17	27	27	1.38
Zinc	5.35	7.33	23	500	20	1.17

Notes:
a R/P ratios can be interpreted as life expectancies at a constant rate of production with no new discoveries
b This reserves ratio has been calculated by dividing 1990 by 1970 world reserves, as given in sources c and d below (— indicates that the ratio could not be calculated from the data in these sources)
c *Source:* Meadows *et al.* (1972: 56–9)
d *Source:* WRI (1992: 320–1)
e *Source:* World Bank (1992: 37)
f This figure came from source d for the year 1975
g This figure came from source e, and is the reserves ratio for 1988 with respect to 1970

fuels are ultimately finite. Oil and natural gas reserves are also unevenly distributed geographically. Seventy-six per cent of known 1996 oil reserves are located in OPEC countries (currently comprising Algeria, Gabon, Indonesia, Iran, Iraq, Kuwait, Libya, Nigeria, Qatar, Saudi Arabia, United Arab Emirates, Venezuela). Seventy-three per cent of known 1996 natural gas reserves are located in the Middle East and former Soviet Union (BP 1997: 4, 20). Practically all countries outside these areas will become net importers of oil and natural gas before the middle of the next century. The World Energy Council's view of the implications of this is emphatic:

> There is a very high likelihood that some time between 2030 and 2080 supplies of oil and natural gas will be severely constrained, with the remaining reserves allocated to privileged users and top premium uses. Perceptions of impending supply shortfalls will cast a shadow forward well into the period between now and 2020.
>
> (WEC 1993: 104)

Interlinkages

One of the most striking observations about the symptoms of unsustainability is the number of interlinkages between them, unfortunately usually tending to reinforce their negative effects. Some of these are specifically noted in Table 1.1 or in the evidence given above, but there are many others. Thus deforestation is a major cause of land degradation and increases in sedimentation and downstream nutrient enrichment of rivers and lakes worldwide (WRI 1992: 169), as well as of species extinction and global warming. Climate change is likely to increase the rate of species extinction. Acid deposition kills forests and pollutes water sources. Two of the most promising non-ozone-depleting potential substitutes for CFCs, HFCs and HCFCs, are potent greenhouse gases. The extra UV-B radiation reaching the Earth due to ozone-depletion may damage fish larvae and juveniles, as well as the phytoplankton at the base of the food web, as noted on p. 11, and cause damage to crops (ibid.: 196). Toxic pollution of freshwater increases its effective scarcity for human purposes.

An example of the complexity of possible interlinkages is given by the following combination of environmental effects in North America:

> Climate change and acidification have led to decreases in dissolved organic carbon concentrations in North American lakes. Carbon absorbs UV radiation, which has, in turn, increased due to depletion of the ozone layer. In combination, these changes have resulted in much deeper penetration of UV radiation into lake waters and higher death and disease rates among fish and aquatic plants. This effect can be compounded by drought when sulfur compounds stored in lake sediments oxidize in response to falling water levels.
>
> (WRI 1998: 183–4)

One hundred and forty thousand lakes are at risk in this way.

Finally, practically all the problems are worsened, and the achievement of solutions to them rendered more difficult, by continuing population growth which adds around 90 million to human numbers each year.

Several of these effects, namely population growth, soil degradation and water depletion, have potentially worrying implications for the adequacy of the global food supply. Brown *et al.* (1996: 7) describe this as 'the defining issue': 'Globally, food scarcity may soon become the principal manifestation of continuing population growth and environmental mismanagement'. In 1995 world stocks of grain had declined to 49 days of consumption, the lowest level on record, largely because grain harvests since 1990 have all been below that year's record yield: 1995's harvest was 5 per cent below. The world's grainland area has declined by 9 per cent since 1981; from 1978–90 the irrigated area per person fell by 6 per cent and since 1990 there has been little or no growth in irrigation at all; there has been a decline in world fertiliser use since 1989; and, as has already been seen, the world fish catch has stopped growing. This is in the context of population growth of 90 million people per year, and the world's most populous country, China, changing from grain exporter to importer, as, in its industrialisation, it grows less grain and eats more meat. The prices of wheat, rice and corn all rose by about 30 per cent in 1995. Further price rises of that order would severely challenge the stability of countries that are both food importers and poor.

This is the complex and challenging context within which environmental economic policy must be formulated. For some analysts, the evidence of environmental damage cited above is either not conclusive enough to warrant action, or they believe that the economy will react appropriately to emerging environmental scarcity without policy intervention (see, for example, Bernstam 1991). Others believe that active intervention is justi-fied in order to achieve a 'sustainable development' that is compatible with continuing economic growth (see, for example, World Bank 1992). Others still believe that the environmental problems are evidence of limits to that growth (see, for example, Meadows *et al.* 1992). This book's prin-cipal purpose is to explore the reasons for and validity of these differences of opinion with a view to making a judgement between them. The next chapter gives some of the historical background to these positions and plots how, and why, they have come to be formulated.

2 Perceptions of environmental scarcity

The obvious importance of natural resources and the environment to economic activity and to human life in general has caused economists to be concerned about these issues since the dawn of economics as a mode of analysis. This chapter provides some insights into ways in which economists have expressed this concern, and how its focus has shifted as different issues have come to seem important. In moving from the early classical economists Malthus and Ricardo to more modern economic treatments of environmental degradation and the exhaustibility of resources, the chapter introduces some of the basic concepts and analytical and empirical techniques of environmental and resource economics, together with some of the controversies surrounding them. These concepts and techniques reappear and are treated in more detail as appropriate in subsequent chapters.

The chapter then surveys the literature that has arisen around the competing ideas of 'limits to growth' and 'sustainable development'. These ideas provide the essential starting point for this book's attempt in the chapters that follow to clarify the relationship between economic growth and environmental sustainability, and to define the conditions for compatibility between them.

2.1 EARLY HISTORY

Two of the earliest classical economists – Thomas Malthus and David Ricardo – were much exercised by the prospect of a growing human population in the context of a fixed quantity of agricultural land of differing fertility.

Malthus' theory of population, for which Ricardo expressed his admiration (Ricardo 1973: 272), contended that:

> The power of population is indefinitely greater than the power in the earth to produce substance for man. Population, when unchecked, increases in a geometrical ratio. Subsistence increases only

in an arithmetical ratio. ... This implies a strong and constantly operating check on population from subsistence.

(Malthus 1970: 71)

Should somehow more food become available, then 'population does invariably increase' (Malthus 1970: 79), maintaining the mass of the population at the basic level of subsistence.

While there were differences between Ricardo's and Malthus' analyses of the economic consequences of these tendencies, both perceived that population could only grow by taking more land into production which, assuming that the most fertile land had been used first, would be of diminishing fertility. The marginal cost of production rises as the fertility of the land decreases. On the least fertile land in production, which determines the minimum price of food, all the revenues are divided between wages and profits and the marginal land rent is zero. Moreover, the profit share is lower on the less fertile land. This can be understood because less fertile land demands more labour and more capital (at constant technology) per unit of product than more fertile land. But this labour requires at least the minimum quantity of food for subsistence. Once wages are at subsistence level, where population growth will tend to keep them, they can fall no further. The lower marginal product must result in a lower return to capital, so profits fall.

With population growth, more land of even lower fertility is required for production. The cost of production on this land, and therefore the price of food, is higher. On all land already in production, this price increase simply translates into higher rents. The profit on the marginal land falls further. Moreover, the increasing price of food raises the subsistence wage, which reduces the profitability of the manufacturing sector as well. The continuing erosion of profitability in both manufacturing and agriculture reduces the incentive to invest, with profits 'sinking to the lowest state required to maintain the actual capital' (Malthus 1974: 282), resulting at length in a 'stationary state' of the economy with stagnant profits and investment and population growth constantly kept in check by starvation. This was the vision that later led Thomas Carlyle to refer to political economy as the 'Dismal Science'.

Both Malthus and Ricardo recognised that the onset of the stationary state could be postponed by technological progress or a halt in population growth before the stationary state was reached. Technological progress could result in either an increase in the productivity of land or in the substitution of capital for labour, thereby increasing labour productivity. Both effects would counteract the tendency for profits to fall and maintain the incentive to invest. Contrary to his 'dismal' image, Malthus even perceived that improvements in agriculture 'may certainly be such as, for a considerable period not only to prevent profits falling, but to allow for a rise' (Malthus 1974: 282).

In retrospect, Malthus' hopes for technological progress have proved justified. Technological advance has permitted more people to live at higher material standards than Malthus ever conceived. His perception of the overwhelming power of population growth has been contradicted by those industrial countries which combine high living standards with more or less zero population growth. Future population growth in other countries, of course, may yet engender Malthus' dismal scenario, though such a scenario is more likely to come to pass through social and political upheaval due to overpopulation, rather than a quietistic submission to natural forces. What the years since Malthus have shown incontrovertibly is that high living standards do not engender population growth; that population growth can be reduced and halted; and that the productive power of technology is enormous. It is even clearer today than it was to Malthus, that his prognosis of a dismal stationary state is not an inevitability.

2.2 ENVIRONMENTAL DEGRADATION

With the increasing scale of industrial activity in the nineteenth century, the effects in terms of environmental degradation soon became obvious. John Stuart Mill was the first economist to recognise that the growth of production might be at the expense of environmental enjoyments:

> It is not good for man to be kept perforce at all times in the presence of his species. A world from which solitude is extirpated is a very poor ideal. . . . Nor is there much satisfaction in contemplating the world with nothing left to the spontaneous activity of nature. . . . If the earth must lose that great portion of its pleasantness which it owes to things that the unlimited increase of wealth and population would extirpate from it, for the mere purpose of enabling it to support a larger, but not a better or happier population, I sincerely hope, for the sake of posterity, that they will be content to be stationary, long before necessity compels them to it.
>
> (Mill 1904: 454)

The unintended and uncompensated loss to one person of natural beauty, pleasantness and solitude in nature due to the economic activity of an another is an example of what, following the analysis of A.C. Pigou, has come to be called an 'externality'. Another more often quoted example is pollution through the discharge of wastes from production or from the disposal of the products themselves.

Although Pigou never used the term 'externality', his description of the effect remains definitive to this day:

> The essence of the matter is that one person A, in the course of rendering some service, for which payment is made, to a second person

B, incidentally also renders services or disservices to other persons (not producers of like services), of such a sort that payment cannot be exacted from the benefited parties or compensation enforced on behalf of the injured parties.

(Pigou 1932: 183)

Environmental externalities arise because property rights to the use of environmental resources are either non-existent – the resources are treated as 'free goods' – or ill-defined. Coase (1960) discusses a range of issues in relation to obtaining optimal outcomes in such situations. In principle the externality problem may be solved by the clear legal delineation of these rights, so that environmental conflicts may be resolved through private negotiation. In practice, it may not be feasible for political or other reasons to give strict definition to property rights over natural resources. It is not clear, for instance, what system of private ownership could realistically encompass the atmosphere or the stratospheric ozone layer. Alternatively, it may be that, even if such resources could be privately owned, their degradation would affect so many people that the transaction costs involved in negotiations would be so great as to prohibit the negotiations taking place; or non-excludability from use of the resources may make it effectively impossible for the property rights to be asserted. Consequently the property rights approach to the resolution of the problem of externalities, while theoretically appealing, is often practically infeasible.

2.2.1 Environmental taxation

Another theoretically attractive approach to resolving the externality problem is to seek to 'internalise' the cost by levying a charge or tax on the activity concerned. Following Pearce and Turner (1990: 86) this approach is illustrated in Figure 2.1.

Private producers gain benefits from an activity which causes pollution, as shown by the marginal net private benefit (MNPB) curve. Left to themselves, they will produce until the MNPB falls to zero, when the level of emissions is Q. Associated with this pollution is a cost, external to the producers, shown by the marginal external cost (MEC) curve, which rises with the pollution level. At Q the marginal external cost is C.

Now it can be seen that at all levels of production that cause emissions higher than Q*, at which MNPB = MEC, the marginal external cost is greater than the marginal net private benefit. In other words, although production causing emissions greater than Q* makes the producers better off, society as a whole is worse off. At Q the total excess cost to society of the externality-induced overproduction is the area *abc*.

The policy problem is to persuade producers to reduce their production such that their emissions fall to Q*. This can be achieved by levying a tax, called a Pigouvian tax, equal to t* per unit of emissions, which will

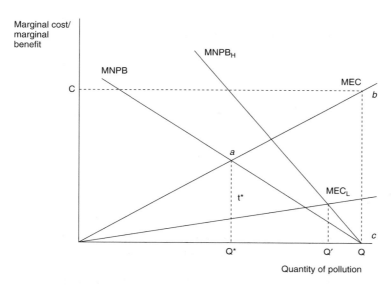

Figure 2.1 External costs of pollution and a Pigouvian tax

cause the producer either to cut production or to abate emissions so that they fall to the efficient level Q*.

There are several important points to be made about this simple solution to environmental externalities. The first concerns the difficulty of establishing the MEC curve. For complex or pervasive environmental problems, such as, for example, global warming or depletion of the ozone layer, it may be so difficult as to be practically impossible to establish the costs of environmental damage. This issue is discussed on pp. 29ff.

In addition to taking account of environmental values, the MEC curve must also include consideration of risk and uncertainty, of discounting over time, and of distributional issues, given that those who bear the costs will often not be those who experience the benefit of the activity that caused them.

A third point to note is that, with a Pigouvian tax, the polluter will experience two effects. First there is the incentive to reduce pollution to the optimal level. This level is unlikely to be zero, as the tax seeks to balance the costs of pollution with the costs of reducing it. Second, the polluter will have to pay the tax on all the emissions that remain. This tends to make environmental taxation less popular with polluters than legislated standards, discussed further below, whereby once the standard has been met no further costs ensue.

A fourth point concerning environmental taxes is that, because they raise revenue, for a given level of government expenditure they allow taxes to be reduced elsewhere. Taxes on labour and profits, which generally raise most government revenue, reduce the incentives to undertake economic activity, thereby causing economic distortions. They also reduce the demand for labour by increasing the wage that has to be paid for a given take-home pay. Insofar as taxes on labour and profits can be replaced by environmental taxes up to the efficient level, economic distortions may be reduced and demand for labour be increased. This is an important consideration when unemployment is a problem.

These and other detailed issues connected with taxation and the environment are surveyed in S. Smith (1992). The systematic shift of the burden of taxation from labour and profits to the use of environmental resources is sometimes called ecological tax reform and is discussed in Weizsäcker and Jesinghaus (1992). It is also the subject of Chapter 8.

2.2.2 Environmental valuation

The environmental effects caused by economic activity often occur outside of market exchanges and are unpriced. One result of this is that they have often been excluded from economic consideration. However, now that environmental issues have risen in perceived importance, there are intensive efforts to give money values to environmental effects and resources, so that they may more easily be taken into account.

Where costs or benefits escape markets and markets cannot be created to capture them, the economic approach is to apply some valuation technique in order nevertheless to express the cost or benefit in monetary terms and so bring it into the calculus. Environmental systems have many different kinds of values, relating to their different functions. D. Pearce (1993: 22) considers that the total economic value (TEV) of these systems can be expressed as:

TEV = Direct use value + Indirect use value + Option value
+ Existence value

where the direct use value relates broadly to the production of at least potentially measurable, marketable outputs; the indirect use value relates to other uses of the environmental functions; the option value relates to people's desire to sustain these functions for possible future use even if they are not being used currently; and existence value relates to people's desire to sustain these functions irrespective of their use. Pearce considers existence value to capture at least part (the humanly defined part) of 'intrinsic' value (ibid.: 15). Turner (1992: 26–7) has written of another existence value, which is 'the prior value of the aggregate ecosystem structure and its life support capacity'. This structure precedes the environmental functions and the TEV values to which they give rise, and the functions are completely dependent on it. However, this existence value is effectively impossible to measure in conventional terms, because it is not based on human preferences.

Within this basic formulation of value, there are several possible ways of trying to calculate at least some of the TEV value of environmental functions, and thence the economic implications of their loss:

- *Costs in surrogate markets:* people's valuation of environmental functions may be deducible from the costs they are prepared to incur to make use of them (e.g. by paying more for well-situated houses or paying to travel to parks).
- *Damage costs:* the impairment or loss of a function may damage economic productivity or human welfare. Such damage may or may not be remedied and may or may not give rise to compensation, which might include actual payments, the provision of substitutes or hypothetical willingness-to-accept valuations. Any of the costs of the damage, its remedy or compensation for it may be used as a valuation of the environmental function.
- *Maintenance and protection costs:* the costs of maintaining and protecting environmental functions (e.g. through pollution abatement) can be regarded as expressions of their worth to human society. These costs may be actual payments made or hypothetical costs, as in willingness-to-pay valuations; or they may be opportunity costs, that is, the costs of forgoing otherwise beneficial activities which would unacceptably impair or destroy an environmental function.
- *Restoration costs:* the costs associated with the impairment or loss of a function may under some circumstances be equated to the cost of restoring that function to some agreed level. These costs normally can be inferred from the relevant market prices.

These methods, when used to value unpriced environmental resources, can be classified slightly differently into *indirect market methods*, which seek to infer environmental values from market choices for other goods, and *direct methods*, which survey people's willingness to pay for the environment.

Cropper and Oates (1992: 703ff.) divide the indirect methods into three kinds:

1   those which derive from behaviour which seeks to avert or mitigate the damage caused (for example, installing pollution abatement equipment, or the purchase of a medicament against the effects of air pollution);
2   those which exploit the complementarity of a purchased good with the relevant environmental good (for example, the cost of travel to a site of environmental quality);
3   'hedonic market' methods, for example, the increase (or decrease) in the price of a house which benefits (or suffers) from an environmental amenity, such as a beautiful view (or disamenity, such as aircraft noise).

In each case the environmental good or bad is valued at the cost of purchase of all or part of some other good.

Direct methods, sometimes called contingent valuation methods (CVM), use the direct questioning of people to establish their willingness to pay (WTP) for environmental goods, or to avoid environmental bads, or to accept compensation (WTA) to forgo the former or suffer the latter. The outcome of such surveys is obviously greatly influenced by the design of the questions and the amount of information about the relevant issue which the respondent either possesses or is given. It is also influenced by whether a WTP or WTA survey is used; Pearce and Moran (1994: 31 (Table 3.2)) have shown over a range of issues that WTA values often exceed WTP values by a factor of four. Clearly which of these two methods is appropriate depends on the property rights involved, but this issue is rarely addressed and WTP is routinely used without prior justification.

The values of environmental functions produced by these techniques can vary enormously. D. Pearce (1993: 166) reports implicit willingness-to-pay valuations for tropical forests that vary by a factor of 400 without any evidence that this difference relates to difference in forest quality. Again, different methods of valuing the potential benefits in OECD countries of medicinal forest plants under threat of extinction produced results that varied between \$17.2 billion and \$720 billion (ibid.: 86). Another example that enters into some environmental valuations is the value of a human 'statistical life', taken in one study to be \$1 million, in another \$4 million (ibid.: 45, 87). Such variations, of course, undermine the credibility and usefulness of the evaluating techniques.

Because WTP survey replies are supposed to be based on existing budget constraints, the use of this method ensures that poor people's valuation of external effects is lower than rich people's. Turning again to Figure 2.1, consider an economic activity with a high MNPB ($MNPB_H$) but involving serious external environmental effects, which primarily or exclusively affect poor people, who are not the beneficiaries of the activity. Contingent valuation surveys may well reveal that these people have a low willingness to pay to avoid these effects, because they have a low ability to pay to do so. The MEC curve will be correspondingly low (MEC_L), so that the optimal level of environmental damage, where the curves intersect (Q'), could be relatively high.

Even where CVM studies have been carefully designed and justified, and distributional issues are not considered problematic, they have been criticised on such grounds as that: there is a difference between professing a willingness to pay and actually paying; people may resent being asked to pay for certain environmental goods and this may influence their answers; or they may seek to 'free ride' on others' professed payments. The evidence also shows that elicited values differ depending on the number of issues that are included in any single survey. Such considerations cast doubt on the appropriateness of comparing values derived from CVM with actual market values, and caused Diamond and Hausman (1994: 46, 62) to conclude that the contingent valuation method 'is a deeply flawed methodology for measuring non-use values' and that reliance on it 'in either damage assessment or in government decision-making is basically misguided'.

The problem is that only CVM can attempt to estimate existence values and those option values for which no well-functioning futures market exists. Such values are of obvious importance with regard to the environment, and despite cautions such as those above, CVM has been used to value such diverse environmental goods as: improvements in water quality to allow fishing or swimming; improvements in visibility from the reduction in air pollution; endangered species; and days free of respiratory ailments. Portney (1994) and Hanemann (1994) believe that CVM has a role to play in valuing environmental goods, providing that clear principles are followed in executing the technique and the results are assessed with care.

These controversies over environmental valuation are not surprising given the common characteristics of the symptoms of unsustainability listed in Chapter 1, which make them most intractable for economic analysis and which include chronic uncertainty often verging on the indeterminate; irreversibility; profound social and cultural implications; actual or potential grave damage to human health, including threats to life; global scope; and a long-term intergenerational time-scale.

There is rarely any generally acceptable way of putting a money value on costs with these characteristics, especially when the characteristics are combined. CVM and other techniques of environmental valuation are not able realistically to assess the costs of displacing millions of people from low-lying coastal areas (global warming); of hundreds of thousands of extra eye-cataracts and skin cancers (ozone depletion); of other processes of large-scale environmental degradation, such as current rates of deforestation, desertification and water depletion, which entail considerable national or international threats to life and livelihood; of the possible unravelling of ecosystems (species extinction); of the persistent release of serious toxins (e.g. radiation) or the effects of major disasters (e.g. Chernobyl, Bhopal). Such costs need to be considered in a different decision-making framework, one possibility for which is provided by the concept of environmental sustainability, which is explored in Chapter 4.

2.3 THE EXHAUSTIBILITY OF RESOURCES

With the exception of solar radiation, which enters the biosphere in a quantity and with a geographic distribution that is beyond human influence, all environmental resources that are used for economic activity are exhaustible. Some resources, such as concentrated mineral ores and fossil fuels, are non-renewable and are necessarily depleted with extraction. Others are conditionally renewable, dependent on rates of harvest and ambient environmental quality.

The economics of resources has traditionally focused on the optimal depletion of the resources, where 'optimal' refers to the maximisation of the profit to the resource's owner from its sale, or of the social welfare to be derived from its consumption. At the optimal rate of depletion, the stock of the resource and the demand for it will fall to zero at the same moment.

From the private owner's point of view, the key economic insight is that, in a perfectly functioning market, the rate of depletion would be such that the price of the resource net of its extraction costs (i.e. its price 'in the ground', or user cost, which is also called its rent) would rise at the same rate as the rate of interest (Hotelling 1931). The intuition behind 'Hotelling's Rule' is easily seen. Were the resource's rent to be rising more slowly than the rate of interest, its price would fall, as owners sought to acquire alternative assets instead. This would tend to restore the resource's rate of rent increase to parity with the interest rate. Were the rent to be rising faster than the rate of interest, the opposite would happen: people would seek to buy stocks of the resource, the net price of which would rise, slowing its rate of rent increase, again until it was equal to the interest rate.

Theoretical results for perfect markets have been modified to try to take into account market imperfections such as non-exclusive ownership (e.g. an oil-field that extends under differently owned plots and is tapped into by differently owned wells) or varying degrees of monopoly. As would be expected, the former condition leads to more rapid depletion than the optimal rate, as each owner tries to maximise their private return; the latter condition leads to slower depletion than the optimal rate, due to the restriction of output that the concentration of ownership brings about. Dasgupta and Heal (1979) is the classic work that reviews and derives many results in such areas.

V.K. Smith (1981) attempts an empirical evaluation of Hotelling's Rule, with the important qualification that lack of data prevented him from using figures of net price, or rent, of the resources considered. Instead, the price used was that of 'natural resources of uniform quality in their rawest form at a uniform distance to markets' (ibid.: 107), i.e. inclusive of extraction costs. After examining the price movements of twelve non-renewable resources – four fossil fuels and eight metals – through the use of five different economic models, including the simple Hotelling model, the study does not support the practical validity of Hotelling's Rule. For four of the metals, none of the models used had any explanatory power. Hotelling's Rule was only accepted by the data for two of the resources. While the best-performing model, Heal and Barrow (1980), was accepted by eight of the resources, in all but three cases even it was outperformed by a simple autoregressive model that related the resource's current price to that in the previous time period. Smith's conclusion is that variables not entering the models, such as extraction costs, new discoveries, and changes in market structure and their institutional environment, for which data are not generally available in suitable form, must also be important in explaining price movements.

The poor empirical performance of the Hotelling model is corroborated by a review of other studies in Slade (1992: 8). Farrow's (1985) careful application of the Hotelling Rule to the actual behaviour of a mining firm, using confidential proprietary data from the firm, found that the Rule was not consistent with the firm's behaviour. Eagan (1987) considers that, at best, the Hotelling Rule is a special case of very little practical application in a real-life situation dominated by institutional, distributional and political considerations, from which it abstracts; at worst the Hotelling Rule may be based on the 'chimera of intertemporal arbitrage' (ibid.: 568), the theoretical application of which has more to do with mathematical tractability than relevance to firms' behaviour.

Where privately optimal depletion seeks to maximise the present value of profits from a resource over its lifetime, socially optimal depletion is concerned with maximising the social utility to be derived from it. Utility is normally (though problematically, as noted in Chapter 1) identified with consumption, so the problem then becomes one of maximising the present value of the consumption of the resource through time. Several conditions affect the optimal depletion path: whether the resource is essential to the production of the consumption good; whether, and to what extent, forms of produced capital can be substituted for the resource; whether technological change either economises on the use of the resource or develops a substitute that renders it inessential; whether a new resource will be discovered that serves the same purpose; and the size of the discount rate, the relative value that is given to present and future consumption.

The core theoretical result in this area is that if the discount rate is positive (i.e. if future consumption is worth less than present consumption), if the resource is essential to consumption, and no technological breakthrough, discovery of substitutable resources or substitutability with produced capital stop it from being so, then it will be optimal to deplete the resource fully and, therefore, drive future consumption to zero. Improvements in the efficiency of resource use (the yield of more consumption goods per unit of resource use), or a reduction in the discount rate, will prolong consumption but will not prevent its eventual decline. This can only be achieved by rendering the resource inessential for consumption by the development or discovery of substitutes. In this case, the resource may still be fully depleted but, as far as the maintenance of consumption is concerned, it will not matter.

The difference between a renewable and non-renewable resource is the capacity of the former for self-regeneration. Provided the harvest-rate does not exceed the rate of regeneration, the stock of the resource will be undepleted. Optimal rates of harvest for renewable resources have been derived by relating reproduction of the resource to its stock, and then maximising the present value of the profit to be derived from the resource, by expressing the harvest as a function of the harvesting effort and then factoring in the effort's associated cost. A standard treatment is given in Pearce and Turner (1990: 244ff.), which yields the following results:

(a) Clearly defined property rights and profit maximisation, with a zero discount rate, will tend to result in a yield that is lower and a stock that is higher than that at maximum sustainable yield.
(b) Open access conditions will reduce the stock from the level in (a), but will not result in extinction provided that the sustainable yield is not exceeded.
(c) A positive discount rate will tend to result in a stock level between that of (a) and (b). The higher the discount rate the closer will the stock level be to (b).
(d) If the discount rate exceeds the net rate of return from the resource as an asset, the resource will be liquidated, perhaps to extinction.
(e) Increasing the price of the resource, or reducing the cost of harvesting it, will reduce the stock level. If the price is above the cost at low population levels, then extinction becomes likely.
(f) The calculated costs of harvesting the resource should include the externalities of both attendant environmental damage costs and forgone option and existence values. They frequently do not do so, increasing harvesting beyond the social optimum.

2.4 EXHAUSTION AND EXTINCTION: THE EVIDENCE

2.4.1 Exhaustion

Malthus and Ricardo were concerned that population levels would outstrip either the available quantity or the fertility of agricultural land, but the first economist who worried about the actual depletion of resources was W.S. Jevons, whose book *The Coal Question* (Jevons 1965, first published 1865) warned of the dire consequences for British industry of, in his view, the inevitable exhaustion of British coal stocks and consequent increases in coal prices. 'The exhaustion of our mines will be marked *pari passu* by a rising cost or value of coal; and when the price has risen to a certain amount comparatively to other countries, our main branches of trade will be doomed' (ibid.: 79).

In the event, Jevons has been proved to have underestimated, as have many conservationists since, the ability of human ingenuity under the influence of market forces to discover new reserves, develop substitutes and increase the efficiency of use of potentially scarce resources. However, this does not guarantee that human ingenuity will always overcome scarcity, the evaluation of which remains an empirical matter. Expert opinion on this issue is divided, with differing definitions and indicators of scarcity being used, and with differing perceptions of the reliability of price movements in this context.

While Hotelling's Rule describes the expected movement of resources' net prices under perfect market conditions, theory certainly suggests that the reason for such a price movement is a resource's actual or possible scarcity. Scarcity is, of course, the *raison d'être* of rent, as Ricardo developed the concept. Marshall argued that 'all rents are scarcity rents' (Marshall 1959: 351). A resource that was not scarce would command a rent, or *in situ* price, of zero. Economic agents would not bother to hold it at all. This being so, it is to be expected that the increasing scarcity of an exhaustible resource, without a perfect, less scarce, substitute, would cause its rent and market price to rise, whether or not the increasing scarcity resulted in an increase in extraction costs. The rise in price would encourage both the economisation of the use of the resource and the development of substitutes, thereby mitigating the increasing scarcity. However, while it may be acknowledged, with Dasgupta and Heal (1974: 4), that: 'This argument clearly has force', their qualification is equally valid: 'In the absence of a well-articulated temporal plan, or a satisfactory set of forward markets, it is not at all plain that market prices will be providing the correct signals', as far as an increase in scarcity or otherwise is concerned.

There has been a sustained effort over the last thirty years to test the hypothesis of increasing scarcity by analysing the movement of resource prices, beginning with Barnett and Morse's classic (1963) investigation, which, using a unit cost indicator, found no increase in scarcity since the late nineteenth century over a wide range of resources, with the exception of forest products. Barnett (1979) updated this work and came to the same conclusion. Hall and Hall (1984) found in contrast that coal increased in scarcity on a unit cost test, but on a relative price test oil, gas, electricity and timber all exhibited scarcity increases through the 1970s.

In the same volume reporting Barnett's updated results, Brown and Field (1979) present compelling arguments why both unit cost (the Barnett and Morse measure) and product price are ambiguous measures of scarcity. In contrast: 'A rising rental rate always portends increasing scarcity and eventual exhaustion, unless there is a "backstop technology"' (Brown and Field 1979: 235). Unfortunately they also note that rental rates for most resources are not readily available. Furthermore, in the same volume Fisher presents a model in which 'rent as an indicator of scarcity has the disturbing property of sometimes decreasing as the resource-stock decreases' (Fisher 1979: 256). Such considerations, theoretical and empirical, suggest that Barnett and Morse's reassuring (1963) conclusions, and Barnett's (1979) restatement of them, should be treated with a great deal of caution.

Other work has confirmed the difficulty of using economic measures to test for increasing environmental scarcity. Slade (1982) seemed to have found a promising specification using a quadratic model, whereby price decreases due to technological progress initially dominated, but were later dominated by, price increases due to increasing scarcity. In this model:

> fitted trends for prices of all the major metals and fuels showed the predicted convex curvature – initially falling but eventually rising –

and all but one of the estimated coefficients of the squared terms were statistically significant at the 90% confidence level.

(Slade 1982: 136)

However, in subsequent work on volatile price behaviour in the 1980s (Slade 1991), the author did not even mention increasing scarcity as a possible contributory factor and concluded the following year that 'there is little evidence of a sustained trend' (Slade 1992: 7).

Three factors can be responsible for price decreases during the depletion of an exhaustible resource: large, new unanticipated discoveries of stocks of the resource, technical change, and the development of substitutes. Slade (1992: 8) considers that: 'Ultimately, the exhaustibility underlying Hotelling's Rule should reassert itself', but this does not by any means seem inevitable. In particular, it is perfectly possible that continuous incremental technical change could yield a rate of price decrease that constantly outweighs any price increase due to scarcity, in contrast to the quadratic timepath exhibited in Slade (1982), which suggests that new technologies are introduced as one-off improvements that eventually exhaust their price-reducing potential and that no further technological improvements are implemented to prevent scarcity-induced price increases from becoming dominant. In this way it is perfectly possible for physical exhaustion, or the extinction of commercial, marketed species (Brown and Field 1979: 232 give the actual example of the passenger pigeon in the US), to occur in the absence of price increases.

Dissatisfaction with economic measures of scarcity, and with other aspects of conventional approaches to environment and resource issues, has led to the emergence of 'alternative views' (Barbier 1989) and, in particular, to a 'biophysical' approach to these issues, the proponents of which 'generally argue that basic physical and ecological laws constrain our economic choices in ways that are not accurately reflected in existing economic models' (Cleveland 1991: 290). This approach has resulted in the development of a biophysical indicator of scarcity, the physical output of an industry per unit of energy (direct and indirect) input (output per energy input, or OEI). For the energy industry this indicator is called the energy return on investment (EROI) and is the ratio of the energy produced to the energy consumed by the industry.

There are three reasons why an extractive industry's OEI might change over time. First, where the extracted resource is exhaustible, depletion of the resource may make further extraction more difficult, *inter alia*, requiring more energy. This is a classic scarcity effect which would tend to reduce OEI, as well as increase the cost and price of extractive output. Second, the discovery or greater availability of new energy sources may result in a substitution in the production process towards energy and away from other inputs (labour and capital). Georgescu-Roegen (1975: 362) observed that 'economic history confirms a rather elementary fact – the fact that the great strides in technological progress have generally been touched off by a discovery of how to use a new kind of accessible energy'. The substitution of energy for labour will reduce OEI unless it gives rise to a proportional increase in output that is equal to or greater than the proportional increase in energy use. However, assuming the substitution leads to cost-reduction (and in a competitive environment there is no other reason why it should take place), it will lead price and other economic measures of scarcity to indicate a decrease in scarcity, despite an underlying change in the availability of the resource and greater depletion of energy. This is one of the reasons why the biophysical and economic indicators of scarcity may tell opposite stories and why price has been criticised as a measure of scarcity.

Third, the more efficient use of energy by an industry is likely to cause its OEI to increase. Energy efficiency, in turn, is likely to be encouraged by high energy prices, which may come about due to a scarcity of energy. Therefore the increasing scarcity of an essential input into the extraction of a resource may lead to a perception that the resource itself is becoming less scarce. This is a perverse result, which can be further illustrated by considering a situation in which an extreme physical shortage and consequently high price of energy lead to a collapse in output of some energy-intensive extractive resource. Despite the fact that the extracted (as opposed to *in situ*) resource would now be scarce in the sense of being in short supply, its OEI would increase, provided that the energy efficiency of its production increased, suggesting that its biophysical scarcity had decreased.

This leads to two conclusions: first, that the effective scarcity of a resource depends not only on its own abundance, but on the scarcity of the inputs that are essential to extract it; and second, that the extractive importance of energy gives it a primacy among resources. If energy became extremely scarce, many other resources would effectively become extremely scarce too, no matter how energy efficient their extraction (how high their OEI) became. Paradoxically, cost and price measures of scarcity (though not rent) perform better than the biophysical, energy-based OEI on this score, because extreme scarcity of energy would result in a high price of energy and energy-intensive resources.

Cleveland (1991) calculates OEI time trends in the twentieth century for the US for many minerals and renewable resources. The results are mixed and few conclusions can be drawn. Metals as a whole show a decreasing OEI from about 1950; for non-metal minerals overall the OEI increases almost continuously from 1920–80. For agriculture the OEI fell almost continuously through the century to about 1970, and then rose, exhibiting the efficiency effect discussed above. For forestry OEI declines from 1950–74 and then rises a slightly greater amount to 1986. For fisheries OEI declined by 80 per cent between 1968 and 1988.

For fossil fuels the results are more interesting and show a clear change of trend in the 1960s, from rising to falling EROI, for oil from 23 to 12, for coal from 60 to 30. Moreover, this biophysical indication of scarcity is confirmed by the economic measures: both the price of crude oil and the cost of US petroleum extraction rise from about 1970 (Cleveland 1993: 140–1). Hall and Hall's (1984: 371) analysis on the basis of relative prices and unit costs led them to conclude: 'The most basic (conclusion) is that *all* primary fuels became more scarce in the 1970s.' It remains to be seen whether this conclusion survives the oil-price collapse of the mid-1980s and the lower level of oil prices since.

2.4.2 Extinction

With regard to extinction, while there is great uncertainty over overall numbers, species loss is generally agreed to be proceeding at a rate unprecedented since the extinction of the dinosaurs 65 million years ago, with a global rate of extinction 10–1,000 times the background rate (Pimm 1995: 35). Even the most conservative estimates suggest that 1–5 per cent of a possible 10 million species (though the number could be as high as 30 million) are being lost each decade. Other estimates put the rate at more than 10 per cent (Barbier *et al.* 1994: 3, 11).

There are several reasons why this matters economically even if no intrinsic value is given to other species. Many people enjoy watching wildlife, or even just knowing that it exists. Plants have been the source of valuable medicinal drugs and as yet undiscovered species which may be extinguished could doubtless yield more. Genetic diversity is important in agricultural breeding programmes. Perhaps most importantly, complex ecosystems, such as rainforests, provide natural services, such as climate regulation, on which many people are dependent. Ignorance about the functions of such ecosystems is still very great. Their destruction, which may be irreversible, could prove catastrophic.

The economics of renewable resources gives a clear understanding as to why extinction is occurring: prices of resources generally do not reflect ecosystem functions or option or existence values; costs of harvesting can be low; discount rates can be above the sum of natural growth rates and rates of appreciation of the natural stock; open access conditions often pertain; and livelihoods are often dependent on continuing unsustainable exploitation. Moreover, it is also clear that, in conditions of open access, if the price of the resource received by the harvester is high, if the cost of harvesting is low, or if the discount rate is high, then it can be *optimal* to drive the resource to extinction.

The experience of Antarctic whaling, discussed in Clark (1990: 20, 21, 49, 313), provides a clear example of how this may occur in practice: stocks of the blue whale fell from 150,000 to probably below 1,000 and the whale's extinction was only prevented by regulation, in this case a moratorium imposed by the International Whaling Commission in 1965. Even so, Clark notes, 'whether the population has increased significantly in the intervening quarter century remains in doubt' (ibid.: 21). Of course, extinction can also occur non-optimally due to uncertainty about stocks or sustainable yields or due to economic pressures. The Grand Banks of Newfoundland provide an example. Once 'the richest cod fishery in the world' (*New Scientist* 1992: 11), Canada banned cod fishing there in March 1992 as 'the only way to save the stock'. Analysis of the fishery collapse blamed too high quotas based on a faulty estimate of stocks, an excessive catch by foreign boats and improved fishing technology (MacKenzie 1992: 8). Similar stories are told of the Pacific mackerel fishery off Ecuador, where catches went from 400,000 tonnes a year to practically zero in a decade (Vines 1994: 15) and the South Atlantic's 'biggest squid fishery in the world', where the catch crashed to 30 per cent of its 1989 high within three years (F. Pearce 1996: 33).

While the theoretical results yield useful insights, their relevance to the actual production of renewable resources by ecosystems may not be very great. Concerning many ecosystems there are profound uncertainties about stocks and the basic processes that give an ecosystem stability and resilience, which are fundamental to the maintenance of sustainable yields. It may not be possible to compute the maximum sustainable harvest for any given stock size (even where the stock is known) with any degree of accuracy, so that attempts to achieve such harvests run the perpetual risk of actually exceeding them and driving the resource to extinction. Given the scientific uncertainties, and the incentives of economic agents to exaggerate the growth potential of a resource in order to justify a greater harvest, there is a very real risk of this happening. Without being able to assign probabilities to the uncertainties, which is often the case, an optimal solution cannot be derived. One possible response to this problem is the adoption of the safe minimum standards approach, or the precautionary principle, which fall outside the conventional territory of resource economics and are discussed further in Chapter 4 on pp. 92ff.

Leaving incalculable uncertainties aside, the analysis above leads to the conclusion that for both renewable and non-renewable resources, optimal use or depletion can be environmentally unsustainable. This was made explicit by V.L. Smith (1977), who concluded from four control theory models of natural and environmental resource use, involving renewable, non-renewable and amenity resources, that: 'Just as exhaustion can be optimal, extinction can be optimal' (ibid.: 1). Optimality and unsustainability are very much compatible in the mainstream resource economics literature that has been developed over the last sixty years. Whether economic growth and environmental sustainability are thus compatible is, however, still very much a matter of dispute, as will be seen.

2.5 LIMITS TO GROWTH AND SUSTAINABLE DEVELOPMENT

The twenty years between the 1972 UN Conference on the Environment in Stockholm and the 1992 Earth Summit, the UN Conference on Environment and Development (UNCED) in Rio de Janeiro witnessed a major change in approach to issues of environment and development. Today the key phrase is 'sustainable development'. Then it was 'limits to growth'.

2.5.1 The limits to growth debate

In order to shed light on the arguments for and against 'limits to growth' that raged so heatedly in the 1970s, not just among economists but in society at large, it is necessary to unpack the concept, in particular by asking 'what sort of limits?' and 'limits to what kind of growth?'. At the outset it may be observed that the limits in question have been perceived to be either ecological or social; while several different kinds of growth can be identified in relation to economic activity: an increase in the physical quantity of resources going through the economy (sometimes called its physical throughput); growth in the production of the economy, measured in the national accounts as the Gross Domestic, or Gross National, Product, GDP or GNP, which is what is usually called 'economic growth'; an increase in the human welfare delivered by the economy; or the growth of biomass brought about by the natural regeneration of renewable resources.

The term 'limits to growth' itself was the title of a book by Donella and Dennis Meadows and a team from the Massachusetts Institute of Technology (MIT), which was the principal fuel for the subsequent debate. For the Meadows team the limits were ecological limits, and they applied to economic growth, understood as growth in production as measured by GNP, which they assumed implied a similar increase in the consumption of resources. They concluded: 'The most probable result (of reaching the limits to growth) will be a rather sudden and uncontrollable decline in both population and industrial capacity' (Meadows *et al.* 1974: 23).

The Meadows' model assumed that population and industrial capital would grow exponentially, leading to a similar growth in demand for food and non-renewables and in pollution. The supply of food and non-renewable resources was, however, taken to be absolutely finite. Not surprisingly, exponential growth within finite limits resulted in systematic breakdown; the expansive nature of compound growth also meant that the finite limits could be raised by a factor of four without significantly affecting the results.

While the 'limits to growth' thesis struck a chord with the general public, economists and other scientists were quick to seek to discredit it. Two of the most comprehensive rebuttals came from a team at Sussex University's Science Policy Research Unit (Cole *et al.* 1973), and from William Nordhaus (1973). They criticised the relationships in Meadows' model, the assumptions on which the model was based and the emphasis on purely physical parameters.

On the basis of their critique, Cole *et al.* reran Meadows' model with different assumptions and produced quite different results. This was also not *a priori* surprising because the key assumption they replaced was that of absolute limits by introducing ongoing exponential increases in available resources (through discovery and recycling) and the ability to control pollution.

> To postpone collapse indefinitely these rates of improvement must obviously be competitive with growth rates of population and consumption so that even if the overall growth is rapid, it is also 'balanced'. In this case some kind of stable but dynamic equilibrium is obtained.
>
> (Cole *et al.* 1973: 119)

The authors also claimed that, at 1 per cent and 2 per cent, the actual numerical values used as improvement rates for the various technologies were compatible with historical experience.

Nordhaus (1973) also reran the model with different assumptions, respecifying the model's population behaviour and its savings assumption, and introducing technological change and substitution possibilities. All the changes in assumptions dramatically changed the behaviour of the model, with the introduction of technical change and substitutability having the greatest effect, either significantly postponing the model's 'overshoot and collapse' trajectory or converting it into one of continually increasing consumption.

Lecomber (1975) admirably expresses the difference between resource optimists, such as Nordhaus and Cole *et al.*, and pessimists such as the Meadows' team. He identifies the three key effects that can reduce depletion or pollution: changes in composition of output; substitution between factor inputs; and technical progress (more efficient use of the same input). If these three effects add up to a shift away from the limiting resource or pollutant equal to or greater than the rate of growth, then the limits to growth are put back indefinitely. But, Lecomber warns:

> [This] establishes the *logical* conceivability, not the certainty, probability or even the possibility in practice, of growth continuing indefinitely. Everything hinges on the rate of technical progress and possibilities of substitution. This is perhaps the main issue that separates resource optimists and resource pessimists. The optimist believes in the power of human inventiveness to solve whatever problems are thrown in its way, as apparently it has done in the past. The pessimist

questions the success of these past technological solutions and fears that future problems may be more intractable.

(1975: 42)

Lecomber looks for evidence in an effort to judge between these two positions, but without success. 'The central feature of technical advance is indeed its uncertainty' (ibid.: 45). This conclusion is of relevance to the contemporary situation with sustainable development, as will be seen, and will be analysed in more detail in Chapter 6.

Many of the same points as those of Cole *et al.* (1973) are made, and the same beliefs about the efficiency of future technical change are held, by Wilfred Beckerman (1974) in his defence of economic growth. However, Beckerman also introduces several other arguments not related to technology. First Beckerman stresses:

> It is essential not to confuse the issue of how consumption should be spread over time, which is the growth issue, with that of how resources should be used at any moment of time. The fact that resources are misallocated at any moment of time on account of failure to correct for externalities does not necessarily mean that the growth rate is wrong.
>
> (1974: 18, 20)

Beckerman's point is that insofar as environmental degradation is caused by externalities, or 'spillover effects', which are failures of resource allocation, they cannot be solved by tinkering with rates of economic growth. This is true as far as it goes, but misses the important point that if these externalities persist to any given extent, their absolute effect in a large economy will be greater than in a small one. Given that failures to remedy externalities are common, opposition to the economic growth that amplifies them would seem a not irrational position on the part of those adversely affected.

The other point about rectifying resource misallocations is that *per se* this may reduce GNP growth. Lecomber says:

> It is misleading to regard environmental policies of this sort as *alternatives* to reducing economic growth since this would be their incidental effect. Benefits which are not included in GNP would be traded for other (smaller) benefits which are. GNP would fall and, during the period of transition to such policies, growth would fall, probably substantially.
>
> (1975: 59)

Of course, there is no certainty that correcting resource misallocations reduces growth, as is shown by some of the analysis in later chapters, but it would be remarkable if no such corrections involved the trade-off effect Lecomber identifies.

Whatever the potential of technological change, there are certain phys-ical constraints, defined by the laws of thermodynamics, that cannot be circumvented. The Second Law – that all activity and transformation of energy or materials leads to an increase of entropy – has been most exten-sively related to economics by Georgescu-Roegen (1971).

In this analysis it is the increase of entropy that is the ultimate limit to growth. Economic activity increases entropy by depleting resources and producing wastes. Entropy on earth can only be decreased by importing low entropy resources (solar energy) from outside it. This energy can renew resources and neutralise and recycle wastes. To the extent that the human economy is powered by solar energy, it is limited only by the flow of that energy. Growth in physical production and throughput that is not based on solar energy must increase entropy and make environmental problems worse, implying an eventual limit to such growth. Growth in physical production based on solar energy is limited by the quantity and concen-tration of that energy. GNP can free itself from these limits only to the extent that it 'decouples' itself from growth in physical production; what Daly (1977: 118) calls 'Angelized GNP'. As will be seen later, such decou-pling has occurred to some extent, but the entropy law decrees that it can never be complete. Optimists believe that the decoupling can be substan-tial and continuous; pessimists are more sceptical, with Daly (ibid.: 119), for example, remarking: 'It would be necessary for us to become angels in order to subsist on angelized GNP.' Such a perception causes Daly to conclude: 'The term sustainable growth should be rejected as a bad oxymoron' (Daly 1990: 1).

Beckerman's argument in defence of economic growth is twofold: poor countries need economic growth to pull them out of poverty (Beckerman 1974: 9); rich countries pursue economic growth because of the net benefits it brings. With regard to the first of these arguments, there is now some doubt, rather more than when Beckerman was writing, whether economic growth *per se* is what poor people in poor countries need to improve their life prospects. Using the terminology introduced by Sen (1983: 754), entitlements such as ensured access to resources and capa-bilities to use those resources, neither of which are the automatic results of economic growth, may be even more important. Where these lead to more secure but non-market subsistence, they will not even show up as economic growth.

With regard to the second argument, it is a view which is diametrically opposed to the views of E.J. Mishan. In the works so far surveyed the emphasis has been on the feasibility or otherwise of economic growth. Its desirability has either been a moot point or, as with Beckerman, strongly asserted. It was the institutionalist economist K.W. Kapp who made the first thorough-going exploration of the social costs of the growth process (Kapp 1950), but it was Mishan (1967, 1977) who first brought these costs to widespread public notice. Mishan identified them thus:

The uglification of once handsome cities the world over continues unabated. Noise levels and gas levels are still rising and despite the erection of concrete freeways over city centres, unending processions of motorised traffic lurch through its main thoroughfares. Areas of outstanding natural beauty are still being sacrificed to the tourist trade and traditional communities to the exigencies of development. Pollution of air, soil and oceans spreads over the globe. The upward movement in the indicators of social disintegration – divorce, suicide, delinquency, petty theft, drug taking, sexual deviance, crime and violence – has never faltered over the last two decades.

(1977: 10)

It is Mishan's thesis that these and other ill effects are the results of economic growth and far outweigh its benefits. Mishan sees the pursuit of such growth as leading western civilisation to its nemesis. As long as these effects remain important, as they undoubtedly still do, Mishan's thesis stands unfalsified. Whether he will be proved right is, of course, a different matter.

The ecologists' concern was with the physical limits to economic growth. Mishan's focus is on the limits to social welfare that can be derived from growth. Hirsch adds to the picture by postulating social limits to growth, distancing himself from the ecologists' critique with the words:

The concern with the limits to growth that has been voiced by and through the Club of Rome [Meadows *et al.* 1974] is strikingly misplaced. It focuses on distant and uncertain physical limits and overlooks the immediate if less apocalyptic presence of social limits to growth.

(Hirsch 1976: 4)

Hirsch's social limits derive from two causes: the increasing importance of positional goods; and the breakdown of individual morality in an affluent, growing economy. The positional economy 'relates to all aspects of goods, services, work positions, and other social relationships that are either (1) scarce in some absolute or socially imposed sense or (2) subject to congestion or crowding through more extensive use' (Hirsch 1976: 27). As incomes rise, the demand for positional goods increases; with fixed or very inelastic supply, the goods are either rationed through price (e.g. desirable resort properties) or criteria of eligibility (e.g. more stringent examinations) or their quality is degraded through overcrowding (e.g. roads). The effect is either to reduce growth, or the welfare to be derived from it or both.

On the subject of morality, Hirsch writes:

The point is that conventional, mutual standards of honesty and trust are public goods that are necessary inputs for much of economic output. . . . Truth, trust acceptance, restraint, obligation, these are among the social virtues which are also now seen to play a central role in the functioning of an individualistic contractual economy.

(1976: 141)

Yet, Hirsch (ibid.: 175) asserts, these are precisely the virtues that are undermined by the selfsame individualism: 'Economic growth undermines its social foundations.' Daly brings the argument full circle by indicting 'growthmania' for errors in both the ecological and moral spheres:

Economics has overlooked ecological and moral facts of life that have now come home to haunt us in the form of increasing ecological scarcity and increasing existential scarcity. . . . Ultimate means have been treated as if they were limitless, and the Ultimate End as if it were unreal.

(1977: 170, 176)

Daly's solution to growthmania is the steady-state economy, 'an economy with constant stocks of people and artefacts, maintained at some desired, sufficient levels by low rates of maintenance "throughput"' (Daly 1977: 17). The throughput is limited by strict quotas, auctioned by the government, on depletion of resources. The population is limited by the equal per capita issue of transferable birth licences. And inequality of income and wealth is limited by the setting of maximum and minimum levels, with redistribution from rich to poor. The dual ecological and social components of Daly's steady-state are explicit in the subtitle to his book: 'The Economics of Biophysical Equilibrium and Moral Growth'.

2.5.2 The aspiration for sustainable development

The 1970s' limits to growth critiques, both physical and social, failed to dent the social consensus in favour of economic growth, so that by the time the Brundtland Commission produced its report, *Our Common Future* (WCED 1987), on environment and development, the emphasis was placed on a perceived complementarity between growth and environment. In her introduction to the report, Mrs Brundtland calls for 'a new era of economic growth – growth that is forceful and at the same time socially and environmentally sustainable' (WCED 1987: xii).

This bullish attitude was justified by statistics which showed that over the period 1972–86 the relationship between energy use and economic growth in industrial countries had undergone a significant change from the broadly proportional relation that had pertained before. In the US, energy intensity (the amount of energy used per unit of GDP) from 1973–86 diminished by 25 per cent. Over the OECD as a whole, it fell by 20 per cent from 1973–85. In the same period for countries belonging to the

International Energy Agency, GDP grew by nearly 32 per cent, but energy use only by 5 per cent (WRI 1990: 146). A 'decoupling' of economic growth from energy consumption was proclaimed.

In an even more optimistic twist to this debate, Bernstam (1991) postulates that industrialisation under free market conditions exhibits a characteristic relationship between output and the environment, as follows. In the early days there is a negative trade-off at the expense of the environment. This effect diminishes as industrialisation proceeds and, at a certain historical moment, there is a positive relationship between the two. At this point 'economic growth can reduce pollution if it increases the productivity of resources (that is, reduces wastes) faster than both resource output and population growth' (ibid.: 33, 34).

Bernstam (1991: 40) asserts that in industrial market economies this condition is now being met by the operation of what he calls the 'Invisible Environmental Hand'. This assertion remains at the level of pure conjecture. In fact, it is flatly contradicted by trends in energy use since 1986. US energy intensity actually increased (that is, more energy was used per unit of GDP) in 1987 and 1988, as did that of several European countries (WRI 1990: 146). There is some limited evidence on air pollution supporting Bernstam's hypothesis, which is examined in Chapter 7, the overall conclusion of which is that there is no evidence that, over a prolonged period, Bernstam's condition for growth to reduce overall environmental impacts is being met.

Beckerman (1992), arguing for economic growth in developing countries, adopts the same line of argument as Bernstam (1991) with an intriguing difference. Bernstam's thesis was that continuing economic growth in industrial countries would reduce their contribution to global pollution, which would go some way towards compensating for the inevitable rise in pollution from growth in developing countries. Beckerman contends that it is *developing countries* that need economic growth to improve their environments, at least in important areas such as access to drinking water, sanitation and air quality. He concludes: 'In the longer run, the surest way to improve your environment is to become rich' (Beckerman 1992: 491).

Beckerman's is not the only important voice from the 1970s, debate to have restated its essential conclusions in the 1990s. A second report from Meadows *et al.* states:

> [The possible paths into the future] do not include continuous growth. The choices are to bring the burden of human activities upon the earth down to a sustainable level through human choice, human technology and human organisation, or to let nature force the reduction through lack of food, energy or materials, or an increasingly unsound environment.
>
> (1994: 12)

The emphasis on continuing limits to growth is also echoed in a publication which includes contributions by two Nobel laureates in economics, one of whom writes:

> Saving the environment will certainly check production growth and probably lead to lower levels of national income. This outcome can hardly surprise. Many have known for a long time that population growth and rising production and consumption cannot be sustained forever in a finite world.
>
> (Tinbergen and Hueting 1992: 56)

It was in response to the new Meadows book that Nordhaus (1993a) also produced an updated assessment of the issues and arguments around the limits-to-growth theme. His critique of Meadows' new model run largely restates his earlier objections, with the extra calculation that introducing a rate of technical change of only 0.25 per cent per annum (in the context of recent historical rates of 1–2 per cent) is sufficient to keep consumption per head rising (ibid.: 16). However, his key new conclusion is that 'the debate about the future of economic growth is an empirical one' (ibid.: 16), so that the second part of his paper is devoted to examining 'insights that economists have gathered from actual economic growth over the last twenty years' (ibid.: 19). His review of long-term trends in resource prices confirms the picture that emerged earlier in this chapter of prices falling to roughly 1970, and then rising or rising and falling. On this evidence at least the era of continually decreasing resource prices would seem to have come to an end.

Nordhaus then goes on to estimate the 'drag on economic growth' that depletion, pollution and defensive environmental expenditures may exert in the years up to 2050, concluding that the growth rate may be reduced by 0.3 per cent per annum, or nearly 20 per cent of the per capita 1.6 per cent per annum growth that he projects (Nordhaus 1993a: 38). Although this is still very far from 'overshoot and collapse', it is a non-negligible effect. If the projected per capita growth rate is overoptimistic, if the estimates of environmental damage are generally too low, or if there is some unforeseen environmental calamity, then the impacts on growth rates could start to look dramatic. Nordhaus' (ibid.: 39) conclusion from these figures is justified: 'It would take either a massive slowdown in productivity growth or a massive underestimate of the constraints to growth before the resource constraints would actually produce a decline in global living standards.' However, he rules out neither eventuality, ending with a sober assessment of both the necessity for and difficulties of sound policy making in this area: 'The peril lies not in the stars but in ourselves' (ibid.: 43).

A comparison between the attitudes of the 1970s and the 1990s shows that the resource pessimists' conclusions are essentially unchanged, but, with the exception of the Bernstam/Beckerman views, there has been a significant shift in the mainstream resource optimists' position since the 1970s. Then, environmental limits were largely perceived to be either non-existent or automatically self-delimiting. Now the broad conclusion of the mainstream optimists, as expressed in Nordhaus (1993a) or in the Brundtland, WRI or BCSD reports quoted in Chapter 1, is that environmental problems are real and threatening and that to be reconciled with continuing economic expansion *active policy* will be required.

This conclusion received one of its most sophisticated restatements in the *World Development Report 1992* (World Bank 1992). This report accepts the gravity of the environmental situation. Further, it accepts that some environmental problems are 'exacerbated by the *growth* of economic activity' (p. 7, original emphasis). Its strategy to achieve both environmental conservation and economic growth advocates a twin focus. Most importantly:

> Some problems are associated with the *lack* of economic development; inadequate sanitation and clean water, indoor air pollution from biomass burning, and many types of land degradation in developing countries have poverty as their root cause. Here the challenge is to accelerate equitable income growth.
>
> (p. 7, original emphasis)

The Report accepts that 'these "win-win" policies will not be enough' (p. 5) and that, in other cases, 'there may be trade-offs between income growth and environmental protection' (p. 1). However: 'The evidence indicates that the gains from protecting the environment are often high, and that the costs in forgone income are modest if appropriate policies are adopted' (p. 1). The gains from 'win-win' opportunities on the one hand, and only modest costs on the other, could, on this analysis, result in both a 3.5-times rise in world output and 'better environmental protection, cleaner air and water, and the virtual elimination of acute poverty' (p. 2).

The greater acceptance now of environmental threat by policy makers and academics compared to the 1970s has resulted in the enormous expansion of analysis of and political interest in the idea of sustainable development. Although it was the Brundtland report that popularised the concept, it was in fact first used in the mid-1970s 'to make the point that environmental protection and development are linked' (Holmberg and Sandbrook 1992: 19).

Barbier (1987) has suggested that sustainable development should be viewed as an interaction between three systems, the biological, economic and social systems. 'The general objective of sustainable economic development, then, is to maximise the goals across all these systems through an adaptive process of trade-offs' (ibid.: 104), although the difficulty of expressing these trade-offs in the same units suggests that the process is likely to be at best one of attempted optimisation through the political process rather than strict maximisation. The same multi-dimensionality is present in the concept of 'primary environmental care' (PEC), which is clearly related to sustainable development and has become widely current among development organisations in their attempts to put sustainable development into practice. PEC is defined as 'the umbrella term for development approaches in the interactive zone between economic, environmental and social systems' (Holmberg and Sandbrook 1992: 31). Its 'integral elements' are:

- meeting and satisfying of basic needs – the economic goal;
- protection and optimal utilization of the environment – the environmental goal;
- and empowering of groups and communities – the social goal.

(ibid.: 32)

The multi-dimensionality and multiplicity of objectives embraced by sustainable development has resulted in it coming to mean different things to different people. By 1989 Pearce *et al.* were able to cite a 'gallery of definitions' (Pearce *et al.* 1989: 173–85), which by 1993 could have been much extended. Such diversity of meaning clearly militates against clarity of discourse. Beckerman is roundly dismissive of the whole debate around sustainability: 'The aggregative concept of global sustainability . . . seems to be either morally indefensible or devoid of operational value', while the question 'how do we achieve sustainable development?' is 'unanswerable and meaningless' (Beckerman 1992: 491–2). One relatively early survey of the sustainable development scene was led to conclude (Lélé 1991: 613): '[Sustainable development] is a "metafix" that will unite everybody from the profit-minded industrialist and risk-minimising subsistence farmer to the equity-seeking social worker, the pollution-concerned or wildlife-loving First Worlder, the growth-maximising policy-maker, the goal-oriented bureaucrat and, therefore, the vote-counting politician.'

Not surprisingly perhaps, Lélé finds that this all-inclusive formulation suffers from significant weaknesses in:

(a) Its characterisation of the problems of poverty and environmental degradation;
(b) Its conceptualisation of the objectives of development, sustainability and participation; and
(c) The strategy it has adopted in the face of incomplete knowledge and uncertainty.

(1991: 613)

The weaknesses in conceptualisation, in particular, have added to the confusion concerning the growth/sustainability relationship. The limits to growth debate has been left hanging in the air, with the resource optimists either dismissing it as *passé* or regarding it as somehow resolved by the mere incantation of 'sustainable development', and the resource pessimists sticking doggedly to their line of 'indefinite growth is not possible in a finite world', without adequate differentiation between different kinds of growth, or specification of what kinds of growth they have in mind. The introduction of the concept of sustainable development into this definitional imprecision has further muddied the waters. What is now needed are clear specifications and clarification of the difference between production, welfare, growth and development, and of what kinds of growth and development it is desired to sustain and why this may prove problematic.

It is the purpose of the next two chapters to provide this specification and clarification. In particular Chapter 3 seeks to establish a clear distinction between:

1   Production and welfare, where the former comprises the goods and services produced by the economy, and is conventionally measured in money terms, while the latter, which economists also call utility, is a term denoting satisfaction or happiness. Where such satisfaction derives from participation in the economy, it may be termed 'economic welfare' and this is the focus of the subsequent discussion. As will be seen, the consumption of produced goods and services is only one of the sources of such welfare.

2   Different kinds of growth, as noted earlier, namely:

   (i)   the growth of the physical throughput of the economy (measured in physical units);

   (ii) the growth of the production of the economy (conventionally measured by GDP and GNP);

   (iii) the growth of human welfare (the measurement of which is still a source of great controversy) as a result of economic activity;

   (iv) the growth of biomass, as part of natural processes.

3   Growth and development, and the relationship between them.

With these essential concepts clarified, and the necessary distinctions made in Chapter 3, Chapter 4 then introduces and develops the idea of sustainability, with environmental, economic and social dimensions, which, as part of the concept of sustainable development, is establishing itself as a new fundamental objective of environmental policy.

3 Wealth creation

Distinguishing between production, welfare, growth and development

3.1 MODELLING WEALTH CREATION

Economic analysis usually depicts the process of wealth creation as in Figure 3.1: land, labour and manufactured capital are judiciously combined in an economic process which produces goods and services, some of which are consumed to give utility to the consumers, and some of which are invested to enhance the capital stocks (or make up for depreciation).

The process which combines the inputs of land, labour and capital is conceptualised in terms of a production function. A common representation used in growth theory (e.g. R. Solow 1991) is:

$$Y = F(K, L, t)$$

where Y is output, K is capital inputs, L is labour inputs, t is time (introduced to reflect technical progress) and F(.) is the function which states how the inputs are combined. Such a treatment abstracts totally from the physical reality of production, even omitting land altogether, so that there is no scope for analysing the environmental contribution to production in such a model. As Nordhaus and Tobin have said:

> [The prevailing standard model of growth] is basically a two factor model in which production depends only on labor and reproducible

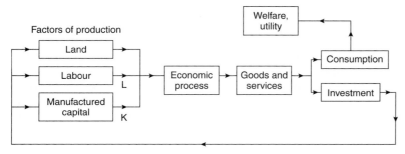

Figure 3.1 A three-factor model of the creation of wealth and utility

capital. Land and resources, the third member of the classical triad, have generally been dropped. The simplifications of theory carry over into empirical work. The thousands of aggregate production functions estimated by econometricians in the last decade are labor-capital functions.

(1973: 522)

More recently there have been attempts to incorporate at least some aspects of the environmental contribution. Thus the work of Jorgenson and Wilcoxen (1993) implies a production function of the form:

$$Y = F(K,L,E,M,t)$$

where the new variables E and M are energy and intermediate material inputs respectively. Such a formulation obviously enables the contribution of energy and raw materials to production to be studied but the range over which substitutions between factor inputs are physically meaningful may be quite small. As Smith and Krutilla (1979: 30) note: 'The adjustments . . . by the factor substitutions represented in an abstract production function may well violate physical laws.' Moreover, they further note that treating natural resources as if they were conventional inputs 'is not necessarily valid for addressing the problem (of environmental scarcity) when it involves services of non-priced common property environmental resources also required in production and consumption processes' (ibid.: 29).

These are severe limitations for the present purpose of understanding and representing both the complexities of the economy and the full contribution of the environment to it. To circumvent the limitations, a diagrammatic, rather than a mathematical, representation of a K,L,E,M production process has been chosen (Figure 3.2), which also includes social/organisational capital, producing services, S. The model of Figure 3.2 is a development of that in Ekins (1992: 149) and is similar to that subsequently put forward by the World Bank (Serageldin and Steer 1994: 30ff.). It is also consistent with the description of production by A. Harrison (1993: 25ff.) and Bartelmus and Tardos (1993: 185), in connection with their discussion of integrated economic and environmental accounting, which will be discussed in Chapter 5.

Figure 3.2 portrays four kinds of capital stock: ecological (or natural) capital; human capital; social and organisational capital; and manufactured capital. Each of these stocks produces a flow of 'services' from the environment (E), from human capital (L), from social/organisational capital (S), and from physical capital (K), services which serve as inputs into the productive process, along with 'intermediate inputs' (M), which are previous outputs from the economy and which are used as inputs in a subsequent process.

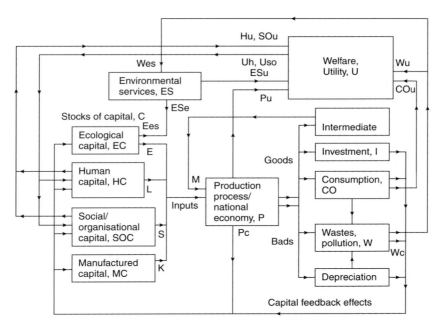

Figure 3.2 Stocks, flows and welfare in the process of production

Note: In the flow descriptors, the upper case letters denote the source of the flow, lower case letters denote the destination. Those relating to the various capital stocks have the C omitted for simplicity

Manufactured capital comprises material goods – tools, machines, build-ings, infrastructure – which contribute to the production process but do not become embodied in the output and, usually, are 'consumed' in a period of time longer than a year. Intermediate goods, in contrast, either are embodied in produced goods (e.g. metals, plastics, components) or are immediately consumed in the production process (e.g. fuels). Human capital comprises all individuals' capacities for work; while social and organisa-tional capital comprises the networks and organisations through which the contributions of individuals are mobilised and coordinated.

Ecological capital is a complex category which performs three distinct types of environmental function (Pearce and Turner 1990: 35ff.), two of which are directly relevant to the production process. The first is the provi-sion of resources for production (E), the raw materials that become food, fuels, metals, timber, etc. The second is the absorption of wastes (W) from production, both from the production process and from the disposal of consumption goods. Where these wastes add to or improve the stock of ecological capital (e.g. through recycling or fertilisation of soil by live-stock), they can be regarded as investment in such capital. More frequently, where they destroy, pollute or erode, with consequent negative impacts on the ecological, human or manufactured capital stocks, they can be regarded as agents of negative investment, depreciation or capital consumption. Either way, the wastes contribute to the capital feedback effects identified in Figure 3.2.

The third type of environmental function does not contribute directly to production, but in many ways it is the most important type because it provides the basic context and conditions within which production is possible at all. It comprises basic 'environmental services' (ES), including 'survival services' such as those producing climate and ecosystem stability, shielding of ultraviolet radiation by the ozone layer, and 'amenity services' such as the beauty of wilderness and other natural areas. These services are produced directly by ecological capital independently of human activity, but human activity can certainly have an (often negative) effect on the responsible capital and therefore on the services produced by it, through the capital feedback effects discussed earlier.

The outputs of the economic process can therefore, in the first instance, be categorised as 'Goods' and 'Bads'. The Goods are the desired outputs of the process, as well as any positive externalities (incidental effects) that may be associated with them. These Goods can be divided in turn into consumption, investment and intermediate goods and services. The Bads are the negative effects of the production process, including capital depreciation and polluting wastes and other negative externalities, which contribute to environmental destruction, negative effects on human health, etc. As noted above, insofar as they have an effect on the capital stocks, the Bads can be regarded as negative investment.

The necessity for a matter/energy balance on either side of the production process means that all matter and energy that feature as inputs must also emerge as outputs, either embodied in the Goods or among the Bads. On disposal of the former, therefore, all these former inputs are returned to the environment, to the stock of ecological capital, where they may have a positive, negative or neutral effect. The essential point is that, for matter, Figure 3.2 represents a closed system; for energy, inputs can be received from the sun, and heat can be radiated from the Earth into space.

The differences between Figure 3.1 and Figure 3.2 can be summarised as follows:

- Land has been redefined as ecological capital, with the identification of its three key sets of environmental functions: resource provision, waste absorption and the direct provision of environmental services as discussed above.
- Wastes and pollution from the production process and consumption have been added. These affect utility directly (Wu, e.g. litter, noise) and through their mainly negative feedback into the stocks of environmental, human and manufactured capital. These feedbacks, Wc, can reduce the productivity of environmental resources (e.g. through pollution) and

affect the ecological capital that produces environmental services (e.g. by engendering climate change or damaging the ozone layer); they can damage human capital by engendering ill health; and they can corrode buildings (manufactured capital). They can also affect environmental services directly (*Wes*, e.g. by reducing the beauty of natural areas).

- Labour has become the service delivered by an expanded concept of human capital, the formation of which Becker (1964: 1) defined as 'activities which influence future monetary and psychic income by increasing the resources in people'. Human capital can therefore be seen to include such aspects of labour-power as knowledge, skills, health and motivation. Specifying human capital thus allows the model to recognise the direct relationships between human capital and welfare: a happy worker will be more productive (*Uh*); and a healthy worker will be happier as well as more productive (*Hu*).

- The addition of social/organisational capital reflects the considerable part played by institutions in wealth creation. The concept was first developed by Tomer (1973: 267–81), and considerably expanded in his book *Organizational Capital* (Tomer 1987). Whereas human capital is embodied in individuals, social/organisational capital derives from their ways of interacting. As with human capital, social/organisational capital has a direct relationship with welfare. Social structures (e.g. the family) are major determinants of welfare (*SOu*), while the welfare of individuals will affect the performance of social structures (*Uso*).

- It is explicitly acknowledged that utility is generated by many other aspects of life apart from consumption. Broadly these can be classified according to the four modes of experience identified by Max-Neef (1991: 30ff.):

Being:	affected by the quality of the environment (*ESu*), the nature and level of wastes (*Wu*) and the quality of human capital itself (*Hu*);
Having:	derived from consumption (*COu*);
Doing:	derived from the work process (*Pu*);
Interacting:	derived from social and organisational structures as well as from the work process (*SOu*).

- Feedback effects are emphasised in Figure 3.2. One that has not yet been mentioned is the joint relationship between the stock of ecological capital (*EC*) and the environmental services (*ES*) deriving from it. In a stable ecosystem, *EC* and *ES* will tend to be symbiotically balanced. Another important feedback is that from the work process to the human and social organisational capital stocks (*Pc*), reflected in the emphasis that has been placed on 'learning by doing' (Arrow 1962) and in the perception that work can 'deskill' workers (Braverman 1974).

- The greater complexity of Figure 3.2. This is a disadvantage in terms of its tractability for formal analysis. However, as has been seen, more

tractable models have undesirable limitations in their physical interpretation. It seems that the complexity of Figure 3.2 is necessary if
the full contribution of the environment to wealth creation and welfare
is to be understood and its relationship to economic growth be
adequately analysed.

There are two resources – space and time – that are crucial to all
economic activity which have not been explicitly included in the model
(see Faber and Proops 1993 and Barker 1996 for recent treatments),
although space can be considered as an aspect of environmental capital,
and will be thus considered in the discussion in Chapter 4. However, the
important difference between these resources and the four capitals that
are included is that space and time are absolutely scarce and cannot be
increased by investment. Investment in the other factors of production can
make space and time more productive, for example miniaturisation in
electronics, time-saving domestic appliances, but no investment or depletion
can increase or reduce the volume of a cubic metre or make a day more
or less than twenty-four hours. The focus of the model is confined to those
production factors that can be augmented or depleted.

Figure 3.2 identifies as a 'production process' any humanly organised
combination of flows from the capital stocks which results in the production
of desired outputs, Goods. It makes no distinction between flows of inputs
that are paid for and those that are not; or between outputs that are
marketed and those that are not. Such distinctions obviously become
important when one wishes to quantify the flows of inputs and outputs,
and are dealt with in detail in Chapter 5. But they are not relevant to
the discussion of the nature of, and distinction between, 'growth' and
'development' which now follows.

3.2 DIFFERENT KINDS OF GROWTH

In the model of Figure 3.2 it is possible to distinguish between four different
kinds of growth:

I   Growth of the economy's biophysical throughput. This is measured
     by the flow E. The first and second laws of thermodynamics dictate
     that the matter which is included in this flow as an input into produc-
     tion will appear in due course as an output from it, while the energy
     in the flow will also be conserved and will join the flux of energy that
     is radiated to and from the earth, with the proviso that high grade
     (low entropy) energy that is used as an input into production will
     emerge as lower grade (higher entropy) energy. Growth in E will there-
     fore be associated with an increase in entropy, which will be manifest
     as a growth in wastes and pollution, impacting negatively on welfare

through *Wu*, *Wes* and *Wc*. The extent of growth type I since 1950 can be illustrated from Brown *et al.* (1996: 4): 'the human population has doubled; demand for water, firewood, grain, beef and mutton has tripled; consumption of fossil fuels has increased by nearly four times, with a corresponding increase in carbon emissions, and of seafood has more than quadrupled; consumption of paper has gone up sixfold.' In a physically finite world governed by the laws of thermodynamics, indefinite, let alone exponentially indefinite, growth type I is not possible. It is in fact quite clear that it is this kind of growth that is responsible for current environmental problems.

II   Growth of production. As stated above, this may be monetary or non-monetary production, organised by markets, governments or households. The system of national accounts computes a subset of this production, mainly comprising marketed goods and services and government expenditure, in its aggregates Gross Domestic and National Products (GDP, GNP), which form the focus of discussion in Chapter 5. Production growth leads to an increase in consumption, in this or subsequent periods, and therefore to an increase in *COu*'s contribution to welfare. Whether and under what conditions it does or does not lead to a growth of biophysical throughput is one of the principal subjects of investigation of this book. Hereafter, production growth, as measured by growth in GNP, will also be called economic growth, in accordance with conventional practice, while recognising this to be controversial (for the controversy, see, for example, Hueting's contention (Hueting 1986: 244) that economic growth means growth in welfare, not production).

III   Growth of economic welfare. In the model of Figure 3.1, the growth of welfare is exclusively dependent on, and can therefore be measured by, the growth of consumption (i.e. growth type II). This is not the case with the model of Figure 3.2 as has been seen. Although there the relation between consumption and welfare is positive, *ceteris paribus*, it is quite possible for the negative feedbacks from production growth, where, for example, they involve more wastes, environmental destruction or erosion of community, to result in a decrease in welfare. Mishan (1967, 1977), Leipert (1989a, b), Daly and Cobb (1989), Douthwaite (1992), Daly (1996) and Parris (1997) all question the extent to which GNP growth now contributes to net economic welfare. The relationship between the growth of GNP and welfare is discussed further below.

IV   Environmental growth. This comprises the addition to some natural resources (ecological capital) that takes place through processes of natural growth and regeneration, leading to an increase both in resources for production and consumption (E) and in environmental services (ES). Ecological capital is the only one of the four capitals to experience spontaneous growth in this way. The tendency of the other kinds of capital is to deplete if they are not continually refreshed through use and/or investment. The generation of biomass through environmental growth leads to the concept of Gross Nature Product (Agarwal 1985: 20ff.), which is not a mere subset of GDP for two reasons. First, a considerable portion of the Nature Product may not enter into money transactions. Second, it generates utility directly (through *ESu*) independently of its consumption.

This kind of growth, including many different kinds of biomass, animal and vegetable, clearly cannot be meaningfully expressed in aggregate form. But, for three reasons, it is probably the most important kind of growth considered here. First, the conversion by plants of solar energy from outside the biosphere to biomass within it is the only means (apart from human-made solar-powered equipment) by which living systems, including humans, can circumvent the Second Law of Thermodynamics and decrease biospheric entropy. Second, the quantity and quality of biomass is crucial to the stability of important natural processes, such as climate regulation or the carbon and water cycles. Third, and most obviously, biomass includes food. The ability of the Earth to support the doubling of the present human population which is in prospect depends on great increases in food production.

The relationship between these four kinds of growth is, therefore, complex. It is also variable. A given flow of environmental resources (E) can produce different structures of production, with different levels of value added (as measured by GDP) with different environmental impacts (W) resulting in different levels of welfare.

The failure to distinguish rigorously and consistently between growth types I and II is the single most important source of the confusion which continues to beset even the most recent writing about growth and the environment, in particular that which stresses the limits to growth. This is clearly exemplified in the recent book on this theme by one of those who has written about it most consistently and influentially, Herman Daly (Daly 1996).

The most frustrating aspect of Daly's treatment of this issue is that he obviously appreciates the distinction between different kinds of growth, asking very early on in the book:

> Does growth mean growth in the total value of goods and services produced during a given time period (GNP, or gross national product)? Or does it mean growth in the rate of flow of matter and energy through a given economic system (physical throughput)?
>
> (Daly 1996: 2)

Clearly Daly is referring to what were earlier called growth types II and I respectively, so that growth can mean either of these two things, but the relationship between these two types is never explicitly addressed in Daly's book and the subsequent confusion pervades the rest of the work, as the following quotations illustrate.

Daly's view of the natural world is as 'an ecosystem which is finite, non-growing and materially closed' (1996: 1). The human economy is a sub-system of this ecosystem. Its physical expansion beyond the size of the ecosystem is therefore impossible and its physical expansion beyond some 'optimal scale' (ibid.: 6) is undesirable. Because the physical demands of the economy are currently beyond that scale, Daly considers that 'physical growth should cease' (ibid.: 3). This argument is very much consistent with that taken in this book. In fact Chapter 6 will argue that the current physical demands of the economy must be substantially reduced if environmental sustainability is to be approached.

However, the clarity of this focus on physical expansion is frequently blurred by reference throughout the book to 'quantitative expansion', with persistent ambiguity as to whether the quantity concerned is physical, i.e. an amount of matter or energy, or a value, such as GNP. Economists, and political and economic institutions, such as the World Bank, are berated for their fixation with 'growth', as if they were concerned to increase the physical size of the economy, whereas in fact they are interested in the growth of its value, GNP.

Daly writes:

> There is much confusion as to what, precisely, is supposed to grow as GNP grows. . . . GNP accounting does not distinguish growth from development – both lead to an increase in the GNP, an increase in the value of annual goods and services, and are counted as 'economic growth'.
>
> (1996: 28)

The confusion should be easily dispelled. GNP, as Daly here makes clear, is a measure of *value* (although on p. 41 he confusingly calls it 'an index of throughput', which implies that it is a physical, rather than a value, measure). Daly rightly insists that the value of GNP has a physical dimension, but he persistently fails to acknowledge the implications of the variability of the relationship between the GNP value and its physical dimension. For example, he applauds the tendency of 'dematerialisation' in the economy to 'reduce the throughput intensity of service', while not seeming to accept that this means that the same quantity of resources can produce a greater value, or GNP. This leads him to make statements that are either confusing or wrong or both, such as: 'The idea that we can save the "growth forever" paradigm by dematerialising the economy, or "decoupling" it from resources, or substituting information for resources, is fantasy.' If by 'growth forever' paradigm, Daly is referring to GNP growth, this statement is clearly wrong. As was noted in Chapter 2 in connection with the Lecomber quotation on p. 41, if dematerialisation with respect to limiting resources proceeds at a rate equal to or greater than the growth of GNP, then GNP can increase indefinitely, and can do so without inflicting increased damage on the environment.

It is not clear whether Daly would dispute this point theoretically, or whether he believes such dematerialisation to be a practical impossibility. Rather he side-steps the issue with 'one really does not have to argue the point. We can simply distinguish growth (quantitative expansion) from development (qualitative improvement) and urge ourselves to develop as much as possible, while ceasing to grow'. The distinction between growth and development is explored further in the next section of this chapter, but it does nothing to resolve the question of whether indefinite GNP growth in a finite world is possible or not, because it is clear from an earlier quotation that Daly's development, as well as growth, can contribute to an increase in GNP. Daly's explicit advocacy of a steady-state, as opposed to a growth, economy, and his position as the most prominent and influential economist advocating 'limits to growth', suggest that he thinks that indefinite GNP growth in a finite world is not possible, but this position cannot be logically deduced from his work, nor is it expressed explicitly there.

The essential issue actually emerges more clearly in three sentences from another recent publication that perceives limits to growth:

> The limits to energy availability, environmental raw materials and sink capacities mean there are very real limits to the growth of the physical scale of the material economy. Insofar as the *value* of the material economy is linked to its physical scale, the economic growth of the material economy also faces limits. This means that the unlimited exponential growth of the money economy is a virtual impossibility.
>
> (Parris 1997: 25, original emphasis)

In fact, the third sentence does not follow logically from the second. Rather the issue should be reformulated thus: If the value of the material economy has a fixed relationship to its physical scale, the economic growth of the material economy also faces limits, so that the unlimited exponential growth of the money economy is an absolute impossibility. If, however, this relationship is variable and, in particular, the material intensity of economic value can be continuously reduced, then the possibility exists of indefinite growth of value, i.e. GNP, even in a context of binding physical limits.

It is clear from past experience that the relationship between the economy's value and its physical scale is variable and that it is possible to reduce the material intensity of GNP. This establishes the theoretical possibility of GNP growing indefinitely in a finite material world. However, neither such a possibility nor previous experience says much about the kind of changes in the physical impacts of current economic activity which are required for that activity to become environmentally sustainable in the real world, or whether the technological and economic opportunities exist for these changes to be brought about such that the value of economic activity (GNP) is increased rather than reduced.

These are the issues which are explored in the rest of this book. The question is whether, in practice, reducing the economy's throughput of matter/energy requires a slowing down of production growth, measured as the rate of growth of GNP, or even a reduction in GNP itself. This is an important question since GNP is the variable of most concern to macro-economists and politicians, and the fear of negative impacts on growth is probably the principal source of resistance to environmental policy. At least part of the reason for policy makers' commitment to GNP growth (growth type II) is that this kind of growth is perceived to be a necessary if not sufficient condition for welfare growth (growth type III). Before addressing the central question of how much GNP growth is likely to be compatible with environmental sustainability, it is helpful to elucidate further the relationship between these two types of growth, and to relate them in turn to the concept of 'development'.

3.3 GROWTH, DEVELOPMENT AND WELFARE

The concept of sustainable development has two components: sustainability, which is the subject of Chapter 4, and development. Now the debate about what constitutes development has a considerable history which has spawned an enormous literature, which is largely outside the scope of this book. For present purposes it is enough to characterise development as a process which results in the increased welfare of the group under consideration, perhaps with special reference to the least well-off members of the group.

Development is therefore most closely related to growth type III (increase in welfare) and therefore also has a complex relationship to growth type II (increase in production). Environmental sustainability is most closely related to growth types I (probably negatively) and IV. The relationship between 'sustainable development' and GNP growth therefore has several levels of complexity.

Other things being equal, increases in per capita income may be considered to contribute positively to development (or welfare), but clearly many other factors are also contributors to economic (and non-economic) welfare, including health, education, income distribution, employment, working conditions, leisure, environmental quality and security, social cohesion and spiritual coherence. There is no numeraire that can evaluate the trade-offs between these various factors, so that at a time when some are changing for the better and others for the worse it becomes very difficult to say whether 'development' is taking place or not.

Table 3.1 Has the UK become more 'developed' from 1961–91?

	1991	1981	1971	1961
Gross domestic product (GDP)[a] (£1985 billion)	345	275	236	183
Unemployment, %[b]	8.7	9.8	3.3	1.3
Income per week: *Bottom tenth:*[c]	(1993)			
Amount (£1993)	175		138	
Index	127		100	
Top tenth:				
Amount (£1993)	567		336	
Index	169		100	
Net income, %[d]	(1990–1)		(1973)	
Bottom fifth	7	10	8	
Top fifth	41	36	37	
Recorded offences (thousands):[e]	(1991)		(1971)	
Violence against the person	190	100	47	17
Sexual offences	29	19	24	15
Burglary	1219	718	452	na[f]
Families headed by lone parents, %[g]	18	12	(1976) 10	
Divorces (thousands)[h]	171	156	(1971) 79	27

Notes:
a At factor cost. The 1971, 1981 figures come from *UK National Income and Expenditure (UKNIE) 1991* (HMSO, London), Table 1.1: 10–11; the 1991 figure comes from *UKNIE 1994*, Table 1.1: 10–11, converted from £1990 to £1985; the 1961 figure from *UKNIE 1974*, Table 8: 10–11, converted from the index number series
b The 1981, 1991 figures come from *Social Trends (ST) 1994* (HMSO, London), Table 4.19, p.62; the 1961, 1971 figures come from *ST 1984*, Table 4.16, p.66
c The bottom tenth figure is the maximum amount earned by men in that part of the income distribution; the top tenth figure is the minimum amount earned by men in that part of the distribution. Figures from *ST 1994*, Table 5.5, p.69
d Before housing costs. Figures from *ST 1994*, Table 5.20, p.77
e England & Wales. Figures for 1981, 1991 from *ST 1994*, Table 12.2, p.152; for 1971 from *ST 1984*, Table 12.1, p.165; for 1961, *ST 1974*, Table 169, p.187
f Recorded under different categories
g Figures from *ST 1994*, Table 2.8, p.36
h Figures from *ST 1994*, Table 2.13, p.38

For example, it is debatable whether the UK is more 'developed' than it was twenty or thirty years ago. Table 3.1 shows that its GDP was certainly much higher in 1991 than in 1971, having grown by 46 per cent. But unemployment is also much higher, income distribution is more unequal, the poorest people have benefited least from growth, in relative as well as absolute terms, and there is more violence, crime and family breakdown. With regard to the environment, one conclusion on the basis of a recent set of measures was 'in many areas the UK environment is in "poor condition", and in some cases the situation is actually deteriorating' (ECG 1994: 76); globally damage continues at a high rate to such resources as forests and fisheries and significant new global threats to the atmosphere have emerged. Such considerations led one calculation of Sustainable Economic Welfare in the UK to conclude:

> Welfare in the UK has not improved over the study period [1950–90] at anything like the rate that a conventional measure of GNP would have us believe. In particular, sustainable economic welfare appears to have declined in this country since the mid-1970s.
>
> (Jackson and Marks 1994: 36)

The weighing of such complex issues, and the striving for balance between them, is the stuff of democratic politics and political debate, of course, so that it is hardly surprising that the 'development' component of sustainable development remains contested and confusing ground.

Identifying development as an increase in welfare and relating this to the model of Figure 3.2, that part of welfare which is economic is conceived as a function of the stocks, flows and processes related to production, and of its social, economic and environmental outcomes (including consumption and income distribution). As shown, it is affected by many factors apart from the consumption of produced goods and services, including the process of production (working conditions), the institutions of production (family, community, firm, political/legal system), people's state of health (part of human capital) and environmental quality (negative externalities and the stock of ecological capital).

This seems to be the approach taken by Pearce *et al.*, who consider 'development' – 'implying change that is *desirable*' (and therefore equivalent to an increase in welfare) – to be

> a *vector* of desirable social objectives; that is, it is a list of attributes which society seeks to achieve or maximize. The elements of this vector might include:
>
> - increases in real income per capita;
> - improvements in health and nutritional status;
> - educational achievement;
> - access to resources;
> - a 'fairer' distribution of income;
> - increases in basic freedoms.
>
> Correlation between these elements, or an agreed system of weights to be applied to them, might permit development to be represented by a single 'proxy' indicator, but this is not an issue pursued here.
>
> (Pearce *et al.* 1990: 2–3, original emphasis)

A very similar approach was taken by Hueting (1986: 243ff.), who identified welfare as having the components production (income), environment, employment, working conditions, income distribution, leisure and safety of the future.

This approach is also compatible with the United Nations Development Programme's definition of human development as

> the process of enabling people to have wider choices. Income is one of those choices, but it is not the sum total of human life. Health, education, a good physical environment and freedom of action and expression are just as important. . . . The distribution of (economic) growth is also important.
>
> (UNDP 1992: 13)

This message was re-emphasised in UNDP (1995: 122–3): 'Economic growth is essential to human development. But to fully exploit the opportunities for improved well-being that growth offers, it must be properly managed, for there is no automatic link between economic growth and human progress.'

Such a view contrasts sharply with that of Daly, who, as noted earlier on p. 60, has tried to draw a clear distinction between development and growth: 'Growth is quantitative increase in physical scale, while development is qualitative improvement or unfolding of potentialities. An economy can grow without developing, or develop without growing, or do both or neither' (Daly 1990: 1). Daly is here clearly identifying 'growth' as growth type I, while his characterisation of development as 'qualitative improvement' is compatible with Pearce *et al.*'s characterisation of development as a 'vector of socially desirable objectives'. It is surely the case that, *ceteris paribus*, income growth (growth type II) contributes to the 'qualitative improvement' of people's lives and therefore to development. If growth type I occurs without growth type II, then the former's negative environmental impact will reduce welfare. If growth type II occurs without growth type I (and without negative impacts on other components of welfare), then welfare will unambiguously increase. If the two kinds of growth occur together, as has historically been the case, then the net effect on welfare is uncertain. It is the need to evaluate such trade-off situations that has led to the formulations of the concepts of sustainability and sustainable development, which are discussed in Chapters 4 and 5. As was seen earlier, Daly's seemingly clear distinction between growth and development actually sheds little light on the crucial growth–environment issue, which is the relationship between growth types I and II.

Income, as measured by GNP or Net National Product (NNP, derived from GNP by subtracting capital consumption), and its growth, may contribute to but are quite distinct from welfare. There is no shortage of pronouncements from economists and statisticians on the inappropriateness of using the national accounts aggregates as welfare indicators. Many years ago Graaff (1967: 92) pointed out that, in general, a heterogeneous collection of goods and services $(X_1, \ldots X_n)$ could not be expected to proxy for the social welfare function $W(u_1, \ldots u_m)$ reflecting the utilities of individuals. The role of an index number such as aggregate output or consumption was, he thought, simply to permit 'a balanced judgement on the relative merits of two years', and such numbers should always be supplemented with information about a range of relevant concerns, such as the distribution of income and wealth. 'The more information made available, the more likely it is that a balanced judgement will be obtained. . . . The chief error of those who have attempted definite welfare interpretations of index numbers is that they have attempted too much' (ibid.: 165–6).

It is worth quoting at some length Herfindahl and Kneese's exposition of the conditions for NNP to be a useful welfare indicator.

> If it were true that all salient goods and services were exchanged in markets; that the degree of competition in these markets did not change; that the programs of government and non-profit institutions did not change in such a way that they produced substantially altered welfare relative to the final goods and services that they absorbed; that population stayed constant; and that the distribution of income did not change; then alterations in real NNP . . . could be regarded as a good indicator of changes in the economic welfare of the population.
>
> This is an imposing string of assumptions, none of which is ever exactly met in reality. . . . In fact, the distance between reality and these assumptions is large and significant in some cases, thus seriously reducing the practical usefulness of NNP as a welfare measure. . . . The designers of the accounts thought that at best they would serve to provide only a rough indicator of one dimension of welfare.
>
> (Herfindahl and Kneese 1973: 446)

Despite the theoretical problems and the heroic nature of the assumptions required to overcome them, GNP and NNP continue to be widely used as indicators of welfare, both in popular discourse and in academic work. Beckerman provides a clear example of academic ambivalence on this issue. He is clear that income and welfare are not the same thing: 'With exactly the same income and prices and quantities today as yesterday, and without any change in my tastes . . . I may still be less happy today than yesterday on account of some change in economic circumstances' (Beckerman 1968: 167). Yet five pages later, without so much as an invocation of *ceteris paribus*, he is proposing to discuss 'how to measure differences in real income, *which we will equate with economic welfare*' (ibid.: 172, emphasis added). There is a continuing robust academic tradition of advocating the practical use of NNP as a welfare indicator (for recent examples of the tradition see Hartwick 1990; Dasgupta *et al.* 1994; Dasgupta 1995), with the proviso, arising from current concerns about the environment, that it is suitably adjusted for environmental effects.

Examples of the use of GDP or GNP as a welfare measure abound in practical work. Thus, to take the global warming issue, Boero *et al.* report in their survey of the CO_2 abatement literature:

> Even if consumption were proportional to GDP, welfare is not proportional to consumption, and so measuring the costs of abatement in terms of GDP is not ideal. However, given that this is *the almost universal metric*, GDP is the main focus of this survey.
>
> (Boero *et al.* 1991: S3, emphasis added)

Similarly, in his influential paper on the economics of the greenhouse effect, Nordhaus explicitly employs the GDP metric as a welfare measure: 'We assume that it is desirable to maximise a social welfare function that is the discounted sum of the utilities of per capita consumption' (Nordhaus 1991a: 925). Consumption in the paper is expressed in terms of GDP.

The theoretical and practical identification of NNP and GNP with welfare contrasts strongly with the views of those like Bryant and Cook (1992: 99), who do not consider appropriate such a use of national accounting aggregates: 'The national accounts measure activity involving economic exchanges. They do not measure, nor claim to measure, sustainable development or welfare.' Such a perception has led to attempts to develop a proxy indicator for welfare or development, despite the difficulties related to the commensurability and aggregation of their various components. Probably the best known and simplest of these is the UNDP's Human Development Index (HDI), calculated annually for its *Human Development Report*. HDI consists of a combination of various measures of income, education and longevity.

The first, and more ambitious, attempt to calculate a proxy for welfare, Nordhaus and Tobin's derivation of a Measure of Economic Welfare (MEW), arose directly from their perception of GNP as an unsuitable welfare measure:

> GNP is not a measure of economic welfare. . . . An obvious shortcoming of GNP is that it is an index of production, not consumption. The goal of economic activity, after all, is consumption. Although this is the central premise of economics, the profession has been slow to develop, either conceptually or statistically, a measure of economic performance oriented to consumption, broadly defined and carefully calculated.
>
> (Nordhaus and Tobin 1973: 512)

MEW was calculated through some reclassification of GNP final expenditure, imputations for capital services, leisure and non-market work and deductions for disamenities of urbanisation. The detail of the calculation need not concern us here, but Nordhaus and Tobin's conclusion is significant, in that it seemed to confirm a rough correlation between GNP and welfare: 'Although GNP and other national income aggregates are imperfect measures of welfare, the broad picture of secular progress which they convey remains after correction of their most obvious deficiencies' (Nordhaus and Tobin 1973: 532).

Sixteen years later Daly and Cobb came to a very different conclusion, both by interpreting Nordhaus and Tobin's figures differently, and on the basis of their own calculation of an Index of Socio-Economic Welfare (ISEW). With regard to the former they note: 'When [Nordhaus and Tobin's] findings are more carefully examined for time frames other than the full period from 1929–65, the relatively close association between per capita GNP and MEW disappears' (Daly and Cobb 1990: 79). In particular, if the period 1947–65 is chosen, the difference between the growth of GNP and MEW (both per capita, hereafter PC-GNP and PC-MEW) is striking: 48 per cent or 2.2 per cent per annum for PC-GNP, 7.5 per cent or 0.4 per cent per annum for PC-MEW. This leads Daly and Cobb to conclude: 'With their own figures, Nordhaus and Tobin have shed doubt on the thesis that national income accounts serve as a good proxy measure of economic welfare' (ibid.: 80).

ISEW makes different adjustments to GNP from MEW, including giving consideration to resource depletion and environmental damage, so the two indices are not strictly comparable, although the general trend in ISEW is similar to that of MEW for the same years (i.e. to 1965). However, from 1950–86 GNP and ISEW differ substantially: PC-GNP growth was 2.02 per cent, while PC-ISEW grew by 0.87 per cent. From 1970–86, while PC-GNP roughly maintained its 2 per cent annual growth rate, PC-ISEW actually declined, at an increasing annual rate (–0.14 per cent from 1970–80; –1.26 per cent from 1980–6) (Daly and Cobb 1990: 453).

From an environmental point of view, one of ISEW's most interesting insights is:

> Efforts to control air pollution and reduce accidents have paid off by improving economic welfare during the 1970s and 1980s. . . . Improvements in both areas have had the effect of countering the generally downward trend in ISEW. They offer evidence that the choice of policies by government can indeed have a positive effect on economic welfare even if they do not increase physical output.
>
> (Daly and Cobb 1990: 454)

However, Daly and Cobb's overall conclusion from ISEW is in stark contrast to the generally rosy GNP record:

> Despite the year-to-year variations in ISEW, it indicates a long-term trend from the late 1970s to the present that is indeed bleak. Economic

welfare has been deteriorating for at least a decade, largely as a result of growing income inequality, the exhaustion of resources, and the failure to invest adequately to sustain the economy in the future.

(ibid.: 455)

Subsequent work along these lines has included Jackson and Marks (1994) for the UK, which came to broadly the same conclusion as Daly and Cobb for the US, although much the largest adjustment for 1980–90 comes, not from environmental factors, but from the increase in inequality over these years. Cobb and Cobb (1994: 83 (Table A1)), extending and largely confirming the earlier US results, find that their ISEW decreased by 7 per cent from 1980 to 1986, although GNP rose by 11.6 per cent over the same period.

The ISEWs of both Daly and Cobb and Jackson and Marks have been subjected to thoroughgoing criticism by Nordhaus (1992a) and Atkinson (1995) respectively. Both critiques call into question the derivation of many of the components of the ISEW calculations (which are similar, but not identical). Nordhaus' alternative calculation of Hicksian income shows that this has grown substantially slower than US GDP, but not as slowly as US ISEW. Atkinson (1995: 20–1) simply finds that the UK ISEW is 'fundamentally flawed' and subject to 'an alarming degree of arbitrariness'.

The diversity of components of welfare in the lists of Pearce *et al.* (1990) and Hueting (1986), and as illustrated in Figure 3.2, the acknowledged difficulty and arbitrariness of attaching either money values or appropriate weights to them for the purpose of aggregation and the failure of such efforts as the calculation of MEW and ISEW to generate a methodological consensus, or even a research programme to generate such a consensus, raise the question as to whether in fact the derivation of a single 'proxy' indicator for development or welfare is a feasible objective. Ruggles and Miles both conclude that it is not: 'No amount of imputation can convert a one-dimensional summary measure such as the GNP into an adequate or appropriate measure of social welfare' (Ruggles 1983: 41–3) and:

Despite many approaches to the modification of GNP, some of which have provided more or less useful statistical innovations, they have not resulted in, and cannot result in, any single indicator which can do for welfare or quality of life comparisons the sort of thing which GNP has achieved for economic output. . . . The search for a single indicator of progress is misguided. Social reality is too complex for it to make any sense to collapse its manifold dimensions into a one-dimensional scale.

(Miles 1992: 288, 296)

Rather, in order to convey more information about the achievement of welfare, as suggested by Graaff, it would seem preferable to promote the adoption of a framework of indicators (as discussed in Ekins 1990 and, in more detail, in Ekins and Max-Neef 1992: 231–310), which would seek to convey the dimensions of social and economic welfare more effectively than any single indicator could hope to do. This appears to be the approach adopted by the UK Government in its publication of a set of 'headline' indicators for the UK (DETR 1998).

In fact GNP is a poor measure, not simply of welfare, but of production itself. This is not just because GNP does not include the great majority of non-monetary economic production and therefore understates production by the huge amount of unpaid and household voluntary work undertaken in the economy; GNP is not even an accurate indicator of monetised production, because of the national accounts' treatment of environmental inputs and impacts, and of the defensive expenditures in environmental and other areas, which are associated with production. The extensions to and modifications of the national accounts which should be made to improve their treatment of these areas are the subject of Chapter 5. First, however, it is necessary to complete the clarification of the concepts of growth, welfare and sustainable development by specifying precisely what is meant by environmental sustainability.

4 The concept of environmental sustainability

4.1 SUSTAINABILITY: GENERAL DEFINITIONS AND DETERMINANTS

The basic meaning of sustainability is the capacity for continuance more or less indefinitely into the future. The past twenty years have seen a substantial accumulation of evidence that, in aggregate, current human ways of life do not possess that capacity, either because they are destroying the environmental conditions necessary for their continuance, or because their environmental effects will cause unacceptable social disruption and damage to human health. The environmental effects in question, as outlined in Chapter 1, include climate change, ozone depletion, acidification, toxic pollution, the depletion of renewable resources (e.g. forests, soils, fisheries, water) and of non-renewable resources (e.g. fossil fuels) and the extinction of species.

A way of life is a complex bundle of values, objectives, institutions and activities, with ethical, environmental, economic and social dimensions. While current concern about unsustainability largely has an ecological basis, it is clear that human situations or ways of life can be unsustainable for social, economic and ethical reasons as well. The pertinent questions are: for the environment, can its contribution to human welfare and to the human economy be sustained? For the economy, can today's level of wealth-creation be sustained? For society, can social cohesion and important social institutions be sustained? And ethically, influencing all the other three dimensions, do people alive today value other people and other life forms, now and in the future, sufficiently highly?

Provided that the interrelatedness of the different dimensions is borne in mind, it can be useful to distinguish between the implications for sustainability of human mores, relationships and institutions (the social dimension); of the allocation and distribution of scarce resources (the economic dimension); and of the contribution to both of these from, and their effects on, the environment and its resources (the ecological dimension). Clearly human relationships may be socially unsustainable (for example, those leading to civil war) independently of economic or ecological factors; and a particular allocation of resources may be economically unsustainable (leading, for example, to growing budget deficits) independently of social or ecological factors. Similarly, a given level of economic growth may be unsustainable for purely economic reasons, insofar as it is leading to increased inflation or balance of payments deficits; on the other hand, it may be socially unsustainable insofar as it is increasing income inequalities or undermining structures of social cohesion such as the family or community; or it may be environmentally unsustainable insofar as it is depleting resources on which the economic growth itself depends.

One way of illustrating the complexities involved is through the matrix shown in Table 4.1, where the rows show the types of sustainability, and the columns the influences on those types, across the same dimensions. In the example above, the sustainability of economic growth would be considered across the second row, with environmental influences (e.g. resource depletion) in box A, economic influences (e.g. inflation, balance of payments) in box B, and social influences (e.g. social cohesion) in box C. Possible ethical influences on the different dimensions of sustainability would be placed in box D (for example, concern for future generations or non-human forms of life), box E (for example, attitudes to poverty and income distribution) and box F (for example, attitudes to the family or the legal system). With regard to environmental sustainability, this may be influenced by purely environmental factors (box G, e.g. earthquakes, volcanic eruptions), by economic impacts (box H, e.g. pollution), or by social arrangements (box I, e.g. systems of property rights).

Environmental sustainability may always be considered a desirable characteristic of a human situation, though some states of such sustainability may be better than others. In contrast, economic and social sustainability have no such happy connotation. As Hardoy *et al.* stress: 'When judged by the length of time for which they (were) sustained, some of the most successful societies were also among the most exploitative, where the abuse of human rights was greatest' (Hardoy *et al.* 1993: 180–1). Also, poverty and the evils which go with it may be all too sustainable. Similarly, in many countries structural unemployment is showing worrying signs of long-term sustainability.

The principal focus of this book is the environment–economy relationship (i.e. boxes A and H in Table 4.1). But such a focus necessarily includes

Table 4.1 Types of sustainability and their interactions

Types of sustainability	Influences on sustainability			
	Ethical	Environmental	Economic	Social
Environmental	D	G	H	I
Economic	E	A	B	C
Social	F			

all the above dimensions, the implications of which for environmental sustainability will now be briefly explored. In a situation of any complexity, the dimensions of sustainability will generally interact in a multiplicity of ways. Any attempt to proceed from the symptoms of unsustainability to their practical remediation which fails to take these interactions into account will be in grave danger of ineffective, and perhaps counterproductive, intervention.

4.1.1 The ethics of sustainability

According to the Brundtland Report:

> Even the narrow notion of physical sustainability implies a concern for social equity between generations, a concern that must logically be extended to equity within each generation. . . . Our inability to promote the common interest in sustainable development is often a product of the relative neglect of economic and social justice within and amongst nations.
>
> (WCED 1987: 43, 49)

The UK Government, in its environment White Paper, also emphasised the moral basis of environmental concern: 'The ethical imperative of stewardship . . . must underlie all environmental policies. . . . We have a moral duty to look after our planet and hand it on in good order to future generations' (HMG 1990: 10).

How a society uses its environment depends first and foremost on its worldview, its perception of the nature of the world and the status of human beings and other life forms within it. It is likely, for example, that a secular, anthropocentric worldview will sanction different uses of the environment, and permit more environmental destruction, than a worldview in which the earth and all life within it is perceived as sacred.

From its worldview a society will derive its concept of environmental justice: the relative rights of non-human forms of life, of future human generations, and of current human generations to benefit from, share or just exist in 'the environment'. Environmental sustainability gains in strength as an imperative the more it is perceived that the well-being and opportunities of future humans and non-human beings should not be sacrificed for present human advantage.

From its worldview, too, a society will derive its means for valuing and taking decisions about the environment. If the environment is viewed primarily as an economic resource, then techniques of environmental economic valuation will be perceived as the most important environmental inputs into decision-making processes.

It is likely that a society's norms of environmental justice will be related to its norms of economic and social justice. If basic personal and civil rights are denied, then environmental rights are unlikely to be respected, or even recognised. Thus sustainability and democracy are related. Further, if non-environmental economic wealth is unequally distributed, access to environmental goods is also likely to be inegalitarian. This has an obvious and direct importance for sustainability, if indeed it is true that poverty is a great destroyer of the environment, as is often asserted.

In exploring how sustainability may be justified on moral grounds, Pezzey (1992a: 333) considers that one of the successful characteristics of humans, which is often given moral force, is their ability to cooperate in, and be loyal to, groups. He speculates that, once unsustainability is perceived as a great enough threat, the elevation of sustainability to an ethical imperative may depend on the ability of humans to transfer their group allegiance from particular tribes or countries to the human species, both present and future generations, as a whole. An ecocentric approach would go further, applying the ethical imperative of sustainability to other species in their own right, and not just insofar as they sustain humanity.

The ethics of sustainability will also determine to a considerable extent where the responsibility for promoting environmental sustainability is perceived to lie, and the degree of coercion in its enforcement that is considered justified. The Polluter Pays Principle, acceded to by OECD countries as early as 1972, but by no means fully implemented, is not only a maxim of economic efficiency; it is also a statement of moral responsibility. If polluters under prevailing economic and social arrangements do not pay, and governments are invoked to make them do so, how governments proceed with this task will depend on the political and social contract between governors and governed, on balances of rights and responsibilities and the institutions that express and enforce them; and, in particular, on how environmental rights are perceived to be distributed. This leads naturally to consideration of sustainability's social dimension.

4.1.2 The social dimension of sustainability

Social sustainability refers to a society's ability to maintain, on the one hand, the necessary means of wealth-creation to reproduce itself and, on the other, a shared sense of social purpose to foster social integration and cohesion. Partly this is a question of having a sustainable economy, as discussed below. Partly it is a question of culture and values. Social sustainability is likely to be a necessary condition for the widespread commitment and involvement which *Agenda 21*, the principal document to emerge from the United Nations Conference on Environment and Development, sees as crucial to the achievement of sustainable development: 'Critical to the effective implementation of the objectives, policies and mechanisms . . . of *Agenda 21* will be the commitment and genuine involvement of all social groups' (*Agenda 21*, Chapter 23, Preamble) (*Earth Summit '92*: 191).

Western industrial societies are often called 'consumer societies', presumably because it is perceived that in these societies consumption is the most important contributor to human welfare. Certainly the principal objective of public policy in these societies is the growth of GNP. The importance that these societies attach to consumption is not only problematic environmentally, because of the level of consumption, and consequent environmental impacts, to which such an emphasis can and often does lead. It is also problematic socially. As per the discussion of Hirsch's work in Chapter 2, a dominant social goal of increasing competitive, individualistic consumption does not seem likely to foster social cohesion, especially in an economic system that is subject to cyclical recession and increasing inequality.

Poverty is always an economic problem both because it denotes chronic scarcity at an individual level and because it can lead to reduced productivity. It is an ethical problem because this scarcity often induces acute suffering and may be the result of social injustice. In some industrialised countries, relative (and sometimes absolute) poverty is also a growing social problem, in terms of its impacts on the social fabric and on the resulting social sense of insecurity, which act to reduce the well-being of the non-poor.

The sense of identity and social purpose of very many people, as well as their income, derives in large part from their employment. Extended unemployment, therefore, not only leads to poverty, but also to the loss of these other characteristics, which is probably more to blame than poverty for unemployment's high correlation with ill-health, mental stress and family breakdown. Unemployment is not just a waste of economic resources, in terms of the unemployed's lost production. It is socially destructive as well, and, at levels not much higher than those presently pertaining in Europe, may be expected to be socially unsustainable. Welfare states were established, both to give practical expression to a sense of social justice and to maintain social cohesion, at far lower levels of unemployment. At current levels they find it difficult to sustain the necessary transfer payments to accomplish these objectives, especially in a climate of growing international competition and taxpayer resistance.

Another contributor to people's sense of identity is their membership of, and involvement in, their local community. In an era of globalisation, the economic life of local communities tends to become increasingly extended. The concept of a local economy that contributes to local livelihoods and responds to local priorities is increasingly unrealistic. To a lesser extent, even national economic options are becoming externally determined. Yet the principal political institutions, that are expected to promote wealth-creation and foster wider well-being, operate at the national and sub-national level. Globalisation damages a sense of social connectedness, of community, while the mismatch between economic and political realities undermines confidence in political processes. Neither phenomenon is helpful for social sustainability. It is possible that local environmental action

– both political and practical – will help to maintain or regenerate local social purpose and identity.

4.1.3 The economic dimension of sustainability

Economic sustainability is most commonly interpreted as a condition of non-declining economic welfare projected indefinitely into the future (Pezzey 1992b). It has already been seen in Chapter 2 that economic optimality (the maximisation of the present value of consumption) is quite distinct from sustainability, and that in fact optimality can be compatible with unsustainability, such that on the optimal path future consumption can decline, even to zero. A number of recent papers have sought to combine optimality and sustainability in some way 'by pruning out of consideration those consumption paths that are ethically indefensible' (Dasgupta 1995: 120), by treating environmental goods as a source of utility in their own right, as well as inputs to production (Beltratti *et al.* 1995) and by making sustainability an extra constraint on the optimal growth path (Pezzey 1994; Baranzini and Bourguignon 1995). The problem with these treatments is that they do not capture the diversity of the contribution of the natural environment to the economy, and they are of very simple economies that are often subject to restrictive assumptions. Such models may yield useful insights, but their application to real economies and environments is inevitably limited.

If considerations of optimality and sustainability lead to different policy prescriptions, then for the purposes of public policy one or other of them needs to be accorded priority. There are a number of reasons for challenging the usual economic perception that optimality should be the dominant policy objective. First it may be noted that optimality is often not the basis for public policy. The existence of welfare states is not optimal, nor, necessarily, are social justice or the observation of human rights. Second, optimality calculations may not be feasible because of the difficulties of environmental valuation. Third, even when optimality calculations are made, they may underestimate environmental damages because the future price of environmental goods may be substantially greater than the present price, given the current rate of environmental destruction, but such possible price increases are routinely left out of account because of uncertainties as to what they might be. Fourth, as Jaeger (1995) points out, calculations of optimality based on consumption will be biased against environmental goods, even when environmental goods are properly accounted for, to the extent that the consumption of produced goods and services is more motivated by a desire for relative position or status than that of environmental goods. This is because consumption to improve relative social position produces no aggregate increase of welfare (one person's gain is another's loss, by definition). Jaeger argues that many environmental goods are public goods which, because of their non-excludability, cannot be consumed in a way that confers relative benefits. Where such goods are sacrificed for the consumption of status goods, the net welfare change will not be accurately reflected by their relative values, whether revealed by prices or willingness-to-pay.

For all these reasons, the approach taken here is to use the same definition of economic sustainability (non-declining welfare) as that used to compute optimality, but then to elaborate in more detail the contribution of the environment to that welfare, such that principles for sustaining this contribution may be formulated. The economic implications of seeking to meet these principles can then be explored in a variety of ways.

As discussed in Chapter 3, economic welfare derives from, *inter alia*, income and from the environment, which performs various functions, some of which contribute to production, and therefore income, others of which contribute to welfare directly. Income is generated by stocks of capital, including manufactured, human and natural (or ecological) capital (see Figure 3.2). Natural capital also performs the environmental functions which create welfare directly. For economic welfare to be non-declining, the stock of capital which generates it must be maintained (Pezzey 1992b: 14ff.). This implies in turn that, for economic sustainability, net investment, i.e. gross investment minus capital depreciation, must be positive.

There is then the issue as to whether it is the total stock of capital that must be maintained, with substitution allowed between various parts of it, or whether certain components of capital, particularly natural capital, are non-substitutable, i.e. they contribute to welfare in a unique way that cannot be replicated by another capital component. Turner (1993: 9–15) identifies four different kinds of sustainability, ranging from very weak, which assumes complete substitutability, to very strong, which assumes no substitutability so that all natural capital must be conserved. The assumption of the former is implicit in the so-called 'Hartwick rule' (Hartwick 1977), namely that, provided that the resource rents from the exploitation of exhaustible resources are invested in manufactured capital, per capita consumption can remain constant indefinitely over time. Very strong sustainability has been called 'absurdly strong sustainability' (Daly 1995: 49) in order to dismiss it from practical consideration. Turner's more interesting intermediate categories are:

- Weak environmental sustainability, which derives from a perception that welfare is not normally dependent on a specific form of capital and can be maintained by substituting manufactured for natural capital, though with exceptions.
- Strong sustainability, which derives from a different perception that substitutability of manufactured for natural capital is seriously limited by such environmental characteristics as irreversibility, uncertainty and the existence of 'critical' components of natural capital, which make a unique contribution to welfare. An even greater importance is placed

on natural capital by those who regard it in many instances as a complement to man-made capital (Daly 1992: 27ff.).

The point at issue is which perception most validly describes reality. Resolving this point should be an empirical rather than a theoretical or ideological matter. However, if weak sustainability is assumed *a priori*, it is impossible to show *ex post* whether the assumption was justified or not, for the following reason.

The assumption underlying weak sustainability is that there is no essential difference between different forms of capital, or between the kinds of welfare which they generate. This enables, theoretically at least, all types of capital and the services and welfare generated by them to be expressed in the same monetary unit. In practice, as was seen in Chapters 2 and 3, there may be insuperable difficulties in performing the necessary monetisation and aggregation across the range of issues involved, but the theoretical position is clear and strenuous efforts are being made to make it operational. But the numbers that emerge from these efforts can only show whether or not weak sustainability has been achieved, i.e. whether overall welfare has been maintained. They cannot shed any light on the question as to whether the assumption of commensurable and substitutable capitals was justified in the first place. In assuming away any differences at the start, there is no way of establishing later on whether such differences were important.

The strong sustainability assumption does not suffer from this severe defect in scientific methodology. In keeping natural capital distinct from other kinds of capital, it can examine natural capital's particular contribution to welfare, distinguishing between its contribution to production (through resource-provision and waste-absorption) and its services that generate welfare directly. The examination may reveal that in some cases the welfare derived from natural capital is fully commensurable with other welfare from production and can be expressed in monetary form, so that in these cases substitutability with other forms of productive capital exists, and the weak sustainability condition of a non-declining aggregate capital stock is sufficient to maintain welfare. In other cases the outcome of the examination may be different. The important point is that, starting from a strong sustainability assumption of non-substitutability in general, it is possible to shift to a weak sustainability position where that is shown to be appropriate. But starting from a weak sustainability assumption permits no such insights to enable exceptions to be identified. In terms of scientific methodology, strong sustainability is therefore greatly to be preferred as the *a priori* position.

There are other theoretical reasons for choosing the strong sustainability assumption, in addition to the practical reason of the sheer difficulty of carrying out the necessary weak sustainability calculations for complex environmental effects. Victor (1991: 210–11) notes that there is a recognition in economics going back to Marshall that manufactured capital is fundamentally different from environmental resources. The former is human-made and reproducible in the quantities desired, the latter is the 'free gift of nature' and, in many categories, is in fixed or limited supply. The destruction of manufactured capital is very rarely irreversible (this would only occur if the human capital, or knowledge, that created the manufactured capital had also been lost), whereas irreversibility, with such effects as species extinction, climate change, or even the combustion of fossil fuels, is common in the consumption of natural capital. Moreover, to the extent that manufactured capital requires natural capital for its production, it can never be a complete substitute for resources.

Victor *et al.* (1995: 206) identify the elements of natural capital that are essential for life as we know it as water, air, minerals, energy, space and genetic materials, to which might be added the stratospheric ozone layer and the relationships and interactions between these elements that sustain ecosystems and the biosphere. Some substitution of these essential elements by manufactured and human capital can be envisaged, but their wholesale substitutability, as assumed by weak sustainability, appears improbable, certainly with present knowledge and technologies. In fact, if the process of industrialisation is viewed as the application of human, social and manufactured capital to natural capital to transform it into more human and manufactured capital, then it is possible to view current environmental problems as evidence that such substitutability is not complete. If our current development is unsustainable, it is because it is depleting some critical, non-substitutable components of the capital base on which it depends. 'Critical natural capital' may then be defined as natural capital which is responsible for important environmental functions and which cannot be substituted in the provision of these functions by manufactured capital.

The difference between weak and strong sustainability is important to the argument about the compatibility of sustainability and GDP growth. In general, it may be said that value added (GDP) is generated by transforming energy and materials from the natural environment into human-made goods and services. Fewer environmental goods can be permanently transformed into human-made capital under strong sustainability than under the weak version. *Ceteris paribus*, strong sustainability principles for the specific maintenance of some natural capital could therefore be expected to make the generation of GDP more difficult. The general conditions for compatibility of GDP growth and environmental sustainability will be explored in more detail later, but it should be noted here that the fewer the substitution possibilities allowed, the more stringent the conditions in practice become.

4.2 CONSIDERATIONS OF ENVIRONMENTAL SUSTAINABILITY

In Chapter 3, the key contribution of the environment to the human economy and to human life in general is perceived to be through the operation of a wide range of 'environmental functions'. This concept was first employed in economic analysis by Hueting (1980) and has been extensively developed by de Groot (1992). De Groot defines environmental functions as 'the capacity of natural processes and components to provide goods and services that satisfy human needs' (ibid.: 7). These 'natural processes and components' can in turn be identified as the stocks of and flows from natural capital (though de Groot does not use the term), which features as ecological capital in Figure 3.2 and in various definitions of sustainability and sustainable development (see, for example, Pezzey 1992b: 55ff.). De Groot identifies thirty-seven environmental functions, which he classifies under four headings: regulation, carrier, production and information (1992: 15).

Chapter 3 used another method of grouping these functions, under three headings:

1 Provision of resources for human activity.
2 Absorption of wastes from human activity.
3 Provision of environmental services independently of or interdependently with human activity.

These two classifications are not contradictory. The resource functions in the second typology correspond broadly to the production functions of the first, but also include some carrier functions. The waste absorption functions are included among the regulation functions; and the provision of services includes the information functions and some regulation and carrier functions.

With the increase of the human population and the scale of its activities, the environmental functions are increasingly in competition with each other. Choices have to be made between them and some functions are lost. Lost functions represent costs to be ascribed to the chosen functions. It is in this sense that the environment has become an economic factor: it is increasingly scarce; the uses to which it is put are increasingly competing; and it is an important ingredient of human welfare. The choices between environmental functions are therefore precisely analogous to other economic choices.

The environmental sustainability of human ways of life refers to the ability of the environment to sustain those ways of life. The environmental sustainability of economic activity refers to the continuing ability of the environment to provide the necessary inputs to the economy to enable it to maintain economic welfare. Both these sustainabilities in turn depend on the maintenance of the requisite environmental functions, according to some classification as above. Which functions are important for which ways of life, and which economies, and the level at which they should be sustained, will vary to some extent by culture and society, although there are obviously basic biophysical criteria for human production, consumption and existence.

Taking an *a priori* position of strong sustainability, for the reasons discussed earlier, *environmental sustainability is here defined as the maintenance of important environmental functions.* The advantage of defining it in this way, rather than as the maintenance of natural capital *per se*, is that such a definition makes explicit the requirements of manufactured or human capital and technical change if they are to be full substitutes for natural capital. Manufactured capital is a substitute for natural capital if it performs the same environmental functions as the natural capital. It is clear that this is more likely to be the case when the natural capital performs a single resource function (e.g. as an energy source) than when it is multifunctional in diverse ways (e.g. a rainforest). Similarly technical change can only be said to compensate for natural resource loss when, through the new technology, a reduced quantity of natural resources can perform the same environmental functions. To the extent that manufactured capital and technical change do not fully perform the environmental functions of the natural capital they replace, then substitutability between them has not been complete and there has been a trade-off between them.

There will be cases when such a trade-off appears justified; environmental sustainability is not here perceived to require the maintenance of *all* environmental functions. But the loss of natural capital to date, combined with ignorance about the importance of what remains, together with threshold effects and irreversibilities that make unwelcome changes impossible both to predict and undo, argue for caution. As Perrings *et al.* observe:

> Ecosystems typically continue to function in the short-term even as resilience declines. Indeed, they often signal loss of resilience only at the point at which external shocks at previously sustainable levels flip these systems into some other basis of attraction and so some other regime of behaviour.
>
> (Perrings *et al.* 1995: 22)

Common (1995: 46ff.) also draws a distinction, as is done here, between economic and ecological sustainability. His definition of the former is the same as that of this book, but with regard to the latter he says: 'Ecological sustainability is not a well-defined state to be attained by following some simple rules. We can say that it is the requirement that the resilience of the system be maintained through time' (ibid.: 54). Unfortunately, sustainability defined like this cannot be measured and, as quoted from Perrings *et al.* in the previous paragraph, its loss may only become evident when it is irretrievable. The advantage of focusing on environmental functions is that whether they are being used sustainably can, in general, be measured. This definition may be linked to Common's, and the concept of resilience, by the not unreasonable assumption that if important environmental functions are being sustained, then so is the resilience of the ecosystem. The advantage of the functions approach is that it can be made operational relatively easily, as outlined below.

Environmental sustainability derives its legitimacy as a fundamental objective of public policy from a number of sources. At the teleological level, Faber *et al.* (1995: 45ff.) regard all organisms, including human beings, as being motivated by three broad goals: individual maintenance and fulfilment; reproduction and thereby species maintenance; and a balanced mutual relationship with other living beings for the maintenance of the ecological whole.

Each of these goals has an element of sustainability in that it is directed towards its subject (the individual, species or ecological whole) being sustained through time. The achievement of any one goal depends on the achievement of the others (individuals will not thrive if their species or supporting ecosystem is in decline), which requires the three goals to be pursued in a balanced fashion. Faber *et al.* (1995: 53) perceive that the current development path overemphasises the first, individualistic, goal, resulting in environmentally damaging production and consumption, and the second, reproductive, goal, resulting in exponential population growth, to the detriment of the third goal, balanced relationships between current people, future generations and nature. They perceive that a rebalancing of these goals, with a greater emphasis on the third rather than the first two, is the only way the overall sustainability of human activity and its encompassing ecosystems can be restored.

An important part of any such rebalancing is likely to be an insistence on intergenerational equity, imposing on present generations an obligation to leave future generations no worse off than the present in terms of environmental functions. But there is also a strong element of self-interest in current concern about unsustainability. The other 'regimes of behaviour' noted by Perrings *et al.* above may be substantially less hospitable to humans than the present one. Munasinghe and Shearer (1995: xviii, xix) consider that 'sustaining the global life support system is a prerequisite for sustaining human societies'. In the Foreword to Munasinghe and Shearer's book, de Souza and Serageldin warn strongly that in the face of current overexploitation of natural resources, 'the quality of the environment and of human life is likely to decline rapidly, accompanied by widespread suffering' (ibid.: ix).

Therefore the concern over the environmental unsustainability of current ways of life partly has an ethical basis: some consider it wrong to diminish the environmental options of future generations below those available today; others consider wrong the impacts on other life forms that unsustainability implies. Partly the concern derives from perceived self-interest. Unsustainability threatens costs and disruption to ways of life in the future that are or may be greater than those incurred by moving voluntarily towards sustainability now. The self-interested concern about unsustainability will obviously become stronger as the time-scale within which the costs and disruption will be experienced is perceived to shorten. This is probably the reason for the current strengthening of public anxiety about the environment.

While some would therefore view environmental sustainability as an ethical imperative, and it is becoming an increasingly important, though not yet dominant, objective of public policy, it is not usually viewed as an end in itself. It is, rather, a present desirability with regard to future human development; and yet implementing sustainability principles could act as a constraint on present development. Sustainability guarantees certain life opportunities in the future at the cost of the modification or sacrifice of life opportunities in the present. The political argument, and the tension in the concept of sustainable development, is over the acceptability of and uncertainties involved in the trade-offs. The task for science is to clarify the uncertainties as far as possible. The task for economic analysis, in this context, is to elaborate the economic implications of moving towards sustainability, and show how the costs can be minimised, once the definition of and need for sustainability have been accepted.

4.2.1 Costs of unsustainability

To apply the standard economic approach to problems of unsustainability, one should seek to equate the marginal benefit produced by the activity causing the unsustainability with the marginal cost of that unsustainability. Where both costs and benefits are expressed in well-functioning markets with socially just property rights, this job can be left to those markets. Unfortunately, as has already been seen, these problems are not usually mediated by such markets.

Figure 4.1 recasts Figure 2.1 in order to illustrate the problem of determining the appropriate level of an environmental function and the use of the sustainability concept in this context. D_E can be viewed as the demand curve for the environmental function(s) affected by the good's production, reflecting the costs of the associated environmental damage. Greater production increases environmental damage, and its associated cost, and reduces the level of the function. S_F is the marginal cost curve for preventing or remedying the environmental damage and can be regarded as the supply curve of the relevant environmental function(s) for this use. Expenditures on preventing environmental damage will change the relationship between output and environmental damage, and thus may enable damage to be reduced proportionately more than output. In this formulation, the

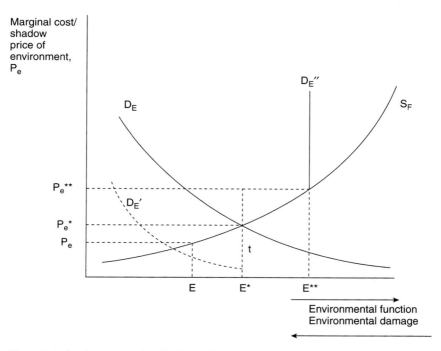

Figure 4.1 Setting a sustainable level for an environmental function

economic problem becomes the location of E*, the optimal level of the environmental function, where the current (too low) level of the function is given by E.

The various techniques for measuring the kinds of costs described in Chapter 2 represent attempts to determine the D_E curves in Figure 4.1, the 'total economic value' (as earlier defined) of the environmental sacrifice. Identifying the D_E curve for a complex environmental effect may simply be unfeasible. De Groot considers that 'accurate economic quantification of existence values attached to ecosystems is quite impossible' (de Groot 1992: 134) and that 'it is quite difficult if not impossible to assign a monetary value to the option value of natural ecosystems' (ibid.: 136). It must also be borne in mind that the environmental costs (or benefits) may be incurred in the future, in which case the calculation of their present value involves the use of a discount rate, the appropriate value of which for distant, large environmental effects is a further matter of great controversy (see Chapter 9 in addition to de Groot 1992 and D. Pearce 1993 for a discussion of this issue).

A danger of seeking to arrive at a money valuation of environmental effects with profound impacts on people or nature is that they will be underestimated and decisions will be taken in favour of the far more certain, near-term benefits that accrue from environmental destruction. In pictorial terms this amounts to the derivation of only a partial demand curve such as D'_E in Figure 4.1, which leads to an excessive level of environmental damage. It is here that the concept of sustainability can be useful, as suggested by Hueting (1992: 66ff.).

Most governments of the world have made commitments, at UNCED and elsewhere, to environmental sustainability. This may be taken to imply a general public preference for the sustainable use of environmental functions. In Figure 4.1, if E** is taken to be the minimum sustainable level of the environmental function(s), then accepting as a priority the public's preference for environmental sustainability amounts to deriving a demand curve for the function(s) of D''_E. E** will not necessarily be the same as the efficient or 'optimal' (in the economic sense) level of the environmental function (E*), for it has already been seen that an efficient use of resources need not be a sustainable one. S_F has already been identified as the marginal restoration or abatement cost associated with supplying the environmental function(s). Unlike environmental damage costs, these costs normally *are* determinable to acceptable levels of accuracy. The point of intersection of the S_F curve with the D''_E curve gives the shadow price of environmental sustainability (P_e**), which in turn puts a value on the extent to which the environment is underpriced (= P_e** – P_e). The E** levels of environmental quality are derived from sustainability standards, as discussed later in the chapter. The first step in deriving the S_F curve is to trace the causes of unsustainability.

4.2.2 Mapping unsustainable processes

Unsustainability arises from activities of production and consumption. At a certain level these cause competition between environmental functions. Following Hueting (1980) again this competition can be quantitative, qualitative or spatial (see Figure 4.2). Quantitative competition results from the extraction and depletion of resources. Qualitative competition results from the emission of substances (or noise) at or resulting in disruptive levels or concentrations. Spatial competition arises from occupation of space resulting in congestion. Unsustainability arises from some of the effects of the depletion, concentration and congestion on living things, including people (biotic effects), or on the human way of life.

All competition between environmental functions entails costs and is appropriate for economic analysis. However, not all such competition results in problems of unsustainability. Noise is an example of qualitative competition which can be disruptive but which is not therefore necessarily a problem of unsustainability as such. It is an environmental and economic problem but need not be a sustainability problem. The boundary between the two is defined by sustainability principles and standards.

It is, however, important to make an evaluation of even non-sustainability problems, because, in the event of them being resolved as a by-product of measures which are directed at sustainability problems, the net cost of these measures is reduced by the resolved (non-sustainability) problem's now forgone cost. Examples are where a transport policy aimed at reducing emissions also reduces noise because of a diminution of road traffic (cost forgone); or where an agricultural policy aimed at reducing pesticide concentrations in groundwater results in a landscape of greater aesthetic or amenity value (benefit gained). While the cost and benefit may be incidental to the achievement of sustainability they should still be accounted for when computing the cost of the sustainability measure itself.

In mapping processes of unsustainability, the following steps are required, with reference to Figure 4.2:

1　The effects on the biota or human way of life (V) must be identified and, if possible, quantified.

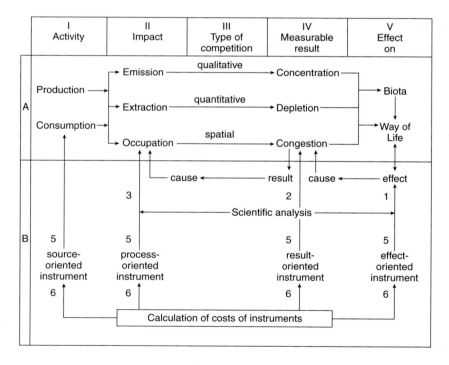

Figure 4.2 Mapping processes of unsustainability

Notes:　A – causal sequences
　　　　　B – analytic sequences
　　　　　Numbers 1–6 refer to the numbered paragraphs

2   The causes of these effects must be determined scientifically: whether they are due to concentration, depletion or congestion (IV) and of what.
3   These causes will themselves be the result of qualitative, quantitative or spatial competition between environmental functions (III) and must in turn be related to the emissions, extraction or occupation patterns of particular human activities (II). The boundaries and levels of these activity patterns and their effects must be established (see below). Thus far the task is one of scientific analysis and the production of appropriate environmental statistics.
4   Standards must be set for the effects on biota and the human way of life which are compatible with sustainability. These standards must then be traced back through the lines of cause and effect established in 2 and 3, to arrive at sustainability standards for emission, depletion and occupation.
5   Instruments, which might be market-based, regulatory or technical, must be devised to meet these standards. These instruments can either be effect-oriented (applied to the effects), result-oriented (applied to the concentrations, depletion or congestion), process-oriented (applied to the emissions, extraction or occupation) or source-oriented (applied to the activity, either reducing its volume or changing its nature). The instruments themselves might have environmental implications (e.g. the quarrying and transport of lime for use in counteracting the acidification of lakes), which should themselves be subject to the mapping process of Figure 4.2. Say, for example, that the unsustainability effect was health problems caused by water-pollution (an example of qualitative competition). An effect-oriented instrument would be the administration of a drug to affected persons; a result-oriented instrument would be water-purification; a process-oriented instrument would be emission-controls; and a source-oriented instrument would be the restriction of production or the replacement or reduction of the pollutant's use. Not all the types of instrument will be appropriate for all problems. Alternatively, effective tackling of a problem may require the use of instruments in several or all categories.
6   The costs of the instruments need to be calculated, first, for comparison between them so as to be able to choose the most cost-effective option; second to estimate, through the use of an appropriate economic model, their sectoral and macroeconomic implications; and third, to permit the computation of a 'sustainability gap' figure that can be compared to GNP. The first objective is obvious. Some results of modelling and the adjustment of the national accounts are discussed in later chapters.

4.2.3 Boundaries of sustainability

Environmental impacts can be felt at global, continental, (bio)regional, national and local levels. To be effective, public policy will have to be formulated at a level appropriate to the impact concerned. Because of the primacy of national governments in political decision making, it makes sense to think of boundaries of sustainability, initially at least, in terms of the nation-state.

Figure 4.3 is a schematic representation of the domestic production and consumption of a country, N, and the environmental impacts caused by these, together with imported pollution.

Of course, the environmental effects will not generally be measurable in the same units, so that the additions are descriptive rather than computable. Most of the environmental effects identified are obvious and need no exemplification here. EIP, EIC, PEX, CEX, the imports and exports of environmental effects, are likely to be in the form of air- or water-borne pollutants. CIE might be exemplified by the destruction of tropical forests due to hardwood imports, CXE by damage to human health or the environment by the export of pesticides or other dangerous chemicals.

It is possible to identify three meaningful sets of environmental impacts:

Set 1   The total environmental impacts in N due to domestic production and consumption. These are:

$$PE + CE - PEX - CEX = PDE + PXE + CED + CEI$$

Set 2   The total environmental impacts in N. These are:

$$PDE + PXE + CED + CEI + EIP + EIC$$

Set 3   The total environmental effects of domestic production and consumption. These are:

$$TPE + TCE = PE + CE + PIE + CIE + CXE$$

Which of these sets is relevant and can be made operational will depend on the issue in question and on possibilities of measurement. The measurement of impacts in N is likely to include the contribution of imported impacts (EIP and EIC, as in Set 2). The measurement of domestic emissions will probably include those that are subsequently exported (PEX and CEX). PIE, CIE and CXE are likely to be impossible to measure without the cooperation of the exporting/importing country, but may be among the principal contributors to unsustainability. The boundaries relevant to the different sets must also be borne in mind in the choice of instruments. Tackling domestic emissions may not improve the domestic concentration of pollutants if the pollutants are mainly imported (EIP, EIC), in which case the cheapest way to improve environmental quality may be to subsidise emission-reduction in the neighbouring polluting countries (though this

Territory, N

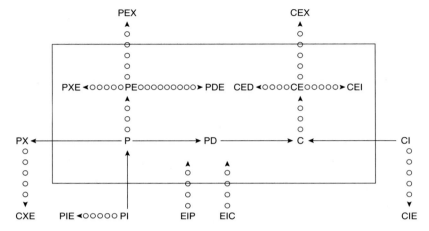

Figure 4.3　Production, consumption and environmental impacts of and in country N

Notes:

Solid lines are processes of production or consumption. Lines of o are associated environmental impacts.

E terms: E appearing in any sequence of letters signifies an environmental impact (i.e. emission, extraction or occupation).

Activity:　　　Production, P Consumption, C

N　　　= Territorial boundary of nation-state
P　　　= Production within N
PE　　　= Environmental impacts due to production in N
PI　　　= Imports for production (capital goods)
PIE　　　= Environmental impacts outside N due to PI
PD　　　= Domestic product for home consumption
PX　　　= Domestic product for export
CXE　　　= Environmental effects outside N due to consumption of exports
PDE　　　= Environmental impacts due to production of home-consumed domestic product
PXE　　　= Environmental impacts due to production of exports

Production equation: P = PD + PX

C　　　= Consumption within N
CE　　　= Environmental impacts due to consumption in N
CED　　　= Environmental impacts in N due to consumption of domestic product
CEI　　　= Environmental impacts in N due to consumption of imports
CI　　　= Imports consumed in N
CIE　　　= Environmental effects outside N due to production of imports of consumer goods

Consumption equation: C = PD + CI

EIP, EIC　= Import of environmental effects due to production and consumption abroad
PEX, CEX　= Export of environmental effects due to domestic production and consumption

Environmental effects equations:

PE　　　= PDE + PXE + PEX
TPE　　　= Total environmental impacts (in and outside N) due to production in N
　　　　　= PE + PIE + CXE
CE　　　= CED + CEI + CEX
TCE　　　= Total environmental effects (in and outside N) due to consumption in N
　　　　　= CE + CIE

has obvious implications for the observation or otherwise of the Polluter Pays Principle). Similarly, purifying domestic soil or water will not decrease the emissions that are exported to neighbours.

In accounting situations involving more than one country only Set 2 allocates all effects to one country and one only. In Set 1, no country is considering the impacts of pollution imports and exports (PEX, CEX, EIP, EIC). In Set 3, more than one country (N, and the countries importing from or exporting to N) will be considering, and perhaps taking responsibility for, CXE, CEI, PXE, PIE, CIE. (CXE for one country is the equivalent to CEI for the other; PXE is similarly equivalent to the sum of PIE and CIE.) While untidy in accounting terms, acceptance of shared responsibility for these effects is likely to produce the best environmental outcome. The environmental impacts arising from trade or transfrontier pollution flows are discussed further on pp. 147–51.

Two methodologies have recently been developed which seek to make actual calculations based on the kind of aggregate impact equations above. Wackernagel and Rees' (1996) ecological footprint analysis 'is an accounting tool that enables us to estimate the resource consumption and waste assimilation requirements of a defined human population or economy in terms of a corresponding land area. . . . The Ecological Footprint . . . represents the corresponding population's "total appropriated carrying capacity"' (ibid.: 9, 11). The analysis in practice computes the extent of six different uses of 'ecologically productive land' (for energy, buildings, gardens, cropland, pasture and forests) for five categories of consumption (food, housing, transportation, consumer goods and services). The resulting per capita land use for the given population can then be compared with the global per capita availability of such land. Wackernagel and Rees claim:

> There is much evidence today that humanity's Ecological Footprint already exceeds global carrying capacity. Such overshoot is only possible temporarily and imposes high costs on future generations. For example, the present Ecological Footprint (EF) of a typical North American is calculated to be 4–5ha, compared to present global availability of ecologically productive land of 1.9ha per person, which will fall to half that if the human population doubles as expected.
>
> (ibid.: 55)

The EF calculations are largely driven by the method of calculating the land area imputed to the use of fossil fuels, which is the area required to absorb the carbon from their combustion. This accounts for 55 per cent of the North American footprint above (Wackernagel and Rees 1996: 83), which reduces to 11 per cent of only 2.2ha if the energy footprint is instead calculated according to the area required for the photovoltaic substitution of fossil fuel (own calculation from figures in ibid.: 69). This would not even be required to be ecologically productive land, but could utilise land in the built environment (e.g. on buildings) or ecologically degraded land (e.g. deserts). Clearly such a substitution is currently limited by the cost of photovoltaics but, were it to become feasible, it is not clear that present 'overshoot' would in fact have imposed 'high costs on future generations'.

The second methodology is based on the concept of 'environmental utilisation space' (EUS). EUS has been defined as 'the locus of all feasible combinations of environmental services that represent steady states in terms of levels of relevant environmental quality and stocks of renewable resources' (Opschoor and Weterings 1994/5: 199), which in fact is the set of sustainable uses of environmental functions, which is the definition of environmental sustainability being employed here. Sips *et al.* (1994/5: 209) consider that making the concept of EUS operational requires three stages:

1   Determining the human demands for environmental functions. This is the process of assessing environmental impacts within given boundaries as analysed above.
2   Determining the sustainable supply of environmental functions. This is tantamount to adopting principles of sustainability and setting sustainability standards, which is the subject of the next section (see p. 92ff.).
3   Matching supply and demand. This is the process of achieving, or at least moving towards, sustainability, the economic implications of which are the subject of later chapters.

The environmental space methodology has been extensively deployed by Friends of the Earth groups and others in a series of publications seeking to establish the degree of unsustainability in some European national economies and in Europe as a whole (Buitenkamp *et al.* 1993; FOE 1995; McLaren *et al.* 1998; Sachs *et al.* 1998). Globally available 'environmental space' is calculated for different environmental functions (e.g. the sustainable yield of timber, agricultural land, absorption of CO_2 emissions), and this is then divided by the projected global human population at a certain date to arrive at a per capita availability of these functions. Multiplying by a country's projected population at that date then gives that country's sustainable use of environmental space with regard to each environmental function.

It can be seen from Table 4.2 that all four studies show that substantial cuts in CO_2 emissions and non-renewable resources are required to bring the countries concerned within their environmental space. For land use, wood and water, while reduction of use is still indicated, there is more variability both for the reductions and the targets themselves.

Finally it may be noted that these environmental space calculations are heavily dependent on projected population growth. In particular, countries with stable populations will have their environmental space reduced over

Table 4.2 Calculations of global environmental space and necessary reductions from four European studies

	Europe[a]		Germany[b]		Netherlands[c]		UK[d]	
	Env. space	Reduc- tion, %	Env. space	Reduc- tion, %	Env. space	Reduc- tion, %	Env. space	Reduc- tion, %
CO_2 emissions, t/head	1.7	−77		−80 to −90	1.7	− 85	1.13[e]	−88
Primary energy use, GJ	60	−50		−50				
Fossil fuels, GJ	25	−75						
Nuclear, GJ	0	−100		−100				
Renewables, GJ	35	+400						
Non-renewable resources, kg/head				−80 to −90				
Cement	80	−85					58	−72
Pig iron/steel (UK)	36	−87					25.7	−83
Aluminium	1.2	−90			2	−80	2	−80
Chlorine	0	−100					0	−100
Aggregates, t/head							2.33	−50
Renewable resources								
Wood, m^3/head	0.56	−15			0.4	−60	0.238	−73
Water, l/day					217	−15	80	−40
Land use, ha/head								
Built up	0.05	−3						
Protected	0.06	+1933						
Unprotected forests	0.14	−16						
Arable	0.1[f]	−58			0.25		} 0.489	−27
Pasture	0.09[f]	−47			0.32			

Notes:

a *Source:* FOE (1995: 102 (Table 6.1))

b *Source:* Sachs *et al.* (1998: 45 (Table 3.1))

c *Source:* Buitenkamp *et al.* (1993: 89)

d *Source:* McLaren *et al.* (1998: 241 (Table C.1))

e The Table cited actually says this is the required reduction in energy use, but the detailed calculation of p.89 makes it clear that it is CO_2 that is intended

f Agricultural land requirements for minimum dietary needs, i.e. not sustainable environmental space

time by population growth elsewhere. Such a variation is likely to be politically controversial and to militate against policy makers' adoption of the
environmental space methodology and targets. This problem would be
eased by the adoption of a reference year (e.g. 1990) for the calculation
of a country's environmental space, which would then be unchanged by
future population change. Then, of course, countries with growing populations would find their environmental space being progressively reduced,
while those with stable populations would not. This would give an incentive
to curb population growth.

4.3 SUSTAINABILITY PRINCIPLES AND STANDARDS

4.3.1 Deriving principles of environmental sustainability

Unsustainability with regard to a human way of life in general has been
earlier defined as a situation in which, because of effects on biota or the
human way itself, cannot with any assurance be projected to continue into
the future. Environmental unsustainability comes about when environmental functions which are important for human ways of life and welfare
are not sustained or put at risk. Given the uncertainties involved in matters
of sustainability, and the possibility of irreversibility, and of the incidence
of very large costs, once environmental functions have been lost, the question of risk is crucial, not least because risk, through insurance premiums
for example, incurs present real, as well as hypothetical future, costs.

The simultaneous coincidence of uncertainty, irreversibility and possible
large costs has long been recognised as an important consideration for
environmental policy. Ciriacy-Wantrup's (1952) classic work prefigured
many of the current concerns of sustainability with his development of the
concept of 'the safe minimum standard'.

First Ciriacy-Wantrup (1952: 38ff.) identifies the existence of 'critical
zones' for many, especially renewable, resources, where such a zone 'means
a more or less clearly defined range of rates [of flow of the resource] below
which a decrease in flow cannot be reversed *economically* under presently
foreseeable conditions. Frequently such irreversibility is not only economic
but also technological' (ibid.: 39, original emphasis) and, one may add
with regard to extinguished species, biological. In the terminology being
employed here, this means that the loss of environmental functions may
be irreversible. The 'critical zone' concept is strikingly similar to that of
the 'critical load' which is employed in modern environmental policy (see,
for example, the discussion of limits on SO_2 emissions in Chapter 10).

Then Ciriacy-Wantrup (1952: 88, original emphasis) identifies the possibility of 'immoderate losses' arising from environmental degradation, with
respect to which: 'One important objective of conservation decisions is to

avoid *immoderate* possible losses – although of small probability – by accepting the possibility of moderate ones – although the latter are more probable.' A decision rule which would achieve this is the 'minimax' criterion, which involves minimising maximum possible losses. The application of this criterion to resources characterised by critical zones leads Ciriacy-Wantrup (ibid.: 251ff. (Chapter 18)) to recommend the 'safe minimum standard' (SMS) as an objective of conservation (what today would be called environmental) policy: 'A safe minimum standard of conservation is achieved by avoiding the critical zone – that is, those physical conditions, brought about by human action, which would make it uneconomical to halt and reverse depletion.'

Despite the fact that the SMS approach was addressed in a practical way at those environmental problems, characterised by chronic uncertainty, and possible irreversibility and immoderate losses, for which more conventional economic approaches based on cost–benefit analysis are either inappropriate or unfeasible, it made little impact on the literature of subsequent decades. The next substantial reference is Bishop (1978), by which time the Total Economic Value framework (discussed in Chapter 2) of use, option and existence values had been developed, and Bishop relates this to the SMS. Bishop (ibid.: 14) considered option and existence value to be unmeasurable, and distinguished between the following benefits: B_d, the net financial benefits of a development which entails environmental losses; B_p, the total value of the losses or, equivalently, the gross environmental value of not proceeding with the development; B_p', that portion of B_p that is measurable. The SMS approach becomes relevant when the losses included in B_p include possible irreversibilities or immoderate costs. These are unlikely to be included in B_p'.

On a benefit–cost rule the development should only proceed if $B_d - B_p > 0$. But B_p is unknown. However, if $B_p > B_p' > 0$, it is clear that the development should also only be considered if $B_d - B_p' > 0$. Strict adherence to a SMS and the minimax criterion would mean that, where irreversibility and the possibility of heavy losses were involved, the development would not be permitted however large $(B_d - B_p')$ was. Bishop (1978: 10) considers such a rule too restrictive and modifies it such that 'the SMS should be adopted unless the social costs [i.e. $B_d - B_p'$] of doing so are unacceptably large. How much is "unacceptably large" must necessarily involve more than economic analysis, because endangered species involve issues of intergenerational equity.' Bishop (ibid.: 17) concludes his article, which focused on endangered species, with the observation 'it is worthwhile to note that problems of irreversibility and uncertainty are not limited to endangered species, that the SMS approach may be applicable to a wider range of resource issues'.

Bishop (1993) brings the SMS approach into the context of current environmental discourse by relating it to sustainability:

To achieve sustainability policies should be considered that constrain the day to day operations of the economy in ways that enhance the natural resource endowments of future generations, but with an eye towards the economic implications of specific steps to implement such policies.

(Bishop 1993: 72)

Here the safe minimum standard has been converted into a sustainability standard. In the terms previously discussed, those activities that entail the possibility of irreversible effects and immoderate costs are now identified as environmentally unsustainable.

Bishop's modification of the SMS approach by introducing the notion of 'unacceptably large' costs actually undermines it. This is because it relocates the SMS in a cost–benefit framework that seeks to compare the potential 'immoderate losses' of proceeding with a course of action with the 'unacceptably large' costs of not proceeding with it, when the former cannot in fact be reliably computed. It was precisely to avoid such situations that the SMS approach, and the sustainability concept, were formulated in the first place. In contrast to Bishop's modification, the SMS approach as interpreted here proposes that policies that constrain or transform human activities towards environmental sustainability should not be considered in a normal benefit–cost framework but one which seeks to achieve the sustainability standard in a cost-effective way. Sustainability is accorded this pre-eminence as a policy objective because of the importance of environmental functions for human welfare, as previously discussed, and because of the irreversibilities and large costs that may be associated with their loss.

The problems of unsustainability arise, as has been seen, from chronic competition between environmental functions:

Qualitative   = excessive emissions lead to excessive concentrations which lead to unsustainable effects.

Quantitative = excessive extraction leads to excessive depletion which leads to unsustainable effects.

Spatial   = excessive occupation (of space) leads to excessive congestion which leads to unsustainable effects.

What counts as an 'unsustainable effect' rather than a sustainable economic cost is a matter of judgement which can only partially be resolved by science. Ethics and the attitude to risk also play a significant role here. It is important that the basis of judgement is articulated clearly, especially as to who is responsible for the effects and who is bearing their costs, and differentiating the contributions played by science, ethics and risk acceptance or aversion.

Detailed sustainability standards will need to be formulated for all the important environmental functions that are perceived to be at risk from human activities, but some general principles for these standards can be posited with regard to the generic functions of resource use, waste absorption and life support. Daly (1991: 44–5) has suggested four principles of sustainable development:

1 Limit the human scale (throughput) to that which is within the Earth's carrying capacity.
2 Ensure that technological progress is efficiency-increasing rather than throughput-increasing.
3 For renewable resources harvesting rates should not exceed regeneration rates (sustained yield); waste emissions should not exceed the assimilative capacities of the receiving environment.
4 Non-renewable resources should be exploited no faster than the rate of creation of renewable substitutes.

These principles are among the rules that Turner (1993: 20–1) has formulated 'for the sustainable utilisation of the capital stock', the others of which are: correction of market and intervention failures; steering of technical change not only to increase resource-using efficiency but also to promote renewable substitutes for non-renewable resources; taking a precautionary approach to the uncertainties involved.

Of these rules, the correction of failures and the steering of technical change are more to do with achieving sustainability than defining standards for it; and in view of the complexity of applying the concept of carrying capacity to human activities, it seems desirable to express it more specifically in terms of those environmental problems that appear most pressing. Such considerations enable the Daly/Turner rules to be reformulated into a set of sustainability principles:

1 Destabilisation of global environmental features such as climate patterns or the ozone layer must be prevented. Most important in this category are the maintenance of biodiversity (see below), the prevention of climate change, by the stabilisation of the atmospheric concentration of greenhouse gases, and safeguarding the ozone layer by ceasing the emission of ozone-depleting substances.
2 Important ecosystems and ecological features must be absolutely protected to maintain biological diversity. Importance in this context comes from a recognition not only of the perhaps as yet unappreciated use value of individual species, but also of the fact that biodiversity underpins the productivity and resilience of ecosystems. Resilience, defined as 'the magnitude of the disturbance that can be absorbed before the system changes its structure by changing the variables and processes that control its behaviour' (Folke *et al.* 1994: 6) depends on

the functional diversity of the system. This depends in turn, in complex ways, not just on the diversity of species but on their mix and population and the relations between the ecosystems that contain them. 'Biodiversity conservation, ecological sustainability and economic sustainability are inexorably linked; uncontrolled and irreversible biodiversity loss ruptures this link and puts the sustainability of our basic economic-environmental systems at risk' (Barbier *et al.* 1994: 41).

3   The renewal of renewable resources must be fostered through the maintenance of soil fertility, hydrobiological cycles and necessary vegetative cover and the rigorous enforcement of sustainable harvesting. The latter implies basing harvesting rates on the most conservative estimates of stock levels, for such resources as fish; ensuring that replanting becomes an essential part of such activities as forestry; and using technologies for cultivation and harvest that do not degrade the relevant ecosystem, and deplete neither the soil nor genetic diversity.

4   Depletion of non-renewable resources should seek to balance the maintenance of a minimum life-expectancy of the resource with the development of substitutes for it. On reaching the minimum life-expectancy, its maintenance would mean that consumption of the resource would have to be matched by new discoveries of it. To help finance research for alternatives and the eventual transition to renewable substitutes, all depletion of non-renewable resources should entail a contribution to a capital fund. Designing for resource-efficiency and durability can ensure that the practice of repair, reconditioning, reuse and recycling (the 'four R's') enables the use of resources to approach the limits of its environmental efficiency.

5   Emissions into air, soil and water must not exceed their critical load, that is the capability of the receiving media to disperse, absorb, neutralise and recycle them, nor may they lead to concentrations of toxins that cause unacceptable damage to human health. Synergies between pollutants can make critical loads very much more difficult to determine. Such uncertainties should result in a precautionary approach in the adoption of safe minimum standards.

6   Landscapes of special human or ecological significance, because of their rarity, aesthetic quality or cultural or spiritual associations, should be preserved.

7   Risks of life-damaging events from human activity must be kept at very low levels. Technologies which threaten long-lasting ecosystem damage should be forgone.

Of these seven sustainability principles, 3, 4 and, to some extent, 2 seek to sustain resource functions. Five seeks to sustain waste-absorption functions; 1 and 2 seek to sustain life-supporting environmental services; 6 is concerned with other environmental services of special human value;

and 7 acknowledges the great uncertainties associated with environmental change and the threshold effects and irreversibilities mentioned above. The principles are clearly an application of the SMS approach, but they seek to reinterpret it explicitly in the context of ensuring the sustainable use of important environmental functions.

The above sustainability principles should be applied together. For example, excessive fossil fuel use violates principle 1 on global warming, and on its own may lead to a perception that nuclear power should be deployed as a substitute energy resource. However, nuclear power is not compatible with environmental sustainability because it violates principle 7 on environmental risk. In this case acceptance of the sustainability principles suggests that the efficiency of energy use should be maximised, and safe renewable energy sources should be developed (as per principle 4), while, in the interim, CO_2 emissions from fossil fuels should be minimised (e.g. by switching to low carbon fuels) and the safety of nuclear power should be a prime concern. In this way, the principles give clear guidance how to approach today's principal perceived environmental problems as outlined in Chapter 1. They may need to be supplemented as new environmental problems become apparent.

The sustainability principles are coming to be reflected in a number of international treaties, conventions and principles, including the Montreal Protocol to phase out ozone-depleting substances (1 above), the Convention on International Trade in Endangered Species and the establishment of World Biosphere Reserves to maintain biodiversity (2 above), the Second Sulphur Protocol to limit SO_2 emissions (5 above, discussed in detail in Chapter 10) and the Precautionary Principle, endorsed by the United Nations Conference on Environment and Development in *Agenda 21*, to limit environmental risk-taking (5 and 7 above). None of these international agreements was the outcome of detailed application of environmental evaluation techniques in a framework of cost–benefit analysis. They rest on a simple recognition that they represent the humane, moral and intelligent way for humans to proceed in order to maintain their conditions for life, and are argued for on that basis.

Interpreting the SMS approach as the setting of sustainability standards to ensure the sustainable use of important environmental functions offers a practical methodology to address those environmental problems where uncertainty, irreversibility or possible large costs make the use of benefit–cost analysis problematic. The methodology was applied in the formulation of the Second Sulphur Protocol, as discussed in Chapter 10. It was applied by the German Advisory Council on Global Change to recommend the necessary level of CO_2 reduction to the First Conference of the Parties on Climate Change in Berlin (WBGU 1995). Hueting *et al.* (1992: 44–52 (Appendix 2)) have also used the methodology to indicate how sustainability standards can be derived for seventeen different environmental problems.

4.3.2 Deriving standards of environmental sustainability

The different forms of competition (qualitative, quantitative, spatial) will need to be addressed by different kinds of standards, which can be clarified by redrawing only those parts of Figure 3.2 that are related to the contribution of ecological capital, as in Figure 4.4. Ecological capital is schematically divided into the parts performing its different kinds of functions: resource providing (*EC1*), service providing (*EC2*), and waste-absorbing (*EC* generally). This division of function facilitates the expression of a few simple sustainability constraints relating to the various environmental inputs and outputs.

Qualitative constraints

Sustainability condition 5 implies:

$Wes \leq Aes$ and

$Wec \leq Aec$

where *Wes* and *Wec* are the waste emissions into the environment which potentially affect the environmental services directly (*Wes*), or which affect the ecological capital which produces those services and ecological

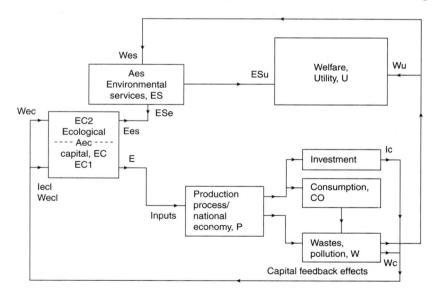

Figure 4.4 The role of ecological capital in production and welfare creation
Note: In the flow descriptors, the upper case letters denote the source of the flow, lower case letters denote the destination

resources (*Wec*), and *Aes* and *Aec* are the environmental absorptive/ neutralising capacities of receiving media.

It is important to emphasise that not all wastes or emissions cause pollution. They only do so when they exceed the extent to which the environment can absorb, neutralise or recycle them, or cause unacceptable health effects on humans. In the non-human bioeconomy there is no such thing as pollution. All emissions or waste products from one process are transformed into resources for another in a multitude of interlinked cyclical processes powered by the sun, which provides the necessary external energy input to decrease entropy in the biosystem overall, as life forms become increasingly varied and complex. Thus *Aec/Aes* for ecosystems or natural processes are the relevant critical loads, while *Aes* for humans is defined by standards relating to human health.

The distinction between *Wec* and *Aec* on the one hand, and *Wes* and *Aes* on the other, is important. Wastes *Wec* impact on the environmental capital stock which produces environmental services; wastes *Wes* may affect the services themselves (and thence, of course, *EC* through *ESe*, but that is a secondary rather than a primary effect). The distinction may be exemplified as that between emissions which cause fundamental atmospheric and climate change (*Wec*) and those which cause smog (*Wes*). Both ultimately interfere with the climatic experiences of those affected, but effects on the capital stock itself tend to be less easily remedied. Against that it may be argued that the capital stock itself is less easily affected than the services it provides (*Aec > Aes*). The emissions that produce a local smog are lower than those needed to cause a global change in climate. One of the more serious characteristics of the present environmental situation is that it derives from fundamental degradation of the basic stock (atmosphere, ozone layer, soil, forest systems) rather than a simple interference with the services they provide. Regenerating this capital stock is likely to be a more formidable task than removing interference with its services.

In general for qualitative constraints, a standard can be set at each of the stages of the unsustainable process:

1 effect (e.g. a tolerated level of sickness from pollution or disruption from noise);
2 concentration (e.g. maximum levels of pollutants in soil, water, air, organisms);
3 emissions (e.g. maximum emission levels).

Quantitative constraints

From Figure 4.4 it can be seen that the basic sustainability equation for resources is

$$E \leq Iec1 + Wec1$$

where E is the total outflow of renewable and non-renewable resources into the economic process, *Iec1* is the generation of new ecological resources by investment and *Wec1* is the addition to the resource stock achieved by recycling. *Iec1* includes the replenishment of renewable resources by human intervention or non-human processes (e.g. the sun), and new discoveries of non-renewable resources or the development of new technologies, materials or processes to substitute for depleting resources.

For renewable resources the basic sustainability standard is clear: the definition of a minimum acceptable stock and then the definition and enforcement of a strictly sustainable harvest. For non-renewable resources, the situation is more complex and various methods can be employed in order to address explicitly the issue of how a non-renewable resource can be used 'sustainably', when all depletion of such a resource must bring closer its exhaustion. The approach of Hueting *et al.* (1992: 15) is to determine the maximum sustainable rate of depletion in any period, according to the improvements in use-efficiency, recycling or development of substitutes for the resource during the period in question. Where $r(t)$ is the total rate of such improvements, $d(t)$ is the rate of extraction (depletion rate) and $S(t)$ is the stock of the resource, they posit the equation

$$d(t) \leq r(t) * S(t) \tag{4.1'}$$

In fact it is not clear that, when it is the sustainable use of the environmental function that is of concern, taking into account recycling, substitutes and end-use efficiency, $d(t)$ is actually the relevant variable. Rather it is the rate of waste disposal, $w(t)$, that indicates the loss of a resource from useful service. Appendix 4.1 derives a relation between w and the stock of the unextracted resource, S, the amount of the resource in current use, C, the level of renewable substitutes for the resource, R, the efficiency of use of the resource, e, and the proportional increase in R between two time periods, a. Then, when the subscripts $_0$ and $_1$ indicate the quantities in two consecutive periods, sustainable use requires:

$$w_0 \leq (1 - e_0/e_1)(S_0 + C_0) + (a_0 - e_0/e_1)R_0 \tag{4.1}$$

If the increases in R are somehow incorporated directly into e, and if $w_0 = d_0$, i.e. as much resource is extracted as is disposed of, then this equation reduces to Hueting *et al.*'s Equation 4.1'.

Another way of seeking to ensure sustainable use is to set a minimum life expectancy of the resource, L_{min}. Where d_1 is the depletion rate in period 1 from a stock level of S_1, then

$$d_1 \leq S_1/L_{min}$$

As is shown in Appendix 4.2, where d_2 is the rate of depletion in period 2, and D_1 is the amount of the resource discovered in period 1, then, operating at maximum depletion rates

$$d_2 = d_1 [1 + (D_1 - d_1)/S_1] \qquad (4.2)$$

The interpretations of sustainability given by Equations 4.1 and 4.2 are quite different. The effect of 4.1, strictly in accordance with the principle of strong sustainability, is to ensure that the stock of the given resource, together with any substitutes that may have been developed, maintain their capacity to perform the relevant environmental function at its current level. The disposal of the resource is only sustainable if technical advances enable the stock remaining (plus substitutes) to perform the same level of function as the initial stock. Discoveries, which add to the quantity of known stock, mean that the stock is able to maintain a higher level of environmental function than was originally thought, and it is this higher level that then becomes the standard for sustainability. Obviously, under Equation 4.1, if no technical advance takes place in a given period, and there is no further development of renewable substitutes for the resource, then, even if there are substantial discoveries, the sustainable level of resource consumption (disposal) in that period is zero.

Equation 4.2 interprets sustainability as the maintenance of the current level of environmental function for a certain minimum length of (finite) time. Discoveries increase the possible depletion rate by increasing the stock, i.e. the sustainable level of environmental function is not adjusted upward as in the Hueting method. With no discoveries, and operating at the maximum depletion rate consistent with the minimum life expectancy, this depletion rate will decline over time, according to the ratio of depletion in the previous period to the undepleted stock (as seen by setting $D_1 = 0$ in Equation 4.2). Technical advance does not enter into Equation 4.2. If it occurs, but depletion stays the same, then the consumed resources will have increased their productivity of useful services delivered. But this will not change the minimum life expectancy of the resource.

In terms of the strict maintenance of environmental functions over an indefinite time period, the Hueting *et al.* method would appear to be correct. For non-renewable resources, the level of environmental function depends only on the stock, whether discovered or not. As discoveries are made, so that the quantity of the known stock is revised upward, so is the level of function that needs to be sustained. Only recycling, more efficient use, or the development of (renewable and renewed) substitutes can add to the environmental function of a given stock, so that it is only by the amount of these advances that the stock can be sustainably depleted. Hueting *et al.* (1992: 15) advocate that an average rate of technical advance for an earlier period should be computed and applied to the present stock to estimate sustainable use rates. Clearly the estimation of advances in recycling, use efficiency and the development of substitutes across a wide range of non-renewable resources is a substantial statistical and methodological challenge.

The minimum life expectancy method, on the other hand, treats discoveries as windfalls which will either enable the stock to last longer or, at constant life expectancy, allow greater annual consumption. Here it is only the current level of environmental function that is to be sustained, and only for a definite period. With no discoveries, the sustainable level of depletion according to this decision rule would gradually decline. The minimum life expectancy method entails relatively simple calculations, requiring no information beyond discoveries, initial stock and depletion rates, which are already widely available.

These differences between the methods perhaps suggest that they are suited for different tasks. The method of Hueting *et al.* would provide a rigorous method for calculating the gap between current and sustainable depletion; the minimum life expectancy method would ensure that sudden resource shocks were avoided and would give guidance as to the resources most in need of the development of substitutes. The method of Hueting *et al.* was developed for a national economy; the minimum life expectancy method would need to be applied with regard to global resource stocks. Setting the minimum life expectancy for different resources would be somewhat arbitrary, but should perhaps be between 30 and 50 years, based on the time-scale required for the development and diffusion of major new technologies, if these were needing to be deployed once a resource was totally exhausted.

How much of a non-renewable resource can be used sustainably is one issue; how receipts from that use should be accounted is another. Given that use of a non-renewable resource amounts to the liquidation of natural capital, it is clearly incorrect that all the receipts from such depletion should be accounted as income, as they are as present. This issue is explored in more detail in Chapter 5, but for the present it can be noted that El Serafy (1989) has proposed that the receipts (net of extraction costs) be divided into two streams, one representing current income, the other to generate a permanent income stream in the future equal to that consumed as income in the present. El Serafy calculated a formula by which this proportion can be computed (derived in Appendix 4.3), relating it to the discount rate and the life expectancy of the resource. The formula is:

$$I/R = 1/(1 + r)^{n+1}$$

where I = that part of receipts to be considered as capital
        R = receipts
        r = discount rate
        n = life expectancy of the resource

For the UK this formula has been applied to the depletion of the UK's North Sea oil and gas reserves by Bryant and Cook (1992) and, more recently, Vaze (1998). Using a discount rate of 5 per cent and the total of proven and probable reserves to calculate the lifetime of the resource, Bryant and Cook (1992: 103 (Table 1)) estimate the depletion cost from 1980–90 to be £44 billion (price year unspecified). Adding possible to proven and probable reserves (and therefore extending the resource lifetime and reducing the depletion cost), Vaze (1998: 73 (Table 4)) arrives at a total depletion cost for 1980–94 of £51 billion for a 3 per cent discount rate, and £21 billion for a 6 per cent discount rate (1990 prices).

It may be noted that, if the Hueting method is an application of the strong sustainability principle, the El Serafy method is an example of the weak sustainability principle. The monetary receipts are divided into two parts, broadly a capital and income component, but there is no requirement for the capital component to be invested such that specific substitutes for the depleted resource are provided. To the extent that the capital component is so invested, of course, the strong sustainability principle will be being followed. The Bryant and Cook and Vaze calculations suggest that, since the beginning of extraction of UK oil and gas in the 1970s, by 1994 £20–50 billion should have been invested in the development of renewable energy substitutes had the UK Government been applying a strong sustainability rule. The lower figure is at least 50 times the amount that was actually invested by the Government in research, development and demonstration of renewables during this period. It goes without saying that an enhanced investment of this kind would have substantially accelerated the development of renewable substitutes for fossil fuels.

The Hueting *et al.* minimum life expectancy and El Serafy methods could be applied as alternatives or together, with their different implications summarised thus. The Hueting *et al.* method would give an indication of the gap between current activities and strong sustainability. The second method would guarantee to future generations a continuing flow of the resource in question but, depending on new discoveries, it could be a diminishing one. Reductions in sustainable depletion would be gradual. El Serafy's method could result in total exhaustion of the resource but should have ensured the development of a substitute or an equivalent income stream from another source. This would only be compatible with strong sustainability where the asset producing the income stream was a perfect substitute for the depleted resource.

Given that the whole notion of sustainable use of a non-renewable resource is somewhat contradictory, a case can be made for applying the methods together as appropriate and therefore benefiting from their different sustainability insights.

Spatial constraints

The principal unsustainability effect from spatial competition is species extinction. Because of its irreversibility and the uncertainties involved, an appropriate standard would appear to be that no species be knowingly extinguished. This is the presumption underlying the US Endangered Species Act, and is rendered the more imperative by the fact that many extinctions are currently occurring, and many more undoubtedly will occur, as a result of processes already underway which cannot be immediately halted (though for sustainability they must be over time). Other potentially unsustainable examples of spatial competition are waste-dumping and traffic congestion. Both these are likely to be much ameliorated by sustainability measures to reduce emissions and depletion, so it may not be necessary to formulate sustainability standards in these areas (although as noted earlier, the cost savings associated with dealing with these problems must be computed and subtracted from the costs of the measures of the sustainability measures in the other areas).

4.4 DERIVING INDICATORS OF SUSTAINABILITY

4.4.1 A framework for sustainability indicators

The conclusion at the end of Chapter 3 was that the search for a single, aggregate measure of human welfare was unlikely to be fruitful and that a number of measures giving insight into different aspects of welfare would be more likely to convey the complex realities involved. Precisely the same considerations apply to measurements intended to indicate the achievement or otherwise of sustainability, of which an essential component is in any case the sustaining of human welfare.

It will be recalled from the beginning of this chapter that the essential relevant questions for sustainability across its environmental, economic, social and ethical dimensions were identified as follows:

- For the environment, can its contribution to human welfare and to the human economy be sustained?
- For the economy, can today's level of wealth-creation be sustained?
- For society, can social cohesion and important social institutions be sustained?
- Ethically, and influencing all three other dimensions, do people alive today value other people and other life forms, now and in the future, sufficiently highly?

As already discussed, environmental sustainability requires the maintenance of important functions, as identified in the seven sustainability principles set out on pp. 95–6. Each of these principles has associated with it a sustainability standard (e.g. stable climate, sustainable harvest, critical load of pollution for an ecosystem, standards of air or water quality to safeguard human health) and a number of possible indicators of environmental pressure (e.g. emissions) or environmental state (e.g. concentration of pollutant) to show whether the standard is currently being complied with. These standards and indicators are discussed on pp. 108ff.

Economic sustainability depends on the maintenance of the capital stock. Here the economic dimension of sustainability is conceived in terms of the four capitals as discussed in Chapter 3, the elements of which may be briefly recapitulated here:

1 *Ecological capital* is defined as stocks and flows of energy and matter, and the physical states, such as climatic conditions or ecosystem characteristics, to which they give rise. The stocks include the gases of the atmosphere, including the ozone layer, renewable and non-renewable resources, the absorptive, neutralising and degrading capacities of the environmental media air, water and land, and countryside and wilderness; the flows include the biospheric cycles of carbon, nitrogen and water, and the nutrient flows of ecosystems. From these stocks and flows derive the environmental functions which are the subject of the sustainability standards above, i.e. an atmosphere that yields climate stability, an ozone layer that filters out ultraviolet light, biodiversity that yields ecosystem stability and resilience, the provision of resources, the degradation of wastes, environmental amenity and inspiration and environmental security.

2 *Human capital* comprises the abilities of individual people to do productive work and therefore includes physical and mental health, strength, stamina, knowledge, skills, motivation and a constructive and cooperative attitude.

3 *Social/organisational capital* comprises the social structures and institutions which enable individuals to maintain and develop their human capital and be productive and include firms, trade unions, families, communities, voluntary organisations, legal/political systems, educational institutions, the health service, other social institutions (e.g. the welfare state), systems of property rights, financial institutions, etc.

4 *Manufactured capital* comprises material goods – tools, machines, buildings, infrastructure – which contribute to the production process but do not become embodied in the output and, usually, are 'consumed' in a period of time longer than a year. Intermediate goods, in contrast, either are embodied in produced goods (e.g. metals, plastics, components) or are immediately consumed in the production process (e.g. fuels).

Economic sustainability is promoted by any activity that maintains or increases the level of any of the four capital stocks, i.e. which maintains or increases productive capacity. Activities that promote environmental sustainability therefore are also likely to contribute to economic sustainability, but need not do so. There will be some environmental functions that under the strong sustainability principle one would wish to conserve, which do not contribute to productive capacity, though they do contribute to well-being.

Social sustainability is promoted by any activity which fosters social cohesion, solidarity and well-being. Clearly there is a large overlap here with economic sustainability, especially with regard to the maintenance/enhancement of social/organisational capital. There may also be an overlap with environmental sustainability, if it is the case that social cohesion fosters environmental awareness. However, the strength of this connection is uncertain. Perhaps the correlation is clearer when expressed negatively: a society that is disintegrating is unlikely to pay much attention to the environment.

As depicted in Table 4.1 (p. 71), the ethical dimension itself is not here conceived as having its own type of sustainability, but of contributing to environmental, economic and social sustainability. The particular ethical attitudes that seem important in this respect are:

- concern for the other, including both people and other life forms;
- concern for the future.

From these attitudes derives a concern for equity and inclusiveness in the current generation, a concern for intergenerational equity among present and future humans, and a concern for the well-being and continued existence of the natural world and other species, now and in the future. An ethical concern for the environment tends to lead to an ecocentric, rather than anthropocentric, worldview.

Environmental functions, wealth-creation from the four capitals, appropriate and well-functioning social institutions and social equity and inclusiveness lead to the generation of human welfare. The welfare deriving from the environment may be economic or non-economic, that deriving from wealth-creation is economic, that deriving from social arrangements or ethical concern is economic, social or spiritual. A full schema of these relationships is shown in Figure 4.5.

The whole concept of sustainable development implies the delivery of environmental, economic and social benefits. The environmental benefits will contribute to bringing human ways of life more into line with the seven sustainability principles. The economic and social benefits may involve a direct contribution to economic sustainability by contributing to the maintenance or increase of the stock of the four capitals; or they may involve the strengthening of non-economic social institutions; or they may enhance a concern for equity, social inclusion or the natural world. Alternatively the benefits may derive from an increase in the welfare to

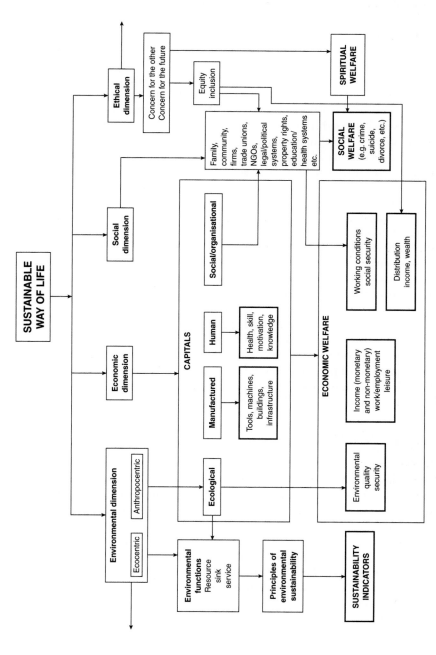

Figure 4.5 A framework for sustainability indicators

Note: Thick-edged boxes denote categories for indicators

which these economic, social and ethical elements give rise. In each case the benefits will need to be expressed in terms of *indicators* (see Figure 4.5), where an indicator may be defined as a measure which gives summary and meaningful information about a situation of interest.

Indicators of manufactured and human capital are readily available and are clearly implied by the description of that capital. The strengthening of social institutions and enhancement of equity are less easily identified in standard data series. With regard to economic and social welfare, there is an enormous variety of possible indicators (e.g. income, employment, work, leisure, working conditions, social security, income and wealth distribution, participation, environmental quality, statistics of crime, family stability, etc.). Improvements in spiritual welfare are more difficult to describe in general terms, but it may be that acceptable indicators can be found.

It should be stressed that a characteristic of the different dimensions of sustainability, and of the indicators in the different categories that have been discussed, is their *incommensurability*. No single numeraire exists into which the different elements of even environmental sustainability can be converted, let alone one which will achieve quantitative commensurability between environmental, economic, social and ethical benefits. This, of course, is the reason for opting for an indicator framework rather than seeking a single aggregated sustainability measure.

The concept of sustainability is complex and multidimensional. However, using an indicator framework such as that in Figure 4.5, the concept can nevertheless be adequately defined and interpreted across its different dimensions in order to be related to measurable indicators. This would allow a picture of progress towards sustainability to be built up. The next section looks in more detail at what the indicators of environmental sustainability in such a framework might be.

4.4.2 Indicators of environmental sustainability

The derivation of indicators of environmental sustainability requires first of all some classification of environmental issues. This is usually done through the categorisation either of environmental media and resources (the UK Government's approach, as in UKG 1994) or of 'environmental themes', as with the approach of the OECD (1995a) and EC (CEC 1992c), and that adopted in Table 1.1 (p. 7) in Chapter 1, where these themes relate to the areas that seem problematic as far as environmental sustainability is concerned. Table 4.3 relates the two approaches.

The distinction between environmental medium and environmental theme is broadly carried over to the various schemes for indicators of environmental 'state' and 'pressure' that have been proposed, which are discussed in some detail below. Here it may only be noted that 'state' indicators refer to the state, or condition, of environmental media, while 'pressure' indicators relate to the pressures or threats to which these

Table 4.3 Alternative classifications of environmental media and themes

Environmental media (Source: UKG 1994)	Environmental themes (Source: OECD 1995a)	Environmental themes (Source: CEC 1992c)
Global atmosphere	Climate change Ozone layer depletion	Climate change Ozone layer depletion
The sea	Natural resources Wastes Toxic contamination	Coastal zones Wastes management
Soil	Natural resources Wastes Toxic contamination	Wastes management
Freshwater	Natural resources Wastes Toxic contamination Eutrophication Acidification Urban environmental quality	Management of water resources Wastes management Acidification and air quality Urban environment
Air quality	Natural resources Wastes Toxic contamination Acidification Urban environmental quality	Wastes management Urban environment
Land use	Wastes Urban environmental quality Landscapes	Wastes management Urban environment Protection of nature and biodiversity
Wildlife/habitats	Urban environmental quality Landscapes and biodiversity	Urban environment Protection of nature and biodiversity

Source: Ekins and Simon (1998: 152)

media are subject, as classified in the environmental themes. (The 'response' component of some of these indicator schemes, intended to show how the pressures on the environmental media are being addressed, is not discussed here.)

It is a straightforward matter to regroup the environmental themes of the EC and OECD approaches into a classification based on environmental functions, in line with the discussion of the previous section. This is the approach taken by the World Resources Institute (Hammond *et al.* 1995) and the World Bank (World Bank 1995) in their classifications of environmental themes, to which they add the category of 'human impacts'. This addition is clearly a significant consideration in the determination of the importance of environmental functions, which is necessary to make the present definition of environmental sustainability operational.

Because of its basis in the concept of the environmental function, the WRI/World Bank classification is the best suited to the approach to sustainability being taken here. Slightly adapted from the original sources to include some of the categories in Table 4.3, and some of the environmental issues identified in UKG (1994), it is set out in Table 4.4, identifying the major environmental functions, together with the principal pressures to which they are being subjected.

Table 4.4 Classification of environmental themes based on environmental functions

Environmental functions

I Source functions (themes: resource depletion; soil erosion; species extinction)

Renewable resources:
1 Soil fertility
2 Forest resources
3 Fish resources
4 Water resources
5 Renewable energy resources
Non-renewable resources:
6 Minerals
7 Fossil fuels
8 Land use

II Sink functions (theme: pollution)

9 Stable climate
   impaired by climate change due to emission of greenhouse gases
10 Ozone shielding
   impaired by emission of ozone-depleting substances
11 Air quality
12 Fresh water quality
13 Marine water quality
14 Soil quality
   impaired by one or more of:
   Acidification
   Eutrophication
   Toxic contamination (including chemicals, radioactivity)
   Solid waste disposal

III Service functions (themes: biodiversity, landscape)

15 Biodiversity
16 Special lands
17 Recreation, scenery, aesthetic enjoyment

IV Environmental functions and particular human impacts

18 Health (air, water and soil quality)
   also impaired by:
   Natural disasters
19 Risks

Source: Ekins and Simon (1998: 153)

The next step in deriving environmental sustainability indicators is to determine which environmental functions should be maintained and at what level. This is done using the seven sustainability principles set out on pp. 96–6. Developed out of a concern to maintain important environmental functions, these principles imply clear standards of environmental performance or quality. For example, for climate to be stabilised, atmospheric concentrations of greenhouse gases must be maintained below a certain level, requiring certain maximum levels of emissions of these gases (with a given global greenhouse gas absorptive capacity). Keeping within an ecosystem's critical load, or maintaining acceptably low impacts on human health, similarly requires certain maximum concentrations or emissions of pollutants.

Table 4.5 sets out the standards implied by the principles and indicates the kinds of changes that are required in a situation of unsustainability if the standards are to be met.

The sustainability standards are put forward as conditions that need to be complied with if environmental sustainability is to be achieved. Whether these standards become the objective of public policy is, of course, a political matter. It is, for instance, possible that governments might decide that other public policy objectives (e.g. economic growth, employment) were more important than environmental sustainability. The advantage of the above standards in such circumstances is that they have the necessary

Table 4.5 Implications of environmental sustainability principles

Function	Standard	Required for sustainability
1a Climate	Stable climate	Reduce emissions of GGs, increase GG sinks
1b Ozone shielding	Undepleted ozone	Reduce emissions of ODS
2 Ecosystem stability and resilience	Biodiversity at current levels	Reduce loss of species and habitat destruction
3 Non-renewable resources	No loss of function	More efficient use; repair, reuse, recycling, renewable substitutes
4 Renewable resources	Sustainable harvest at desired level	Reduce harvest/increase stock where necessary
5 Waste absorption	Critical load (ecosystems), human health	Reduce emissions where necessary
6 Amenity, inspiration	Unspoilt countryside	Conserve landscape
7 Environmental security	Low level of risk	Reduce risks where necessary

Source: Ekins and Simon (1998: 156)

objectivity to judge whether this is in fact the case. Application of the standards enables rhetoric about environmental sustainability to be tested in an unambiguous way.

If governments adopt environmental sustainability as an objective of public policy, then the standards of sustainability become sustainability *targets*. Intermediate targets, such as the UK Government's target of reducing CO_2 emissions by 20 per cent from 1990 levels by 2010, may also be set as part of a strategy of achieving environmental sustainability over time. The sustainability standards are also examples of sustainability indicators, which are part of the larger set of general environmental indicators. The sustainability indicators are chosen because of their clear relationship to the seven sustainability principles.

Despite its name the UK Government publication *Indicators of Sustainable Development* (DOE 1996a) largely steered clear of setting out sustainability indicators. In contrast, the approach taken by the Netherlands National Environmental Policy Plan (NEPP) (MOHPPE 1988), as further developed by Adriaanse (1993), gives clear targets for the reduction of the environmental pressures that are causing unsustainable environmental effects. The targets are to be achieved over twenty-five years, in line with the insight that environmental sustainability requires this generation to bequeath a broadly sustainable environment to the next.

4.5 CONCLUSION

The preceding sections set out a methodology for making the concept of environmental sustainability operational by tracing out the causes of unsustainability and identifying instruments to bring economic activity within defined and measurable standards of sustainability. The determined application of these instruments across the whole range of activities implicated in unsustainability could have profound implications for the macroeconomy, as well as for economic growth, as is explained in later chapters.

Standards of sustainability derived from the principles set out earlier would set clear directions and targets for changes in the economy's biophysical throughputs and in the production of biomass. The costs of the instruments necessary to achieve these targets can serve as inputs into an appropriate macroeconomic model to estimate the instruments' impacts on GNP growth and other macroeconomic variables. Some results of modelling exercises of this kind will be given in later chapters.

The actual calculation of GNP and GNP growth is carried out through an internationally agreed system of national accounts which itself needs to be modified in order to reflect better the contribution of the environment to production. How such a modification should be effected is the subject of Chapter 5.

A4 APPENDIX

A4.1 Deriving the strong sustainability formula for the depletion of non-renewable resources

In a two-period sequence, where $_i$ refers to the relevant period, let:

S_0 = Stock of unextracted non-renewable resource at beginning of first period

S_1 = Stock of unextracted non-renewable resource at beginning of second period (excluding discoveries in first period)

d_i = Depletion (extraction) during period

R_i = Stock of renewable substitutes for the resource

C_i = Stock of the non-renewable resource in use

e_i = Level of economic/environmental service delivered by one unit of the resource

w_i = Quantity of resource disposed of as waste during period

a_i = Multiplication factor to reflect increase in renewable substitute during period

ES_i = Total environmental service delivered by the resource

$\Rightarrow ES_0 = e_0(S_0 + R_0 + C_0)$

$S_1 = S_0 - d_0 \; ; \; R_1 = a_0 R_0 \; ; \; C_1 = C_0 + d_0 - w_0$

$ES_1 = e_1(S_1 + R_1 + C_1) \qquad = e_1(S_0 - d_0 + a_0 R_0 + C_0 + d_0 - w_0)$

$\qquad = e_1(S_0 + a_0 R_0 + C_0 - w_0) = e_1(ES_0/e_0 + (a_0 - 1) R_0 - w_0)$

For sustainability, $ES_1 \geq ES_0$

$\Rightarrow e_1(S_0 + a_0 R_0 + C_0 - w_0) \geq e_0(S_0 + R_0 + C_0)$

$\Rightarrow w_0 \leq (1 - e_0/e_1)(S_0 + C_0) + (a_0 - e_0/e_1)R_0$

A4.2 Deriving the formula for the depletion rate at minimum life expectancy

Let: S = Resource reserves (stock)

d = Depletion in a given time period, then

L = Life expectancy $\qquad = S/d$

L_{min} = Agreed minimum life expectancy

D = Discoveries

Subscripts $_{1,2}$ refer to time-periods, then

$S_2 = (S_1 - d_1) + D_1$

At L_{min}:

$L_{min} = S_1/d_1 = S_2/d_2 = [(S_1 - d_1) + D_1]/d_2$

$\Rightarrow d_2 = d_1[(S_1 - d_1) + D_1]/S_1 = d_1[1 + (D_1 - d_1)/S_1]$

A4.3 Derivation of capital/income shares of receipts from depletion of a non-renewable resource (after El Serafy 1989: 17)

Let: R = Constant stream of receipts in each year from total depletion of a resource over n years

X = Constant income derived from R in each year of depletion, and indefinitely thereafter from capital fund, S

I = Constant capital component of R, which contributes to S in each year of depletion

$\Rightarrow$ R = X + I in each period

r = Interest rate

The task is to convert a finite stream of income, R in each year for n years, into an indefinite stream of income, X in each year. This can be done by converting each stream to a present value, and equating the present values.

For X: $\displaystyle\sum_{0}^{\infty} X/(1 + r)^i \quad = \quad \frac{X}{1 - 1/(1 + r)}$

For R: $\displaystyle\sum_{0}^{\infty} R/(1 + r)^i \quad = \quad \sum_{0}^{n} R_i/(1 + r)^i + \sum_{n+1}^{\infty} R_i/(1 + r)^i$

Now present value of $R_{n+1} = R/(1 + r)^{n+1}$

$\Rightarrow \qquad \displaystyle\sum_{n+1}^{\infty} R/(1 + r)^i \quad = \quad \frac{R/(1 + r)^{n+1}}{1 - 1/(1 + r)}$

$\Rightarrow \qquad \displaystyle\sum_{0}^{n} R/(1 + r)^i \quad = \quad \frac{R}{1 - 1/(1 + r)} - \frac{R/(1 + r)^{n+1}}{1 - 1/(1 + r)}$

$\qquad\qquad\qquad\qquad = \quad \dfrac{R[1 - 1/(1 + r)^{n+1}]}{1 - 1/(1 + r)}$

Let $\displaystyle\sum_{0}^{\infty} X/(1 + r)^i \quad = \quad \sum_{0}^{n} R/(1 + r)^i$

$\Rightarrow \qquad \dfrac{X}{1 - 1/(1 + r)} \quad = \quad \dfrac{R[1 - 1/(1 + r)^{n+1}]}{1 - 1/(1 + r)}$

$\Rightarrow \qquad X/R \quad = \quad 1 - 1/(1 + r)^{n+1}$

$\Rightarrow \qquad I/R \quad = \quad 1/(1 + r)^{n+1}$

5 Accounting for production and the environment

5.1 THE CASE FOR ADJUSTING THE NATIONAL ACCOUNTS

At the end of Chapter 3 it was suggested that one of the reasons why the national accounts aggregates are a poor measure of production is because they fail to give an adequate account of uses of, and impacts on, the environment as a factor of production, or ecological capital in the terms of Figure 3.2 (p. 53). In this chapter this critique will be further developed and suggestions made as to how the national accounts should be adjusted to treat ecological capital consistently in the framework of the national accounts.

A standard introduction to the topic has defined national accounting thus: 'National accounting is simply a systematic way of classifying the multitude of economic activities that take place in the economy in different groups or classes that are regarded as being important for understanding the way the economy works' (Beckerman 1968: 68). Beckerman acknowledges that 'there is an arbitrary element in many of the decisions that have to be made in drawing up a classification system for the national accounts', and is at pains to stress that there is nothing sacrosanct about the present way the accounts are structured:

> It must be emphasised that there is a constant evolution and change in the questions the economists are asking, in the institutional structure of the economy, and in the working hypotheses that economists use for purposes of analysing the behaviour of the economy. In accordance with these changes so it will be necessary to modify and adapt the classification system used for national accounting. It would be useless to persist with a classification system, for example, that no longer corresponded to the institutional and social categories of society, or to the latest knowledge about how the economy operated and so about which relationships were important for analytical purposes. . . . It is to be expected that the appropriate national accounts classification will, as the years go by, be subject to far-reaching modifications.
>
> (ibid.: 5–6)

This is also the view of Robert Eisner, who noted in his authoritative survey of proposals to amend or extend the national accounts:

> [T]he accounts are not set in concrete. . . . From the early days of their formulation there have been lively debates as to just what they should include, how items ought to be measured, and how they are to be put together. They have been modified over the years.
>
> (Eisner 1988: 1611–12)

When the national accounts were being systematised in the 1940s, environmental issues had a low perceived importance, and the accounting structure adopted simply ignored environmental issues, as one of the essentially 'arbitrary' judgements referred to by Beckerman. The national accounts have now matured into the fundamental instrument of macroeconomic management and, more controversially, means of indicating economic progress. The 1992 Earth Summit in Rio de Janeiro committed countries to producing national strategies for sustainable development, but it is most unlikely that these will carry economic weight unless they are integrally related to the national accounting system. The European Community certainly recognised the importance of this when, in its Fifth Action Programme on the Environment, it stated categorically: 'Environmentally adjusted national accounts should be available on a pilot basis from 1995 onwards for all Community countries, with a view to formal adoption by the end of the decade' (CEC 1992b: 97).

This political imperative for environmental adjustment of the national accounts reinforces the intellectual and economic imperatives. Omitting the environment from the national accounts can only be justified intellectually if environmental issues are economically unimportant. If these issues are now of central importance to humanity, and are intimately related to economic activity, as was generally accepted at the Rio Summit, then the national accounts' treatment of them is bizarre and indefensible. Moreover, it is economically misleading. As discussed below, a number of studies (e.g. Repetto *et al.* 1989 for Indonesia; Solórzano *et al.* 1991 for Costa Rica; Adger 1992 for Zimbabwe; Bartelmus, Lutz and Schweinfest 1993 for Papua New Guinea; Van Tongeren *et al.* 1993 for Mexico) have shown that GNP growth rates and net capital formation can be greatly overstated by failing to account properly for natural resources.

Over the past ten years it has gradually been accepted by both policy makers and national statistical offices that environmental impacts due to economic activities need to be incorporated in some way into the national accounts which provide a systematic way of reporting on and monitoring those activities. Expressions of this consensus may be found in the Handbook on Integrated Environmental and Economic Accounting produced by the United Nations Statistical Division (UNSD 1993), the Communication from the European Commission to the Council and

European Parliament (CEC 1994) and EUROSTAT's statement on the 'Present state and future developments' of environmental accounts (EURO-STAT 1997). However, before coming to the methods of integrating economic and environmental accounting, it is necessary to explain briefly how the national accounts themselves are constructed.

5.2 CONSTRUCTION OF THE NATIONAL ACCOUNTS

The first, and perhaps most important, question the national accounts are intended to answer is: 'How much does the national economy produce?' To answer this question the national accounts must be, and are, based on a clear theory of production and definition of national product, which, according to Beckerman, is 'the unduplicated value of the flow of goods and services produced by the nation in the time period concerned (usually a year)' (Beckerman 1968: 31). If the environment is to be included in the accounts, then it must be incorporated consistently into this theory and definition as they are made operational in the quantification of the flow of goods and services in order to arrive at a figure for 'national product'.

The national accounts are presently constructed by defining a 'production boundary', which distinguishes between 'productive' and 'non-productive' activities. As Beckerman notes, 'the dividing line between what is and what is not a productive activity is necessarily arbitrary in any system of national accounts' (1968: 8). The current dominant convention is that where the flows of goods and services are accompanied by corresponding flows of money (in the opposite direction), then they are part of national product. Where they are not thus accompanied, they are not part of national product. The principal exceptions to this rule are the residential services provided by buildings to owner-occupiers and the home-grown food consumed by farmers, the values of both of which are estimated ('imputed') according to reigning market prices and added into national product. With few such exceptions a flow of goods and services that is not accompanied by a money flow is not considered part of national product, or GNP. Similarly, any flow of money that is not matched by a flow of goods and services (such as the payment by government of old-age pensions or unemployment benefit) is called a 'transfer payment' and is not added to national product.

Finally, care must be taken in the accounting of intermediate goods and services. If their value is counted as part of national product; and if the value of the goods and services to the production of which they contribute (which will include their value) is also counted as part of national product, then the value of the intermediate goods will have been counted more than once – 'double-counting' will have occurred. Therefore national product must be counted *either* from the value only of 'final' goods and services, those which are sold directly for consumption or investment (which will include the value of all intermediate goods); *or* it must be calculated by summing the value added by each industry, the payments only for capital (including rents) and labour services in each industry. National product computed in either of these ways will include the value of intermediate goods only once.

This method of constructing national product is shown in Figure 5.1. The double lines show the flow of goods and services into and out of the production sector, which produces intermediate, consumption, investment and export goods. The single lines show flows of money, in the reverse direction to the flow of goods. Households comprise people as workers, who provide labour services (L), and as owners (of firms and property), who provide capital services (K, E′, where E′ is the flows from ecological capital which are marketed). For these services workers are paid wages (W), shareholders receive profits (P) and property-owners receive rents (R). These comprise household factor incomes. There then take place various transfer payments between people and government (taxes, T, and government benefits, Tr), from which households and governments emerge with net incomes H and G respectively. Household income (H) is spent on consumption (C), which includes imports (M_H), or investment (I), according to whether households spend or save (S) their incomes. Government expenditure (G) is also spent on investment or consumption goods, also including imports (M_G). Total imports are M (= M_H + M_G). Exports are bought with the money of foreigners (X).

The flows of money, adjusted for imports and exports, are circular: the production sector pays out incomes (W + P + R) from the value added (Vi + Vf, where Vi is the value added in the intermediate goods sector, and Vf is the value added in the final goods sector) which it generates, which it receives from expenditures on its products (C + I + G +X − M).

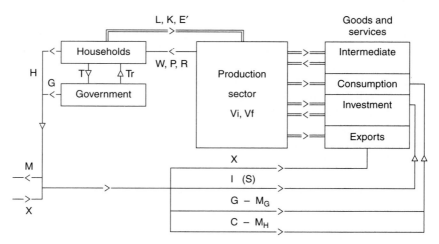

Figure 5.1 Flows of money as they are entered into the national accounts

The value of the national product is the value of the expenditures on it, but, because of the circular flow of the money concerned, this must be equal to the factor incomes and the value added generated in production. The figure obtained by calculating any of these totals is called Gross Domestic Product (GDP), according to the triple identity between incomes, value added and expenditure:

$$GDP \equiv W + P + R \equiv Vi + Vf \equiv C + I + G + (X - M) \qquad (5.1)$$

GNP is obtained from GDP by adding in net property income from abroad.

Factor incomes as identified above are a gross income measure in that no allowance has been made for the capital depreciation that has taken place in generating them. This is in contrast to the income measure as defined by Hicks (1946: 172): 'We ought to define a man's income as the maximum value which he can consume during a week, and still expect to be as well off at the end of the week as he was at the beginning.' In other words, Hicksian national income is the total of the factor incomes less (plus) any capital depreciation (capital accumulation) which may have taken place. The national accounts do not always maintain a rigorous distinction between these two measures, sometimes referring to 'national income' as the sum of factor incomes (HMSO 1985: 1 (para. 1.4)) and sometimes specifying it as Net National Product (NNP), which is GNP less a deduction for depreciation, or capital consumption (ibid.: 1, 3 (paras. 1.5, 1.19)). Hereafter the term income is used in the Hicksian sense, i.e. net of depreciation (or including capital accumulation).

5.3 CAUSES FOR CONCERN IN THE NATIONAL ACCOUNTS

Comparing the full model of production described in Chapter 3 (Figure 3.2) and the method of calculating the National Income described above, it can be seen that there are three major ways in which the national accounts fail to give a correct assessment of income, as defined by Hicks.

The first is the summary exclusion of practically all non-monetary production, so that GDP as calculated will be substantially less than a 'Total Product' which included non-monetary, including household, production. But the error introduced by excluding non-monetary production goes further than this, for monetary and non-monetary production are not independent of each other. One of the main characteristics of industrial economic development has been the transfer of activities (e.g. cooking, washing, cleaning, child-care, education) from the household, family and community, where they were not paid for, to market-settings (e.g. restaurants, launderettes, cleaning firms, nurseries, schools) where they are paid for. The national accounts calculated as above show the whole of the new market activity as growth in production, whereas the actual net product of the transfer is the difference between the value of the new market activity and the value of the non-monetary production it replaced.

It was to avoid such an anomaly of this sort that the decision was taken to include in national product the imputed rents of owner-occupied households. Otherwise GDP would have decreased by the amount of the rent every time a tenant bought the house he or she was renting (and increased every time an owner-occupier became a tenant). This would obviously have been an absurd situation. It is, however, precisely analogous to the situation identified by Pigou (1932: 32–3), whereby, under current conventions, GDP decreases by the amount of her pay when a man marries his housekeeper, even if she performs the same tasks after her marriage as before, though without a wage. More contemporaneously, one might ask by how much GDP overstates the increase in production when a single-income married couple is divorced, and both individuals get full-time jobs and start paying for services which before they rendered freely to each other and their children.

Therefore the exclusion of non-monetary production from GDP not only understates real production. Given the shift of activities towards the market that occurs with modern economic development, it also systematically overstates economic growth. It also denies the value of non-monetary work, which discourages and discriminates against those who do it, still mainly women. For all these reasons non-monetary production should be brought into the national accounts. Goldschmidt-Clermont (1992, 1993) has described clearly how this could be achieved by shifting the production boundary to include these activities as 'productive', and then calculating their value, on the basis of comparison with their nearest market equivalents, in accordance with current national accounting conventions.

The second major area of omission in the national accounts is their failure to assess changes in human and social/organisational capital. Growth accounting has now developed very detailed ways of differentiating between different qualities of labour input. For example, the model described in Jorgenson (1990) cross-classifies labour inputs 'by the two sexes, eight age groups, five educational groups and two employment statuses – employee and self-employed' (Jorgenson 1990: 35). Clearly these different qualities of labour input, which have different productivities, issue from a heterogeneous human capital stock, which could, in principle, be valued either according to the productivity of associated labour services, as expressed by the present value of the streams of incomes to which the stock gives rise; or according to the inputs required to create, maintain and increase it. In practice, however, the task appears too ambitious. While it is beyond contention, for example, that malnutrition degrades human capital, that does not mean that all food expenditures should be regarded as investment in such capital, nor would it be possible to distinguish between food 'consumption' and food 'investment' without making a plethora of arbitrary assumptions and running into huge data problems (similarly with expenditures on health and education, the other principal components of human capital creation and maintenance).

If human capital is statistically intractable, social and organisational capital is even more so. Harrison is in no doubt about the importance of this kind of capital, which she calls institutional capital:

> Economic behaviour does not take place in a vacuum. Rather it consists of a large number of agents interacting according to a known set of norms and conventions. These are enshrined in the laws and customs of the country through the formal and informal activities of the governing body.
>
> (A. Harrison 1993: 26)

In addition to political and legal institutions, social and organisational capital includes firms, business associations, trade unions, voluntary groups and families, for all these institutions play an important role in monetary and non-monetary production. But, as Harrison says:

> Just because the importance of institutional capital is recognised, however, does not mean it can be represented in economic terms. . . . Even less than human capital (to which of course it is linked) can it be associated with specific expenditures or approximated in money terms.
>
> (ibid.: 26)

The issues of human capital and non-market production are discussed in great detail in Eisner's (1988) survey of proposed national accounting extensions. What is notable is that Eisner practically ignored the third great area of failure of the national accounts, their treatment of the environment. Partly this was due to the lack of worked-out environmental adjustments for Eisner to include in his empirical review. But the virtual omission of the environment from the conceptual and methodological discussion also indicates the low profile this issue had among national income accountants at that time. The change of attitude in relatively few years has been striking, and restores the issue of the treatment of the environment in the national accounts to an importance it had in an earlier period of environmental awareness, the 1970s. Then, one of the fathers of national accounting had written:

> Pollution, depletion and other negative by-products of economic production were greatly accelerated because of the very rapid rise of total output. . . . Economic production, and the technology that it employs, may be viewed as interference with the natural course of events, in order to shape the outcome to provide economic goods to man. All such

interference has potential negative economic consequences – pollution and the like – the more lasting, the higher the level of production technology as measured by its capacity to produce goods.

(Kuznets 1973: 585)

Herfindahl and Kneese were confident about the implications of these 'negative ecological consequences' for the national accounts:

> The exclusion of the services of clean air, clean water, space etc. from the list of final goods probably is not the result of disagreement that the services provided by nature are a factor in true welfare, but rather of the judgment on the part of the income accountant that obtaining acceptable estimates for these values would be too difficult and costly. It is clear, however, that any reduction in the service flows of common property resources that is viewed as a loss of real product by consumers means that NNP overstates any increase in final product as compared with the total flow from the truly relevant and larger list of final goods and services. In the extreme case the 'true' service flow could actually decrease while NNP rises.
>
> (Herfindahl and Kneese 1973: 447–8)

Juster (1973: 66) agrees: 'The environment is clearly worse today than it was in the mid-1950s, and comparison of real output between these two periods is already over-stated because environmental deterioration has been permitted to occur.' The ISEW calculations given in Chapter 3 provide an empirical (if controversial) example of Herfindahl and Kneese's theoretical hypothesis that true service could decrease while NNP rises.

This situation can be considered in terms of the concept of ecological capital developed in Chapter 3. As was then seen, the economic functions of the environment include the provision of resources, the absorption and neutralisation of wastes and the provision of other services independently of human agency. In the process of economic activity, resources can become depleted (and, in the case of non-renewable resources, are bound to become so) and the environment can become degraded through pollution or occupation (change of use). Exactly analogously to the consumption of manufactured capital, continuing depletion and degradation imply that the environment will in the future be able to fulfil its functions less effectively or not at all. Yet in many cases these functions are of vital importance to economic, and wider human, life. It is for this reason that current use of the environment is perceived as 'unsustainable': it cannot be envisaged to continue.

The calculation of GNP and National Income (NNP) give no inkling of this increasingly serious unsustainability, which is far more pronounced now than in the early 1970s, despite the fact that, as discussed earlier, income in the Hicksian sense is defined as a sustainable quantity. It is this inconsistency in the accounts' treatment of the environment that is one of the components of the recent upsurge of concern over the issue, which has led one economist, a Nobel Laureate who, like Kuznets, was among those responsible for the early development of the accounts, to say that, because of them, 'society is steering by the wrong compass' (Tinbergen and Hueting 1993: 52).

5.4 ENVIRONMENTAL ADJUSTMENTS TO THE NATIONAL ACCOUNTS

It is the sense of chronic misdirection of the economy, and chronic misallocation of environmental resources, which has motivated the current impetus to adjust the national accounts for environmental effects. There are several possible responses to this situation. One is to redefine the production boundary of the national accounts to include all environmental services. According to Hartwick:

> It only makes economic sense to deduct economic depreciation from GNP for those stocks whose flows are priced appropriately in GNP. . . . [T]he correct approach would be to re-price the environmental services by appropriate scarcity or shadow prices and revise GNP upwards. Then any annual declines (increases) in the corresponding *stocks* should be valued and netted out (added to) GNP to obtain NNP.
> (Hartwick 1990: 292, original emphasis)

Faber and Proops (1991: 225ff.) have shown how the pollution degradation services provided by the natural environment can be treated in the same way as the pollution abatement provided by economic investment. The 'real' national income, consisting of both natural goods and services and those produced by the economy, would then be higher than the 'measured' goods and services recorded in the macroeconomic aggregates of the national accounts. Continuing pollution which damaged the pollution degradation capability of the natural environment, and so reduced the services it could deliver, would then show up as a deduction from this 'real' national income. If investment in pollution abatement were to be diverted from other economic opportunities in order to take the place of these lost natural services, 'measured' output would stay the same, but there would in fact have been a real economic loss. If such a diversion were not to take place, the loss of natural services would be experienced as reduced environmental quality. In either case the loss of natural services has reduced 'real' output. This is of relevance to the correct treatment of pollution abatement, and other environmental protection, expenditures, in the national accounts, as will be seen below.

Faber and Proops (1991: 228ff.) go on to extend this model to the depletion of natural resources, noting that such resources are a 'wealth asset

. . . with the same status as labor and capital goods'. In other words natural resources are a form of capital as per the model of Figure 3.2. Faber and Proops consider that currently the national accounts measure the services from this capital at much too low a level, so that it is overexploited, and 'real' national income is underestimated for this reason too. However, it would also be possible to treat the depletion of natural resources as capital consumption in the same way as the depreciation of manufactured capital is treated.

This may be a theoretically appealing approach, but it is practically unfeasible for all the reasons concerning uncertainty about and difficulties in valuing environmental functions discussed earlier. For practical reasons it seems preferable to continue to take the production boundary to be the human economy, with the current conventions of the national accounting system, but to treat any depletion of ecological capital due to economic activity as capital consumption and seek to deduct it from GDP to form an adjusted NDP. This was the approach recommended by the UN Statistical Division in its system of integrated environmental and economic accounting (Bartelmus, Stahmer and Van Tongeren 1993; UNSD 1993). The approach sticks resolutely to the treatment of the national accounts aggregates as measures of production and not welfare. In contrast to Hartwick (1990), Mäler (1991), Hamilton (1994) and Dasgupta (1995), it does not attempt to adjust GDP or any of the other national accounting aggregates in order to improve them as welfare indicators. This is in line with the discussion in Chapter 3 concluding that welfare is too complex to be capturable by any adjustments to the national accounting framework.

5.4.1 Examples of national accounting for the environment

Bartelmus, Lutz and Schweinfest have set out the three basic shortcomings of the national accounts with regard to the environment:

> National accounts have certain drawbacks that cast doubt on their usefulness for measuring long-term environmentally sound and sustainable economic development. For one thing they neglect the scarcities of natural resources that can pose a serious threat to sustained economic productivity. For another they pay only limited attention to the effects of environmental quality on human health and welfare. In addition, they treat environmental protection expenditures as increases in national product, which could instead be considered social costs of maintaining environmental quality.
>
> (Bartelmus, Lutz and Schweinfest 1993: 108)

One of the differences between the 1990s and the 1970s is that there now exists a number of quantitative estimates of adjustments that would need to be made to the national accounts for them to reflect environmental depletion and degradation. These estimates, some of which are reported below, give an idea of the quantities that have so far been calculated in pursuit of the aim of estimating the value of the depletion and degradation of the ecological capital stock that occurred as a result of economic activity in a given period.

With regard to the first of Bartelmus *et al.*'s points, several studies have now computed a partial estimate of the depletion of natural resources. Van Tongeren *et al.* (1993) calculated the value of the depletion of oil and forests in Mexico in 1985. They find that this depletion amounted to 5.7 per cent of Mexico's GDP. More seriously, perhaps, for Mexico's future production prospects, they found that net capital accumulation fell from 11 per cent to less than 6 per cent of NDP when depletion was accounted for. The sectoral effects are, predictably, even more pronounced. Forestry and oil extraction made a contribution to unadjusted NDP of 0.54 per cent and 3.50 per cent respectively. When depletion was taken into account their contribution fell to 0.15 per cent and 0.00 per cent – that is, this study accounted all of oil extraction's contribution to NDP as capital consumption rather than the generation of income (figures from Van Tongeren *et al.* 1993: 100 (Table 6.9), 105 (Table 6.12)).

Adger (1992) produced estimates for Zimbabwe for 1987. He found that depletion of ecological capital due to soil erosion and forest loss reduced the net product of Zimbabwe's commercial and communal agriculture sector by 30 per cent and Zimbabwe's NDP by 3 per cent. Adger further analysed the true economic results of a surge in minerals production in 1991 following the devaluation of the Zimbabwean dollar. In nominal terms the sector's conventionally calculated net product grew by 18 per cent; but depletion grew from 20 per cent to 27 per cent of this net product. When this is taken into account the adjusted net sectoral product only grew by 7 per cent (rather than 18 per cent) (figures from Adger 1992: 19 (Table 4)).

The World Resources Institute has also done two studies of this kind. Solórzano *et al.* (1991) found for Costa Rica that the loss of three resources – forests, soil and a fishery – grew from 5.67 per cent of NDP in 1970 to 10.5 per cent in 1988. Capital formation was even more drastically affected: net capital formation was lower by 38 per cent in 1970 and 48 per cent in 1988, if depletion is taken into account (figures from Solórzano *et al.* 1991: 7 (Table 1.2), 9 (Table 1.3)). For Indonesia, Repetto *et al.* (1989: 6) found that subtracting the depletion of oil, forests and soil from the country's GDP reduced its average growth rate over the years 1971–84 from 7.1 per cent to 4.0 per cent. The study also showed that in some years, using these calculations of the depletion of just these three resources, and contrary to the conventional accounts, net investment in the Indonesian economy was negative: 'A fuller accounting of natural resource depletion might conclude that in many years depletion exceeded gross investment, implying that natural resources were being depleted to finance current consumption expenditures' (ibid.: 6).

Repetto *et al.* spell out the implications of their study, which are also applicable to the other studies cited. Under the current system of national accounting:

> a country could exhaust its mineral resources, cut down its forests, erode its soils, pollute its aquifers, and hunt its wildlife and fisheries to extinction, but measured income would not be affected as these assets disappeared. . . . [The] difference in the treatment of natural resources and other tangible assets confuses the depletion of valuable assets with the generation of income. . . . The result can be illusory gains in income and permanent losses in wealth.
>
> (Repetto *et al.* 1989: 2–3)

Bartelmus *et al.*'s second basic environmental shortcoming of the national accounts was their failure to account properly for economically induced environmental degradation and its effects on human health and welfare. The effects on human health and welfare can entail two types of costs: actual monetary expenditures incurred to 'defend' against the effects; and losses of health, production or welfare due to a lack of such 'defensive expenditures'. The defensive expenditures due to degradation are simple to calculate in principle because they represent actual monetary flows, although data in the required disaggregation may not always be available.

The other losses are clearly a more difficult category of ecological capital consumption to measure than either the defensive expenditures or the depletion of such resources as oil, timber and fish that was investigated earlier. Because there are no corresponding monetary flows, monetary values have to be imputed to these losses using a variety of methods none of which is totally satisfactory.

One calculation of the costs of ecological degradation comes from Cobb and Cobb (1994) for the US, as part of their calculation of an Index of Socioeconomic Welfare (ISEW), which also included the calculation of some depletion costs. For 1986 their calculated costs of air, water and noise pollution plus long-term environmental degradation amounted to 17 per cent of US GNP (15 per cent of the 17 per cent was long-term environmental degradation, which was a largely speculative figure, but the pollution costs were conservative). Their costs of depletion of non-renewable resources and loss of farmland and wetlands amounted to 7 per cent of US GDP. Thus, even leaving long-term degradation out of account completely, ecological capital equivalent to about 10 per cent of US GDP was consumed in 1986 (figures from Cobb and Cobb 1994: 82–3 (Table A.1)).

The study of Van Tongeren *et al.* (1993) that has already been cited also makes an estimate for Mexico in 1985 of the costs of a variety of forms of land, water and air degradation and pollution. The authors find that these costs are 7.6 per cent of NDP and no less than 67 per cent of net capital accumulation. When these costs are added to the resource depletion costs given earlier, to give a figure of ecological capital consumption that includes both depletion and degradation, this figure is 13.4 per cent of NDP and capital accumulation becomes −2.3 per cent of NDP, i.e. instead of the economy having net investment of 11.2 per cent, as the conventional accounts showed, it had net disinvestment of 2.3 per cent, when ecological capital was accounted for.

Pearce and Atkinson (1992, 1993) use the characterisation of environmental losses as the consumption of natural capital to deduct the figure for such losses from the net investment (savings less depreciation) of different countries to compute a figure for 'net savings', which they identify as an indicator of weak sustainability. Hamilton (1994) further adjusted net savings by adding education expenditures (as investment in human capital), to arrive at a 'genuine savings' indicator. He regards the adjustment of savings as of more policy relevance than the adjustment of income, because 'net savings rates that are near zero or negative would indicate clearly that development is not sustainable' (ibid.: 166).

The Pearce and Atkinson (1992: 12 (Table 1)) figures for twenty-one different countries indicate that eight are unsustainable according to the authors' net savings rule. Surprisingly, developing countries that have experienced and are experiencing great environmental degradation (Brazil, Costa Rica and Zimbabwe), as well as a number of industrial countries, are all shown as sustainable by this rule. In Hamilton (1994: 166), OECD countries are shown to have positive genuine savings rates. Hamilton and Atkinson (1996), in contrast, show that of sixteen European countries, Greece, Ireland, Portugal and the UK all had periods of negative net savings in the 1980s. The improvement in this figure in the UK during the 1980s was due to the fall in the oil price which reduced the estimates of UK depletion costs.

These results show the limitations, as well as the uses, of such weak sustainability indicators. The environmental data presented in Chapters 1 and 7 do not lend support to the hypothesis that industrial economies are environmentally sustainable. Moreover the influence of the oil price on the sustainability indicator, irrespective of depletion rates, emphasises that what is being measured is economic, and not environmental, sustainability, as defined in the previous chapter. Such considerations suggest that adjusted savings indicators should at most be used as indicators of environmental unsustainability, when they are negative, but positive net or genuine savings do not necessarily indicate the reverse.

Bartelmus *et al.*'s third category of national accounts anomalies was the treatment of environmental protection expenditures. These are expenditures that prevent environmental degradation rather than trying to defend against or compensate for it. However, they are normally included in calculations of defensive expenditures. Leipert (1989a: 852 (Table 1)) has calculated that environmental protection expenditures in Germany in 1985 were 1.48 per cent of GDP. The costs of environmental degradation, excluding health costs, were less, 0.80 per cent of GDP. This is in stark contrast to the Mexican case, where Van Tongeren *et al.* (1993: 98) estimated that environmental protection expenditures were only 5 per cent of the value of the environmental degradation cost.

There is a long and still unresolved debate over the correct treatment of defensive expenditures in the national accounts, to which this chapter will later make a contribution (see p. 138). But, however they are to be accounted, no-one denies that they are costs arising from unintended effects of production and consumption. If the economic activity was not going to or did not bring about the unintended effect, then there would be no need to incur the costs.

Finally, it must be remembered that in all the studies cited above the authors are cautious about the accuracy of the actual numbers calculated. However, it is also true that they only try to measure a small fraction of the environmental depletion and degradation in the economies concerned, so that the total ecological capital consumption could be very much higher than their estimates. To arrive at the full environmental costs incurred by the economy, omitted health and welfare effects of the depletion and degradation would have to be considered as well.

5.4.2 Theoretical and methodological issues in environmental accounting

The three environmental shortcomings in the national accounting system identified by Bartelmus, Lutz and Schweinfest (1993), of which the examples in the preceding section gave numerical estimates, essentially amount to a failure to account properly for the depletion and degradation of scarce ecological capital, and for environmental protection expenditures. The discussion of the estimates makes clear that the theoretical and methodological issues in remedying these shortcomings are complex. So much so that it was arguments over the correct way of quantifying in physical terms the depletion of resources and degradation of the environment, and then valuing them in a manner consistent with the other calculations in the national accounts, as well as the practical difficulties involved, that for long impeded progress on the environmental adjustment of the accounts. However, sufficient agreement was reached to enable the UN Statistical Division to make detailed recommendations in this area (UNSD 1993) shortly after the 1992 Rio Summit.

The first item of relative agreement (with one significant point of dissension to be mentioned later) is that the accounting for ecological capital should be carried out in a satellite account rather than in the System of National Accounts (SNA) proper. A satellite account is a system of 'ancillary calculations around (the SNA) that allows other areas of interest to be explored within a broadly compatible frame' (Harrison 1993: 26). The advantage of proceeding initially with such an account is that it brings previously excluded areas within the frame of reference of the SNA, while permitting further experimentation and redefinition in the light of experience, without disturbing existing data series. Goldschmidt-Clermont's proposal for including non-monetary production in the national accounts, mentioned earlier, was to do so via a satellite account, and this is now also a UN recommendation. On environmental adjustments, too, this is the view that has been taken by the UN in its suggested revision of the SNA, which states that the objective of the Handbook is 'to provide a conceptual basis for implementing a SNA satellite system for integrated environmental and economic accounting (SEEA) that describes the interrelationships between the natural environment and the economy' (UNSD 1993: iv).

The first required component of an environmental satellite account is a systematic description of natural resources and the state of the environment in quantitative physical terms, and of changes in these quantities over time. Many countries now have extensive experience with such physical environmental and resource accounts (see Lone 1992 for a review and Alfsen *et al.* 1987 for a more detailed description of the Norwegian system, which is one of the most advanced). The second required component is a monetary valuation of the natural resources and environmental qualities, and of changes in them, calculated in such a way that the figures generated are directly comparable with the quantities in the conventional national accounts.

Financial accounts commonly have two parts: a stock account (balance sheet), listing assets and liabilities, and changes in them during the accounting period, and a flow account (income and expenditure) describing the flow of financial resources during the same period. It is, of course, the flow account in the national accounts that provides figures for the calculation of GNP, with an estimate of capital consumption from the stock account converting this to NNP (National Income).

For the environment to be fully integrated into the national accounting framework, the same procedure must be followed in the environmental satellite account. The flows in this case correspond to environmental depletion and degradation (capital consumption) or environmental regeneration (capital formation); the stock comprises land (including subsoil deposits), air and water and the plants and animals (biota) they support. An environmental balance sheet, together with the steps for calculating from opening to closing stocks in both physical and monetary units, is set out in Table 5.1.

Rows 2, 3 and 4 in Table 5.1 are changes in assets that correspond to flows and which would need to be accounted for in any adjustment to NNP. New findings of subsoil deposits are not included as flows, although they add to stocks, because they do not result from the production process, and are accounted for under Row 6. Row 7 accounts for the effects of natural disasters (e.g. floods, fires, earthquakes, etc.).

Table 5.1 Schema for an environmental balance sheet

Physical units	Multiplied by price	Monetary units
1 Opening stocks	× opening price	= value of opening stocks
2 + natural growth		
3 − offtake/depletion		
4 − net degradation		
5 2 + 3 + 4 = change in stocks due to economic activity	× opening price	= value of change in ecological capital
6 ± changes due to economic reappraisal (e.g. discoveries)		
7 ± changes due to non-economic events (e.g. earthquakes)		
8 = closing stocks	× closing price (revaluation)	= value of closing stocks

Source: Derived from Harrison (1993: 34)

While the ultimate aim in environmental accounting is to produce a complete balance sheet for each kind of environmental asset, of more immediate importance for the assessment of sustainability of current production are the flow items, depletion and net degradation. These represent consumption of environmental assets and their value must be subtracted from NNP to arrive at an income figure which is environmentally sustainable in terms of Hicks' definition given earlier. The nature of, and various differences between, the various estimates that need to be made to calculate an environmentally sustainable national income figure, and gain other insights into the relation between the macroeconomy and its environmental impacts, are illustrated in Figure 5.2, which shows possible paths of development of environmental capacity during a reporting period, T.

The level of environmental capacity (E_c) is the ability of the environment to perform environmental functions and is measured by both the quantity of resources (as affected by depletion) and their quality (as affected by pollution and degradation). At the beginning of the period this level is at point X. Clearly Figure 5.2 is extremely stylised and, of course, no aggregate measure of 'environmental capacity', encompassing depletion and pollution of all kinds, exists or could be meaningfully constructed. However, it can be used to illustrate various environmental accounting procedures, and their associated methods of valuation. It may then be considered in more detail how the adjustments to the national accounts may be made.

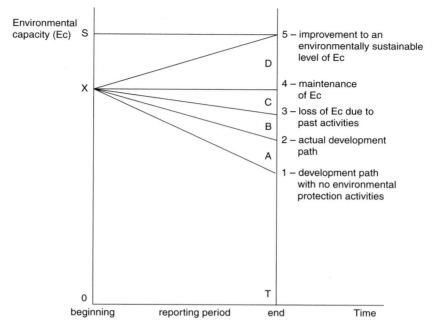

Figure 5.2 Development of environmental capacity in period t
Source: Adapted from Van Dieren (1995: 248)

In Figure 5.2 the lowest line (to point 1) indicates the hypothetical environmental capacity that would have been achieved had there been no attempts at environmental protection during the period. However, there are likely to have been such attempts, from government, consumers and firms. Point 2 indicates the actual achieved environmental capacity, resulting from these expenditures, with distance A (between points 1 and 2) up the axis being the environmental difference made by the expenditures.

Figure 5.2 shows (as is likely) that the environment protection efforts did not succeed in totally protecting the environment, so that some deterioration from X due to activities in the reporting period took place. Point 3 indicates the level of environmental capacity that would have been achieved if all current economic activities had resulted in no consumption of natural capital (again considering both resource and waste-absorption capacities). Where this was not the case, the loss of environmental capacity due to current activities is indicated by distance B (between points 2 and 3).

However, if the environment has been damaged by past activities, then it may deteriorate even if current activities do not damage it further. The distance C indicates environmental deterioration over the period, because of a legacy of past environmental damage.

When the losses in environmental capacity represented by (B + C) could potentially be compensated for by investments in manufactured capital, then these losses can be treated as capital consumption in the normal way, i.e. after valuation (see p. 134), and deducted from gross capital formation, to indicate the economic sustainability of the use of the environment. However, when some or all of the losses represented by (B + C) entail the loss of important environmental functions for which there is no effective manufactured substitute, then the activity during the period has contributed to environmental unsustainability. Moreover, it is possible that the period began from a position of environmental unsustainability, in the sense that the initial environmental capacity was below some environmentally sustainable level, S. In this case, if point 5, at S, represents a sustainability standard, then investment in the appropriate environmental capacity corresponding to D may be required if environmental sustainability is to be achieved.

In Figure 5.2 the distance up the vertical axis is measured in physical units appropriate to the resource being considered. The availability of current and reliable physical data about the environment is essential for effective environmental policy and management, whether or not adjustment of the national accounts is being considered. This does not mean that comprehensive data about all aspects of the environment must be generated before the environment can be related to economic activity as described in the national accounts. Indeed Norway, with a highly developed system of environmental resource accounts, which are used regularly and effectively in both economic and environmental analysis, has specifically rejected a comprehensive approach to data collection, preferring to concentrate on those areas that are most important for environmental and economic policy. This would appear also to be a sensible approach for those countries with small statistical offices just starting out on environmental accounting. On the other hand, any selective approach may detract from the usefulness of integrated accounts for overall (macroeconomic and environmental) policy analysis.

The core of the production (supply and use) accounts in the System of National Accounts (SNA) is an input–output structure organised according to a standard industrial classification. For policy purposes it is useful if the environmental data, whether in physical or monetary units, and whether of resources (an input into industries) or pollution (an output from industries and final demand) can also be organised in this manner. This greatly helps the relation of environmental impacts to particular economic sectors, which is useful both for understanding the causes of environmental problems and for developing policy to address them. It also permits the integration of the environmental data into the national accounts.

As already mentioned, the environmental effects represented by the distances up the vertical axis of Figure 5.2 are measured in physical units. However, to integrate these effects fully into the national accounts, it is necessary to ascribe a monetary value to them. There are several possible methods of valuation, which were mentioned in Chapter 2 and discussed further below. Table 5.2 sets out and describes the distances up the vertical axis of Figure 5.2. It distinguishes between physical measurement and monetary valuation. It should be noted that prior physical measurements of pollution (or emissions) and depletion are always required in order to derive a monetary measurement of the costs associated with them. As already noted, such physical measurements are required for effective environmental management whether or not they are subsequently to be used to adjust the national accounts. Table 5.2 also indicates different possible methods of valuation.

As indicated in Table 5.2, environmental distance A is expressed by its monetary valuation only, namely the monetary expenditure by economic agents to prevent or mitigate environmental damage arising from economic activity. It would be both difficult and unnecessary to estimate in physical units how much damage had been prevented in this way. Environmental expenditures may be made by firms, government or households. Environmental expenditures may be to prevent or reduce pollution, or to reduce the net depletion of renewable resources (e.g. planting trees, restocking rivers with fish, plugging leaks in water distribution systems) or of non-renewable resources (e.g. investment in recycling, development of substitutes, such as

Table 5.2 Environmental distances and methods of valuation

Environmental distance	Description	Units		Method of valuation of costs		
		Physical measurement	Monetary valuation	Damage	Abatement/ avoidance	Restoration
A	Environmental expenditures	n.a	+	n.a	+	+
B	Damage/ depletion from current activities	+	+	+	+	+
C	Damage/ depletion from past activities	+	+	+	+	+
D	Avoidance/ abatement/ restoration to reach sustainability	+	+	n.a	+	+

Notes:
+ signifies that the relevant unit or method of valuation may be calculated for this environmental quantity
n.a. signifies that the relevant unit or method of valuation is not appropriate for this environmental quantity

renewable energy to replace fossil fuels). It is important to ensure that the expenditures calculated are exclusively those concerned with counteracting in some way the negative environmental side-effects of production and consumption, rather than adverse environmental conditions (e.g. earthquakes), that are unrelated to human activity. Some environmental expenditures will relate to damage caused before the current accounting period. This may be thought of as reducing distance C below what it would otherwise be, rather than B.

If not all environmental damage caused by the economy in the accounting period is repaired, then the environment deteriorates during the period. In physical terms environmental distance B is the increase in concentration of pollutants in environmental media, the harvesting of renewable resources beyond their growth or the depletion of non-renewable resources. In monetary terms environmental distance B can be expressed as the monetary cost associated with the loss of environmental capacity during the accounting period. UNSD (1993: 91ff.) distinguishes between environmental cost *caused* by activities that took place during the accounting period (i.e. damage B in Figure 5.2), and environmental cost *borne*, i.e. damage realised during that same period, but caused by activities carried out during previous and the current periods (which also includes damage C in Figure 5.2). Clearly damages are borne and caused by different people at different places and times.

The valuation of the costs associated with the environmental deterioration associated with distances B and C in Figure 5.2 is often not straightforward, but can be effected or approximated in a number of ways as follows:

1   *Pollution* may be valued in two main ways:

 a   According to the cost of the damage incurred. Where the damage is to marketed goods (e.g. crops, fish), then the economic damage can be valued in principle as the loss of production and income resulting from the damage. Where the damage is to non-market goods or to non-economic (environmental) functions of natural assets, the valuation may be carried out by various techniques, including those involving surrogate markets or contingent valuation, but, as described in Chapter 2, these techniques can be controversial and can yield wide ranges of valuations. Moreover, contingent valuations contain consumer surplus, which renders them incomparable with GNP data based on market prices. Although intensive work on environmental valuation of this kind continues, including that which has the eventual objective of being incorporated into a national accounting framework (for example, Markandya and Milborrow 1998), at its present stage of development it does not command the necessary consensus among statisticians to be used by national statistical offices for this purpose.

b   According to the abatement/avoidance/restoration cost that would
be required to achieve a certain standard of emissions, or maintain
or restore certain standards of environmental quality. Sometimes
collectively called 'maintenance costs' (UNSD 1993: 105ff.), these
costs have been divided into five types: reduction in or abstention
from economic activities; changes in economic outputs or consumption patterns; changes in economic inputs or processes; prevention
of environmental deterioration without changing products or
processes (e.g. by end-of-pipe abatement); environmental restoration or protection from harmful effects. Thus distances B and C in
Figure 5.2 may be valued by a combination of measures needed to
prevent loss of environmental capacity from current or past activities or, in the case of C, to restore past environmental degradation.
Such costs may only be a very rough estimate of the damage cost
that distance B represents. The advantages of using such an approx-
imation are purely pragmatic: where non-market damages are
concerned, it is often easier to calculate abatement or restoration
costs than damage costs, because they can often be derived through
the investigation of actual environmental expenditures.

2   With regard to *depletion*, according to Harrison (1993: 36): 'It is the
inclusion in income of th[e] liquidation of an asset that has provoked
the criticisms of the national accounts from environmentalists.' Yet:
'No single method of determining the value of subsoil assets has been
agreed upon, and controversy surrounds the alternatives that have
been proposed.' The starting point for the valuation of depletion for
all resources is their economic rent, defined by Bartelmus and Tardos
(1993: 183 (note 5)) as 'gross value added minus annual depreciation
minus a total labour cost minus a "normal return" on invested assets'.
In other words, the value of a resource before extraction, for both
renewable and non-renewable resources, is the value of the resource
on the market less all the costs of extraction and distribution to the
point of first sale.

Techniques proposed for the valuation of the depletion of a natural
resource include the net price, present value and user cost methods.
The net price method is used in Repetto *et al.* (1989), whereby the
depletion cost is obtained by multiplying the unit rent by the net
change in the quantity of the resource during the time period (if discoveries exceed resource extraction over the period, this method will
therefore show depletion as negative). The income adjustment of the
present value method is the same as that of the net price method
except that the former ignores discoveries for the purpose of the adjustment, valuing as depletion only the total economic rent of the resource
extracted over the period, so that positive extraction can never result
in negative depletion. The user cost method is advocated by El Serafy
(1989) and, as described in Chapter 4, entails splitting the economic

rent into two streams according to a formula which involves the rent, the discount rate and the expected lifetime of the resource. One stream represents the depletion (or user) cost. The other represents the permanent income which could be generated if the user cost was invested at the rate of interest used for the calculation. From this brief description it can be seen that, in general, the methods give costs of depletion such that:

present value > user cost

Depletion according to the net price method may be more than by the present value method, if there is a downward revision of reserves during the period, or less than the user cost if there are substantial discoveries of the resource during the period. While there is no clear consensus as to which valuation method for depletion should be used, the present value method is that preferred by the UK Office of National Statistics (Vaze 1998: 71).

Many of the difficulties and complexities associated with measuring and valuing environmental distance B apply to attempted measurements and valuation of environmental distance C. Identifying the current damages associated with, for example, the past contamination of land, acidification of soil or atmospheric pollution is likely to be even more difficult than identifying current damages from current emissions. Abatement/avoidance costs are not relevant in this case, because the damage has already occurred in a previous period. Restoration costs would appear to offer the best prospect of approximating the value of C. In practice with the calculation of restoration costs, no distinction can usually be made between environmental distances B and C, the damages that relate to present and past activities. Clearly there is a simplifying attraction in combining B and C to arrive at a cost figure that relates simply to environmental deterioration over the reporting period, but it must be remembered that this combination figure cannot strictly be ascribed to current activities.

Finally, with regard to environmental distance D, its size depends on the extent to which environmental capacity started the accounting period below the environmentally sustainable level, because of past economic activities. The methodology of Hueting et al. (1992) has been explicitly formulated to address this:

accumulated burden from the past. . . . [It] is intended to supply information on the costs of measures required for bridging the distance between a sustainable level of activities and the level reached in a given year in the past. In so doing we encounter the burden that has mounted up in the environment over an often long period.

(Hueting *et al.* 1992: 14)

The only way of valuing environmental distance D is through restoration costs, namely the costs of measures required to restore environmental capacity to levels defined by sustainability standards, as discussed in Chapter 4, over the whole range of environmental functions that have been diminished by past economic activities. These costs can be regarded as ecological capital formation, to compensate for ecological capital consumption in the past.

5.4.3 Relating environmental accounts to GDP

The overarching reason for seeking to adjust the national accounts for environmental effects is to gain a clearer understanding of the contribution made to production and human welfare by the environment, and of the way the environment's ability to continue to make that contribution is being undermined by the scale and nature of economic activity. More particularly, four specific purposes and intended outcomes of integrated environmental and economic accounting (IEEA) may be identified:

1 To identify the scale of environmental protection expenditures that are made necessary by current processes of production and consumption. Such expenditures are a burden on the economy imposed by the modes and processes of economic production and consumption, but they also give some indication of the level of social importance attached to environmental protection. Domestic industrial expertise in environmental protection, which may result from stringent regulations related to it, may also be an important possible source of export earnings in a context where commitment to environmental protection is increasing worldwide.

2 To make some assessment of the value of the ecological capital stock that has been degraded as a result of economic activity, in a given period. As already discussed, this is analogous to the perceived need to account for manufactured capital in the computation in the present national accounts of real (Hicksian) national income.

3 To estimate the level, given current technologies and economic processes, of the maximum environmentally sustainable national income (ESNI).

4 To give a quantitative estimate of the gap that exists, as a result of economic activity, between current environmental conditions and those which might be deemed sustainable. Without some estimation of such a 'Sustainability Gap', and how it changes over time, it is not possible to know whether 'sustainable development' is being achieved.

Each of these outcomes of IEEA may be related in some way to the aggregates of the economic accounting system, principally GNP and GDP. The various possible relationships that have been proposed will now be explored in turn.

Accounting for environmental defensive expenditures

'The term "defensive expenditures" is commonly understood as the expenditures associated with the negative social and environmental impacts of economic production and consumption patterns' (Brouwer and Leipert 1998: 1 (footnote 1)). This explicit identification of defensive expenditures with the negative impacts of economic activity disposes of the objection to the concept that has been raised by Jaszi (1973) and Repetto *et al.*, the latter of whom have written: 'The notion of "defensive" expenditures is elusive, since spending on food can be considered a defence against hunger, clothing a defence against cold, and religion a defence against sin' (Repetto *et al.* 1989: 17).

Both Jaszi and Repetto *et al.* misunderstand the defensive expenditure concept. The whole point of such expenditures is that they defend against externalities, *unwanted side-effects of production and consumption*. Hunger, cold, rain, headaches and sin (rain and headaches are Jaszi's (1973: 91) additions to the list) are not, in general, unwanted side-effects of production. They are part of the normal human condition, and expenditures to counter them are not defensive in the sense in which the term is predominantly used. Of course, insofar as *extra* hunger etc. were produced by a production process, i.e. were negative externalities of production, then their cost *should* be deducted from the output of that process as a cost of production, or as a depletion of human or ecological capital.

Jaszi and Repetto are thus wide of the mark. Defensive expenditures are a valid and useful concept to describe expenditures that are made to defend against externalities of production or consumption.

The other defining characteristic of defensive expenditures is that they only act to offset, partly or wholly, the negative effects with which they are associated. At most they maintain the *status quo ante*, the social and environmental situation that existed before the economic activities with the negative effects took place.

There is continuing debate as to how defensive expenditures should be dealt with in the System of National Accounts (SNA). It is clear that defensive expenditures are beneficial in themselves, they add to welfare, and some have used this fact to argue that they should be included in GNP and NNP, as at present (e.g. Mäler 1991).

However, this is only part of the necessary argument. As was seen earlier in the work of Faber and Proops (1991), the 'real' output of the total economy-environment system comprises both economic and environmental goods and services. If the production of economic goods and services reduces the output of environmental goods and services (which is what 'a negative impact on the environment' means in economic terms), then 'real' output from the economic activity should be accounted net of this reduction. Alternatively, the economic goods that only serve to offset this reduction, to maintain the output of environmental goods at their level before the damaging economic activity took place, should not be included in the net output of the economy during the accounting period.

This characterisation of the relationship between GNP and defensive expenditures illustrates an important point that is valid when considering any adjustment to the macroeconomic aggregates: the adjustment must be consistent with the interpretation being given to the aggregate and with the use to which it is being put. Thus if GNP is being used to represent the money flows through the economy, then clearly defensive expenditures should be included in GNP. If, on the other hand, GNP is intended to be interpreted as the net output of the economy during the accounting period, then defensive expenditures should be deducted from it, as, of course, should capital depreciation. Similarly defensive expenditures should be excluded from any figures of net output that are being considered as a contribution to economic welfare. Such a treatment would appear to be consistent with the conclusions of EUROSTAT:

> In one sense it can be argued that environmental protection expen-ditures are aimed solely at maintaining the particular quality of the environment and avoiding its degradation. They would not therefore lead to real additional output and should be deducted from domestic product.
>
> (EUROSTAT 1994: 20)

Environmental defensive expenditures are defined in UNSD (1993: 42) as expenditures which prevent environmental damage; restore environmental damage; avoid damage (e.g. to humans, buildings) from an environment which has been damaged; and repair damage (e.g. to humans, buildings) from a damaged environment. Schäfer and Stahmer (1989) have identi-fied four distinct kinds of environmental defensive expenditure: fixed capital formation (e.g. water purification plants); purchase of external environ-mental services by firms; provision by firms of their own (internal) environmental services; purchase of environmental services by government. To these categories may be added defensive expenditures by households, where these have not already been accounted for. Dividing environmental defensive expenditures into these categories ensures that their accounting is consistent with national accounting conventions and that no double counting occurs.

The first of the UNSD categories has now been systematised in detail in the Environmental Protection Expenditure Account (EPEA) of the European System for the Collection of Economic Information on the Environment (SERIEE) (EUROSTAT 1994). ECOTEC (1993: iv) estimates 1990 UK Environmental Protection Expenditures (EPE) to be £14 billion, about 2.5 per cent of GDP. It should be remembered that these are calculations only of the EPE component of environmental defensive expenditures, as defined above. They do not include other environmental defensive expenditures (such as restoration costs) or non-environmental defensive expenditures, such as the health costs of commuting, smoking or traffic accidents. A figure for all defensive expenditures related to the organisation and activities of an industrial society would clearly amount to a substantial proportion of GDP. For example, Leipert's study of defensive expenditures in the Federal Republic of Germany found that, as a proportion of GNP, they had increased by 150 per cent from 5.6 per cent to 10 per cent from 1970 to 1985. GNP itself only increased by 39.4 per cent in the same period, drawing Leipert to the conclusion: 'The genuine growth that was still achievable in providing new economic options for private households, without simultaneously disadvantaging them in other spheres, is being bought at an ever higher economic price' (Leipert 1989a: 853–4).

Making deductions from GNP/GDP

As has been seen, there have been a number of proposals to make deductions from GNP/GDP, or one of its constituent parts, consumer expenditure. Aaheim and Nyborg (1993: 12) consider: 'In the ongoing debate on this issue, little weight has so far been put on defining *which question a corrected national product is really meant to answer*' (original emphasis).

In fact a number of answers to this question have already been suggested in this book. The ISEW and MEW calculations discussed in Chapter 3 were seeking to adjust consumer expenditure to clarify perceptions of its contribution to human welfare. Another approach mentioned earlier, associated with Hartwick (1990), Faber and Proops (1991) and others, seeks to deduct the depreciation of ecological capital, analogously to that of manufactured capital, to arrive at a more accurate figure of net production, or income. More broadly, bearing in mind the symbolic nature of GDP as a general indicator of 'progress', it may simply be desired, as advocated by Tinbergen and Hueting (1993), to adjust GDP to improve the 'compass' according to which society is steered.

The basic equation for the environmental adjustment of GDP to improve it as an indicator of production (as distinct from welfare), is put forward in UNSD (1993: 99), and is also described by its authors in Bartelmus, Stahmer and Van Tongeren (1993) as follows:

GDP – Consumption of fixed capital   =   NDP
NDP – (Imputed) environmental costs   =   EDP   (5.2)

where EDP = Eco, or Environmentally adjusted, Domestic Product
            (Bartelmus, Stahmer and Van Tongeren 1993: 54)

(The validity of the equation is unchanged by substituting GNP, NNP and ENP for the equivalent domestic quantities.)

It can be seen that the above equation does not, as recommended in the previous section, advocate the subtraction of environmental defensive expenditures from NDP in its computation of EDP. UNSD (1993: 5) notes that such a deduction is still considered controversial.

In equation (5.2) the 'imputed environmental costs' are the costs of environmental depletion and degradation. With regard to depletion costs, insofar as they relate to marketed resources there is no problem in subtracting these costs from NNP, although it was seen above that there is still no final consensus as to the method of valuation that should be employed. Such subtraction is analogous to the treatment of the depreciation costs of manufactured capital.

The situation with regard to environmental degradation is not as straightforward, and the two methods of calculating the relevant costs may be considered in turn. Where NNP is regarded as a measure of welfare, then (marginal) damage costs are the theoretically correct measure to use to calculate the reduction in environmental services, and loss of welfare, due to environmental damage, to be subtracted from NNP. However, it was seen earlier that this procedure is problematic on two counts: first, as described in Chapter 3, there are strong methodological objections to treating NNP as a measure of welfare, rather than as an indicator of production; second, it is not practically possible to estimate the damage costs in a way that yields figures robust enough (quantitatively or methodologically) to be combined with national accounting figures. These problems are so deep and intractable that they seem effectively to rule out the calculation of ENP by this route.

Turning to the second method, the calculation of maintenance costs, their subtraction from NNP, as UNSD (1993) suggests, seems of doubtful validity. GNP and NNP are aggregates of value added, income and expenditure (depending on which of the three equivalent ways has been used to calculate them) based on market values that pertain simultaneously in a fully interconnected economy. Maintenance costs are aggregates of hypothetical costs based on available technologies. Although measured in money terms, they are therefore a quite different kind of number to the macroeconomic aggregates which reflect the equilibrium prices in the economy.

The rationale for subtracting maintenance costs from NNP is that this would give an estimate for the level of economic activity that was feasible while maintaining environmental quality. If maintenance costs were small, this might be true because the actual implementation of the maintenance technologies would not significantly affect the prevailing economic conditions. But then ENP would not be materially different from NNP. If maintenance costs were large, however, then their implementation could be expected to change every other price and quantity in the economy, as other economic activities adjusted to take account of the new imperative that was being given to environmental protection. Maintenance costs and NNP are incommensurably different kinds of numbers and subtracting the former from the latter would be statistically invalid.

Nor can the analogy with the subtraction of the depreciation of manufactured capital be used in this case. As Keuning (1996: 13ff.) has pointed
out, the depreciation of manufactured capital is a cost that has been taken
into account by economic actors during the accounting period, and it
relates to actual expenditures that have been made in the past. The prices
and quantities that go into the construction of GNP and NNP can therefore be expected to have taken this capital consumption into account.
None of this is true for environmental degradation, which will normally
have been omitted entirely from firms' financial accounts (and from the
national accounts, which is why an adjustment is being sought in the first
place). Keuning concludes: 'The situation would have been completely
different if a completely new cost item had been introduced at the company
level. . . . the appearance of such a new cost item would have affected
output prices' (ibid.: 13).

To conclude, there would seem to be no way to arrive at a practical
and robust estimate of EDP/ENP, as defined in equation (5.2), simply by
subtracting cost figures from the relevant macroeconomic aggregate. While
such a procedure may be theoretically sound, whether NNP is regarded
as an indicator of welfare or net production, in the former case there is
no way to arrive at credible estimates of the damage costs, and in the
latter case it is not valid to deduct the maintenance costs, which might be
credible, from NNP. The best that can be achieved in terms of adjusted
macroeconomic aggregates is a Partial ENP, obtained by deducting from
NNP the environmental defensive expenditures and the depletion costs
that have been incurred during the period concerned. This may be
expressed as a ratio (Partial ENP)/GNP to give an indication of the extent
of environmental defensive expenditures and resource depletion relative
to economic activity overall.

ENP has been one interpretation of the often ill-defined concept 'Green
GNP'. It should now be recognised that, if conceived in terms of making
deductions from NNP, it is not an operational concept. Another interpretation of Green GNP has been as an Environmentally Sustainable
National Income (ESNI), that is, the income that could be generated by
an economy using currently available technologies while respecting
constraints of environmental sustainability. The next section considers how
an ESNI might be derived.

Modelling environmentally sustainable national income

GNP is calculated from prices and quantities in the economy that take
account of economic interactions and interconnectedness. Using the
maintenance cost approach it is possible to define the least cost way of
achieving environmental standards that are deemed to be compatible with
environmental sustainability. As noted in the previous section, because
these are static cost calculations, rather than being derived in the context

of full economic interaction, they cannot simply be deducted from GNP. Rather, any calculation of Green GNP (ESNI) using the costs of technologies that would have to be implemented to bring environmental performance within sustainability standards requires the implementation of these technologies to be simulated in the context of an economic model that contains these interactions and which projects the economic implications of progressively meeting the sustainability standards over time. Once the standards had been met, the model's economic output could be regarded as the ESNI, offering an estimate 'of the level and composition of environmentally respectful economic output that, for each accounting period being considered, may be feasible with currently known technology or under hypotheses about future technological innovation' (ECDGXII 1997: 8).

Such modelling is a major undertaking, requiring integrated economy-energy-environment modelling that is disaggregated enough to enable the various technologies and environmental effects to be adequately modelled. However, there have been a number of modelling simulations of this kind, carried out with varying degrees of detail and sophistication. An early attempt was De Boer *et al.* (1994), which found that reducing the impacts across five environmental themes (climate change, ozone depletion, acidification, eutrophication, waste disposal) to sustainability levels reduced GNP by 64 per cent. However, as the paper acknowledges, this is not a very realistic result, because it does not, in fact, model technical abatement measures at all, but reduces environmental impacts simply by reducing the activities that are responsible for them. Such a procedure gives very little insight into the economic implications of reducing environmental impacts by bringing about technical change over time. More satisfactory approaches to such modelling are taken by Faucheux *et al.* (1998) and Meyer and Ewerhart (1998), both of which permit more sophisticated economic adjustments in response to imposed restrictions on carbon emissions, the costs of which are therefore much reduced from those obtained by De Boer *et al.* (1994).

Estimating the sustainability gap

Given an indicator of an environmental state or pressure that shows the current environmental position for some environmental issue, and a sustainability standard for the same indicator that shows a sustainable state, or the maximum pressure that is compatible with a sustainable state, with regard to that environmental theme, it is possible to determine a 'Sustainability Gap' ($SGAP_p$), in physical terms, between the current and a sustainable situation.

$SGAP_p$ indicates the degree of consumption of natural capital, either in the past or present, which is in excess of what is required for environmental sustainability. For the state indicators, the gap indicates the extent to which natural resource stocks are too low, or pollution stocks are too high. For pressure indicators, the gap indicates the extent to which the flows of energy and materials which contribute to environmental depletion and degradation are too high. $SGAP_P$ indicates in physical terms the extent to which economic activity is resulting in unsustainable impacts on important environmental functions.

$SGAP_P$ can give useful information as to the environmental impacts which need to be reduced, and by how much, but it does nothing to relate these impacts to the economic activities which are responsible for them, and which will need to be changed if the impacts are to be reduced. It would therefore seem desirable to link the sustainability indicators, and hence $SGAP_P$, to the national accounts, specifically by allocating the physical impacts responsible for the sustainability gap to the different sectors in the national accounts.

The sectoral disaggregation of environmental effects has been pioneered by the NAMEA (National Accounting Matrix including Environmental Accounts) system developed in the Dutch Central Bureau of Statistics. This system so far covers the depletion of three types of natural resources – crude oil, natural gas and wood – and five types of environmental degradation: the greenhouse effect, depletion of the ozone layer, acidification, eutrophication, generation of wastes (Keuning 1996: 4–5). These environmental themes are related to seven aggregate economic sectors, which overall are responsible for generating the unsustainable environmental effects: agriculture; manufacturing (including oil refineries, chemical industries, basic metal industry, other manufacturing); electricity generation; construction; transport; services and other; and households. The NAMEA system has been recommended by the European Commission as the model for a European System of Integrated Economic and Environmental Indices (ibid.: 2). Sweden and the UK have also decided to adopt NAMEA as the organising framework for their work.

The Sustainability Gap indicators represent the physical improvements in the state of, or the reductions in the pressures exerted on, various environmental media and resources that are required in order to comply with the relevant sustainability standard. The NAMEA matrix can allocate the pressures among the various sectors that appear in the national accounts, but in order for the Sustainability Gap indicators to be compared directly with economic activity and output, they need to be given a monetary valuation. Consideration of technologies of abatement/avoidance and restoration, by sector or with regard to different environmental media, enable, for each environmental theme, a series of cost curves to be built up, so that the cost of attaining each of the sustainability standards can be derived. These costs may then be aggregated to arrive at a full monetary figure for the Sustainability Gap ($SGAP_M$). Table 5.3 sets out the general schema, relating it to the normal input–output structure of the national accounts. It can be seen that in general abatement/avoidance costs are

Table 5.3 Matrix for the construction of the Sustainability Gap

	Economic sectors	*Environmental impacts*		
		Current, C	*Sustainable,* S	*SGAP*
Economic sectors	Input–output tables	**NAMEA pressure indicators**	Sustainability standards	S – C
Totals			***physical***	***monetary***[a]
Environmental quality		**state indicators**	***physical***	***monetary***[b]

Notes:
a Calculated using abatement/avoidance costs
b Calculated using restoration costs
Source: Ekins and Simon (1998: 161)

used to calculate the costs of reducing environmental pressures (e.g. emissions) to sustainable levels, while restoration costs are used to calculate the costs of restoring environmental states to sustainable levels. For renewable and non-renewable resources the restoration costs will be different from the depletion costs discussed earlier, because they need to reflect the cost of maintaining the current level, or returning to a sustainable level, of the relevant environmental function. For renewable resources this entails valuing the $SGAP_P$ according to the expenditures required to restore the resources to their condition at the beginning of the period, or to a minimum sustainable level if they started the period below this. Calculation of the non-renewable resource component of $SGAP_M$ is less straightforward.

As discussed in Chapter 4, the only strongly sustainable use of non-renewable resources is that which is matched by increases in recycling or end-use efficiency, or the development of substitutes. Strict adherence to the principle of strong sustainability (the level of environmental function must remain constant) would mean that resource depletion above this level should be costed at the expenditure that would be necessary to provide a substitute resource that would provide the same function as the depleted one. For some resources this could either prove difficult (where only imperfect substitutes exist) or very expensive (e.g. the replacement of the fossil fuels used in the period with renewable energy capacity). Such considerations indicate the rigour of the strong sustainability principle, but also its practical limitations.

However, a compromise between the 'strong sustainability' and 'user cost' treatments of the depletion of non-renewable resources can be struck along the lines suggested in Chapter 4, despite the fact that they proceed from different conceptual bases, whereby the former is physically grounded on the strong sustainability principle, while the latter is more concerned with financial sustainability and depends on such monetary quantities as the interest rate. The compromise entails treating the capital component of the El Serafy calculation as the amount of money that should be invested in the development of physical substitutes for the resources being depleted. For it to be said that the resource was being used sustainably, the 'user cost' element would need to be invested such that either a substitute (preferably renewable) for the resource was developed that could provide the same environmental functions once the resource was depleted, or, where such a (inexhaustible) substitute already existed, a permanent income was guaranteed by other means.

It may here be stressed, in line with the argument of the previous two sections, that $SGAP_M$ is not commensurable with GDP or the other national accounting product aggregates, and could therefore not be subtracted from, say, NDP, in order to produce a 'sustainable income', or 'Green GDP' figure. $SGAP_M$ also does not represent the amount of money that would have to be spent to achieve sustainability. The latter amount could only be estimated from whole-economy modelling using the $SGAP_M$ calculations, which would take account of economic feedbacks and interactions, as noted above. Actually closing $SGAP_P$ would probably cost substantially less than $SGAP_M$, because of the economy's adjustment to the expenditures entailed. $SGAP_M$ is very much a static, partial equilibrium calculation, representing at a moment in time the aggregation of expenditures that would need to be made to reduce the various dimensions of $SGAP_P$ to zero.

However, $SGAP_M$ would still be an expressive indicator of the potential of an economy, at a certain moment in time, to achieve environmental sustainability. It would reflect both the physical distances from environmental sustainability and the economic possibilities of reducing those distances. Over time, $SGAP_M$ would decrease if either the physical Sustainability Gaps decreased, or new technologies, processes or materials were developed which enabled those gaps to be reduced at lower cost in the future. $SGAP_M/GDP$, either in aggregate or for each environmental theme, would also be an interesting indicator with which to make inter-country comparisons of environmental efficiency, in much the same way as energy intensity (Energy Use/GDP) is currently used.

The concept of Hicksian income, and thence environmentally sustainable income, have been important organising ideas for the methodologies of adjustment of the national accounts that have been developed, so it is a matter of some regret that no methodology can at present yield a convincing number for 'Green GDP' in the current or past periods, or seems likely to be able to do so. However, as Young (1992: 12) points out, this may turn out to be just as well, because: 'There is a risk that resource-modified accounting systems may develop a false sense of policy security by implying that all the environmental problems faced by the nation are being adequately dealt with.'

It may in any case be that the (Partial EDP)/GDP and $SGAP_M/GDP$ ratios, which can be calculated and which will be responsive to both economic growth and environmental policy, will fulfil the objectives of trying to calculate Green GDP in the first place. For it is these numbers that monetarily represent, for the former, the relative economic burden of countering environmental degradation and some, at least, of the consumption of ecological capital; and, for the latter, a continuing failure to achieve standards of sustainability.

5.4.4 The environmental impact of trade

The Sustainability Gap calculations would give some indication of the sustainability or otherwise of the impact of a country's production and consumption on its environment and on the global commons. But SGAP says nothing about the environmental impacts abroad of its imports (impacts PIE, CIE in Figure 4.3), which contribute to its 'ecological footprint' on other countries, or its occupation of environmental space, using the terms described in Chapter 4. The size and nature of a country's use of other countries' natural environments is obviously of importance to consideration of whether it is importing environmental sustainability or not, which is relevant to whether its production and consumption are environmentally sustainable overall.

As noted in Chapter 4 (Figure 4.3), the environmental impacts abroad of a trading country may be due to one of three distinct causes:

1   The export of pollutants, especially transported by air or water (PEX, CEX in Figure 4.3).
2   The consumption of imports (PIE, CIE in Figure 4.3).
3   The consumption of exports (CXE in Figure 4.3).

Before examining how these three causes of impacts abroad might be treated in environmental economic accounts, it may be noted that the treatment depends on the purpose for which it is being carried out as well as on which country is perceived to be 'responsible' for the impacts. Bosch and Ensing (1995: 220ff.) make a distinction between the different types of 'environmental burden' that can be conceptualised. The first type, which they call 'the own activities approach', is the burden arising from a country's own production and consumption (set 1 of environmental impacts in Chapter 4 in relation to Figure 4.3 (pp. 88–9), plus PEX, CEX). In this case the country would be responsible for the first of the three causes of pollution listed above, but not the other two, where it would lie with the countries in which the production and consumption respectively took place. This approach would be an appropriate focus for environmental policy that is seeking to reduce environmental pressures arising from domestic production and consumption activities, jurisdiction over which is predominantly at the national and sub-national levels.

The second type of environmental burden is called 'the environmental quality approach', which only takes account of environmental impacts within the territory of the country in question (set 2 in Chapter 4). It therefore includes the import of pollutants from abroad, but excludes all three causes of environmental impact listed above. This approach is appropriate for policy seeking to improve domestic environmental quality, irrespective of the source of the impacts which are affecting it. The third type focuses on the total burden that arises from providing for, or as a result of, the consumption of the country in question (set 3 in Chapter 4, less PXE, CXE). It would therefore include the first two of the three impacts listed above, but not the third, or the import of pollutants from abroad. This approach is often invoked when responsibility for environmental effects is being assigned in some ultimate or moral sense. It may be noted that all three of these approaches are exhaustive and mutually exclusive, in that the application of each of them results in all impacts being considered, and assigns each impact to one country and no more. However, the distribution of the responsibility for impacts between countries is, of course, different for each of the approaches.

It is now possible to examine in more detail how each of the three causes of environmental impacts abroad identified above tend to be treated in terms of both policy and environmental economic accounting.

Transfrontier pollution flows

Responsibility for transfrontier pollution flows is generally perceived to lie with the country that generates the pollution, whether it is the result of domestic production or consumption, and, if the former, whether the goods were produced for domestic consumption or exports (in the latter case this is potentially contradictory with the view that consumers of imports are responsible for the environmental impacts caused by their production, as discussed in the next section). Most commonly the reduction of such pollution is sought through international agreements, such as the UNECE Protocols on sulphur dioxide and nitrogen oxide emissions, or, in the case of hazardous waste, the Basel Convention.

The accounting of the imports and exports of pollutants can in principle be carried out in an exactly analogous way to that of goods and services, simply by adding rows and columns to the standard input–output framework of the national accounts. How this is done in the NAMEA framework is set out in de Haan *et al.* (1993: 3 (Table 1)).

The consumption of imports

The environmental impacts in the producer country of goods produced for export are subject to the environmental policies of the producer country. Nevertheless it can be argued, as noted above, that the ultimate responsibility for these impacts lies with the consuming country, whose effective demand has caused the production for export to take place. Such arguments tend especially to be applied when the importing country is much richer and/or has more economic power than the exporting country, perhaps on the grounds that the importer can more easily take steps to reduce the environmental impacts concerned.

However, this argument is subject to a number of complicating factors. First, it is clear that the benefits from the production of exports are, in general, shared between the producers (who gain jobs, income and producer surplus) and consumers (who gain consumer surplus). If responsibility is deemed related to benefit, then it should be shared. Second, presumably the purpose of assigning to consuming countries responsibility for the environmental impacts caused by the production of their imports is to encourage them to reduce those impacts. However, they have no jurisdiction in the producer country, and attempts to change the conditions of production there, even as part of an aid programme, may be regarded as unwelcome conditionality or unacceptable interference in the internal affairs of the producer country. Even more unwelcome to the producer country, probably, would be a decision in the consumer country either to reduce its consumption of imports or to switch to an alternative, and less environmentally intensive, source of supply, or to encourage consumers to do so through some sort of eco-labelling. In any case, if mandated by government, all these actions could be construed as constraints on trade that are potentially incompatible with the articles of the General Agreement on Tariffs and Trade (GATT).

However the responsibility for these environmental impacts may be assigned, it is clear that policies to address them may have implications for competitiveness. The producer country, which is likely to suffer most from the impacts (though some portion may be exported, as noted in the previous section), may nevertheless derive a competitive advantage from weak environmental regulation. Conversely preferences in a consuming country for imports with low environmental impacts may reward producers who can satisfy this. IIED (1997) contains ten case studies of market success (though on a small scale) in manufacturing, tourism, agricultural commodities and forest products.

Proops *et al.* (1993: 174ff.) use input–output analysis to distinguish between a country's CO_2 emissions and its CO_2 'responsibility', defined as the emissions from domestic demand plus those embodied in its imports. Using the nomenclature of Figure 4.3:

$$CO_2 \text{ emissions} = PE + CE$$
$$CO_2 \text{ responsibility} = PE + CE + (PIE + CIE - PXE)$$

They find that UK responsibility for CO_2 from 1968 to 1984 is always less than UK emissions, the proportion lying between 94 per cent and 97 per cent (ibid.: 177 (Figure 10.10)). In other words, UK exports are more carbon-intensive than its imports.

Proops *et al.* (1996) also use input–output analysis to extend the net savings concept discussed earlier in this chapter, but only considering resource depletion and not environmental deterioration, to consideration of trade. The method used is the same as in the CO_2 case, that is a distinction is made between the use of natural capital *by* a country and that *attributable to it*, when trade flows are taken into account. They find that Western Europe is the world's major importer of sustainability (ibid.: 272 (Figure 6)). They also find that the world's 'quantity of sustainability . . . is globally positive and increasing' (ibid.: 254) through the 1980s, and 'most of the growth in global sustainability can be attributed to Japan, particularly through its very high savings ratio' (ibid.: 260). Such a conclusion illustrates the limitations of this weak sustainability indicator, as discussed earlier, as regards yielding insights into environmental sustainability (the capacity for continuance of environmental functions), rather than just comparing rates of saving and dis-saving for investment in manufactured and natural capital.

At present in the national accounts the import and export of goods and services is accounted only in value terms. Bellis and Barron (1997), extended by Vaze *et al.* (1998), have attempted in the UK context to account for trade in terms of the material flows which it embodies. Bellis and Barron (1997: 7) considered forty-six commodities aggregated into twenty commodity groups and thence into four broad themes: agricultural products, wood and related products, metals and fuels. Vaze *et al.* (1998) separated fish from agricultural products and included non-metallic minerals as a separate category. In both cases the commodities selected represented over 81 per cent of imports by mass, but less than 34 per cent by value. Bellis and Barron (1997: Figure 5) found that in the twenty groups the UK was a net exporter by mass only of petroleum, non-metallic minerals and cereals. Of the imports into the UK considered by Vaze *et al.* (1998: 99), 72 per cent were from OECD countries. Few commodities from non-OECD countries accounted for a significant share of imports, the most important being non-coniferous wood. By making certain assumptions the mass of the commodities can be converted to the same units for each of the broad themes: hectares for agricultural products, tonnes of fuel equivalent for fuels, wood raw material equivalent for wood products and tonnes of metal content or pure extracted material for metals and non-metallic minerals respectively. Since 1976 only in fuels and non-metallic minerals has the UK ever had a trade surplus by mass. In principle the material flows embodied in imports can be allocated to domestic production sectors or final demand, using input–output tables in the normal way. In practice, Bellis and Barron (1997) found that the data were not available for this.

Both papers make the point that the material flows associated with trade are not the same as the environmental impacts of trade, which depend in addition on the production processes, environmental policies and local environments of the producing countries. However, there is clearly some relation between material flows and environmental impacts, and there are absolute limits for the sustainable use of some resources, including the environment's absorptive capacity of pollutants. As already discussed in Chapter 4, two methodologies in particular seek to relate a country's use of resources, including those imported, to these limits. 'Ecological footprint' calculations (set out in Wackernagel and Rees 1996) convert a country's use of energy and land for food, forest products and buildings (including that from imports of food and forest products) to an area of 'consumed and used' land and then identify how much land people in one area are appropriating from another, which is called their ecological footprint. This can be compared in turn with the global per capita availability of land of a certain kind. Alternatively the ecological footprint from the production of different traded goods can be calculated. IIED (1995) carried out a preliminary assessment of the ecological footprints of bananas, forest products, cotton and prawns.

The 'environmental space' methodology (utilised in Buitenkamp *et al.* 1993 and McLaren *et al.* 1998) computes a country's per capita resource use and pollution and compares this with global per capita levels that are deemed consistent with environmental sustainability. Both this and the ecological footprint methodology assume that the responsibility for resource use and pollution rests with the consumer, and implicitly or explicitly allocate global rights to resource use on an equal per capita basis.

The consumption of exports

It is normally assumed that the environmental impact of consumption is the responsibility of the consumer, but there are some situations where this need not be the case, notably where trade takes place between two parties of very unequal economic power. The most obvious, and most tightly regulated, instance of this concerns the export of hazardous waste, which is controlled by the Basel Convention. Less regulated, but still controversial, is the export of potentially hazardous products, such as pesticides, especially those that have been banned in their country of production. In national environmental economic accounting the environmental impacts of the consumption of such products would be included as part of the environmental degradation account.

5.5 CONCLUSION

The basic techniques of integrated environmental economic accounting are now being implemented in a number of countries, and such implementation is now a formal recommendation of the United Nations and the policy of the European Union.

With regard to the accounting of physical stocks and flows associated with economic activity, there is now a broad consensus that the methods to be employed should be consistent with both the accounting conventions and the input–output structure of the national accounts. The NAMEA framework first developed in the Netherlands is being extensively adopted.

The valuation of the impacts of economic activity on the environment is much more difficult and controversial. Several techniques for the valuation of resource depletion exist, with no consensus as to which should be used. With regard to environmental damage there seems to be agreement among statisticians, if not economists, that the problems of valuing environmental damage are such as effectively to rule out the incorporation of such valuations in the national accounts. Arriving at acceptable estimates of maintenance costs is less problematic conceptually, but is still a formidable practical task.

One of the motivations for seeking to value the environmental impacts of economic activity has always been to use the valuations to adjust the macroeconomic aggregates to arrive at a figure for 'Green GNP' that better expresses both the net production, and the economic welfare, that derive from the economy. A deduction of the depletion costs from either GNP or NNP seems methodologically justifiable. It is argued above that environmental defensive expenditures can also justifiably be deducted. However, there are insuperable theoretical problems with the deduction from NNP of either damage costs or maintenance costs. These problems mean that, at best, only a Partial ENP, or Green GNP, can be calculated, by subtracting from GNP environmental defensive expenditures and resource depletion costs. This is most likely to be of policy relevance for those countries whose economies have a large component of natural resource production.

Instead of Green GNP this chapter has advocated the derivation of a 'Sustainability Gap' figure in both physical and monetary terms. This would enable the system of integrated environmental and economic accounting to relate the environmental impacts from the economy to the concept of sustainable development, which now provides the framework for much environmental policy, and would give policy makers a simple indicator which would show over time what progress towards sustainable development was being achieved and how far there was to go. The first stage in the development of a Sustainability Gap indicator is the derivation of a NAMEA accounting framework, as is now underway in a number of countries. Only the Netherlands has so far sought to relate the environmental impacts in such a framework to sustainability (Adriaanse 1993: 78ff.). This would seem to be the next frontier in the use of the national accounting system to help show whether or not the human use of the environment is becoming more sustainable.

There is a sense among researchers that the time is ripe for the implementation of adjustments to the national accounts for environmental factors. As Lutz has said, 'the pressing need is not to devise more theory or techniques, but to apply the existing methodology to concrete problems' (Lutz 1993: 10).

As far as the value of the environment is concerned, there is, of course, much still to be learned. But much is also known and now needs to be brought formally into the accounting framework. As El Serafy (1993: 21) has said: 'Our approach should be gradual and we should attempt to bring measurable elements into the process as our knowledge improves. But to wait until everything falls properly into place means that we shall have to wait forever.'

This is an echo in an environmental context of the earlier call by Eisner:

> There is more to economic activity than what is measured in conventional accounts. . . . [P]erhaps the private research has shown enough in the way of possibilities for presenting a systematic set of accounts of a greater totality. . . . It is time for the major resources of government to be put to the task. The payoff can be great, for the economy as a whole as well as for national income accounting.
>
> (Eisner 1988: 1669)

Perhaps the largest payoff of all would be greater operational clarity in the vexed relationship between the economy and the environment, and in the extent to which environmentally sustainable development is being approached.

6 Population, affluence, technology and environmental impacts

6.1 THE COMMONER-EHRLICH EQUATION

There is no dispute that the negative environmental effects of production are associated with the economy's biophysical throughput: its conversion of energy and material resources into wastes. However, this process is not part of production's desired objective, which is to add value to its resource and energy inputs. As has been seen, when aggregated this added value becomes Gross Domestic Product. The key consideration as to whether GDP growth is or can be environmentally sustainable is the extent to which production processes can add more value without increasing associated environmentally negative biophysical throughputs.

As has also been seen, all economic activity requires three groups of functions from the environment:

1   raw materials and energy as factor inputs;
2   the assimilation of wastes;
3   the maintenance of life support systems (such as climate regulation and maintenance of genetic diversity).

Historically it can be observed that as production has increased, increasing stress has been placed on these three functions, leading to environmental degradation.

In order to examine how this trend might be reversed, use can be made of the concept of the *environmental impact coefficient* (EIC) of output, which is defined as 'the degree of impact . . . caused by an increase of one unit of national income' (Jacobs 1991: 54). Thus defined EIC is a marginal concept, but it can as easily be defined as the average impact on the environment of national income (i.e. I/Y, where I is the impact and Y is national income) due to the consumption of resources and production of wastes, and it is the average concept that is employed hereafter, unless otherwise specified. The three systematic changes in production processes which can theoretically reduce the EIC and thus enable value-added to increase while reducing environmental impacts are, as earlier quoted from Lecomber (1975):

1 changing the composition of output towards less damaging products (for example, goods to services);
2 substituting less damaging factor inputs for more damaging ones (for example, renewable energy sources for fossil fuels);
3 increasing the efficiency of resource use through technical progress (for example, energy conversion efficiency).

The same idea is expressed thus by the World Bank: 'Whether [environmental] limitations will place bounds on the growth of human activity will depend on the scope for substitution, technical progress and structural change' (World Bank 1992: 9).

By reducing the EIC, each of these changes can put off the moment when growth runs up against environmental limits. FOE (1995: 139) makes a useful distinction between 'relative delinking', where EIC falls, but at a lower rate than the growth of GDP, so that overall environmental impacts increase, and 'absolute delinking', where EIC falls faster than GDP grows, so that environmental impacts decrease. In principle, in this latter case the environmental limits can be postponed indefinitely.

Environmentally sustainable GDP growth thus depends on the achievement of substitution and technical and structural change in order to keep environmental impacts within conditions of environmental sustainability. However, this is not sufficient, since first a state of environmental sustainability must be achieved, and, as shown previously, the global economy is far from such a state. Remedying the environmental damage caused by past economic activities (e.g. contaminated land) is likely to reduce growth from what it would have been had no damage taken place. In addition, because of the environmental unsustainability of current activity, substitution and change must reduce the environmental impact of current output *as well as* of further growth in that output, if environmental sustainability is to be attained. Where environmental damage is irreversible, of course, improving EIC will not be effective.

The relationship between environmental impact and human activity was expressed by Ehrlich and Holdren (1971) as

$$I = P.F$$

where I is environmental impact, P is population and F is impact per head. Commoner (1971a: 175–6) expressed the relationship verbally thus: 'Pollutant emitted is equal to the product of the three factors – population times the amount of a given economic good per capita times output of pollutant per unit of the economic good produced' and it appeared thus in equation form in Commoner (1971b: 37). Holdren and Ehrlich appear to have accepted this formulation, because in a later article (1974: 288) the relationship appears as

$$I = P.C.T$$

where C is consumption per head, and T is impact per unit of consumption, i.e. the environmental impact coefficient, EIC, which will be called T hereafter. In this form the equation featured significantly in the authors' textbook *Ecoscience* (Ehrlich *et al.* 1977: 728) and by 1990 was referred to in another book as 'the all-important equation' (Ehrlich and Ehrlich 1990: 228). It was also referred to as an element of the defining context of the UK research programme on Global Environmental Change (UKGER 1993: 23).

Although as written the equation is a simple identity, its terms need some explanation. Population, as the number of people, is straightforward. Consumption per head in the aggregate could be proxied by GDP per head, which includes consumer, government and investment expenditures. This measure would not include consumption that is excluded from GDP (e.g. subsistence agriculture) and therefore the equation will not include environmental impacts from such consumption (e.g. some deforestation). T can be thought of as indicating the technology of consumption (and production). In some cases it will mainly reflect the inputs of production, the processes of transformation of production and consumption, and the disposal of wastes; in other cases it may be influenced by social arrangements such as property rights and the effectiveness of legal systems.

I (and therefore the numerator of T) could be one of a large number of environmental impacts. These impacts will be measured in diverse, normally physical, units, such as the weight of a resource used, or of a pollutant released into the environment, or an area of land degraded. While there may be ways of aggregating such measures into an overall impact, or pressure, indicator (see, for example, the index in MacGillivray 1993, as used in Chapter 7), the weights applied in such an aggregation are bound to be somewhat arbitrary. To express multiple impacts and keep them distinct, the equation could be written in vector form

$$I = P.C'.T$$

where I, T are column vectors of individual impacts, C is a vector of consumption quantities per head relating to those impacts and P is a scalar.

Commoner put the equation to its first practical use by estimating the proportionate contribution made to the increase in I in the US from 1946–68 by the three factors P, C, T. He presents data that show that the percentage increase in I over this period for six different pollutants ranges from 200–2000 per cent (Commoner 1971b: 36 (Table 1)). Elsewhere Commoner expresses this range as an average increase by a factor 10 (i.e. a 900 per cent increase). With population having increased by 43 per cent, he ascribes a 600 per cent ($1.43 \times 7 = 10$) increase to T (Commoner 1971a: 136), ignoring the 50 per cent increase in GNP as a contribution to pollution on the grounds that it 'is vastly inflated'. Commoner concludes:

The chief reason for the environmental crisis . . . is the sweeping transformation of productive technology since World War II. . . . Productive
technologies with intense impacts on the environment have displaced
less destructive ones. The environmental crisis is the inevitable result
of this counterecological pattern of growth.

(ibid.: 177)

The above decomposition of I into its contributions from P, C, T depends
for its validity, as Amalric (1995: 94ff.) notes, on the assumption that P,
C, T are independent. Commoner seems to realise this at the end of his
decomposition, when he asks: 'Is there some functional connection in the
economy between the tendency of a given productive activity to inflict an
intense impact on the environment . . . and the role of this activity in
economic growth?' (Commoner 1971b: 65). But he does not explore the
question and lets the decomposition of doubtful validity stand.

The relationships and interdependencies between P, C and T are of
crucial importance in gaining insights into how these variables affect environmental impacts. Obviously if one increases and the others stay the
same, then so will I. But if there are interdependencies the outcome could
be much more complicated.

Ehrlich and Holdren recognise that P, C and T are not independent.
They analyse several situations in which

$$T = f(P), \quad C = g(P) \text{ and } T = h(PC)$$

and

$$dT/dP, \quad dC/dP, \quad dT/dPC > 0$$

(i.e. technology tends to become more environmentally damaging per unit
of consumption as population or absolute consumption rise and per capita
consumption also rises with population). These interdependencies have the
effect of magnifying the increase in I for an increase in any of the other
variables, i.e. I will rise more than proportionately with the other variables.

In addition to this Ehrlich and Holdren identify threshold effects and
synergies which mean that environmental impacts increase more than
linearly with population and consumption over an important part of the
range ($\partial^2 I/\partial P^2$, $\partial^2 I/\partial C^2 > 0$).

It is not difficult to think of counter-examples: environmental economies
of scale (dT/dC, $dT/dPC < 0$); situations in which an economy cannot
productively absorb population increases, or where population growth acts
as a negative externality on consumption ($dC/dP < 0$, Birdsall (1994)
stresses the latter effect); situations where population growth leads to environmentally conserving technological innovation ($dT/dP < 0$, see Amalric
1995: 95); or, even, contradicting the Commoner-Ehrlich equation, where

poverty increases environmental damage ($\partial I/\partial C < 0$ over some range of very low incomes), as it is widely recognised to be able to do, for example, in the South Commission report, which states 'poverty is also a great degrader of the environment' (South Commission 1990: 279).

Baldwin (1995: 52) posits the hypothesis that 'people make pollution and poverty makes people' ($\partial I/\partial P > 0$ and $dp'/dC < 0$, where $p' = dp/dt = p(C)$, over a range of low incomes). $dp'/dC < 0$ for low incomes is a simple expression of the demographic transition theory, whereby increasing poor people's incomes reduces their population growth. Baldwin couples this theory with the theory that there is also an 'ecologic transition', such that $\partial^2 I/\partial C^2 < 0$ and that, once C has reached a certain level, $\partial I/\partial C < 0$. Considering the two theories together leads him to the conclusion that sustainability needs growth. Because of its importance to this study, the evidence for such an ecologic transition is exhaustively examined in the next chapter. In the context of the Commoner-Ehrlich equation, what this overall relationship between I, P, C, T would mean, given that the equation itself shows that the influence on I of consumption (and therefore income) *per se* is positive, is that an increasing C has a negative effect on the T variable which, combined with any effect on the P variable, causes I to fall overall.

Algebraically, if $T = T(C)$ such that $dT/dC < 0$, and $P = P(C)$, then

$$I \quad = \quad P(C).C.T(C)$$

$$\Rightarrow \quad dI \quad = \quad (dP/dC).C.T + P.T + (dT/dC).P.C \text{ (for } dC = 1)$$

$dT/dC < 0$ by assumption. dP/dC is unlikely to be negative (few even of the richest countries show falling population with continuing economic growth). For $dI < 0$, the (negative) third term must outweigh the sum of the other two. This is an extremely strong hypothesis. The theoretical basis as well as the evidence for it are explored in Chapter 7.

The other complicating factor connected with the Commoner-Ehrlich equation is the possibility of heterogeneity within the P, C, T aggregates. Amalric (1995: 94 (Table 5.3)) shows that, on the basis of a world-level calculation, population growth seems to have contributed 64 per cent of the growth of world CO_2 emissions from 1960–88. However, disaggregation of the population growth between developed and developing countries reduces its contribution to 41 per cent, while that of developing countries alone falls to 17 per cent.

On the basis of such complicating factors, some consider the Commoner-Ehrlich equation to be 'physically indisputable' but 'politically naive' (Meadows 1995: 8). This seems unnecessarily dismissive. Provided the possible interdependencies between the variables are kept in mind, the Commoner-Ehrlich equation seems to yield useful insights over a wide range of environmental impacts and levels of P, C and T.

At the end of his study indicting technology as the principal cause of environmental damage, Commoner (1971b: 65) expressed the view that, for economic and biological survival, much of the post-war technological transformation of the US would need to be 'redone in order to bring the nation's productive technology much more closely into harmony with the inescapable demands of the ecosystem'. Certainly technology is now more often regarded as a possible solution for environmental problems than their cause. In what follows, the Commoner-Ehrlich equation is used to indicate the scale of the technological challenge if both sustainability and GNP growth are to be achieved. Five scenarios are explored through calculations based on $I = PCT$ to indicate the improvements in the environmental impact coefficient (reductions in T) required to achieve environmental sustainability. The scenarios envisage no growth in P or C; growth in P and no growth in C; and growth in P, combined with growth in C only in the South, growth in C only in the North and growth in C in both.

In accordance with the reports already cited in Chapter 1 and the widespread agreement at UNCED, it is assumed that current levels of I are unsustainable. As was seen in Chapter 1 with regard to global warming, the IPCC's 1990 report calculated that carbon dioxide emissions would quickly have to fall by a minimum of 60 per cent from 1990's level to stabilise atmospheric concentrations of CO_2 at 1990's level, and three other greenhouse gases – N_2O, CFC-11, CFC-12 – need cuts of more than 70 per cent. With regard to other environmental problems, the Dutch National Environmental Policy Plan (NEPP) (MOHPPE 1988: 107 (Table 5.1.1)) considers that cuts in emissions of 80–90 per cent for SO_2, NO_X, NH_3 and waste-dumping, 80 per cent for hydrocarbons and 100 per cent for CFCs are necessary to attain a level of environmental quality in 2010 that corresponds to the definition of sustainability in Chapter 4. These targets were essentially confirmed in NEPP2 (MOHPPE 1994). Using the environmental space methodology discussed in Chapter 4, FOE (1995: 42 (Table 2.16)) calculated that the desirable reduction in the European Union in the use of cement, pig iron, aluminium, chlorine, copper, lead and fertiliser was in every case 80 per cent or more. Thus with regard to I overall, it seems conservative to suggest that sustainability demands that it should fall by at least 50 per cent. With regard to consumption, what is considered a moderate economic growth rate of 2–3 per cent per year results in a quadrupling of output over 50 years. With regard to population the UN's projections indicate a global figure of around twice today's level, by about 2050 (Sadik 1991: 3), with 95 per cent of population growth in the Third World. Using this assumption and classifications and data from World Bank (1997), the necessary reductions in T (T_R) in order to reduce environmental impacts to 50 per cent of the current value by 2050 can be calculated as in the Appendix to this chapter.

The results of the calculations can be summarised as follows for convenience, where T_{Ri} is the necessary reduction in T in scenario i:

1   No growth in P or C $T_{R1} = 50\%$

2   Growth in P, no growth in C $T_{R2} = 66\%$

3   Growth in P and C in South $T_{R3} = 81\%$

4   Growth in P and C in North $T_{R4} = 89\%$

5   Growth in P and C in North and South $T_{R5} = 91\%$

These figures clearly illustrate some important aspects of the technology/ sustainability relation. Comparing T_{R1} and T_{R2}, expected population growth at existing consumption levels increases the required cut in T from one-half to two-thirds. Although 95 per cent of the population growth takes place in the South, the calculation shows that the far higher level of consumption in the North means that the growth of population in the North (5 per cent of total population growth) accounts for well over one-half of the increase in environmental impact due to population growth as a whole and thus over one-half of the extra required reduction in T due to that growth.

Comparing T_{R4} with T_{R2} (89 per cent to 66 per cent) shows the extent to which growth in the North makes the achievement of environmental sustainability more technologically demanding. Comparison of T_{R4} with T_{R3} shows that the sustainable quadrupling of just the North's consumption per head, from a high base with very little population growth, demands considerably greater technical change than sustainably quadrupling the South's consumption per head for more than double its present population (89 per cent as opposed to 81 per cent reduction in T). In the latter case the calculation shows that even after quadrupling the South's per capita consumption, this is still only about one-sixth of current levels in the North. It is also clear that the required technological improvement in the North, even without Northern growth, is substantial if the South is to have 'ecological space' for environmentally sustainable growth, a point also made by Goodland and Daly (1992: 130).

Finally, the size of the necessary reduction in T (91 per cent) given growth in both North and South, which remains the principal, practically unchallenged global aspiration, must be noted. This necessary Factor 10 improvement for environmental sustainability is substantially lower than that required according to FOE (1995: 145), which sees the need for such a reduction in environmental intensity even without economic growth. With 2 per cent growth per annum, the required improvement factor increases to 27, and with 3 per cent growth to 46. FOE (ibid.: 147) regards such 'dematerialisation' of the economy as 'barely conceivable'.

Much of the rest of this study is devoted to examining the feasibility and implications of changes on this scale, amounting to a Factor 10 or more improvement in resource productivity. First, however, the variable T needs to be unpacked to differentiate between reductions due to economic structure (the first of Lecomber's three changes listed at the beginning of this chapter) and technical change (incorporating the other two).

Recasting the $I = PCT$ equation somewhat, and expressing it in sectoral form, for any economic sector, i, the environment/income relationship can be expressed as:

$$E_i = a_i y_i$$

where E is the environmental effect (e.g. emission of a pollutant), y is the output of the sector and a is a technical coefficient of the sector's environmental intensity. Where the sector produces multiple, say n, environmental effects, then E and a will be $(n \times 1)$ vectors.

The total environmental effect of production can then be expressed as:

$$E = \Sigma E_i = \Sigma a_i y_i$$

$$\Rightarrow E = Y.\Sigma a_i \frac{y_i}{Y} = Y.\Sigma a_i s_i$$

where s_i is the share of sector i in total output.

Differentiating with respect to time:

$$E' = \Sigma a_i s_i.Y' + Y.\Sigma s_i a_i' + Y.\Sigma a_i s_i'$$

where E' is dE/dt, Y' is dY/dt etc. Dividing by E $(= Y.\Sigma a_i s_i)$:

$$\hat{E} = \frac{E'}{E} = \frac{Y'}{Y} + \frac{1}{\Sigma a_i s_i} . \Sigma s_i a_i' + \frac{1}{\Sigma a_i s_i} . \Sigma a_i s_i'$$

$$\Rightarrow \hat{E} = \hat{Y} + \frac{Y}{E} (\Sigma s_i a_i' + \Sigma a_i s_i') \tag{6.1}$$

Equation 6.1 can be interpreted as follows. It states that the percentage rate of change of the environmental effect ($\hat{E}$) equals the percentage rate of change of output plus two terms incorporating the rate of change of technology (a') and the rate of change of the sectoral composition of output (s'). Therefore, given an increase in output and no change in sectoral composition or technology, one would expect a proportional increase in environmental effect, However, this increase could be reduced by introducing an environmentally improved technology ($a_i' < 0$) or by the sectoral composition shifting away from relatively environmentally intensive sectors ($s_1' < 0$, $s_2' > 0$ where $a_1 > a_2$).

If e_i is the sectoral share of the environmental effect, then

$$e_i = \frac{E_i}{E} = \frac{a_i y_i}{E} = \frac{a_i s_i Y}{E}$$

$$\Rightarrow \quad \frac{Y}{E} = \frac{e_i}{a_i s_i}$$

From Equation 6.1:

$$\hat{E} = \hat{Y} + \sum \frac{e_i}{a_i} a_i' + \sum \frac{e_i}{s_i} s_i'$$

$$\Rightarrow \quad \hat{E} = \hat{Y} + \sum e_i \hat{a}_i + \sum e_i \hat{s}_i \tag{6.2}$$

This is the form in which the equation appears in Grossman (1993: 2). Following Grossman and Krueger (1991: 3–4), the first term in Equation 6.2 can be termed the *scale* effect, the second term the *technique* effect and the third term the *composition* effect of economic development on the environment.

Economic growth *per se* (increases in Y) can then be expected to have a destructive effect on the environment through the scale effect. Three questions then arise:

1   To what extent can reductions in a and s, the technique and composition effects, be expected to counteract the scale effect?
2   Will these reductions come about more or less automatically as part of the process of economic growth, or will they need to be brought about by government policy?
3   If they need to be achieved by policy, will such policy itself incur costs that will inhibit economic growth?

The answers to these questions are likely to vary from issue to issue and from one environmental impact to another. Some evidence on all three of the questions is presented in subsequent chapters. The rest of this chapter is taken up with the issue of costs in question 3: how reasonable is it to expect that the necessary technical changes and policy measures to counteract the scale effect, that tends to increase environmental impacts, will come about or be implemented such that the growth of the economy is not constrained? As was seen in Chapter 2, Lecomber believed:

> It is misleading to regard environmental policies of this sort as *alternatives* to reducing economic growth since this would be their incidental effect. Benefits which are not included in GNP would be traded for other (smaller) benefits which are. GNP would fall and, during the period of transition to such policies, growth would fall, probably substantially.
>
> (1975: 59, original emphasis)

What follows explores the extent to which Lecomber is likely to be right.

6.2 THE COSTS OF ACHIEVING ENVIRONMENTAL SUSTAINABILITY

Reducing T in the Commoner-Ehrlich equation provides the basic *physical* condition for the compatibility of sustainability and growth. But there is also an economic condition. Reducing T may well require resources, in new capital and in more expensive inputs. If the cost of reducing T is positive, then reduced environmental impacts will, as Lecomber envisaged, have been bought only at the expense of retarding growth. Therefore for sustainability not to constrain GDP growth, the net costs of reducing T must be zero or negative.

There are two broad ways in which improving the environmental efficiency of production might also involve raising general productivity (i.e. where policy for environmental sustainability will also promote GNP growth):

1   Situations in which governments change policies which are economically inefficient as well as environmentally damaging.
2   Situations in which public or private sector businesses introduce changes in methods, processes or products, including systems of resource and waste management, which both improve environmental quality *and* turn out to be cost-saving or product-improving.

The first kind of situation may be considered an example of double government failure (policies that are economically and environmentally flawed), and the second exhibits a kind of double market failure (environmental externality and economic inefficiency). There is substantial evidence, some of which will be reviewed below, that both these kinds of failure are surprisingly widespread.

If some environmental improvement measures may in themselves be net cost-reducing, while others are net cost-increasing, this gives us three broad scenarios:

I   T is reduced to counteract environmental impacts and this raises general productivity – growth increases and environmental quality improves ('win–win'). This effect could occur as a result of correcting either government or market failures as part of implementing environmental policies.
II   T is reduced to counteract environmental impacts but this raises costs – growth, as currently accounted, declines, but some aspects of environmental quality improve, or decline less slowly ('win–lose'). Where the environmental gains were greater than the opportunity costs of the environmental measures, an NNP correctly adjusted for these gains would, as discussed in Chapter 5, be higher than without the environmental measures.

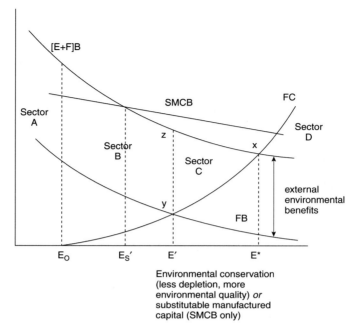

Figure 6.1 Benefits and costs of environmental policies
Source: Adapted from World Bank (1992: 66)

III Nothing is done to counteract the costs from rising environmental damage – environmental quality declines and, if it falls far enough, so does growth (the 'lose–lose' scenario).

The financial implications of scenarios I and II are shown in sectors A, B and C of Figure 6.1. (E + F)B represents the sum of the marginal external and financial benefits deriving from the environment and can be regarded as the 'demand curve' for environmental quality. FC represents the financial costs of maintaining environmental quality at different levels and can be regarded as environmental quality's 'supply curve'. Where they intersect, point x, gives the optimum level of environmental quality, E*. FB represents only the (privately appropriable) financial benefits deriving from the environment. Where FB and FC intersect, point y, gives the non-optimal, market-determined level of environmental quality, E′. The gap between FB and (E + F)B indicates the environment's external non-monetary benefits. If environmental quality is reduced (e.g. from E* to E′), the net cost is the area between the (E + F)B and FC curves (i.e. xyz).

The cost implications of improving the environment can be considered with reference to three sectors under the (E + F)B curve. Sector A, between the vertical axis and E$_o$, represents opportunities for environmental improvement that cost nothing, and result in both financial and environmental gains, because they represent the correction of government policy that was economically inefficient as well as environmentally damaging. In sector B, between E_0 and E', the policies have a financial cost which is outweighed by the financial gain, in addition to the external environmental gain. In sector C, between E' and E^*, the policies have a net financial cost which is outweighed by the external environmental gain. The first two cases may be characterised as 'win–win changes' corresponding to scenario I, and the third as a 'trade-off situation' corresponding to scenario II. In sector D, beyond E^*, in contrast, the financial cost of the environmental measures outweighs the total benefits to be gained from them.

The greatest uncertainty in determining the optimal environmental quality, E^*, attaches to the valuation of the environment's external benefits, which in turn determines the position of the $(E + F)B$ curve. Where, because of this uncertainty, or for political or ethical reasons, environmental sustainability is chosen as the goal of environmental policy, then E^* will be set at the perceived 'sustainable' level for different environmental resources and functions, with each one having its own Figure 6.1-type representation, and the 'environmental quality' being measured in a unit appropriate for that resource or function. Where there are extensive possibilities for equally effective manufactured substitutes for a resource or function, shown in Figure 6.1 by a high marginal benefit from some substitute manufactured capital, SMCB, then the sustainable level of environmental quality, E_s', may be quite low, increasing the sizes of sectors A and B relative to C (as shown in Figure 6.1, sector C in this case has disappeared altogether; above E_s' only substitute manufactured capital, SMC, will be used). Where possibilities for substitution are low or nonexistent, and the sustainability of the environmental function depends on a high level of environmental quality, say up to or to the right of E^*, then the size of sector C may be large relative to A and B. Where the environmental resource is complementary to manufactured capital, SMCB, and where the amount of manufactured capital is such that it is the environmental resource that is the limiting factor on production, this will tend to increase FB and hence the sizes of sectors A and B relative to sector C.

In this framework, the question of whether sustainability and GDP growth are compatible essentially becomes one concerning the relative sizes of sectors A, B and C.

Some empirical evidence on this will be reviewed below. First, however, it may be helpful to summarise the theoretical position. There are two requirements for growth not to run up against environmental limits:

1   The average environmental impact coefficient (T) must be reduced.
2   This must be cost-neutral or must positively increase general productivity.

Three further conditions must be met:

a   The improvements in T and productivity gains must be continuous (and exponential); if not, continuing growth will soon overcome the gains made. It should be noted that if an improvement in T relaxes a constraint, this will itself encourage growth, thereby wiping out at least part of the gain.

b   The improvements in T and productivity must occur across all environmental impacts relevant to the environmental sustainability of GDP growth. If recycling of materials requires more consumption of fossil fuel energy, for example, the environmental constraint will simply be relocated, not removed.

c   The growth-retarding effects of any environmental impacts caused by past actions must be cleared up along with current impacts: for example, hazardous waste treatment, ozone depletion, desertification, etc.

There is no question in principle, both that each of the three methods for reducing T is possible, and that some methods of reducing T will also lead to general productivity improvements. But, as per the quote from Lecomber in Chapter 2 (see p. 41), the theoretical possibility of 'delinking' biophysical throughput from GDP growth does not guarantee its practical achievability. Ultimately it is an empirical matter whether the two requirements for reconciling sustainability and GDP growth, under the three given conditions, can be achieved in practice.

6.2.1 Empirical evidence

In a Background Paper for the World Bank's *World Development Report 1992*, Anderson (1992) provides impressive evidence that the potential exists, or soon will exist, to reduce environmental impact coefficients on the scale required by the Commoner-Ehrlich equation in each of the major fields of global environmental impact: water, food production, pollution from energy, global warming and pollution from industry (Table 6.1). His analysis focuses on substitution between factor inputs and raising technical efficiency; only in energy production is changing the composition of output considered. Anderson further argues that many of the identified measures themselves raise productivity. On the basis of this analysis Anderson concludes that – so long as the correct policies are put in place – growth over the next thirty to forty years need not be constrained, and indeed can be enhanced, by protection and improvement of the environment; while he also acknowledges that time lags in investment will mean that environmental problems, particularly in the South, will get considerably worse before they get better.

    Anderson does not attempt to integrate the results in the different fields, so it is not clear whether (for example) the additional commercial energy

Table 6.1 Relative pollution (or damage) intensities of polluting or low-polluting practices

Source	Basis of index of damage	Practice Polluting	Practice Non-polluting	Nature of alternatives
Particulate matter	Emissions	100	< 0.1	Natural gas; clean coal technologies; scrubbers; low-sulphur fuels
CO	"	100	< 0.1	
SO_2	"	100	0 to < 5	
NO_x	"	100	5 to < 10	
CO_2	"	100	0	Renewables New octane enhancers; catalytic converters
Pb	"	100	< 0.1	
VOCs	"	100	< 2	
Marine pollution (oil)	Spills & wastes	100	< 10	
Surface water pollution	Volume of wastes	100	negligible	Sewerage works; effluent control technologies
Soil erosion	Soil loss	100	negligible	Agro-forestry; soil erosion prevention practices
Forestry	Areas cleared in damaging ways	100	negligible	'Sustainable' practices
Industrial effluents & wastes	Emissions & wastes (by weight & volume)	100	small	Effluent control technologies; waste reduction or 'prevention'

Source: Anderson (1992: 6)

and industrial inputs required to improve agricultural productivity can be accommodated within the win–win energy and industrial pollution scenarios. Nor is it clear whether the gains in general productivity made in some sectors outweigh overall the losses acknowledged in others. In effect the losses are regarded as so small in relation to total output that they are deemed not to be sufficiently serious to inhibit growth.

On the basis of this evidence, the potential of new technologies to enable production to be considerably less damaging environmentally would seem indubitable. Whether such potential is realised in practice depends on whether and how fast these new technologies can be deployed and whether the government and market failures that either hinder their deployment or cause environmental damage directly can be successfully addressed.

Government failure

The notion that government is in some sense a natural protector of the environment was dealt a probably terminal below by the revelations of environmental damage in Central and Eastern Europe and the former Soviet Union (see WRI 1992: Ch. 5 for a survey). It is clear that governmental contributions to environmental destruction that are also economically inefficient were not, and are not, confined to these countries.

One of the largest examples of such governmental lose–lose policies is the Common Agricultural Policy (CAP) of the European Community. The basic mechanism of the CAP is price support of marketed farm products, which, because of intensification of production involving greater specialisation and greater use of chemicals and machinery, has lead to a number of adverse environmental effects including soil degradation, water pollution and the loss of amenity and diversity (OECD 1991a: 184). In aggregate the energy intensity of OECD agriculture increased by 39 per cent over the period 1970–88 (ibid.: 173).

In 1984 the net economic costs of the CAP, including losses to taxpayers and consumers, were nearly 14 billion Ecu, leading a study in 1990 to conclude: 'What is certain, therefore, is that ... on narrow economic grounds a fundamental reform of current policy would be beneficial, even before the environmental benefits of reform are taken into account' (Jenkins 1990: 47). In terms of Figure 6.1, such a policy reform is in sector A, where both economic and environmental benefits can be obtained at zero or negative net overall cost. However, such a reform may have significant distributional implications (for example, farmers may become, or may believe they may become, worse off), which could make the policy change difficult to bring about despite its overall benefits.

Just as price supports for output can inefficiently increase both output and associated environmental damage, so can subsidies for inputs. As the World Bank (1992: 68) notes, 'both economic and environmental benefits will be achieved by removing subsidies that encourage the use of coal, electricity, pesticides and irrigation and promote expansion of grazing and timber extraction on public lands'. Such subsidies are common. In China, Poland and Mexico users pay less that 40 per cent of the production cost of electric power; the figure for coal in the former USSR is 10 per cent, and for Sri Lanka for nitrogen fertiliser is about 60 per cent; in India and Bangladesh irrigation water is practically free (ibid.: 68–9).

A string of publications from the World Resources Institute (Repetto 1985, 1986, 1988; Kosmo 1987) gives many other examples of inefficient, environmentally damaging policies in energy, agriculture and forestry. In Europe taxpayers subsidised fossil fuels and nuclear energy on average by $15 billion per year from 1990–5 (Ruijgrok and Oosterhuis 1997: i). Myers (1998: 328) has estimated that globally environmentally perverse subsidies in five sectors – agriculture, fossil fuels and nuclear energy, road transport, water and fisheries – total $1.1 trillion per year. For the same sectors excluding fisheries, Maddison *et al.* (1997: 111) estimate the subsidies to be in the range of $614–738 billion per year, with the UK share being more than $20 billion (ibid.: 114). Policies to rectify these economic and environmental inefficiencies also fall within sector A of Figure 6.1.

Another possible source of economic inefficiency due to government intervention in the economy is the taxation system that is used to raise government revenue. It has been seen in Chapter 2 that, where there are environmental externalities, imposing taxes on the sources of the externalities is a way of 'internalising' them, and moving towards both environmental and economic efficiency. These environmental taxes will raise revenue, which raises the possibility of reducing other taxes by a similar amount, thereby reducing these other taxes' distortionary impact on the economy and achieving further economic gains. This possibility is explored in some detail in Chapter 8.

Of major importance to both environmental conservation and poverty alleviation in developing countries is the regeneration of degraded land, of which India has some 69 million ha. Chambers has written:

> Paradoxically, degradation often protects potential for the poor. Because land is degraded – deforested, eroded, waterlogged, saline, bare from overgrazing, flooded or unsustainably cropped – it has low value, especially where current management practices seem likely to persist. But again and again, when management priorities are changed, remarkable bioeconomic potential is revealed.
>
> (Chambers 1992: 222)

Conventional 'development' practice has to date been more concerned with harvesting biomass, or even destroying it through industrial projects, than with regenerating it, so a focus on such regeneration would mark a significant change of development direction and approach. It is generally perceived to require two essential ingredients. The first is a high level of motivation and commitment of both individuals and communities, both to carry out the environmental reparations concerned and to go on caring for the renewed environment on a long-term basis. Such commitment will only be forthcoming if the people involved have assured rights to use the biomass they have produced. Inalienable rights of tenure, usufruct and control over the regenerated land is an essential condition for the regeneration to take place.

This is a fundamental policy issue for countries with skewed land distribution and a history of concentrated ownership, unsustainable use of land and biomass, and exclusion of peasant farmers from land or their insecure title to it. The World Bank identified the clarification and enforcement of property rights as a key zero cost (sector A, Figure 6.1) policy geared to both development and environmental conservation (World Bank 1992: 66, 68–70).

Second, the regeneration of biomass often demands low rather than high levels of financial investment, offering the prospect of sector B gains, in terms of Figure 6.1. However, development 'projects' based on biomass regeneration will only succeed if they are rooted in communities' skills, technologies and own perceived priorities. Participation, of course, has been a feature of development parlance for some years, but it rarely extends to 'beneficiary' communities both setting the agenda for their development and playing the principal decision-making role in achieving it. Biomass regeneration demands both.

Where these ingredients are present, there is no doubt, on the basis of successful examples from different countries, that biomass generation is both feasible and yields large, sustainable benefits to the populations concerned. Conroy and Litvinoff (1988) report successful experiences of this kind from north India, Nepal, Honduras, Niger, Burkina Faso and Haiti. P. Harrison (1987) gives many examples from Africa. Pangare and Pangare (1992) give an in-depth account of regenerative success in Maharashtra, central India.

A relevant question for this study is whether, if biomass regeneration were to be achieved on a large scale by participatory processes under the control of the rural poor, this would result in GDP growth. To the extent that the new biomass found its way onto the market, it obviously would, but it is likely that a considerable portion of the output would be consumed for the producers' own subsistence and so would not be thus recorded. It is essential, therefore, that measures of the effectiveness of such processes take account of subsistence production if they are not seriously to understate the results achieved.

Market failure and business successes

With regard to market failures, a number of case studies now attest to corporate improvements in environmental performance which have also yielded economic benefits. Thus the Business Council for Sustainable Development states: 'Many of the waste reduction and environmentally positive programs in business are economically viable and are providing positive rates of return in relatively short time periods' (Schmidheiny 1992: 96). Sometimes the benefit comes in the form of straight cost-reductions, a well-known example of which is the Pollution Prevention Pays (3P) programme of the 3M Corporation, which from 1975–90 cut air pollutants by 122,000 tons, water pollutants by 16,000 tons, solid waste by 400,000 tons and waste water by 1.6 billion gallons – and saved $482 million (Business International 1990: 188).

Similarly, Northern Telecom, in phasing out its use of ozone-depleting CFC-113 between 1988 and 1991, spent $1 million putting a substitute in place, but saved $4 million on purchasing the CFC, associated taxes and waste-disposal (Schmidheiny 1992: 230). In India Harihar Polyfibres implemented 200 projects at its pulp mill between 1983 and 1989, aimed at resource efficiency. Although its production increased by 20 per cent in this period, energy consumption fell by 60 per cent, chemical consumption by 55 per cent and the effluent load by 55 per cent; $69.5 million was invested in the projects, but the payback period was under two years (ibid.: 272–3). In California several companies have found that investment in industrial water conservation can result in substantial savings of water with a payback period of a year or less. For example, the California Paper-Board Corporation cut its water consumption by 72 per cent from 2.5 to 0.7 million cubic metres per year with a payback period on investment of only 2.4 months (Brown *et al.* 1993: 34). In another example, Ayres and Walter (1991: 251) report that the average return on investment for 167 energy-savings projects undertaken by the Louisiana Division of Dow Chemical Co. over the years 1982–8, as part of an 'energy-contest' initiative, was 198 per cent.

Three other examples of reduced effluents, reduced water usage and cost-saving are given in Centre for the Exploitation of Science and Technology (CEST) (1991: 40). A subsequent project of CEST in the UK's Aire and Calder valley resulted in eleven participating companies identifying 542 options for cost-saving waste-reduction that saved over £2 million almost immediately with the prospect of similar savings in future, with over 70 per cent of the measures having a payback of less than a year (CEST 1994: 6–7).

All these examples fall within sector B of Figure 6.1. Some investment is required (which could be public as well as private), but it yields net financial as well as environmental gains, and so can be justified in terms of financial return irrespective of environmental considerations. In a competitive market it is surprising that there are so many opportunities for profitable investment that appear to have been overlooked. It appears that business managers have been widely unaware of the *economic*, let alone the environmental, costs of resource use and waste disposal, and needed the pressure of public opinion drawing attention to the latter before they gave serious consideration to the former. As it happens, Harihar Polyfibres' environmental improvements failed to keep up with public opinion, and it was taken to court in 1988 – it has now installed a comprehensive waste-water treatment plant (Schmidheiny 1992: 273).

Environmental pressure can also achieve economic benefits by stimulating creativity and innovation which results in new products or new business opportunities. Thus the Costa Rican firm RICALIT developed a fibre cement in 1981–2 to replace its asbestos cement which was subject to increasing concern over safety. The substitute proved both less expensive and more manageable than asbestos cement, and was highly profitable, with sales more than doubling to over $6 million in 1991 (Schmidheiny 1992: 215–16). An example of a new business opportunity is that presented by energy conservation in contrast to traditional energy supply companies. The New England Electric (NEE) company realised as long ago as 1979 that energy conservation made more economic sense than providing new supply, but it was not until 1989 that the utilities' regulatory system permitted the company to make a financial return on investments in conservation. In 1990 NEE spent $71 million on energy conservation projects, saving 194,300 MW-hours of electricity and $161 million. NEE retained $8.4 million (9 per cent) of this $91 million net saving, the rest being passed on to customers. NEE projects that it could spend $100 million a year to the year 2000 on economically viable conservation projects in its service area (ibid.: 187–8).

Such experiences have caused Porter to hypothesise that environmental regulations may be good for economic competitiveness:

> Stringent standards for product performance, product safety, and environmental impact contribute to creating and upgrading competitive advantage. They pressure firms to upgrade quality, upgrade technology and provide features in areas of important customer (and social) concern. . . . Particularly beneficial are stringent regulations that anticipate standards that will spread internationally. These give a nation's firms a head start in developing products and services that will be valued elsewhere.
>
> (Porter 1990: 647–8)

In a later publication Porter and Van Der Linde (1995: 111) emphasise market-based instruments, instead of or as well as regulation, as very often the most effective way to give firms the incentive to overcome the various obstacles to corporate innovation and technological change, including lack of information and organisational inertia.

The Porter 'win–win' hypothesis of the economic, as well as environmental, benefits of environmental regulation runs clearly counter to economists' normal assumptions of efficient, competitive markets. It has been attacked as being at best a marginal phenomenon with regard to the costs of environmental regulation as whole. Palmer *et al.* (1995: 127–8) estimate that Porter's 'innovation offsets' amount to only a few per cent of the total costs of conforming to environmental regulations, which in the US have been estimated by the EPA at $135 billion in 1992. They contend that the vast majority of these costs conform to the standard economic trade-off model, whereby environmental benefits are gained at the sacrifice of economic growth. This point is discussed further on p. 174.

Even if Palmer *et al.* are right, the environmental protection industry that has sprung up at least partly as a result of environmental regulation is now a major industrial sector in its own right, which OECD (1991a: 198) and Business International (1990: 157) value at $70–100 billion in OECD countries and probably half as much again worldwide (though this seems low compared to the EPA figure for the US above). It is surely plausible that there should be a first-mover advantage to environmental regulation, in that those countries which develop new technologies early in response to stringent domestic regulations will be well placed in world markets if those regulations are imposed in other countries. Porter (1990: 648–9) gives examples where Japan, Germany, the US and Switzerland have, in different instances, all benefited from first-mover advantages and thereby improved their national economic performance.

The Porter hypothesis has found aggressive advocates in Weizsäcker *et al.* (1997), whose slogan of 'Factor Four' proclaims the possibility 'to double the global standard of living while cutting resource use in half' (Weizsäcker *et al.* 1997: xxii). They give fifty examples of 'quadrupling resource productivity' in energy production, the use of materials, and transport, writing: 'The economic value involved in implementing those 50 examples of the expected efficiency revolution on a world-wide scale could be immense' (ibid.: 139).

In fact not all the examples exhibit the 'great business opportunities' (Weizsäcker *et al.* 1997: 139) that are claimed for them. 'Low energy beef', it seems, offers consumers the prospect of eating less and paying higher prices (ibid.: 50–1). The scheme to reuse bottles, cans and large containers that is put forward (ibid.: 106–7) clearly depends on activist commitment rather than the profit motive. Reducing the transport of processed food turns out to involve, for strawberry yoghurt, the consumer developing local preferences and re-engaging in home production (ibid.: 119), and, for fruit juice, allowing the recent German preference for orange juice from overseas to be denied in favour of home-grown blackcurrants (ibid.: 120–1). 'Car-free mobility' simply involves living without a car, rather than some fundamental increase in 'transport productivity'. Finally, the 'perennial polyculture' that is put forward as an alternative to agriculture (ibid.: 97–9) will not even be available for fifty years.

Even in those cases where the technologies exist to achieve Factor Four increases in resource productivity, Weizsäcker *et al.* acknowledge 'a very large iceberg of modern underlying problems', and 'a daunting array of practical obstacles', standing in the way of their realisation. The obstacles include 'the conventional education of nearly everybody dealing with natural resources', lack of information, vested interests, perverse financial incentives, existing regulatory structures and consumer inertia (Weizsäcker *et al.* 1997: xxvi–xxvii). Overcoming such obstacles, where it is possible at all, may require substantial resources over and above those that are necessary to introduce the technology itself. It is possible that this extra required investment would even take a potential 'Factor Four' technology out of Figure 6.1's Sector B into the trade-off zone of Sector C.

Trade-off situations

In contrast to sectors A and B in Figure 6.1, sector C involves real trade-offs between the production of goods and services for the market and the production, or conservation, of non-market environmental goods and services. Economic resources are allocated for the production of the latter rather than the former which must, as a first-round effect at least, have a negative effect on GDP growth. It is important to recognise that, because the environmental and other benefits from such an allocation are greater than the costs, it still represents an increase in economic efficiency, being a correction of an externality or some other resource-misallocation. It would show up as an increase in environmentally adjusted NNP. But it would reduce NNP as currently accounted, as envisaged by Lecomber in the quote earlier in the chapter.

As has been seen, it is the trade-off situation which best characterises economists' expectations of the effects of moving towards environmental sustainability. In their review of studies in this area, Christainsen and Tietenberg (1985: 372–3) identify five reasons which have been put forward why environmental policy may constrain the growth or productivity and, therefore, income:

1   Investments in more pollution control may crowd out other investment.
2   More stringent abatement requirements for new plant may prolong the life of older, less productive, plant.
3   Pollution control equipment requires labour to operate and maintain with no contribution to saleable output.
4   Compliance with environmental regulations absorbs managerial and administrative resources with no contribution to saleable output.
5   Uncertainty about present and possible future regulations may inhibit investment.

Against this, Christainsen and Tietenberg only cite one possible positive influence of environmental regulation on output, the protection and improvement of the health of workers, but this is extremely difficult to assess and is routinely excluded from models of this issue.

In the model they construct to try to capture some of these influences, Christainsen and Tietenberg (1985: 373) posit a production function of the form

$$Q = F(X_1, X_2, .. X_n, R, t)$$

where Q is output, X_i are inputs, R is the level of regulation and t is time, proxying for technical change.

The rate of growth of total factor productivity, n_G, is then shown to be:

$$n_G = A(n_Q - 1) + n_R(dR/dt) + n_t$$

where A is a constant, n_Q is a measure of the returns to scale of the production function ($n_Q = 1$ means constant returns to scale), n_R is $\partial Q/\partial R$ and n_t is $\partial Q/\partial t$, the effect of technological change. This equation gives the direct effect of environmental regulation on productivity growth, but regulation itself may affect scale economies, technological change and the composition of output, with secondary effects on the rate of productivity growth. Regulation may also affect inflation, with further macroeconomic impacts.

The direct effect of regulation on productivity growth depends on n_R. If n_R is positive, regulation promotes productivity growth, if negative it impedes it. Christainsen and Tietenberg (1985: 378) note: 'The extent to which past increases in regulation caused productivity to decelerate – and price increases to accelerate – remains controversial.' However, the studies they survey permit the conclusion, with regard to the US in the 1970s, that:

> environmental regulations cannot escape some of the blame for the slowdown in the rate of productivity growth. . . . A reasonable estimate would attribute, say, 8–12 percent of the slowdown in productivity growth to environmental regulations. This amounts to a reduction in the growth rate of labour productivity of 0.2–0.3 percentage points.
> (ibid.: 378)

A later study by Jorgenson and Wilcoxen (1990: 315) found that environmental regulation reduced the US GDP growth rate by an average of 0.19 per cent per annum between 1973 and 1985. The authors say that: 'This is several times the reduction in growth estimated in previous studies', but it actually appears very close to the range identified by Christainsen and Tietenberg as above. Jorgenson and Wilcoxen's interpretation of the significance of their numbers is also very different to the earlier study's, for they consider their results 'show that pollution abatement has emerged as a major claimant on the resources of the US economy' (ibid.: 315), while Christainsen and Tietenberg (1985: 380) say that the adverse effect on economic performance in the US 'has not been large in magnitude'. Further comments on the different interpretations that can be accorded to such numbers are made in Chapter 9.

Another review of the macroeconomic effects of environmental policy covers the same literature as Christainsen and Tietenberg, and notes their overall conclusion, but considers: 'There are numerous methodological and practical criticisms that throw doubt on the accuracy and validity of the aggregate productivity measures showing the negative impact' (OECD

1985: 88). It also draws attention to the facts that: 'For a number of other OECD countries, less comprehensive studies indicate that the negative effects are much smaller' (ibid.: 87); and that some disaggregated industry studies suggest that some results from or changes in pollution control, such as cost-saving, the development of cheaper pollution control technologies and the accelerated development of new production processes, 'have either added to productivity growth or helped to reverse the earlier falling trend' (ibid.: 87). In other words, the OECD study specifically acknowledges the possibility of sector B gains.

Reviewing the reported effects of environmental policy on economic growth and employment, the OECD study identifies several conflicting forces at work on the macroeconomy as a result of environmental programmes. First the extra investment and operating expenditure creates extra demand, boosting output and employment, which is further reinforced by the multiplier effect. However, in due course the costs of the programme feed through into higher prices which constrain GDP growth. Overall, the study concludes that the effect on growth is indeterminate, being positive in some studies and negative in others, while the effect on employment is positive. But overall:

> The main conclusion which emerges from [these results] is that the macroeconomic effect of environmental policies is relatively small. Most of the figures reported . . . are in the range of a few tenths of a percentage point per year. Furthermore, it is important to recall that these small effects were registered during a period (the 1970s) of peak pollution control activity, when efforts were directed not only at limiting ongoing pollution, but also at cleaning up the backlog caused by the neglect of the environment during the 1950s and 1960s.
>
> (OECD 1985: 10)

The passage of time seems to have confirmed the early OECD view of low costs from environmental regulation rather than the reverse, with a subsequent OECD study concluding in 1996: 'The trade and investment impacts which have been measured empirically are almost negligible' (OECD 1996: 45). Jaffe *et al.*'s (1995: 157) review concludes that 'studies attempting to measure the effect of environmental regulation on net exports, overall trade flows, and plant-location decisions have produced estimates that are either small, statistically insignificant or not robust to tests of model specification'. Curiously, despite these results, they persist in believing that 'the long-run social costs of environmental regulation may be significant' (ibid.: 157) and that regulation imposes 'large direct and indirect costs' (ibid.: 159), when their review of the relevant studies seems to have shown just the opposite. If the costs were large, they surely would feed through into competitiveness effects. Because their dismissal of the Porter hypothesis is largely based on this continuing belief in large costs, it does not carry conviction. Rather than market failure, Jaffe *et al.* (ibid.: 158) cite data limitations, the low proportion of environmental expenditures in firms' overall costs, the small difference between US regulations and those of its major competitors, and the preference of many companies to standardise their pollution controls to those of the most stringent countries, as the probable reasons for the lack of any significant effects of environmental regulation on competitiveness.

Both Christainsen and Tietenberg and the 1985 OECD study stress that the macroeconomic costs are only one side of the environmental policy picture. According to the former:

> One basic and overriding point should be made with respect to environmental regulations. The contributions to economic welfare which they are intended to make are, by and large, not reflected in marketed or measured output. . . . Although they are difficult to quantify, let alone value, numerous studies have indicated marked increases in these outputs from environmental policy. . . . If this is in fact the case, the effect of these regulations on 'true' productivity would be positive and not negative, and the inclusion of the outputs of these regulations in the numerator of the standard productivity measures would both offset the negative effects of other factors on productivity growth and change the *sign* of the effect attributable to environmental regulations.
>
> (Christainsen and Tietenberg 1985: 388, original emphasis)

The OECD study divides the benefits from environmental policy into three categories: 'output-increasing' (which are included in the Financial Benefits, FB, curve in Figure 6.1); 'cost-saving' (which will be included in the FB or external sector, depending on whether the saved costs were external or not) and 'utility-increasing' (which are the external benefits in Figure 6.1). The study estimates the last category of benefits for the US for 1978 at $25 billion and notes that, had they been taken into account in measured GDP, 'the true productivity change from 1970 to 1978 would have been 0.19 per cent per annum higher than that reflected in the conventional measure' (OECD 1985: 87). Comparing this estimate with the Christainsen and Tietenberg range of 0.2–0.3 per cent suggests that during the 1970s the great majority of environmental policy, even when it incurred net financial costs, operated in sector C of Figure 6.1 rather than sector D.

For sustainability to be approached, environmental policy in the future is likely to have to be more stringent than that in the past, which by no means succeeded in curbing environmental degradation, while the past legacy of environmental damage has by no means been adequately addressed. Brown *et al.* (1993) identifies the US as facing clean-up costs of $750 billion for hazardous waste sites and $200 billion for nuclear weapons manufacturing facilities (Brown *et al.* 1993: 10). Such clean-up problems face all industrial countries to some extent; the costs involved are almost certainly sector C (constraining growth) rather than sector B costs.

There has been substantial modelling of possible future environmental policies in order to gain insight into the likely macroeconomic costs. The important issue of the likely macroeconomic effects of abating carbon emissions is the subject of Chapter 9, following a discussion in Chapter 8 as to whether environmental taxes, by permitting other taxes to be reduced, can yield an improvement in economic efficiency over and above its environmental benefits.

More generally, and in contrast to the Jorgenson and Wilcoxen (1990) retrospective study, several modelling projections have found negligible negative effects on GDP from future environmental policies. Thus Barker and Lewney (1991) have combined a carbon tax designed to reduce UK CO_2 emissions back to 1990 levels by 2005, a four-fold rise in industrial pollution abatement expenditures by 2000, and an intensified water clean-up policy. This reduces GDP in 2010 by less that 1 per cent (Barker and Lewney 1991: 35 (Table 7)). Similarly the Netherlands National Environmental Policy Plan (NEPP) projected the decrease of a number of emissions and waste discharges by between 70 per cent and 100 per cent, and a doubling of environmental expenditures: by 2010 GDP had grown to 95 per cent above its 1985 level, in contrast to a 99 per cent growth with a base case of unchanged policy (MOHPPE 1988: 110 (Table 5.2.3); when other countries implement the same measures as the Netherlands, Dutch GDP actually grows by 0.5 per cent). These effects seem small, and, where they are negative, certainly seem less than the environmental benefits achieved. The DRI (1994) study, reviewed in Chapter 8, produced similar results.

6.3 CONCLUSION

Whether the achievement of environmental sustainability is compatible with GDP growth depends on the manner of calculation of GDP and on the relative size of Figure 6.1's sector C (which represents expenditures which do or can restrain GDP growth) to sectors A and B, which represent policies or expenditures which do not. Whether it is practically feasible depends on it being politically possible to address government and market failures.

The question of the relative sizes of sectors A, B and C is still open to conjecture, and is at the heart of the debate about sustainability and growth reviewed in Chapter 2, which has been characterised by often heated conflict between optimists and pessimists.

The major difference between the optimist and pessimist views is that optimists such as Anderson and the World Bank project win–win scenarios up to about 2030 in which strong environmental policy protects the environment, but helps growth as much as it hinders it, so that growth proceeds largely unconstrained. Meadows *et al.* agree that growth may be able to continue until 2030, but only at the cost of great environmental degradation, which precipitates catastrophe soon thereafter. They perceive that effective environmental policy will constrain growth.

This latter viewpoint is well expressed by Tinbergen and Hueting:

> Saving the environment without causing a rise in prices and subsequent check of production growth is only possible if a technology is invented that is sufficiently clean, reduces the use of space sufficiently, leaves the soil intact, does not deplete energy and resources . . . *and* is cheaper (or at least not more expensive) than current technology. This is barely imaginable for our whole range of current activities . . . From the above it follows that saving the environment will certainly check production growth and probably lead to lower levels of national income.
>
> (Tinbergen and Hueting 1992: 55–6, original emphasis)

Tinbergen and Hueting clearly believe sector C to be the one most often relevant to environmental policy.

The World Bank, though not unambiguously, believes that sectors A and B have more to offer. Thus: 'The evidence indicates that the gains from protecting the environment are often high, and that the costs in forgone income are often modest if appropriate policies are adopted' (World Bank 1992: 1). The gains from 'win–win' opportunities on the one hand, and only modest costs on the other, could, on this analysis, result in both a 3.5 times rise in world output and 'better environmental protection, cleaner air and water, and the virtual elimination of acute poverty' (ibid.: 2). Such quotations illustrate a clear perception of the dominance of sector A and B opportunities, but the World Bank's report ends its Overview with a classic statement envisaging sector C-type costs: 'Accepting the challenge to accelerate development in an environmentally-responsible manner will involve substantial shifts in policies and priorities and will be costly. Failing to accept it will be more costly still' (ibid.: 24).

Whatever the balance of empirical evidence, the mainstream of both optimists and pessimists accept the analysis in Chapter 1 about the potentially disastrous environmental effects of continuing present patterns of economic growth. Both acknowledge that reducing the material intensity or environmental impact of economic activity is possible. In this they both differ from certain fundamentalist Greens, e.g. Irvine (1990). Both moreover argue that this will only happen if proactive governmental policies are put in place. In this they differ from free market economists such as Simon (1981), and Simon and Kahn (1984) and Bernstam (1991).

The need for environmental policy has been put in question by some interpretations of the recent evidence that has been presented that, for some pollutants at least, there is an 'environmental Kuznets curve' for pollution and income, i.e. the relationship between them is on an inverse-U shape, whereby pollution initially increases with rising income, but then reaches a maximum and falls thereafter. Chapter 7 is devoted to an examination of this evidence.

A6 APPENDIX

A6.1 The calculation of the necessary reduction of T in the Commoner-Ehrlich equation on various assumptions

Where subscript 1 indicates the quantity now, subscript 2 indicates the quantity in fifty years' time, superscript H indicates high income countries, superscript L low and middle income countries (the 'Third World'), according to the World Bank's classification and using data from World Bank (1997), and superscript W indicates the whole world, and using the assumptions for population growth and sustainability given earlier, we have:

$I_2^H = I_1^H/2$, $I_2^L = I_1^L/2$ for sustainability

$P_1^W = P_1^H + P_1^L$
$P_2^W = P_2^H + P_2^L = 2 \times P_1^W$;   Population growth $= P_1^W$
(i.e. population is assumed to double)

$P_2^H = P_1^H + 0.05 \times P_1^W$; $P_2^L = P_1^L + 0.95 \times P_1^W$

$P_1^H = 902$ million; $P_1^L = 4771$ million; $P_1^W = 5673$ million

$P_2^H = 1186$ million; $P_2^L = 10160$ million; $P_2^W = 11346$ million

$C_1^H = \$24,930$; $C_1^L = \$1,090$

$P_1^H C_1^H = \$22.49 \times 10^{12}$; $P_1^L C_1^L = \$5.20 \times 10^{12}$; $(P_1 C_1)^W = \$27.69 \times 10^{12}$

$I = (PC)^W.T$
where $(PC)^W = P^H C^H + P^L C^L = $ Total global consumption.

Using this formulation and the earlier assumptions about population and sustainable environmental impact, the environmental implications of five different development paths can be analysed.

1   No growth in population or consumption:

T must be reduced by 50 per cent

Growth in population, and, with regard to consumption

2   No growth in consumption: $C_2{}^H = C_1{}^H$, $C_2{}^L = C_1{}^L$

$P_2{}^H C_2{}^H = 1186 \times 24930 \times 10^6 = \$29.6 \times 10^{12}$
$P_2{}^L C_2{}^L = 10160 \times 1090 \times 10^6 = \$11.1 \times 10^{12}$

$(P_2 C_2)^W = P_2{}^H C_2{}^H + P_2{}^L C_2{}^L = \$40.7 \times 10^{12}$

$$T_2 = 1/2 \times (P_1 C_1)^W / (P_2 C_2)^W \times T_1 = 1/2 \times (27.69)/(40.7) \times T_1$$
$$= 0.35 \times T_1$$

So T must be reduced by 66 per cent

3   Growth only in the South: $C_2{}^H = C_1{}^H$, $C_2{}^L = 4 \times C_1{}^L$

$C_2{}^L = \$4360$

$P_2{}^H C_2{}^H = 1186 \times 24930 \times 10^6 = \$29.6 \times 10^{12}$
$P_2{}^L C_2{}^L = 10160 \times 4360 \times 10^6 = \$44.3 \times 10^{12}$

$(P_2 C_2)^W = P_2{}^H C_2{}^H + P_2{}^L C_2{}^L = \$73.9 \times 10^{12}$

$$T_2 = 1/2 \times (P_1 C_1)^W / (P_2 C_2)^W \times T_1 = 1/2 \times (27.69)/(73.9) \times T_1$$
$$= 0.19 \times T_1$$

So T must be reduced by 81 per cent

4   Growth only in the North: $C_2{}^H = 4 \times C_1{}^H$, $C_2{}^L = C_1{}^L$

$C_2{}^H = \$99720$

$P_2{}^H C_2{}^H = 1186 \times 9720 \times 10^6 = \$118.3 \times 10^{12}$
$P_2{}^L C_2{}^L = 10160 \times 1090 \times 10^6 = \$11.1 \times 10^{12}$

$(P_2 C_2)^W = P_2{}^H C_2{}^H + P_2{}^L C_2{}^L = \$129.4 \times 10^{12}$

$$T_2 = 1/2 \times (P_1 C_1)^W / (P_2 C_2)^W \times T_1 = 1/2 \times (27.69)/(129.4) \times T_1$$
$$= 0.11 \times T_1$$

So T must be reduced by 89 per cent

5   Growth in North and South: $C_2{}^H = 4 \times C_1{}^H$, $C_2{}^L = 4 \times C_1{}^L$

$C_2{}^H = \$99720$; $C_2{}^L = \$4360$

$P_2{}^H C_2{}^H = 1186 \times 99720 \times 10^6 = \$118.3 \times 10^{12}$
$P_2{}^L C_2{}^L = 10160 \times 4360 \times 10^6 = \$44.3 \times 10^{12}$

$(P_2 C_2)^W = P_2{}^H C_2{}^H + P_2{}^L C_2{}^L = \$162.6 \times 10^{12}$

$$T_2 = 1/2 \times (P_1 C_1)^W / (P_2 C_2)^W \times T_1 = 1/2 \times (27.69)/(162.6) \times T_1$$
$$= 0.09 \times T_1$$

So T must be reduced by 91 per cent

7 Review and critique of the Environmental Kuznets curve hypothesis

7.1 INTRODUCTION

There has been a spate of research in the last few years deriving econometric relationships between income and various indicators of environmental quality. As will be seen, a wide variety of results has been obtained, including for some environmental indicators an inverse U-relationship, where environmental degradation is seen to increase at low incomes, reach a peak and then improve as income increases beyond this threshold. This pattern is sometimes described as a 'Kuznets curve', following the observation by Kuznets (1955) that it appeared to describe the relationship between the level of income and income inequality.

The observation of an 'environmental Kuznets curve' (EKC) for some environmental indicators has led to a variety of conclusions from the researchers and others about the overall growth-environment relationship, such as:

> We find that while increases in GDP may be associated with worsening environmental conditions in very poor countries, air and water quality appears to benefit from economic growth once some critical level of income has been reached.
>
> (Grossman and Krueger 1994 (hereafter GK1994): 18–19)

> The evidence suggests that it is possible to 'grow out' of some environmental problems.
>
> (Shafik and Bandyopadhyay 1992 (hereafter SB1992): 23)

> We have found, through an examination of air-quality measures in a cross-section of countries, that economic growth tends to alleviate pollution problems once a country's per capita income reaches about $4,000 to $5,000 US dollars.
>
> (Grossman and Krueger 1991 (hereafter GK1991): 35–6)

> Environmental degradation overall (combined resource depletion and pollution) is worse at levels of income per capita under $1,000. Between

$1,000 and $3,000, both the economy and environmental degradation undergo dramatic structural change from rural to urban, from agricultural to industrial. A second structural transformation begins to take place as countries surpass a per capita income of $10,000 and begin to shift from energy intensive heavy industry into services and information-technology intensive industry.

(Panayotou 1993 (hereafter P1993): 14)

The inverted U-shape is consistent with a scenario in which industrial development initially leads to greater raw emissions of these pollutants, but net emissions eventually decline as the increase in income associated with further development raises the demand for health and environmental quality. . . . [This literature] raises the tantalizing possibility that instead of there being a *trade-off* between greenhouse gases and economic growth, faster growth could serve as part of the *solution* to the worldwide emissions dilemma.

(Holtz-Eakin and Selden 1992 (hereafter HES
1992): 3 (original emphasis))

Growth promoting liberalization of trade will often lead to improved environmental standards.

(Radetzki 1992: 134)

These are strong conclusions. They create the impression that economic growth and the environment are not only not in conflict – the former is necessary to improve the latter. They invite an emphasis on achieving economic growth rather than on environmental policy, because the former is perceived to be able to achieve both economic and environmental objectives, while the latter may impede the former. This turns the 'limits to growth' argument on its head. Instead of the environment setting limits to growth, these conclusions suggest that growth is a requirement of environmental improvement. And these conclusions apply especially for rich countries which have already gone over the hump of the inverted-U because for them growth seems to promise environmental improvement all the way.

P1993 gives the most unequivocal expression to the conclusions that can be drawn from a general acceptance of an EKC relationship between growth and environmental quality:

It suggests that as the development process picks up, when a certain level of income per capita is reached, economic growth turns from an enemy of the environment into a friend . . . Economic growth appears to be a powerful way for improving environmental quality in developing countries . . . If economic growth is good for the environment then policies that stimulate growth such as trade liberalization, economic restructuring and price reform ought also to be good for the environment. This in turn would tend to suggest that the environment needs no particular attention, either in terms of domestic environmental policy or international pressure or assistance; resources can best be focused on achieving rapid economic growth to move quickly through the environmentally unfavourable stage of development to the environmentally favourable range of the Kuznets curve.

(P1993: 14)

It is important to stress that Panayotou himself warns that there are other reasons why such a policy may not be optimal, nor do the other researchers who derived EKC results tend to push their conclusions as far as this. The papers also include caveats and qualifications, as will be seen. But the fact that these studies can be used to support the kinds of interpretations as that of P1993 above, with profound implications for environmental policy making, suggests that their results need to be subjected to careful comparative evaluation. This is the purpose of this chapter.

The next section summarises and compares the relationships between certain environmental indicators and levels of income which have been suggested by econometric estimation. It finds that the evidence for an EKC, even for any single environmental indicator, is inconclusive, and certainly cannot be generalised across environmental quality as a whole. Section 7.3 examines the robustness of the estimations. Several contradictions between the different studies are identified and discussed. Section 7.4 moves on to see whether other sources of environmental data suggest an EKC relationship, particularly with regard to whether the overall environmental quality of richer countries is now improving as the EKC hypothesis would suggest. Neither OECD nor European Commission data offer support for a general EKC hypothesis. Nor does a dataset that aggregates twelve environmental indicators for twenty-two OECD countries. Section 7.5 explores some of the underlying determinants of the income–environment relationship, distinguishing between scale, composition and technique effects. While it is clearly theoretically possible for the composition and technique effects positively to outweigh the negative effect of the scale effect on environmental quality, there is no evidence that this is a systematic occurrence or that the level of income is an especially relevant variable in this regard. Section 7.6 considers the implications of such EKC relationships as have been derived continuing into the future. Because of the skewed nature of the global population distribution towards low incomes, the continuance of these relationships would cause massive further environmental damage through the first decades of the twenty-first century that is clearly incompatible with the objective of sustainable development. Section 7.7 concludes.

7.2 THE ECONOMETRIC RELATIONSHIPS

The studies have generally estimated an equation of the following general form:

$$f(E_{it}) = \alpha_0 + \alpha_1 g_1(Y_{it}) + \alpha_2 g_2(Y^2_{it}) + \alpha_3 g_3(Y^3_{it}) + \alpha_4 g_4(Y^n_{it-a})$$
$$+ \beta.B + \gamma t + \varepsilon_{it}$$

where E_{it} is an environmental indicator for country i at time t; α, β, γ are the parameters to be estimated; Y_{it} is the per capita income of country i at time t, with Y_{it-a}^n being some polynomial of lagged income; B is a vector of other explanatory variables, possibly including dummies to capture specific influences of demography, geography or particular years; and f(.), g(.) are functional forms which are predominantly, but not exclusively, logarithmic or linear.

If $\alpha_3 \neq 0$, then the equation is cubic in income; if $\alpha_3 = 0$, $\alpha_2 \neq 0$, then the equation is quadratic; if $\alpha_3 = \alpha_2 = 0$ and $\alpha_1 \neq 0$, then the equation is linear. The overall shape of the curve generated by the relationship will depend on the signs and relative values of α_1, α_2, α_3. The shapes that have been generated by the studies are given in Figure 7.1 a–f, where:

a   linear, downward sloping: $\alpha_1 < 0$, $\alpha_2 = \alpha_3 = 0$
b   linear, upward sloping: $\alpha_1 > 0$, $\alpha_2 = \alpha_3 = 0$
c   quadratic, inverted U: $\alpha_1 > 0$, $\alpha_2 < 0$, $\alpha_3 = 0$; $|\alpha_2| << |\alpha_1|$
d   quadratic, normal U: $\alpha_1 < 0$, $\alpha_2 > 0$, $\alpha_3 = 0$; $|\alpha_2| << |\alpha_1|$
e   cubic: $\alpha_1 > 0$, $\alpha_2 < 0$, $\alpha_3 > 0$; $|\alpha_3| << |\alpha_2| << |\alpha_1|$
f   cubic: $\alpha_1 < 0$, $\alpha_2 > 0$, $\alpha_3 < 0$; $|\alpha_3| << |\alpha_2| << |\alpha_1|$

In Figures 7.1 c, d, e, f, TP marks the turning-point per capita income(s).

Table 7.A1 in the Appendix gives the results of the main econometric studies of the relationship between environmental quality and income that had appeared up to 1996. Table 7.1 abstracts the main results, focusing on environmental indicators that have been the subject of investigation by more than one researcher or group of researchers, grouping the results by pollutant, which is how they will now be discussed. Before doing so, it may be noted that some of the econometrics involved in the estimations is quite complex. In the discussion that follows technical terms have been used only when necessary, but without explanation, to avoid much detailed exposition. The general reader may pass over these terms without fear of not understanding the main thrust of the argument.

The most studied pollutant is SO_2, for which three of the results show an unambiguous inverse-U (c shape) relationship. The Grossman (hereafter G) and Grossman and Krueger (hereafter GK) results show a cubic relationship, with SO_2 urban concentrations starting to increase again at high incomes, but the researchers tend to discount this because 'the

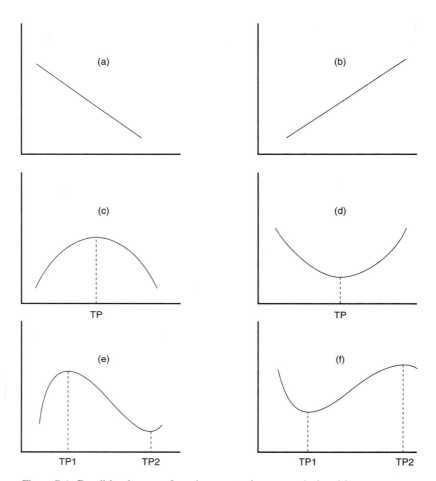

Figure 7.1 Possible shapes of environment–income relationships

relatively small numbers of observations for sites with incomes above $16,000 means that we cannot have much confidence in the shape of the curve in this range' (GK1994: 14). The studies estimate widely differing incomes on the downward turning point, ranging from $3,000 (P1993) to about $4,000 (SB1992; GK1991, 1994), through about $9,000 (Seldon and Song 1994 (hereafter SS1994)) to over $13,000 (Grossman 1993 (hereafter G1993)). The P(Panayotou) and SS estimates have *emissions per capita* as the dependent variable; SB/GK use urban *concentrations*. Several possible reasons have been given for the SS emissions turning points being higher than the SB/GK concentrations turning points. Urban incomes may be higher than the average national incomes used in the SB/GK studies, so that the estimated SB/GK turning points may be downward-biased; urban concentrations may give rise to stronger pressure for political action than general emissions, because urban pollution affects large populations, while urban residents, with greater than average incomes, are likely to have greater than average political power; and urban air quality can be improved more cheaply (e.g. by building tall chimneys or relocating urban power plants) than reducing emissions. However, environmental damage, as opposed to damage to human health, is more likely to be related to aggregate emissions than urban concentrations, so that insofar as such damage is the object of concern, the SS estimates are the most relevant. Even higher than the SS turning point is that of the G1993 (20) study comparing SO_2 concentrations across different counties in the US. The turning point is more than $13,000. This result is simply inconsistent with that of SB/GK, from which one would have expected monotonically decreasing SO_2 concentrations throughout the income range in G1993 (> $5,000). G1993 also estimates a cubic upturn at incomes greater than $24,000 but makes no comment as to the significance of this. Finally, one may note in passing that, using cross-sectional estimators, like P1993, SS generated opposite results for all their pollutants (i.e. d as opposed to c shaped curves, see row 53 of Table 7.A1), which they dismiss as 'inefficient at best' (SS1994: 151). This point is discussed further below.

The relationship between suspended particulates, including dark matter, and income has also been extensively studied. The results of P, SB, SS and G1993 are similar to those for SO_2 (except that the G1993 relationship is now quadratic, not cubic), with an even greater range of downward turning points, so that the earlier comments apply more forcefully. P regards his result as 'clearly unsatisfactory' (P1993: 12) in that the regression only explains 12 per cent of the differences in SPM emissions (see the R^2 figure in Table 7.A1). The GK1991 results are contradictory, in that a random effects model shows particulates monotonically decreasing with income (shape a), while a fixed effects model shows them monotonically increasing (shape b). GK1991 presents this outcome (GK 1991: 19) without comment or explanation. Differences between countries that might be correlated with the explanatory variables suggest a fixed effects model, and indeed SS (1994: 151) find in their study that their test statistics mostly 'argue in favour of fixed effects estimation'. This seems to add weight to the GK1991 result of monotonic increase. The suspended particulates data include the dark matter that is separated out in the GK and G1993 studies, all of which show a cubic relationship between dark matter and income, with an upward turning point around $10,000 (except GK1994), considerably lower than in the SO_2 case, but neither GK nor G say whether it is subject to the same caveat as the SO_2 result.

Both $NO_{2,x}$ and CO show the inverted-U shape in the studies conducted for those pollutants but with turning points at relatively high levels of income, compared to the air pollutants so far discussed. CO_2 shows a monotonic increase in the SB study and a nominal inverted-U in the HES study,

Table 7.1 Environment–income relationships for different indicators from different studies

Medium	Pollutant	Study (row[1])	Shape[2]	Turning point(s)[3], $	
Air	SO_2	GK1991 (1)	e	1	4,100
				2	14,000
		GK1991 (4)	e	1	~4,300
				2	n.a.
		SB1992 (12)	c		3,700
		G1993 (17)	e	1	4,100
				2	14,000
		G1993 (20)	e	1	13,400
				2	24,000
		GK1994 (35)	e	1	4,100
				2	14,000
		SS1994 (49)	c	1	8,900[4]
				2	10,700
		P1993 (58)	c		3,000
	Suspended particles	GK1991 (3)	a		n.a.
		GK1991 (6)	b		n.a.
		SB1992 (13)	c		3,300
		G1993 (19)	c		16,000
		GK1994 (37)	a		n.a.
		SS1994 (50)	c	1	9,800
				2	9,600
		P1993 (60)	c		4,500
	Dark matter (smoke)	GK1991 (2)	e	1	5,000
				2	10,000
		GK1991 (5)	e	1	~4,000
				2	10,500
		G1993 (18)	e	1	4,700
				2	10,000
		GK1994 (36)	e	1	6,200
				2	n.a.
	$NO_{2,x}$	G1993 (23)	c		18,500
		SS1994 (51)	c	1	12,000
				2	21,800
		P1993 (59)	c		5,500
	CO	G1993 (22)	c		22,800
		SS1994 (52)	c	1	6,200
				2	19,100
	CO_2 (or C)	SB1992 (15)	b		n.a.
		HES1992 (54)	1. c		35,400
			2. c		> 8 mill.
Water	Clean water	SB1992 (7)	a		n.a.
	Sanitation	SB1992 (8)	a		n.a.
	Dissolved oxygen	SB1992 (10)	a[5]		n.a.
		G1993 (31)	d[6]		8,500
		GK1994 (38)	d[6]		2,703
	Fecal coliform	SB1992 (11)	e	1	1,400

Table 7.1 (continued)

Medium	Pollutant	Study (row[1])	Shape[2]	Turning point(s)[3]	
				2	11,400
		G1993 (24)	c		8,500
		GK1994 (42)	c		8,000
	Total coliform	G1993 (25)	e		no downturn[7]
		GK1994 (43)	e	1	3,043
				2	8,000
Land	Deforestation	SB1992 (9)	insig.[8]		n.a.
		CG1994 (55)	1. c[9]		4,760
			2. c		5,420
			3. insig		n.a.
		P1993 (61)	1. c[10]		823
			2. c		1,200

Key to studies:
CG   Cropper and Griffiths   G Grossman   GK Grossman and Krueger
HES Holtz-Eakin and Selden   P Panayotou   SB   Shafik and Bandyopadhyay
SS   Selden and Song

Notes:
1   The row number refers to that in the full Table 7.A1 in the Appendix
2   The shape letter refers to those identified in Figure 7.1
3   The turning points are as identified in the relevant shape in Figure 7.1
4   The turning points given from the SS study are those for both the fixed effect (1) and
      random effect estimations (2)
5   Because this is an indicator of environmental quality rather than degradation, this shape
      indicates continually *worsening* environmental quality with income
6   Because this is an indicator of environmental quality rather than degradation, this shape
      indicates *improving* environmental quality after the turning point income
7   The cubic function is continuously rising in income
8   'None of the income terms is significant in any specification' (SB 1992: 7)
9   The three results in this row are for Africa (1), Latin America (2) and Asia (3)
10 The two results refer to two regressions on different samples, one containing forty-one
      developing countries only (1), the other adding twenty-seven developed countries to
      these (2)

but with a turning point at such high incomes that it is projected to increase
for many years.

The HES study is worth analysing in a little more detail, because it
shows many of the difficulties of interpretation, and inconsistency of result,
that are characteristic of these environment-income estimations. HES estimate equations in both levels and logs that are quadratic and cubic in
income, of the general form:

$$E_{it} = a_0 + a_1 Y_{it} + a_2 Y_{it}^2 + a_3 Y_{it}^3 + g_t + f_i + e_{it} \qquad \text{(levels)}$$

$$E_{it} = b_0 + b_1 \ln Y_{it} + b_2 (\ln Y_{it})^2 + b_3 (\ln Y_{it})^3 + g_t + f_i + e_{it} \quad \text{(logs)}$$

where E_{it}, Y_{it} are CO_2 emissions and income respectively, both per
capita, for country i at time t, g and f are fixed year and country effects,

a and b are to be estimated and e are the residuals. For the quadratic estimations, a_3 and b_3 are set to zero.

The four equations estimated have the following general properties (see HES1992: 27 (Table 2)):

1   Quadratic levels: shape c, the inverted U, with downward TP at $35,428.
2   Cubic levels: shape e, with upward TP at $28,010.
3   'Quadratic' logs: in fact the quadratic term in this estimation was insignificantly differently from zero at the 10 per cent level, while the linear term was highly significant, implying a monotonically increasing slope b. However, HES retain the quadratic term despite its insignificance, which yields an inverted-U shape c, with a downward TP at above $8 million.
4   Cubic logs: shape e, with downward TP at $13,594.

It is not at all clear what interpretation should be given to this wide range of results. In HES' subsequent analysis, they determinedly focus on the quadratic equations, despite the insignificance of one of the quadratic parameters, as noted above. They reject both the linear interpretation of equation 3, because 'the nature of the modeling exercise argues against imposing monotonicity' (HES1992: 11), and the two cubic estimates, despite the significance of both cubic parameters at the 1 per cent level, on the grounds that they have 'unattractive out-of-sample properties, and because they contribute so little to the explanatory power of the regression' (HES1992: 12). The 'unattractive properties' are the upturn in equation 2 (at a lower income than the downturn in equation 1). It might also be noted that the equation 4 result is belied by the fact that in 1990 no country with an average per capita income above $13,000 had a trend of decreasing CO_2 emissions (had this trend been established, there would have been little point in the UNCED Climate Change Convention setting as a target for industrial countries the return of emissions to 1990 levels by the year 2000).

HES' choice of the quadratic estimates and their interpretation of these as inverted-Us would therefore seem to derive more from their prior judgement as to plausibility than from the econometric results, which are indeterminate. The quadratic results show that 'global emissions of CO_2 will continue to grow at an annual rate of 1.8 per cent' (HES1992: 22) and, while poorer countries have a higher marginal propensity to emit, even the richest countries will continue to increase their CO_2 emissions until their per capita income is nearly double its present level. In anything but the very long term, therefore, CO_2 emissions are forecast by HES to be monotonically increasing with income, as with the SB results. This is also consistent with Horvath's (1997) finding for a sample of 114 countries that per capita energy use increases with per capita income.

The results for water pollutants are no clearer than for air pollutants. The first two SB indicators are not strictly of environmental quality, but of households which lack basic services (clean water, sanitation). It is not surprising that this lack diminishes monotonically with income, as SB find. With regard to water quality as indicated by the amount of dissolved oxygen, the results are contradictory, with SB finding it monotonically decreasing, and GK and G1993 increasing after the turning point, with income. With fecal coliform, SB found a cubic relationship, and G1993 and GK an inverted U. Shafik (1994), reporting the SB result, is categoric that the cubic relationship (unlike that of GK1994 for SO_2) is robust:

> The cubic shape of fecal content is not an artifact of the functional form. The increase in fecal pollution which occurs at incomes above $11,500 *per capita* is based on 38 observations from seven rivers in three countries (Australia, Japan and the United States). This cubic relationship held even after some extremely high observations of fecal content were dropped from the sample.
>
> (Shafik 1994: 765)

The SB upturn in fecal pollution occurs at income levels not much higher than the level at which G1993 and GK found such pollution to be falling. The studies of total coliform do nothing to clarify this picture. G1993 finds that, despite the overall cubic relationship, 'the concentrations of total coliform in the sample of rivers rise with national income over the entire range of incomes (up to $12,209) found in our sample' (G1993: 22); GK1994 also derive a cubic relationship which they find 'rather baffling' (GK1994: 16), but which quite closely resembles SB's result for fecal coliform (but with an upturn at even lower incomes), an explanation for which is given on pp. 200–1.

The only land-related environmental degradation studies by more than one group of researchers is deforestation. P finds an inverse-U relationship with a turning point at relatively low per capita incomes (approx. $1,000). CG find an inverse-U relationship for deforestation in Africa and Latin America, with turning points around $5,000, but no significant relationship for Asia. SB find that for their estimates of both annual deforestation (sixty-six countries) and total deforestation (seventy-seven countries), 'none of the income terms are significant in any specification' (SB1992: 7; Shafik 1994: 761). Shafik (1994: 765) further concludes: 'This is fairly consistent with other attempts to estimate the causes of deforestation, which find little role for *per capita* incomes and a significant role for agricultural settlement and timber use.' The P and CG results cannot, therefore, be considered conclusive.

The results for other pollutants are reported in G1993 and GK1994 and, for municipal waste, SB1992 (see Table 7.A1 in the Appendix). Biological and chemical oxygen demand (BOD, COD) and nitrates all show inverse-U relationships with downward TPs of \$8–10,000 (ignoring the initial section of the G1993 nitrates result). Most of the rest of the pollutants (airborne lead, arsenic, mercury in one study) show cubic relationships with pollution rising, falling and then rising again at the highest incomes. Waterborne lead has the other cubic shape (falling, rising and then falling at the highest incomes), as do nickel and cadmium in one study, although the relationships for nickel (and mercury) are insignificant, and cadmium decreases monotonically with income, in other studies. Municipal waste rises monotonically with income.

Also listed in Table 7.A1 is the study by Lucas *et al.* (1992), also reported in Hettige *et al.* 1992 (rows 56, 57). This suggests that while there may be an EKC for the toxic intensity of GDP, there is not one for the toxic intensity of manufacturing. That is, income grows with two structural implications: non-manufacturing output (assumed non-toxic) after a certain level of income grows faster than manufacturing output, so that GDP's overall toxic intensity falls; but the toxic intensity of the manufacturing sector *increases* with income; a shift occurs within manufacturing towards more toxic industries. An implication of this is that there is no EKC for toxic pollution; because manufacturing output increases with total output (albeit at a slower rate), so does the absolute amount of pollution generated. Absolute levels of pollution do not fall but go on rising with GDP at the highest incomes.

Turning briefly to the other columns of Table 7.A1, it can be seen that the time trends on the pollutants, where reported, show no clear pattern, being variously positive, negative or insignificant; and the R^2 values are sometimes rather low, e.g. rows 1, 2, 7, 8, 57, 58, 59; indicating the influence of factors unspecified by the equation.

From these results of econometric estimations of the relationship between income and various measures of environmental quality, the main conclusion is that none of the pollutants unequivocally shows an inverse-U relationship where studies have been done by more than one group of researchers. $NO_{2,x}$ and CO do if SS's cross-sectional estimates are ignored. SO_2 does if, in addition, the cubic upward-turning tails of the G1993 and GK estimations are discounted. Suspended particles and dark matter do if, in addition, the GK1991 fixed effects estimation is ignored. Indicators of water quality generally show contradictory results. CO_2 is monotonically increasing over relevant incomes if the HES cubic equations are ignored.

Shafik (1994: 769) concluded from the SB results: 'Some very clear patterns of environmental degradation emerge from the previous analysis.' This is definitely not the case when all the available studies are examined together, as above. More specifically, it is not possible to conclude from these results that an inverse-U relationship exists between income and pollution or other kinds of environmental degradation. Rather it can be concluded in aggregate that the studies so far conducted fail clearly to show such a relationship. As a generally applicable notion, the 'environmental Kuznets curve' (EKC) hypothesis can be deemed invalid.

7.3 THE ROBUSTNESS OF THE RELATIONSHIPS

The first consideration in assessing the robustness of the estimations is the reliability of the data used. The GK studies use data from the Global Environmental Monitoring System of the World Health Organisation and United Nations Environment Programme, which measure concentrations of pollutants in selected cities and rivers over time. 'Multiple sites in the same city are monitored in recognition of the fact that pollutant concentrations can vary dramatically with local conditions that depend in part on land use' (GK1991: 9). G1993 cautions: 'Despite the intentions of the GEMS organisation, there may be reasons to suspect the representativeness of these data' (G1993: 7). SS use GEMS data on countries' aggregate emissions, constructed from estimates of fuel use, commenting: 'It is likely that emissions are measured only imperfectly and that measurement errors for a given country persist across time' (SS1994: 150). SB1992 uses data from a number of different sources, concerning which Shafik (1994: 757) notes: 'The data on environmental quality are patchy at best ... Comparability across countries is affected by definitional differences and by inaccuracies and unrepresentative measurement sites.' He also notes (ibid.: 761) that 'there are a number of serious controversies concerning the data on deforestation', which has implications for the Cropper and Griffiths (CG1994) and P1993 studies.

These data considerations obviously counsel caution against too much faith in the detailed quantitative results of the estimation exercises, such as the turning points. For example, it is unlikely that the data are robust enough to support GK's conclusion (GK1991: 19–20) that environmental measures taken by Mexico in the run-up to the NAFTA agreement were due to Mexico having reached the 'critical juncture' (ibid.: 35–6) of $4–5,000 per capita income. One might conjecture, from a political economy perspective, that it is rather more likely that the timing and extent of these measures reflected President Salinas' desire to achieve a NAFTA agreement in the face of intense opposition from US environmentalists.

However, there is little indication that the data problems are serious enough to cast doubt on the basic environment/income relationship for any particular environmental indicator, but the results in fact suggest that this might be the case. Can the opposite relationship given by SS's cross-sectional estimators to those derived from their panel data really be dismissed on the grounds that the former estimators are 'inefficient at best'? If so, what are the implications for P1993's cross-section results showing EKCs (discussed further below)? One might expect inefficiency of this kind to yield instability or inconsistency but not to generate systematically opposite results to the panel estimations. This indicates that something may be more fundamentally awry and casts considerable doubt on the inverse-U relationships to which SS and others have given some significance.

Similarly the opposite results for suspended particulates that emerge from different estimations in GK1991; and the contradiction between the SB1992 and G1993/GK1994 results for dissolved oxygen suggest that serious uncertainties remain about the basic shapes of the relationships and not just about the quantitative details. The point is reinforced by experiments by Stern *et al.* (1994) in which they regress income against two sets of data for per capita energy consumption, one from UNDP, the other from the World Bank. Using purchasing power parity income, the UNDP figures show an inverse-U relationship, those from the World Bank a linearly increasing relationship. They conclude:

> The most interesting thing about these regressions is that they demonstrate the sensitivity of the results to the data sources. For income reported in purchasing power parity dollars, UN data can be represented as an EKC type relationship, whereas World Bank data cannot.
>
> (Stern *et al.* 1994: 7)

The other aspect of robustness of the estimates concerns the econometrics. Clearly the potential pathways of influence between economic growth and the environment are many and various and act in either direction. Stern *et al.* (1994: 3) consider that this bidirectionality of influence means that 'economy and environment are jointly determined ... so that it is inappropriate to estimate a single equation model where there is unidirectional causality from income to environment'. Were the estimations seeking to establish structural relationships, this criticism would be telling. However, the studies are explicit (see, for example, HES1992: 2; G1993: 10; GK1994: 9; SS1994: 149) that they are using a reduced form approach in order to capture all the direct and indirect effects of the income-environment relationship. This seems fair enough as long as the full implications of the procedure are borne in mind. As HES say: 'Our approach carries a cost as well: reduced forms are not well-suited for policy analysis' (HES1992: 2). GK are even more forthright: 'A limitation of the reduced form approach, however, is that it is unclear why the estimated relationship between pollution and income exists' (GK1994: 9).

Stern *et al.* (1996) made a number of other criticisms about the econometric techniques used in the studies described here. In a subsequent review of as yet unpublished work, Stern (1997) considers that the econometrics employed has improved, but, as noted below, this does nothing to validate the EKC hypothesis.

One of the clearest contradictions to emerge from the studies is that between P1993's cross-section estimates of the air pollution/income relationship for SO_2, NO_x and SPM and the SS cross-section estimates of the same variables. P finds the relationship categorically inverse-U shaped; SS find an opposite, U-shaped, relationship. The econometrics of SS is meticulous; that of P is rough and ready (no alternative functional forms are tested; no tests for mis-specification or bias are reported). On the basis of their analysis, SS dismiss cross-sectional estimators as 'inefficient at best', as we have seen. If this is so, then it casts doubt on the reliability of the P results. If it is not so, then the contradiction between these results becomes more difficult to explain.

7.4 OTHER ENVIRONMENTAL EVIDENCE

If the inverse-U relationship between income and environmental quality is generally valid, and if high income countries are already over the hump, then one would expect widespread overall improvements in rich country environments to have taken place in recent years. Conversely, if the EKC relationship is generally invalid, or the hump is projected to lie at still higher incomes than those yet achieved by rich countries, as in the quadratic estimates of HES1992, then continuing income growth may be expected to lead to continuing environmental degradation.

Both the OECD and the European Commission have produced in the early 1990s detailed surveys of the state of their member-countries' environments (OECD 1991a; CEC 1992c). These surveys present a wide variety of environmental data, on the basis of which conclusions are drawn, which are reported here.

In its Conclusions on the State of the Environment, the OECD acknowledges that 'OECD countries have made progress in dealing with a number of the most urgent environmental problems identified over the last two decades' (OECD 1991a: 283) and lists specific achievements in reducing some kinds of air and water pollution and toxic chemical release, and in increasing nominally protected areas and the afforested area. However, the report then both identifies substantial 'remaining problems from the *unfinished agendas* of the 1970s or 1980s' (ibid.: 284–6), across all areas of environmental concern, and points to the emergence of new problems, both from a 'change in substances of concern' (ibid.: 287) and the emergence of new sectors and industries 'with new kinds and degrees of pollution problems' (ibid.: 288). In general, 'In the 1990s OECD countries will thus have to face more intractable problems than those solved in previous decades' (ibid.: 287). A later assessment of the OECD environment overall from the OECD's Environment Director confirmed that one of the reasons for the 'sea change' in the willingness of OECD countries to confront the challenge of consumption-production head-on' was: 'The continued growth of environmental problems and associated risks to human health and natural ecosystems – despite heavy investments by OECD nations in counter measures over three decades' (Long 1994: 159). While OECD

(1995a) does not draw such conclusions from the data it presents, its message is very much the same.

The CEC report measures the state of the European environment across seven dimensions: air, water, soil, waste, quality of life, high-risk activities and biological diversity. The relevant indicators cannot be presented here in detail, but the conclusions will be summarised (all quotations are from CEC 1992c, page numbers as given):

1   'Some progress has been made towards reducing emissions of sulphur dioxide, suspended particulates, lead and CFCs at the Community level. But serious problems persist or are beginning to strongly emerge, particularly with the greenhouse gases such as carbon dioxide, oxides of nitrogen, atmospheric ozone and methane' (p. 10).
2   'Despite the investments made over the last twenty years or so, generally, the state of the Community's water resources has not improved. The situation varies ... but there are far more examples of deterioration in quality than of improvement' (p. 19).
3   'Physical degradation of the soil is widespread throughout the Community. . . . [I]t is becoming increasingly difficult for it to perform its many vital functions ... An increase in the pollutant content has been observed at many sites' (p. 30).
4   'The volume of waste generated is increasing far faster than treatment and disposal capacity. . . . The dangers for man and the environment are increasing' (p. 36).
5   Quality of life is forecast to come under further pressure due to the twin trends of urbanisation and rural deterioration (p. 40).
6   With regard to high-risk activities, no areas of risk reduction are identified, while several industries and activities are highlighted as posing 'new risks' (p. 44).
7   'Without substantial reinforcement of existing measures and of the steps taken to implement them, the already severe depletion of the biological heritage will continue in most of the Community' (p. 47).

More recently, the largest ever assessment of the European environment concluded that 'human activity ... must now be regarded as a significant perturbation of the critical biogeochemical cycles of the planet' (EEA 1995: 10) and concludes that there are continuing, and in some cases increasing, environmental problems in Europe across a range of issues, including urban air quality, abstraction and nitrate pollution of freshwater, coastal zone pollution, soil erosion, habitat loss and municipal waste (EEA 1995: 601ff.).

These messages, based on official statistics of the richest countries' environmental quality, seem almost completely to negate the EKC hypothesis. Despite improvements in some indicators, notably of some air pollutants, these countries seem to be experiencing continuing, serious environmental degradation on all fronts. Part of the inconsistency between these state-of-the-environment reviews and the conclusions of the EKC studies is explained by the fact that the most convincing evidence of EKC has tended to come from the few indicators that have improved. Another part would seem to lie in the fact that environmental problems and pressures change over time and the EKC studies have noted some improvements in past pollutants without picking up more recent concerns. What the wider environmental assessments indicate is the complete lack of justification of conclusions that seek to use the improvements that have occurred to argue that there is as yet any correlation between income growth and increasing environmental quality overall.

Further evidence for this conclusion is derived from examination of an environmental performance measure for twenty-two OECD countries, calculated by MacGillivray (1993), using OECD data. This measure comprised an aggregation of twelve different environmental indicators:

1 CO_2, SO_2, NO_x (all emissions per capita).
2 Water abstraction per capita.
3 Percentage of population with sewage treatment.
4 Protected areas as a percentage of total land area.
5 Imports of tropical timber and cork.
6 Threatened species of mammals and birds as a percentage of all such species in the country.
7 The generation of municipal solid waste per capita.
8 Energy intensity (primary energy per unit of GDP).
9 Private road transport (passenger kms in private vehicles per capita).
10 Nitrate fertilizer application per km^2 of arable land and permanent cropland.

The procedure adopted for each indicator was to give a score of 100 to the country with the least (B), and 0 to the country with the most (W), environmental impact according to that indicator. Other countries were then scored according to how close they were to the two extremes, as per the formula:

$$S_{i,j} = 100 - 100 * (I_{i,j} - I_{B,j}) / (I_{W,j} - I_{B,j})$$

where S is the score, i is the country, j is the indicator, I is the indicator performance and W, B are the worst and best performance for any indicator. The scores were then totalled across all the indicators, to give a score of total points for each country:

$$S_{T,i} = \sum_{j}^{12} S_{j,i}$$

This total score can then be expressed as a percentage of the possible score (1,200 for twelve indicators) and the countries ranked according to their overall performance.

Of the indicators selected only number 3 could clearly be expected to improve monotonically with income growth (as per the SB1992 result). The others could all go either way as incomes increase, and so the indicator set as a whole provides a reasonable test of the EKC hypothesis.

Table 7.2 gives the total points scores for the 22 countries, for two sets of 11 and 12 indicators, as well as the rankings for these sets. Figure 7.2 plots the total scores against the countries' incomes. No strong relationship between the environmental performance and income is discernible. If anything, the environmental performance in both cases seems to drift

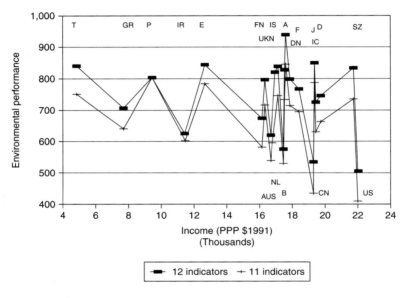

Figure 7.2 Relationship between income and environmental performance for twenty-two OECD countries

Note: The letters are located roughly above or below their respective points, from which the points can be identified according to the following key:

T	Turkey	GR	Greece
P	Portugal	IR	Ireland
E	Spain	FN	Finland
UK	United Kingdom	AUS	Australia
NL	Netherlands	I	Italy
N	Norway	S	Sweden
B	Belgium	A	Austria
DN	Denmark	F	France
CN	Canada	J	Japan
IC	Iceland	D	Germany
SZ	Switzerland	US	United States of America

Table 7.2 Income and environmental performance

	Twelve indicators		Eleven indicators	Twelve indicators			Eleven indicators		
Country	Environmental performance Total points	GDP pc 1991 PPP $I	Environmental performance Total points[a]	Rank	Country	Score,[b] %	Rank	Country	Score, %
Turkey	843.9	4840	753.8	1	Austria	78.5	1	Austria	77.0
Greece	706.0	7680	642.6	2	Japan	71.0	2	Portugal	73.2
Portugal	805.5	9450	805.5	3	Spain	70.6	3	Japan	71.8
Ireland	627.1	11430	603.7	4	Turkey	70.3	4	Spain	71.4
Spain	847.1	12670	785.5	5	Norway	70.2	5	Turkey	68.5
Finland	678.3	16130	583.2	6	Switzerland	69.7	6	Norway	68.4
UK	800.5	16340	718.5	7	Sweden	69.5	7	Italy	68.3
Australia	619.8	16680	541.7	8	Italy	68.7	8	Switzerland	67.1
Netherlands	619.1	16820	596.8	9	Portugal	67.1	9	Sweden	67.0
Italy	824.7	17040	751.7	10	Denmark	67.0	10	UK	65.3
Norway	842.8	17170	752.3	11	UK	66.7	11	Denmark	65.2
Sweden	834.2	17490	736.5	12	France	64.3	12	France	63.4
Belgium	580.3	17510	533.2	13	Germany	62.5	13	Germany	60.5
Austria	941.9	17690	847.5	14	Iceland	60.9	14	Greece	58.4
Denmark	804.2	17880	717.7	15	Greece	58.8	15	Iceland	57.5
France	771.8	18430	696.9	16	Finland	56.5	16	Ireland	54.9
Canada	536.7	19320	436.7	17	Ireland	52.3	17	Netherlands	54.3
Japan	852.6	19390	789.9	18	Australia	51.6	18	Finland	53.0
Iceland	730.7	19529[c]	632.8	19	Netherlands	51.6	19	Australia	49.2
Germany	750.0	19770	665.2	20	Belgium	48.4	20	Belgium	48.5
Switzerland	836.5	21780	737.6	21	Canada	44.7	21	Canada	39.7
USA	507.6	22130	408.7	22	USA	42.3	22	USA	37.2

Sources: The environmental performance indicators come from a data set supplied by Alex MacGillivray (1993). The results here differ slightly because MacGillivray (1993) reported for eleven indicators and excluded Iceland. The GDP data are the Purchasing Power Parity figures given in WRI (1994: 256–7 (Table 15)), with the exception of Iceland

Notes:
a The indicator omitted from this column is imports of tropical timber and cork
b This is the percentage of the total points obtained out of 1,200 (twelve indicators) or 1,100 (eleven indicators)
c The GDP figure for Iceland, absent from WRI (1994), comes from Summers and Heston (1991), scaled up in the same proportion as Denmark

downwards with income, but this movement is unlikely to be statistically significant (some initial linear regressions confirmed this impression of a statistically insignificant downward drift). Certainly there is no support in this dataset for an EKC relationship.

In addition to the direct evidence of continuing environmental deterioration in rich countries, further doubt on the EKC hypothesis has been cast by a paper by De Bruyn and Opschoor (1997). They investigated and extended work by Jänicke *et al.* (1989, 1993) which had suggested that a kind of EKC applied to the energy and material intensity of economies. Specifically Jänicke *et al.* constructed an aggregate environmental index (EI) for thirty-one COMECON and OECD countries for 1970 and 1985, based on data for environmentally intensive activities (consumption of energy and steel, production of cement, weight of freight transport). They found that for some of the richer countries the EI improved absolutely over the period considered; for other of the richer countries the EI improved relatively to GDP (i.e. the environmental impact per unit of GDP decreased); while for the poorer countries the EI increased, both absolutely and relative to GDP. They interpreted these changes as evidence of structural economic change brought about by the process of economic development (rather than by government policy, a distinction discussed further below), from which they infer an endogenous 'delinking' between economic growth and environmental impact. The similarity of this conclusion to that of the EKC studies discussed earlier is obvious.

De Bruyn and Opschoor (1997) question several aspects of Jänicke *et al.*'s analysis and therefore their conclusions but, more relevant here, they extend the time interval considered and divide it into four periods: 1966–72 (pre-oil shock), 1972–8 (post-first oil shock); 1978–84 (recession post-second oil shock), 1984–90 (strong economic growth in western countries). During the first three periods there was, for most OECD countries, a pronounced tendency for environmental impact to diminish relative to GDP and, for several countries, to decrease absolutely. However, during the fourth period for most of the countries the environmental intensity of GDP either stayed nearly constant or increased. De Bruyn and Opschoor conclude:

> There are strong reasons to believe that [the trend of developed economies to 'delink'] is coming to an end and that we may now enter a phase of relinking, at least as far as materials inputs are concerned. The levels of aggregate materials consumption through time may show an 'N-shape' rather than an inverted-U curve, with several Western European countries now finding their aggregate material consumption again increasing faster than GDP.
>
> (De Bruyn and Opschoor 1997: 266)

Heintz and De Bruyn (1997: 20) suggest that an explanation might be 'the difficulty of ongoing efficiency improvements to keep up with continuing growth of production'. This suggestion of an N-shaped curve strikingly reflects the cubic shape that was the best estimate for many of the EKC studies listed in Tables 7.1 and 7.A1. As we have seen, GK tended to dismiss the upturn at high incomes (although Shafik did not). The De Bruyn and Opschoor result suggests that it may be significant. However, there has been little further work in this area. In his recent review of as yet largely unpublished work, Stern (1997: 19–20) notes: 'The current crop of studies shows surprisingly little interest in looking at whether impacts begin to rise again at high income levels for the indicators where a mid-income turning point has been identified.'

7.5 THE DETERMINANTS OF THE INCOME – ENVIRONMENT RELATIONSHIP

The following equation was derived (as Equation 6.2) in the previous chapter (see p. 162):

$$\hat{E} = \hat{Y} + \Sigma e_i \hat{a}_i + \Sigma e_i \hat{s}_i$$

in which the first term was characterised the *scale* effect, the second term the *technique* effect and the third term the *composition* effect of economic development on the environment.

Here two of the questions which were there raised but passed over will be addressed, namely:

1   To what extent can reductions in a and s, the technique and composition effects, be expected to counteract the scale effect?
2   Will these reductions come about more or less automatically as part of the process of economic growth, or will they need to be brought about by government policy?

In consideration of question 1, Table 7.3 reproduces various statistics to show how the environmental impacts of the G7 countries have changed with GDP since 1970. Numbers greater than 100 indicate an increase in the quantity in this period and, because the indicators chosen have a negative environmental impact, suggest environmental deterioration. Had all these environmental effects grown pro rata with GDP, then the numbers would be the same as those in the GDP column. This would be the scale effect. However, it can be seen that most of the environmental effects have grown less than GDP, showing that they have been offset to some extent by the technique and composition effects. Where the numbers are less than 100, the technique and composition effects have more than offset the scale effect, so that the environment has actually improved. It is easy to see that emissions of SO_2 have fallen markedly in all countries despite the growth of GDP. For CO_2 and NO_x the record is mixed. In some countries

Table 7.3 Growth of GDP, energy and fertiliser use, various emissions and municipal waste, 1970[e]–93, unless otherwise stated

Country	GDP	Energy	CO_2	SO_2	NO_x	Nitrogen fertilisers	Municipal waste[e]
Canada	209	158	134	45[c]	142[c]	477	122
France	171	152	83	41[c]	115[c]	130	152
W.Germany	169	116[a]	95[b]	23[c]	102[c]	92[a]	100[a]
Italy	183	125	123	59[a]	145[a]	131	136
Japan	249	155	137	18[d]	89[a]	102	116
UK	155	103	83	50	98	145	108[a]
USA	184	124	122	69	116	151	128

Source: Calculated from OECD (1995a) and OECD (1991b) for all except energy use (OECD 1991a)

Notes:
Index numbers: 1970 = 100, except CO_2 (1971 = 100) and municipal waste (1975 = 100)
a Figure for 1990
b Figure for 1988
c Figure for 1992
d Figure for 1989
e 1975 for municipal waste

emissions have decreased (Japan and UK for NO_x, UK, France and W. Germany for CO_2), but in most emissions have increased but less than GDP. For energy use and municipal waste, only the UK (more or less) and W. Germany respectively have maintained quantities at 1970 levels; in all other countries they have increased. Nitrogen fertilisers offer the only example here of use increasing faster than GDP (in Canada). It was from data such as these that the OECD and EC reports cited earlier drew their conclusion that despite progress on some fronts, rich country environments were still deteriorating overall.

As noted above, the difference between GDP growth and the environmental effects is due to the joint operation of the technique and composition effects. These effects are brought about by the following changes:

1　*Technique*: more efficient use of inputs, substitution of less for more environmentally intensive inputs, less generation of wastes, transformation of wastes to less environmentally harmful forms, containment or recycling of wastes, a shift within a sector towards new, less environmentally harmful products or processes.
2　*Composition*: shift in production and/or consumption patterns towards existing or new sectors or industries that are less environmentally damaging.

Clearly it is possible that the substitutions and new processes, products and industries may introduce different environmental problems of their own. The OECD report quoted earlier indicated that this was indeed the case, so that such data as in Table 7.3 should not be considered the whole story. It is also necessary to ask of the composition effect whether the shift in production patterns has been accompanied by a shift in consumption patterns, or whether the same consumption of environmentally intensive goods is increasingly being met by imports. If the latter, two conclusions follow. The first is that the environmental effects due to the composition effect are being displaced from one country to another, rather than reduced. The second is that this means of reducing environmental impacts will not be available to the latest-developing countries, because there will be no countries coming up behind them to which environmentally intensive activities can be relocated.

Some interesting light is shed on this issue by the Lucas *et al.* (1992) study which was briefly discussed earlier. In addition to finding that there was no EKC for toxic pollution, as already mentioned, they found that the growth rate of the toxic intensity of manufacturing was both higher in the poorest countries and increased through the 1970s and 1980s. The authors consider that this is consistent with the hypothesis that 'stricter regulation of pollution-intensive production in the OECD countries has led to significant locational displacement, with consequent acceleration of industrial pollution intensity in developing countries' (Lucas *et al.* 1992: 80). This result showing the absolute and relative growth of pollution-intensive industry in poor countries is confirmed by Low and Yeats (1992) through quite different non-econometric analysis of trade statistics. However, while Low and Yeats agree that the result is consistent with the Lucas displacement hypothesis, they stress that there are a number of other possible explanations, including that the strong growth of 'dirty' industries is a normal occurrence at an early stage of development.

It must be emphasised that the Lucas *et al.* result is only concerned with compositional, and not technical, effects. Its 'toxic intensity' was calculated using constant technologies, so that the increase in such intensity refers only to a proportional increase in the output of the toxically intensive sectors. The environmental impact of this compositional change would be reduced, and could be completely counteracted, if improvements in technique rendered the environmentally intensive sectors less toxic. Moreover, a different conclusion from the Low and Yeats analysis is provided by an input–output study of CO_2 emissions from the UK and W. Germany by Proops *et al.* (1993). Their results indicate that the CO_2 embodied in the net imports of these two countries increased only marginally from 1970–90, and, as noted in Chapter 5, that at the end of the period both countries still exported more embodied CO_2 than they imported (Proops *et al.* 1993: 177). This does not suggest the displacement of energy-intensive industries from those countries.

Other studies, surveyed by Dean (1992: 16–20), give conflicting results, but overall do not suggest that the forces for displacement are very great. One study since Dean's survey, however, examined the effect of pollution abatement expenditures on the productivity of factories in the paper, oil and steel industries, finding that:

> Plants with high compliance costs have significantly lower productivity levels and slower productivity growth rates than less regulated plants. The impact of compliance costs is stronger for total factor productivity than for labour productivity, and stronger for productivity growth rates than for levels. The magnitude of the TFP impacts indicates that the compliance costs have a larger than expected effect.
>
> (Gray and Shadbegian 1993: 2)

Jaffe *et al.* (1995: 152) say that subsequent work by Gray and Shadbegian has shown these effects on productivity to be 'largely an artifact of measurement error in output'.

With regard to the composition effect, therefore, the evidence suggests:

1   that it adds to the scale effect at lower levels of income, i.e. it causes environmental damage to increase faster than income;
2   that it acts against but does not fully counteract the scale effect at higher levels of income;
3   that the effects in 1 and 2 may be due to some small extent to the displacement of dirty industries from high to low income countries due to stricter environmental regulations in the former, which erodes high-income countries' competitive advantage in these industries.

With regard to the technique effect, many examples could be cited of increasingly efficient resource use, substitutions between resources and containment of wastes. The three most dramatic reductions in Table 7.3, SO_2 emissions for Japan, W. Germany and France, can be explained by the instalment of flue-gas desulphurisation (FGD) equipment (W. Germany), a switch to nuclear power (France) and a combination of the two (Japan). This example illustrates the kind of secondary environmental effects that can arise from such developments. FGD requires the quarrying and transport of large quantities of limestone, and, by reducing the energy efficiency of power stations, increases their CO_2 emissions. Nuclear power has its own environmental impacts (waste disposal, radioactive emissions, risk of accidents) which make it a cause for public concern.

From the above discussion, it is clear that the combination of (negative) technique and composition effects is able to completely counteract the (positive) scale effect on environmental impact. It is also clear that emissions of SO_2 are the only impact of G7 countries for which this has unequivocally been the case; and, insofar as the composition effect is due to displacement, later developing countries will not be able to benefit from it, for lack of other countries to which environmentally intensive activities can be displaced. The question now arises as to whether these changes come about more or less automatically as part of the process of growth and development or whether they have to be brought about by government policy. In the latter case it is assumed that, while policy may be linked to the process of growth and development in some complex way, it is not completely determined by it.

Because they deal with reduced form rather than structural equations, the EKC estimations themselves can shed no light on this question. Relevant hypotheses discussed in the papers, include the following:

1   Cost-saving pressures induced by market-competition will tend to increase the efficiency of the use of purchased resource inputs and therefore reduce the pollution to which this use gives rise.

2   There is a normal trajectory of economic development such that societies move from subsistence to more intensive patterns of agriculture to industrialisation and then to more service-based economies. The quote from Panayotou (1993) early in this chapter (see pp. 182–3) expresses this view. This development path is not seen to be brought about by policy but by the increasing importance of capital accumulation and knowledge-based industries.

3   Insofar as environmental damage arising from economic activity affects people's health or threatens society in other ways, freedom to cause such damage is reduced as people become more aware of, and concerned about, the problems (see, for example, Radetzki 1992: 130). Prohibitions, regulations and sanctions are introduced to protect environmental quality.

4   The poor have little demand for environmental quality, and are constrained by their present consumption needs to degrade their environment. But as people get richer their demand for environmental quality increases more than proportionately to their income (i.e. the income elasticity of environmental quality is greater than one). GK1991 make this point thus: 'As a society becomes richer its members may intensify their demands for a more healthy and sustainable environment, in which case the government may be called upon to impose more stringent environmental controls' (GK1991: 7).

All these points have some validity, but they are all also subject to qualification. With regard to 1, market pressures only act on inputs that are priced. Many environmental functions are not priced and are therefore immune from this pressure. Moreover, substitution between inputs depends on their relative price. If another input such as labour is relatively more expensive than a polluting resource, then substitution may result in more of the resource being used rather than less.

With regard to 2, it has been seen that the composition effect reduced the intensity of environmental impact per unit of output, rather than its absolute level. With regard to 3, it is clear that legal developments to protect environmental quality are the direct result of policy. History shows that the enactment of such policy is often neither painless nor automatic but is the outcome only of public pressure and campaigning. The effectiveness of such pressure obviously depends on the political structure of society: the more democratic the structure, the easier it is likely to be for public pressure to lead to legislative change. SB (1992: 20) sought to illustrate this effect by regressing their indicators of environmental quality against indices of political and civil liberties, but no clear patterns emerged. This may have been due to the difficulty of defining such liberties quantitatively.

With regard to 4 the issue needs more careful specification than it receives in most of the EKC papers. First, Heintz and De Bruyn (1997) note that most studies have found the income elasticity of demand to be positive, but less than unity, against any hypothesis that environmental quality is a luxury good. Second, poor people, especially rural poor people, are often the most directly dependent on their environment, and its resources, and the most vulnerable to its degradation. Such people do not need to become richer to become concerned about the environment, for as Shafik (1994: 757) has said: 'There are some environmental problems where thresholds like survival are at stake. Here the willingness to pay to avert damage is close to infinity and the level of *per capita* income only affects the capacity, not the willingness, to pay.' Not surprisingly, therefore, especially where their survival may be at stake, many low income societies, such as those of some indigenous peoples as studied by Davis (1992), have evolved both conserving and sustainable patterns of use of the resources on which they depend. Such patterns, however, depend on these societies preserving their control over the resources in question, yet they have little capability to defend them against outside expropriation. When external agents degrade poor people's environments, such people can become environmental activists, as Broad and Cavanagh (1993) discovered in the Philippines. Specifically with reference to the Grossman and Krueger position given under 4 above, Broad writes: 'Our research suggests that looking at growth and poverty alleviation as the means to instil environmentalism misses a key point: in the Philippines environmentalism was a demand of the poor, not of the rich' (Broad 1994: 814). The mechanism here is not one whereby getting richer stimulates people to look for environmental improvement, however valid this may be in other situations. Rather it is one whereby some people get richer through the degradation of the environment (e.g. logging, unsustainable fishing), which impoverishes other, already poor, people who are dependent on the degrading resources, and stimulates them to take actions for environmental protection.

Third, rising incomes may result in the flight of better off people from environmentally degraded areas rather than their improvement. It is a matter of common observation as well as *a priori* expectation that degraded areas will impact more on the poor, who cannot afford to leave them, than on the relatively rich, who can. Fourth, the kind of environmental quality which people wish to buy (e.g. solitude, tranquillity, beauty) may be degraded when more than a few people seek and are able to purchase it (this is the problem of Hirsch's positional goods, discussed in Chapter 2). Such a degradation of the environment by increasing effective demand is clearly a problem that affects the tourist industry. Fifth, when the environmental quality desired is not a private good, it may need to be obtained through political means (public regulation or expenditure), the availability of which depend, as with point 3, on the presence of a relatively democratic political structure able to prevail against any powerful interests which may be benefiting from the environmental degradation. Sixth, not all important environmental problems are amenable to resolution by self-interested aspiration, private or public. The popular appeal of an environmental issue may have little to do with its ecological importance. Moreover, as Shafik has noted:

> Action tends to be taken where there are generalised local costs and substantial private and social benefits. Where the costs of environmental degradation are borne by others (by the poor or by other countries), there are few incentives to alter damaging behaviour.
>
> (Shafik 1994: 770)

This may be thought to apply even more strongly where the costs fall on future generations.

All these qualifications point to the necessity of determined public policy to achieve environmental improvement in a context of rising incomes: policy to internalise environmental costs to move towards market efficiency by making environmental damage subject to market pressures; policy to stimulate technical and structural change to increase the counteraction of the scale effect by the technique and composition effects; policy to give effect to increasing desires for environmental quality that cannot be privately bought; and policy to bring about a distribution of environmental goods, both within and between generations, that is both fair and provides incentives for their sustainable use.

Such is also the conclusion even of the EKC studies which give more weight to the existence of environmental Kuznets curves than this survey deems warranted. Thus Shafik (1994: 770) concludes: 'The evidence suggests that it is possible to "grow out of" some environmental problems. But there is not necessarily anything automatic about this – in most countries, environmental improvement has required policies and investments to be put into place to reduce degradation.' Grossman and Krueger seem to concur:

> Even for those dimensions of environmental quality where growth seems to have been associated with improving conditions, there is not reason to believe that the process has been an automatic one. In

principle, environmental quality might improve automatically when countries develop if they substitute cleaner technologies for dirtier ones, or if there is a very pronounced effect on pollution of the typical patterns of structural transformation. . . . However, a review of the available evidence on instances of pollution abatement (see e.g. OECD, 1991[a]) suggests that the strongest link between income and pollution in fact is via an induced *policy response*; . . .

> (Grossman and Krueger 1994: 19, original emphasis)

This echoes the conclusion from the World Bank's *World Development Report 1992* (World Bank 1992: 24) quoted in the previous chapter.

7.6 THE IMPLICATIONS OF THE EKC STUDIES FOR THE FUTURE

The EKC studies deduce a certain historical relationship between income and environmental quality. This section explores the implications of these relationships being continued into the future. Figure 7.3 shows the 1988 distribution of global income among world population and marks in the various turning points that have been estimated for certain types of environmental damage.

It is at once obvious that, with the exception of P1993's deforestation estimate, discussion of which is below, most of the world's population lies on the upward-sloping portion of the EKCs that have been estimated. This implies that, even if these EKCs are valid, income growth across the global population will increase environmental damage before it reduces it. This is precisely the conclusion of the two studies that have projected EKC relationships into the future. Thus Selden and Song find from such a projection: 'The global flows of all four emissions remain at or above their 1986 levels throughout the entire next century, even in the most optimistic scenarios' (SS1994: 158). These most optimistic scenarios show that at 2050 the levels of their emissions are as in Table 7.4.

Stern *et al.* (1994) perform a similar calculation for P1993's estimated relationships for SO_2 and deforestation. They find for SO_2: 'Emissions of SO_2 per capita rise from 73kg to 142kg from 1990 to 2025. Global emissions rise from 383 million tonnes in 1990 to 1181 million tonnes in 2025' (Stern *et al.* 1994: 13); and for deforestation:

> Despite the maximum rate of deforestation at P's sample mean population density occurring at $823, global forest cover declines until 2016 when mean world income is $5962 . . . However, tropical forest cover continues to decline throughout the period from 18.4 million km² in 1990 to 9.7 million km² in 2025.

> (ibid.: 13)

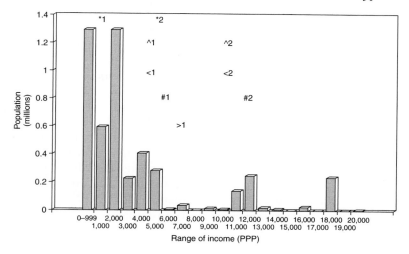

Figure 7.3 Income/population distribution and EKC turning points

Sources: Summers and Heston (1991), series POP (population) and RGDPCH (1988 purchasing power parity, PPP, income) except for some Eastern European (EE) countries and countries of the former Soviet Union (FSE), for which the source was WRI (1994: 257 (Table 15.1) (1991 PPP GDP, deflated by a factor of 1.35 to account for growth and deflation) and 269 (Table 16.1) (1990 population, reduced by a factor of 1.02 for EE, 1.04 for FSU)

Notes:
The symbols roughly mark the downward turning point incomes estimated by some of the studies reported in Table 7.1, according to the following key:
*1   Deforestation, P1993
*2   Deforestation, CG1994
^1 SO_2 urban concentrations, GK1991, GK1994, SB1992
^2 SO_2 per capita emissions, SS1994
<1   Suspended particles (inc. dark smoke) urban concentrations, GK1991, G1993, P1993
<2   Suspended particles per capita emissions, SS1994
#1 NO_x urban concentrations, P1993
#2 NO_x per capita emissions, SS1994
>1   CO per capita emissions, SS1994

Table 7.4 Emissions of four pollutants in 2050, 1986 = 100

SO_2	SPM	NO_x	CO
> 200	300	> 150	150

Source: Selden and Song (1994: 158–9 (Figures 1–4))

These projections place the EKC results in an entirely different light. They suggest that, if these historical relationships continue to hold, far from future economic growth yielding environmental improvement, it will result in serious further environmental decline. The projections drastically change the EKC relationships from sources of optimism from future economic growth to warnings of continuing environmental damage. In particular they do not permit the optimistic conclusion quoted earlier from P1993: 'Economic growth appears to be a powerful way for improving environmental quality in developing countries' (P1993: 14); nor that from Baldwin (1995: 76) that 'sustainability necessitates *per capita* income growth, at least among the world's poor'. On the contrary, economic growth in developing countries, if proceeding according to past patterns and trends, will cause enormous further environmental degradation. The EKC studies do not presage a benign environmental future from business-as-usual, but a stark environmental prospect, unless past growth–environment relationships can be substantially changed.

7.7 CONCLUSIONS

Those environmental indicators for which the EKC hypothesis is most plausible, or least unconvincing, are various indicators of air pollution: $NO_{2,x}$, CO, SO_2, suspended particles, dark matter. However, the principal conclusion of this investigation into the relationship between environment and income as revealed in various econometric studies is that the hypothesis that there is an environmental Kuznets curve is not unequivocally supported for any environmental indicator and is rejected by the OECD and EC studies of environmental quality as a whole. This conclusion accords with those of the already cited reviews of the issue carried out by Stern (1997: 19) and Heintz and De Bruyn (1997: 21). The former concludes: 'Evidence continues to accumulate that the inverted U shape relation only applies to a subset of impacts, and that overall impact . . . rises throughout the relevant income range.' The latter conclude that, on the evidence available, the EKC 'remains a loosely defined hypothesis. There exists no evidence that the EKC has, or will become, a "stylised fact" on the patterns of pollution associated with a particular stage of economic development.'

The studies themselves shed little light on the causation, as opposed to the correlation, that might be embodied in the environment–income relationships. However, this chapter's discussion of the issues, as well as that of the researchers of the studies, suggests that any improvements in environmental quality as incomes increase is likely to be due to the enactment of environmental policy rather than endogenous changes in economic structure or technology.

Finally, setting the turning points of the various EKC studies in the context of the current distribution of world population shows that a continuation of the relationship that produced the turning points would result in very great further environmental damage for a number of decades into the future. Such damage is clearly incompatible with the political commitments that have been made to the achievement of sustainable development. In fact, insofar as the EKC studies permit any conclusions at all, they provide evidence of unsustainable development rather than the reverse. Sustainable development requires the modification of the historical environment–income relationship, as much where there is limited evidence of an inverted-U relationship between income and environmental quality as where there is a clear positive relationship between these variables. There is no evidence that such a modification will emerge endogenously from the growth process. It seems likely to require determined environmental policy.

APPENDIX

Table 7.A1 Econometric relationships between income and various environmental indicators

Row no.	Study	Range/ medium	Environment indicator	Shape	TP, US$ (1985)	Time trend g^1	R^2
1	GK1991	Global/air	SO_2, uc[2]	e	1. 4,100[3] 2. 14,000	–	0.125– 0.166
2			D.m.[4], uc	e	1. 5,000 2. 10,000	n	0.21– 0.352
3			SP[5], uc	a[6]	n.a. (in)	– 0.590	0.569–
4[7]			SO_2, uc	e	1.~4,300 2. n.a.	–	0.76
5			D.m., uc	e	1.~4,000 2. 10,500	–	0.87
6			SP, uc	b	n.a.	–	0.91
7	SB1992[8]	All global/water	Cl.w.[9]	a	n.a.	–	0.43
8			Sanit.	a	n.a.	–	0.22
9		land	Defor.	in[10]	n.a.	n	0.00
10		water	D.o., c	a[11]	n.a.	n	0.99
11		water	F.col., c	e	1. 1,400 2. 11,400	+	0.96
12		air	SO_2, uc	c	3,700	–	1.00
13		air	SPM, uc	c	3,300	–	0.99
14		land	M.w.p.c.	b	n.a.	n	0.60
15		air	Carb.p.c.	b	n.a.	n	0.85
16		various	Six indic.[12]	same			
17	G1993	Global/air	SO_2, uc[13]	e	1. 4,100 2. 14,000	nr[14]	nr
18			D.m., uc	e	1. 4,700 2. 10,000	nr	nr
19		US/air	SPM[15]	c	16,000[16]	nr	nr
20			SO_2, c	e	1. 13,400 2. 24,000	nr	nr

Table 7.A1 (continued)

Row no.	Study	Range/ medium	Environment indicator	Shape	TP, US$ (1985)	Time trend g[1]	R²
21			lead, c	e	1. 14,000 2. 22,000	nr	nr
22			CO, c	c	22,800	nr	nr
23			NO_2, c	c	18,500	nr	nr
24		Global/water	F.col., c	c	8,500	nr	nr
25			T.c., c[17]	e	none[18]	nr	nr
26			Lead, c	e	none[19]	nr	nr
27			Cd, c	a	n.a.	nr	nr
28			Hg, c	e	1. 5,800 2. 12,900	nr	nr
29			As, c	e	1. 5,300 2. 14,000	nr	nr
30			Ni, c	f	1. 5,900 2. 11,900	nr	nr
31			D.o.	d[20]	8,500	nr	nr
32			B.O.D.[21]	c	10,000	nr	nr
33			C.O.D.	c	10,000	nr	nr
34			Nit., c	f	1. 2,000 2. 10,000	nr	nr
35	GK1994	Global/air	SO_2, uc	e	1. 4,100 2. 14,000	–	nr
36			D.m.,uc	e	1. 6,200 2. none[22]	–	nr
37			SPM, uc	a	n.a.	+	nr
38		Global/water	D.o.	d[20]	2,703	–	nr
39			B.O.D.	c	7,600	+	nr
40			C.O.D.	c	7,900	+	nr
41			Nit.	c	10,500	–	nr
42			F.col.	c	8,000	+	nr
43			T.col.	e	1. 3,043 2. 8,000	+	nr
44			Lead	e	1. 1,887 2. 14,000	+	nr
45			Cd	f	1. 5,000 2. 11,600	+	nr
46			As	e	1. 4,900 2. 15,000	+	nr
47			Hg	in	n.a.	n.a.	n.a.
48			Ni	in	n.a.	n.a.	n.a.
49	SS1994	Global/air	SO_2, epc[23]	c	1. 8,900[24] 2. 10,700	n.a.	0.95
50			SPM, epc	c	1. 9,800 2. 9,600	n.a.	0.99
51			NO_x, epc	c	1. 12,000 2. 21,800	n.a.	0.98
52			CO, epc	c	1. 6,200 2. 19,100	n.a.	0.96
53			All[25], epc	d	n.a.	n.a.	n.a.
54	HES1992	Global/air	CO_2,	1. c	1. 35,400	n.a.	0.76

Table 7.A1 (continued)

Row no.	Study	Range/ medium	Environment indicator	Shape	TP, US$ (1985)	Time trend g[1]	R^2
			epc[26]	2. c	2. 8m.+[27]		0.84
55	CG1994	Regional/land	Defor. rate	1. c[28]	4,760	+	0.63
				2. c	5,420	–	0.47
				3. in	n.a.	+	0.13
56	LWH1992	Global/all	Toxic intensity	1. c[29]	1. n.a.	n.a.	n.a.
				2. b	2. n.a.		
57	HLW1992	Global/all	Toxic intensity	1. c[29]	1. n.a.		
				2. b	2. n.a.		
58	P1993	Global/air	SO_2, epc[30]	c	3,000	n.a.	0.33
59			NO_x, epc	c	5,500	n.a.	0.35
60			SPM, epc	c	4,500		0.12
61		Global/land	Defor. rate	1. c[31]	823	n.a.	0.75
				2. c	1,200		0.63

Key to studies:

CG Cropper and Griffiths
GK Grossman and Krueger
HLW Hettige, Lucas and Wheeler
P Panayotou
SS Selden and Song

G Grossman
HES Holtz-Eakin and Selden
LWH Lucas, Wheeler and Hettige
SB Shafik and Bandyopadhyay

Notes:

1 Given as + (positive), – (negative), n (no clear trend) or in (insignificant)
2 uc stands for urban concentration; c for concentration
3 50th percentile
4 Dark matter, also called smoke
5 Suspended particles
6 Here $\alpha 1 < 0$, $\alpha 2 > 0$, $\alpha 3 < 0$, but $|\alpha 3| << |\alpha 2| << |\alpha 1|$ gives shape a (rather than f) overall over the income range considered, flattening out at $Y = \$9,000$
7 Rows 1–3 are random effects models; rows 4–6 are fixed effect models
8 This study estimated three models – log linear, quadratic, cubic in income – for each environmental indicator. The model with the most explanatory power is reported here
9 The new environmental indicators in this and the other SB rows are lack of clean water (row 7), lack of sanitation (8), deforestation (9), dissolved oxygen (10), fecal coliform (11), suspended particulate matter (13, the same as SP), municipal waste per capita (14) and carbon emissions per capita (15)
10 'None of the income terms is significant in any specification' (SB 1992: 7)
11 Because this is an indicator of environmental quality rather than degradation, this shape indicates continually *worsening* environmental quality with income
12 Rows 7–15 report SB's estimations on panel data (i.e. times-series for different countries). This row reports their cross-sectional results for 1985 for six indicators – clean water, sanitation, SO2, SPM, municipal waste and carbon emissions per capita, which were the results given wide coverage by being quoted in World Bank (1992: 11). All the cross-section estimates gave the same general results as the panel estimates. SB believed the panel estimates to be more robust
13 Taken from a subsequent reworking of GK1991, which was then published as Grossman and Krueger (1993).
14 nr stands for not reported
15 This and the following four rows are taken from a study using exclusively US data from different states
16 1987 US$ for TP in this and following four rows
17 Total coliform
18 The cubic function is continuously rising in income

19 No turning point in the reported range, \$8,000–\$15,000
20 Because this is an indicator of environmental quality, this indicates environmental improvement after the turning point income
21 Biological oxygen demand; the indicators of the next two rows are chemical oxygen demand and nitrates
22 The second turning point of this cubic equation was outside the range of income reported

Table 7.A1 (notes continued)

23 Here the environmental indicator was SO_2 emissions per capita rather than concentrations
24 The turning points given are those for both SS's fixed effect (1) and random effect estimations (2)
25 This row refers to estimates for each of the SS environmental indicators derived using cross-sectional estimators. They all showed d-shaped 'emissions-GDP relationships that are concave upward (i.e. they exhibit increasing marginal propensities to emit at higher levels of income' (SS1994: 151). SS reject these estimates as 'inefficient at best'
26 Emissions per capita
27 These are estimates of two quadratic equations. The quadratic term of the second is insignificantly different from zero, which explains the very high turning point of over \$8 million. This study is discussed further in the text
28 The three results in this row are for Africa (1), Latin America (2) and Asia (3). In after 3 stands for insignificant.
29 The two results in this row are for toxic intensity per unit of GDP (1) and toxic intensity per unit of industrial output (2)
30 The regressions in P1993 use cross–section data across countries in a given year
31 The two results refer to two regressions on different samples, one containing forty-one developing countries only (1), the other adding twenty-seven developed countries to these (2)

8 The dividends from environmental taxation

8.1 INSIGHTS FROM THEORY

8.1.1 The environmental dividend

It is generally agreed among economists that, in a situation where the production or consumption of some good results in a negative external effect (i.e. one that is not reflected in the price of the good in question), then social welfare can be improved by imposing a tax on the good.

Figure 8.1 revisits Figure 2.1, in which the output of a good, Q is associated with damaging pollution, P, which imposes a marginal external cost given by the MEC curve. The producer of the good derives a marginal net private benefit from production given by the MNPB curve. The figure is stylised in the sense that it assumes that the curves can be measured and remain stable as prices and outputs change, which may not in practice be the case, but it illustrates the basic theoretical position.

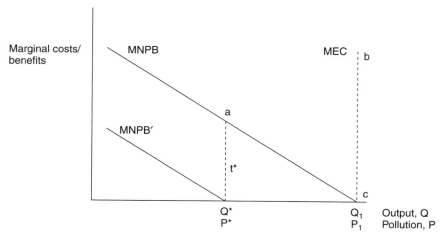

Figure 8.1 Optimal environmental taxation with no abatement

Without intervention the producer will produce at Q_1, P_1. However, this is clearly not socially optimal, because beyond Q^* all output incurs a net social cost. At Q_1 the total net cost of production beyond Q^* is given by the triangle abc. Conversely, this triangle abc becomes the net benefit gained – the environmental dividend – of reducing output and pollution to Q^*, P^*. A tax, t^*, levied on the producer's output, such that t^* is equal to the MEC and MNPB at the point they intersect, will reduce the producer's net benefit to MNPB', giving the producer the incentive to reduce output to its optimal level, so that social welfare is maximised.

However, it is not the output *per se* that is responsible for the environmental damage, but the pollution associated with it, so that it is really the pollution which should be taxed. Of course, given the pollution/output relationship, a tax on output acts as a tax on pollution. But if the tax is levied directly on pollution (e.g. through an emissions tax), then the producer has the opportunity of reducing pollution by abating it directly, rather than by reducing output. How much abatement will be undertaken depends on the marginal abatement cost (MAC) of reducing pollution below P_1.

In Figure 8.2(a) and (b) three possible MAC curves are shown, MAC_1, MAC_2 and MAC_3. MAC_1 lies everywhere above MNPB. No abatement will take place. Given an optimal tax on pollution, t^*, pollution will be reduced only by reducing output, as in Figure 8.1, to reach the optimal pollution level P^*. MAC_2 lies partly above, and partly below, MNPB. Following Pearce and Turner (1990: 90), pollution reduction will take place along the arrowed line, through abatement up to P_2 (where MAC_2 lies below MNPB), and then through output reduction (where MAC_2 lies above MNPB). Where the environmental damage is given by MEC_1, optimal pollution will be P_2, achieved by a tax t_2^* through abatement only. Where the damage is higher, MEC_2 say, optimal pollution will be P_2', achieved by a tax t_2^* through a combination of abatement and output reduction. With the tax t_2^*, the producer's MNPB will fall to $MNPB_2$, with the tax t_2^*, it will fall to $MNPB_2'$.

In Figure 8.2(b), MAC_3 lies wholly below MNPB, so that pollution reduction will be only through abatement. Here the optimal pollution is P_3, achieved by tax t_3^*, reducing the MNPB (per unit of pollution) to $MNPB_3$.

In Figure 8.1 the cost of the pollution reduction in terms of lost output is $Q_1 - Q^*$. In Figure 8.2(a),(b), with abatement curves MAC_2, MAC_3, the possibility of abatement at lower cost than output reduction means that the same pollution reduction as in Figure 8.1 can be achieved at lower cost. The lower the cost of abatement, the lower the level of pollution that can be achieved with a given tax; or the lower the tax that is required to achieve a given level of pollution.

Yet even this is only a partial equilibrium result. Several other effects can be identified which make the overall macroeconomic effect much more difficult to compute. First, the output of pollution abatement companies

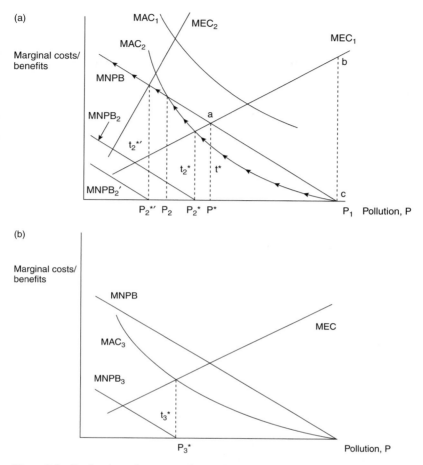

Figure 8.2 Optimal environmental taxation with abatement

will have increased. Second, the price of the abating firm's output may have increased, with further knock-on effects through the economy. Third, in response to any increase in the price of the abating firm's output, substitution towards other products will take place. Fourth, it may be that the productivity of people or other firms will have increased due to the reduction in pollution. Fifth, it may be that the rise in price of the use of the environmental resource will hasten the depreciation of the capital equipment affected; on the other hand it may be that the shift in relative prices will stimulate research, innovation and investment with a view to economising on the resource, which may be economically beneficial. Sixth, the tax will yield revenue, which will allow other taxes to be reduced, with yet more knock-on effects through the economy. Assessing the overall costs of pollution abatement even in this simple case is therefore no simple matter. The last point is revisited in some detail below.

The environmental dividend arises solely from the benefits of reducing negative externalities, although its value depends, as has been seen, both on the valuation given to the externality and to the marginal cost of abating it. It is sometimes perceived that environmental taxes introduce economic distortions. Thus Gaskins and Weyant (1993: 320) write of 'the distortions to the economy caused by the imposition of the carbon tax', and Jorgenson and Wilcoxen (1993: 518) write of the 'introduction of distortions resulting from fossil-fuel taxes'. But the whole point of an environmental tax is that it corrects a distortion from a pre-existing environmental externality. The adjustment to the new relative prices, and the resulting shift in resource allocation, should not be regarded as a 'distortion' due to the tax, but as a desirable adjustment to a higher level of allocative efficiency, whereby a distortion is removed through the externality's internalisation. As D. Pearce (1991: 940) has emphasised: 'While most taxes distort incentives, an environmental tax corrects a distortion, namely the externalities arising from the excessive use of environmental services.'

The cost of achieving the environmental dividend is the loss of real economic output incurred. Given that the environmental improvement can be envisaged as being brought about through the diversion of economic resources from producing marketed goods or services to the production of unmarketed environmental goods or services, in the absence of other economic inefficiencies a loss of marketed output is to be expected. In the modelling of an environmental tax, if the base run is considered non-distortionary and at full equibrium, then, as Boero *et al.* (1991: 34) note, 'any deviation from a "no distortions" base run necessarily involves economic costs'.

However, no economy is at a point of non-distortionary equilibrium. There are distortions due to current taxation patterns, which bear most heavily on labour; and there are distortions due to market or government failure, such as, perhaps, in the market for energy efficiency, or as a result of inefficient government regulation. The macroeconomic effect of an environmental tax will depend on whether its introduction, or other associated policy, affects these distortions.

The revenues from an environmental tax can be substantial. Thus the levels of the carbon taxes proposed as necessary to make substantial reductions in carbon emissions are between \$100 and \$400 per ton of carbon (see Boero *et al.* 1991: 87–9 (Table 5)). A \$250 tax is equivalent to \$0.75 per gallon on petrol or \$30 per barrel on oil (Cline 1992: 147). A \$100 per ton global tax rate would raise on the order of \$500 billion annually, and about \$130 billion from the US alone (ibid.: 151). Schelling considers that 'a carbon tax sufficient to make a big dent in the greenhouse problem would have to be roughly equivalent to a dollar per gallon on motor fuel . . . [which] would currently yield close to half a trillion dollars a year in revenue' (Schelling 1992: 11).

This revenue can be rebated in some way, either directly or through the reduction of other taxes. If this can be done in such a way as to yield economic benefit through the removal of an existing economic inefficiency, quite apart from the environmental benefit discussed earlier, then it may be said that there is a 'revenue-recycling' dividend from the tax, in addition to the environmental dividend. It is to the investigation of the possibility of such a second dividend that we now turn.

8.1.2 The revenue-recycling dividends

A revenue-recycling dividend is here defined as an economic (and non-environmental) benefit resulting from the revenue-neutral imposition of a tax (i.e. all the revenue from the tax is returned to taxpayers by cuts in other taxes or lump-sum rebates, rather than saved or spent by the government). Such a dividend can arise if the tax-plus-rebate (TPR) improves economic distribution (a distributional dividend), reduces involuntary unemployment (an employment dividend) or increases economic efficiency (thereby increasing output, an efficiency dividend).

It may be immediately noted that the possibilities for all these dividends depend on the economy being in a non-optimal state to start with: •the existing tax structure must be non-optimal in some sense, for example, because the tax base is related to employment; or there must be existing deficiencies in distribution and market failures in the labour and other markets. Any perception or assumption that the initial condition of the economy is characterised by perfectly competitive markets operating in equilibrium with taxes imposed on a per capita basis (as sometimes assumed in, for example, general equilibrium modelling of such measures as a carbon tax), will *a priori* rule out the existence or possible achievement of such dividends (except for those related to improvements in distribution). However, with a less ideal initial economic configuration, the existence of such dividends cannot be ruled out, and they will be investigated in turn.

The distributional dividend

There have been a number of proposals (reviewed in Atkins and Wilson 1984) for TPR measures in order to achieve distributional goals with less disruption than the alternatives seemed to entail. They mainly concern the distribution of scarce goods that are also regarded as basic needs (e.g. food, housing) at times when the supply of the goods is particularly constrained. The TPR measure essentially involves a tax on the good in question, which increases its price and constrains the demand for it, accompanied by a distribution of the tax revenues that relatively favours the group perceived to be needy so that they can afford to purchase more of the good than they could have done without the tax, should they wish to do so.

The advantage of such a measure over alternatives is that it permits the market to operate in its normal way, while effectively rationing the good in question so that everyone can afford basic access to it, without being forced to consume it against their preferences (as happens with non-transferable ration coupons). Obviously the perceived distributional benefit would have to be high enough to justify the administrative costs of the scheme.

The proposals for explicitly distributional TPR schemes came shortly after the last World War when the supply of specific goods to satisfy basic needs was constrained. As supplies have increased, the need to reduce demand for the goods has decreased or vanished, so that redistribution is now normally carried out through general taxation or the granting of entitlements to specific goods (e.g. food stamps).

Perhaps more relevant in the context of the current discussion of environmental taxation is the possibility that environmental taxes, where they fall proportionately more heavily on the poor than on the rich, will cause a distributional disbenefit (effectively a negative distributional dividend). Detailed discussion of this issue is outside the scope of this book, but there is some evidence that a carbon tax, for example, could bear disproportionately on low income households (Pearson and Smith 1991). There is also evidence that it does not need to do so (Barker and Johnstone 1993). The overall desirability of an environmental tax, as well as its likely political and ethical acceptability, depends on regressive effects being avoided.

The employment dividend

Involuntary unemployment is a condition in which people who want to become employed cannot find a job at a wage which they are willing to accept. Because it is perceived that, if their asking wage were low enough, they would be able to find a job, unemployed people are thence assumed to have a 'reservation wage', set by the social security system or their perceptions of what is fair or worthwhile, below which they are not prepared to take a job.

Figure 8.3 shows (again in a stylised way, with assumptions about the stability, measurement and existence of the curves shown) how the existence of a reservation wage, R, leads to unemployment, where L_s and L_d are respectively the curves of labour supply and labour demand. At R L_1 people want to work, but firms only wish to employ L_2 people. Unemployment of $(L_1 - L_2)$ is the result. If wages were to fall to w*, then the labour market would clear, with resulting employment at L*.

Now consider a situation in which there are no taxes on labour and firms are subject to an environmental tax, all the revenues from which are returned to them in the form of a labour subsidy (the more realistic equivalent case of a cut in non-wage labour taxes is discussed later). In

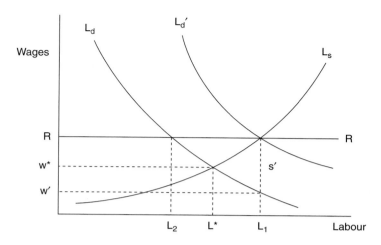

Figure 8.3 The effect of wage subsidies on unemployment

aggregate, and ignoring adjustment and administration costs, firms would not experience net costs, by definition. Firms that are more than averagely environmentally intensive and less than averagely labour-intensive would be net losers, while more labour-intensive and less environmentally intensive firms would be net gainers. There should be no change in the overall price level. Because of the labour subsidy, all employers would experience an outward shift in their labour demand curve, as it became cheaper to employ people. If the subsidy was s', the L_d curve would shift to L_d'. If the reservation wage and labour supply curve did not shift, employment would rise to L_1 and unemployment would disappear. This has occurred through employers now being prepared to pay the reservation wage R, because it is only actually costing them w', the difference s' being covered by the labour subsidy.

If it is not practical to focus the wage subsidy only on those parts of the labour market that are subject to the imperfection of a reservation wage, then the subsidy will still result in an outward shift in labour demand and employment will increase. The extra employment will, however, be at least partly the result of increased labour supply rather than reduced unemployment.

Returning to the situation with a reservation wage, the crucial question is whether with a wage subsidy R and L_s would remain unchanged. Although the environmental tax would raise firms' costs, the lower labour costs would lower them. Overall there should be no increase in the price level and so no increase in either the reservation wage or other wages would be justified on inflationary grounds.

However, if nominal wages were to rise to absorb the subsidy, the result would be quite different. Firms' labour demand curves would not shift outwards, because their labour costs would not change. There might be some initial movement up the L_s curve as workers initially perceived their returns from labour to have increased, but there would be general inflation as labour costs failed to fall to balance the rise in prices due to the environmental tax and the labour supply would drop back down as it became clear that inflation was eroding the value of the nominal wage increase. However, to the extent that the environmental tax was passed on by firms in their prices to non-employed consumers, there would be a redistribution of income from the non-employed to wage-earners, and to this extent real wages and labour supply would rise, *increasing* unemployment (because L_d is unchanged).

If R remained nominally the same, then in real terms the increase in the price level would have caused it to fall, and some increase in employment might result. However, it is more likely that nominal R would rise with the price level, leaving real R the same. Moreover, the price increase would feed through into further wage rises and adverse competitiveness effects, leading to general macroeconomic deterioration.

Whether the wage subsidy increased nominal wages or not, there would be a further effect tending to increase employment. Relative to labour, the price to firms of the taxed environmental input would have increased, and this effect would be greater where wages did not increase and firms' labour costs fell to w′. This would lead to firms seeking to substitute other inputs, including labour, for the taxed environmental input. Moreover, the price of output which embodied the taxed environmental input would rise relative to that which did not (even if the aggregate price level remained unchanged). Insofar as firms' labour costs fell because of the wage subsidy, the price of labour-intensive output would tend to fall relative to other output. All these shifts in relative prices would increase the demand for labour, tending to increase employment and reduce unemployment. The shift in relative prices would also alter the productivity of the affected capital stock and, perhaps, hasten its depreciation. This adjustment effect could be minimised by introducing the taxation in a gradual, pre-announced way, so that the new relative prices were anticipated and allowed for in investment schedules.

To summarise this discussion of the employment dividend, the key question which would determine the extent to which this dividend would arise is whether or not the wage subsidy results in higher wages. If it does, then the implications for employment are ambiguous, being negative because of inflation and macroeconomic deterioration, and positive through the substitution effects in both production and consumption.

If it does not, then employment would unambiguously increase, through both the substitution effects and firms' falling labour costs. Although the higher employment would probably mean that overall labour productivity in the economy was lower, it is also likely that output would increase somewhat. Reaping an employment dividend would have resulted in an efficiency dividend as well. It is important to recognise that these dividends are not due to reducing distortions arising from the existing tax system (which will be discussed in the next section) but from removing the labour market imperfection caused by the reservation wage, as illustrated in Figure 8.3, and increasing the employment of resources (in this case labour) in the economy. To achieve these dividends, and reduce unemployment perhaps substantially, it is only required that social dialogue and economic understanding prevent wage demands from absorbing the labour subsidy from the tax-plus-rebate. Achieving such dialogue and understanding would need to be a political priority in the introduction of such a measure.

The efficiency dividend

Where the existence of a (negative) externality means that the marginal cost of the responsible activity exceeds the marginal benefit, then that activity is underpriced. This is the rationale for environmental taxation, as has been seen. But the underpricing of something in one market affects other markets, as well as its own. The income effect of the underpricing will cause all other goods to be overconsumed compared to the undistorted case. The sign of the substitution effect will differ depending on whether the other goods are substitutes (less will be consumed) or complements (more will be consumed). The environmental tax will not only remove the distortion in the market causing the externality (the environmental dividend), it will also cause the other markets to adjust. Whether these other adjustments are viewed as part of the move towards internalisation and environmental optimality, or as distortions due to the environmental tax, makes a crucial difference as to whether the environmental tax is perceived able to deliver an efficiency dividend or not, as will be seen.

An efficiency dividend from environmental taxation is here defined as an improvement in non-environmental economic welfare because of an increase in output caused by a reallocation of resources that is consequent on the imposition of an environmental tax. Such a dividend may be yielded by an increase in employment, here called an employment dividend, brought about by an environmental tax. But there are a number of other possible sources.

The possibility of an efficiency dividend associated with an employment dividend arose only because the labour market was distorted by the existence of a reservation wage. In general, the possibility of an efficiency dividend exists only where there is such a market distortion, meaning here an allocation of resources that results in lower than potential economic output, prior to the imposition of the environmental tax.

That taxation (apart from impractical lump-sum or poll taxes or taxes internalising externalities) leads to distortions in the economy, is generally and uncontroversially accepted. According to the static perfect competition model, distortions arise from the taxes changing the prices facing both producers and consumers, so that factors no longer receive their marginal product and the cost of output does not reflect its true economic cost. Where the tax falls on labour, whether directly as a labour tax or indirectly as an expenditure tax which reduces the real value of the wage, it introduces a wedge between what the producer pays for labour and what the employee either gets or is able to purchase. Either labour demand or labour supply or both are lower as a result, and so are employment and output (it may be that unemployment is not higher, because this is the difference between labour supply and demand at a given wage).

Figures from the US suggest that distortions from taxation are substantial. Thus Ballard *et al.* calculate the marginal excess burden (MEB) of taxation in the US to be in the range 17 to 56 cents per dollar of extra revenue (Ballard *et al.* 1985: 128). Jorgenson and Yun (1990) find that the MEB of the US tax system as a whole, even after the tax reform of 1986, which was widely held to have reduced the excess burden, is 38 cents per dollar of revenue raised. Some components of the tax system had far higher costs, for example, the MEB for individual capital taxes was 95c/$ (Jorgenson and Yun 1990: 20). Jorgenson and Yun (ibid.: 6) acknowledge that their MEB estimates 'are considerably higher than previous estimates. This can be attributed primarily to the greater precision we employ in representing the US tax structure.' Nordhaus (1993b: 316) notes that 'some have estimated [the marginal deadweight loss of taxes in the US] as high as $0.50 per $1.00 of revenue'.

While there are no comparable figures for Europe, the European Commission makes the point:

> Marginal costs of taxation increase more than proportionally with the level of taxation. In view of the much higher share of tax revenues in the Community than in the USA (the tax burden in the Community is nearly 50 percent higher than in the USA and Japan) it would appear that the costs of fiscal systems in terms of forgone GDP and hence employment might be particularly high in the Community. Only if the structure of the Community's fiscal system were much more efficient than in the USA, would this not hold true.
>
> (EC 1994: 145)

In the absence of grounds for believing European tax systems to be more efficient than that of the US, it seems likely that the distortions from taxation in Europe are at least as great as those in the US.

The key question then becomes whether the substitution of an environmental tax for a distortionary tax can reduce the distortions from the tax system as a whole and lead to an efficiency dividend. The focus here will be on substituting an environmental tax for a labour tax of two kinds: an income tax on employees and a social security tax levied on employers.

Finally some brief consideration will be given to the so-called erosion and interdependency (or tax interaction) effects, which have been the object of some recent analysis in the literature.

Substituting for a personal income tax

Two immediate first-round effects of substituting an environmental tax for a personal income tax (here considering only labour income) will arise:

S1 The environmental tax will raise the price of the affected items; the reduction in income tax will increase the disposable income of employees. Insofar as the higher prices are paid by non-employees (unemployed, pensioners, other non-employed, foreigners), and income tax rebates are received by employees, the substitution will raise the real wage. This will increase the labour supply.
S2 The price increases will be concentrated in the goods or activities subject to the tax. Where the tax falls on inputs, producers will tend to substitute away from the taxed input. Where it falls on final demand, consumers will shift demand away from the affected sectors to others that are relatively less environment-intensive and so less affected by the tax. It is, of course, the intention of the tax to bring about this substitution by both producers and consumers, and it will occur irrespective of how the revenue from the tax is recycled.

Insofar as there is an inverse correlation between labour-intensity and environment-intensity, the demand for labour-intensive goods and services will increase. Barker (1994: 20–1) has shown that such a correlation exists for the production and industrial use of energy (energy-intensive industries tend to use relatively little labour; labour-intensive industries tend to use relatively little energy). A revenue-neutral energy tax would therefore be expected to increase labour demand.

The increase in labour demand as a result of S2 will either reduce unemployment (if it exists) or put to work the increased labour supply induced as a result of S1. Either way employment and output would increase, yielding both an employment and an efficiency dividend. The increased employment and output would result in second-round macroeconomic improvements (lower benefits, higher tax revenues so lower tax rates, etc.). The only way these positive benefits would fail to materialise would be if S2's increase in labour demand were far stronger that S1's increase in labour supply in the context of a tight labour market. The increased labour demand would then engender wage inflation with generally negative effects on employment and output.

The effect S1 comes about as a result of a reduction of a distortion in the labour market (employees' disposable income moves closer to their marginal product as paid by their employers), through the simultaneous reduction or removal of a distortion in the market of the taxed good (an externality has been wholly or partially internalised). It is important to recognise that the labour market distortion has *not* been reduced through the introduction of another distortion, but through the reduction or removal of one. However, the possibility has been addressed in a number of recent papers (e.g. Bovenberg and de Mooij 1994; Goulder 1995a, 1995b; Parry 1995) that, through interdependencies in the tax system, or the erosion of the environmental tax base, the reduction of the environmental distortion in the context of a labour market with pre-existing labour taxes could lead to more labour market distortion rather than less. This possibility is considered below.

Substituting for an employers' social security tax (SST)

Consider an average firm using energy E_1 and employing labour L_1, which is subject to a SST of t_L. The firm pays tax of $L_1 t_L$.

Now let a tax t_E be imposed on energy, with full compensation by way of reduction in SST. Then, initially, the firm will pay energy tax of $E_1 t_E$, with a reduction in its SST rate to:

$$t_L - (t_E E_1)/L_1$$

Now, with energy relatively more expensive and labour relatively cheaper, the firm changes its proportion of inputs, say to L_2 ($> L_1$) and E_2 ($< E_1$).

The tax paid on energy use is now $t_E E_2$. Let the new tax rate on labour, t_L', be set so that the total tax paid by the firm is unchanged, so:

$$
\begin{aligned}
t_L L_1 &= t_L' L_2 + t_E E_2 \\
\Rightarrow t_L' &= t_L(L_1/L_2) - t_E E_2/L_2 \\
\Rightarrow t_L' &< t_L
\end{aligned}
\tag{8.1}
$$

The first term on the right-hand side (RHS) of equation 1 can be thought of as the result of the substitution effect. The firm's tax rate on labour will be reduced in proportion to its increased employment. The second term is the revenue effect of the energy tax, further reducing the effective tax rate on labour.

The reduction in the effective tax rate on labour will reduce the overall marginal cost of labour to the firm, as long as the wage paid to labour is unchanged. If this is so, then the greater is the fall from t_L to t_L', the greater is the fall in labour's marginal cost to the firm.

This situation is analogous to that analysed earlier using Figure 8.3. In this case, instead of s' being a wage subsidy, it is a reduction in the employers' SST, which has the same effect of reducing the marginal cost of labour and thereby increasing labour demand. The reduction in labour costs may also enable firms to cut the price of their output, thereby compensating for any price increases due to the imposition of the environmental tax.

As in the earlier case, if all the SST decrease is passed through to employees as an increase in wages, then evidently the marginal cost of labour to employers will not fall and so labour demand will not rise. Even so, because of the increased cost of energy, a substitution effect still takes place, but less strongly. The situation then becomes identical to where the recycling was achieved by reducing a personal income tax, as in S1 and S2 above.

Situation S1 above described how the substitution of an environmental tax for a personal income tax could, by reducing the distortionary effects of the latter, bring about an efficiency dividend. However, there are a number of reasons why this might not be the whole story, namely the so-called erosion and interdependency effects (explored in Bovenberg and de Mooij 1994; Goulder 1995a; Parry 1995) and possible distortionary effects due to the environmental tax *per se*. These possible effects are discussed in the next two sections.

Erosion and interdependency effects between environmental and labour taxes

The interdependency effect has been discussed in detail in Parry (1995). Parry constructs a model that includes a good, the production or consumption of which entails a negative environmental externality, and labour taxes which distort the labour/leisure market, such that more than the optimal amount of leisure is taken.

Imposing an environmental tax raises the price of the polluting good and, where this good is a substitute for leisure, this causes still more leisure to be taken, thereby increasing the distortion in the leisure market. This not only imposes a welfare cost *per se*, but reduces revenue from the labour tax so that more labour taxes are required, thus increasing the welfare burden from that source. This combined effect Parry calls the 'interdependency effect' (IE) of environmental taxation.

Parry acknowledges that recycling the revenue from the environmental tax will reduce the welfare burden from the pre-existing labour taxes, which he calls the recycling effect (RE). However, his analysis finds that, where the polluting good is an average or greater than average substitute for leisure, RE/IE < 1 always. This means that the 'efficiency dividend', as defined above, cannot exist in such a situation. It means, moreover, that the optimal environmental tax will be less than the marginal environmental damage.

Where Parry talks of an interdependency effect, Bovenberg and de Mooij (1994) find that the erosion effect of an environmental tax rules out an efficiency dividend. Their model shows that the imposition of an environmental tax has a negative effect on employment:

The negative effect on employment is due to a decline in the real after-tax wage eroding the incentives to supply labour. The drop in the real after-tax wage comes about because the lower tax rate on labour income does not fully compensate workers for the adverse effect of the pollution levy on their real after-tax wage. This incomplete offset is due to the erosion of the tax base of the environmental tax. In particular, the higher environmental tax induces households to switch from dirty to clean consumption commodities. If the initial tax rate on the dirty commodities is positive, this behavioral effect erodes the base of the environmental tax and, therefore, produces a negative tax base effect.

(Bovenberg and de Mooij 1994: 1087–8)

In other words, imposing the environmental tax (on final commodities) causes consumers to switch away from the affected goods. The price of the goods rises by the amount of the tax, but the erosion of the tax base means that not enough revenue is raised to fully compensate consumers by adequately reducing their income taxes. Consumers are worse off, their real wage has declined and so they will work less. This reduces employment and output (and, in Bovenberg and de Mooij's framework, would have further knock-on effects through raising reduced revenues from the labour tax, necessitating a further rise in tax rates and even greater losses in the after-tax wage).

Goulder (1995a) basically endorses these results and then extends the discussion of the possible effects of incorporating other issues into the analysis, such as intermediate inputs, capital and emissions taxes. These extensions serve to complicate the results of the other papers, without fundamentally altering them.

Pethig (1996: 1, original emphasis) describes these results as an 'obvious *discrepancy* between informed common sense and theoretical analysis', and considers that it may be due to a failure to understand the complexities of multiple distortions or a lack of robustness in the models used. Elsewhere Ekins (1996b, 1997) has subjected the analysis of Parry and Bovenberg and de Mooij to a detailed critique, only the conclusions of which will be given here. Essentially, both papers, while acknowledging the distortion caused by the environmental externality in the market of the polluting good, ignore the distortion that this brings about in the labour/leisure market. Thus Parry's negative interdependency effect derives from ignoring the distortion in the leisure market due to the externality (i.e. ignoring the interdependence between the markets) before the environmental tax is imposed, and then regarding the tax's effect on the leisure market as the imposition of a distortion instead of the removal of one. With a more consistent treatment of the interdependency between the two markets, an efficiency dividend emerges as the most likely outcome from the substitution of environmental taxes for distortionary labour taxes.

Bovenberg and de Mooij also do not consider that the undistorted position of the labour/leisure market is that *after* the internalisation of the environmental externality by the environmental tax, but this does not affect their basic outcome of an erosion effect. However, they also do not take into account two other considerations, which could counteract it. The first is the point made under S1 above, that some of the price increase from the environmental tax will be paid by non-employees and this will act to counter the reduction in the real wage from the erosion effect. The second is the possibility, again discussed above, that a reduction in employers' social security taxes, again discussed above, may enable firms to cut the price of their output, thereby counteracting the price increases from the environmental taxation and preventing the reduction in the real wage which reduced the labour supply.

Although Goulder (1995a: 168) very briefly considers involuntary unemployment, neither he, Parry nor Bovenberg and de Mooij consider a situation in which a reduction in voluntary unemployment could result in an efficiency dividend.

The distortions introduced by an environmental tax

It has been repeatedly argued in this chapter that, unlike other taxes which tend to introduce distortions, environmental taxes at (or below) their optimal level (partially) correct an economic distortion. As far as the environmental dimension is concerned this argument is uncontroversial.

While accepting this argument, Goulder (1995b) puts the environmental dimension on one side and subjects the carbon tax to the standard insights of the optimal taxation literature (e.g. Diamond and Mirrlees 1971; Stiglitz and Dasgupta 1971). His conclusions, which are quantified by the use of a general equilibrium model, are that, leaving aside its environmental benefits, a carbon tax is substantially *more* distorting than personal income, corporate or payroll taxes. The distortions it introduces arise from its non-uniformity across energy carriers (precisely the characteristic that makes it an efficient environmental tax), the narrowness of the tax base, and the fact that it falls on intermediate inputs as well as final output. Goulder's model also broadly endorses Bovenberg and de Mooij's theoretical conclusions described above.

Goulder's result that the distortionary effect of a tax on energy is likely to be greater than that of the other taxes it replaces has itself been challenged. INFRAS (1996) points out that the size of the distortionary effect of a tax depends not only on the tax rate (which, for a given revenue, will tend to be higher and more distortionary the narrower the tax base), but also on the elasticities of demand and supply of the taxed quantity. The net effect of increasing energy and, for example, reducing labour taxes will therefore depend on the relative elasticities of labour and energy. Using the ECOPLAN computable general equilibrium model for Switzerland,

INFRAS (1996: 141) finds that the distortionary effects of a carbon tax are substantially less than the reduced distortions from lowering employers' labour taxes, yielding a positive efficiency dividend even before the extra output from reducing unemployment is considered.

The conclusions of the Goulder, Parry and Bovenberg and de Mooij papers discussed above may, as Pethig suggests, conflict with 'common sense' about environmental taxes and doubtless will continue to be challenged both theoretically and empirically, including with such arguments as have been presented here. But formal economic analysis can sometimes yield insights of more validity than 'common sense', and certainly the arguments of Bovenberg and de Mooij about the possible significance of pre-existing taxation distortions, and of Goulder about the possible non-environmental distortions introduced by, for example, a carbon tax, cannot simply be dismissed. To the extent that the arguments are valid, they reduce the optimum level of the carbon tax. Furthermore, if the distortions postulated by Bovenberg and de Mooij and Goulder are of a comparable size to the environmental dividend, they undermine the case for Pigouvian taxation completely. Under these circumstances the prospects of using efficiency gains in the tax system to offset the costs of environmental improvement are practically non-existent.

8.1.3 Conclusion on the three main dividends

1   Where there is an environmental externality, the imposition of a tax directed at the externality, at a level equal to or below the Pigouvian level, will yield an environmental dividend. If the tax falls on the commodity related to the externality, the environmental dividend will derive purely from a reduction in output, which is the cost of achieving this dividend. If the tax falls directly on the environmental externality (e.g. on an emission), and if there are possibilities of abating the externality at a marginal cost lower than the tax levied, then some abatement will take place, the output/externality relation will be changed, the environmental dividend will be greater and the loss of output will be less than if there is no abatement or a commodity tax is levied.

2   Where there is involuntary unemployment, it can be reduced by the imposition of an environmental tax with the revenues used to subsidise wages in the part of the labour market where wages are inflexible, providing that the wage subsidy is not passed on to employees as a wage increase. Where the labour market imperfection is due to an employer's labour tax, then unemployment can be reduced by using the revenues from the environmental tax to reduce the labour tax, again providing that this reduction is not passed on to employees in the form of higher wages. In both cases the increase in employment, the employment dividend, will result in increased output, an efficiency dividend.

An employment dividend also arises from the shift towards relatively labour-intensive production and consumption caused by the reduced price of labour relative to taxed environmental inputs. Where there is involuntary unemployment this will also lead to an efficiency dividend in the form of increased output.

3   It is possible that an efficiency dividend will arise from using environmental tax revenues to reduce other distortionary taxes. The most recent theoretical work suggests, however, that not only is such an efficiency dividend unlikely, but that the environmental tax may be both more distortionary (apart from its environmental effects) than the taxes it replaces and may 'exacerbate rather than alleviate pre-existing tax distortions' (Bovenberg and de Mooij 1994: 1085). These effects would mean that the optimal environmental tax rate would be below that suggested by the environmental dividend alone.

The theoretical analysis on which these last conclusions are based is complex and yet highly stylised. Even if it is relevant to the operation of a real economy, it may still be that a net efficiency dividend could emerge from the reduction in involuntary unemployment, as noted in the previous point. However, literature that is sceptical of the possibility of achieving an efficiency dividend has probably served a useful purpose in dampening down excessive expectations of cost-free improvements to the environment simply from a reduction in the distortionary effects of other taxes.

8.2 EVIDENCE FROM SIMULATION MODELS

The discussion so far has been purely theoretical. Another way of gaining insights into the dividends of environmental taxation is from computer models that simulate the effects of such taxation on the economy. The link between theory and simulation is that the relationships in the simulation models are derived from theory. In a general equilibrium model the simulations are normally exclusively driven by the specified theoretical relationships, in that the values of the parameters of the model are calibrated from a single year, and all markets, including the labour market, are constrained to clear, which means, among other things, that these models show no unemployment. Macro-econometric models, on the other hand, which are also based on theory, derive their parameters from time-series estimation so that they are based on a whole range of past data which has been accepted by the model. While their markets may be constrained to clear in the long run, they can have non-clearing markets in the short and medium terms, so that they do yield insights into unemployment.

All models produce results that are determined by the relationships between variables that are specified in the models, so that these results are entirely dependent on the assumptions and specifications of the modellers.

8.2.1 The environmental dividend

All models agree that, where there is a negative environmental externality, environmental taxation can yield an environmental dividend. The size of the dividend from a given environmental tax depends on the size of the elasticity of substitution of the affected input in production, and of the elasticities of demand and substitution of the affected products in consumption: the higher the elasticities the higher the environmental dividend.

The variety of dividends that can be simulated by different models with regard to the same issue is well illustrated by the exercise undertaken by the Energy Modeling Forum (EMF) at Stanford University, which specified standardised scenarios for fourteen widely differing economic models of the US economy. In these models a carbon tax of $80/tonne carbon brought about a change in CO_2 levels with respect to 1990 of between −35 per cent and +20 per cent (Gaskins and Weyant 1993: 319). Obviously, had no carbon tax been levied, emissions in all cases would have been greater, but the range of these simulations is very great.

More general evidence of the environmental dividend from environmental taxation came from the wide-ranging report from DRI and other consultancies, commissioned by the European Commission (DRI 1994). DRI modelled three scenarios for six of the larger European Union economies (EU-6): a Reference scenario (REF) containing 'all policy measures and actions agreed by the end of 1992' (ibid.: 27); a Policy-in-the-Pipeline scenario (PIP), incorporating policies or proposals that had been the subject of a directive, mainly comprising 'command and control' measures, except for the European Commission's carbon-energy tax; and an Integrated scenario (INT), mainly using market instruments, including environmental taxation, to internalise environmental costs.

Table 8.1 shows the environmental results of the scenarios, in terms of changing environmental pressure in various areas. Much of the positive difference between PIP and INT may be attributed to environmental taxes and considered the taxes' environmental dividend.

8.2.2 The employment dividend

DRI also modelled a variant of the INT scenario, called INT+, in which all the revenues from INT's environmental taxes were used to reduce employers' non-wage labour costs such as social security payments or, in the UK, employers' National Insurance Contributions. This was the situation that was analysed theoretically earlier. The scenario results showed that the employment dividend was not insubstantial. INT showed an increase over REF by 2010 of 1.1 million jobs (an employment increase of 1 per cent), while INT+ showed an increase of 2.2 million jobs (DRI 1994: 53). The increase in INT will have come about from the substitution of now relatively cheaper labour for environmental resources in

Table 8.1 Changes in environmental pressures between 1990 and 2010 across themes

Theme	REF	PIP	INT
Climate change	−30	−10	0
Regional air quality			
• acid deposition	+10	+40	+70
• photochemical	−10	+20	+60
Urban environment			
• air pollution	+10	+30	+80
• other	−70	−40	−20
Toxic substances	+30	+20	+20
Nature and biodiversity	−20	−10	+10
Water quality	−20	+30	+50
Water resources	−20	−10	−10
Waste			
• hazardous	−60	0	+50
• non–hazardous	−30	−10	+40
Oil in the coastal zone	−20	+10	+30

Source: DRI (1994: 62)
Note: a + indicates an environmental improvement, and a − an environmental deterioration (i.e. a decrease or increase in environmental pressure) of the percentage indicated

production, and a shift away from environmentally intensive goods and services in consumption, as discussed earlier. The further effect in INT+ is due to an intensification of these effects through the reduction in firms' labour costs from the recycling of the environmental taxes' revenues.

A number of other studies, reviewed by Majocchi (1996), have produced similar results. The QUEST model indicated that a 10 per cent reduction in employers' social security contributions (SSCs), financed by a carbon-energy tax, would after seven years increase employment by 1.0 per cent, reducing unemployment by 0.9 per cent (Majocchi 1996: 384). Financing the cut by increasing personal income taxes only increased employment by 0.7 per cent (because of the lack of any shift away from energy-intensive commodities), while increasing VAT brought no employment increase at all. Another study, using the HERMES model, found that a similar cut in SSCs, also financed by a carbon-energy tax, produced a 0.64 per cent rise in employment in the EU-6 by 2001 (ibid.: 386).

The employment dividend can be made even greater by targeting the SSC reductions on the lower paid. Several studies suggest that such targeting could increase employment by 2–3 per cent (Majocchi 1996: 388–93). For example, the QUEST model shows that, with full recycling of revenues to achieve budget neutrality, employment could increase by 3.0 per cent and unemployment decrease by 2.7 per cent across the EU from such a measure (ibid.: 393 (Table VIII); see also EC 1994: 160).

INFRAS (1996) is another recent review of the now substantial literature in this area. Its conclusion from this review is: 'The revenue-recycling through a reduction of SSC [employers' social security contributions] has positive, [or] in the worst case, no *employment effects.* . . . A targeted cut in SSC for low skilled labour forces has a strong positive employment effect' (INFRAS 1996: 52, original emphasis).

The positive employment effects of a carbon tax are not only due to the lower relative price of labour compared to energy. It also derives from the relative labour-intensity of non-carbon-intensive sectors, which can expect to experience increased demand due to the relative price shift. The effect is brought out clearly in the detailed study by Proops *et al.* (1993). In order to provide insights into the implications of a changed structure of final demand due to measures to limit CO_2 emissions, they used input–output techniques to calculate the embodied energy and CO_2 emissions of different industrial sectors. In one of their simulations they impose, on an underlying growth rate of 2 per cent, an extra 8 per cent per annum increase in the demand for commodities in the tertiary sectors (e.g. telecommunications, financial and other services), and cut demand in energy-intensive sectors proportionally to maintain the overall 2 per cent growth rate. They find that, in the UK, CO_2 emissions fall by 3.45 per cent per annum and employment rises by 4.60 per cent per annum, reflecting the tertiary sector's higher labour intensity (Proops *et al.* 1993: 206–7).

All these studies tend to confirm the theoretical conclusions discussed earlier that an employment dividend from environmental taxation is probable and may be significant.

8.2.3 The efficiency dividend

It is to be expected that the increase in employment shown by the models as discussed in the previous section would lead to an increase in output, and the models do indeed show this too. Thus the INT and the INT+ scenarios in the DRI report indicate GDP increases over REF by 2010 of 0.9 per cent and 1.06 per cent respectively. For the untargeted case using the QUEST model, the GDP increase after seven years was 1.0 per cent, rising to 1.8 per cent in the targeted case.

QUEST's albeit small increases in GDP from an imposition of a carbon tax are in contrast to the GDP decreases, or costs, from such a tax that many other models have found and which tend to predominate in discussion of this issue. For example, the Stanford Energy Modeling Forum exercise mentioned earlier found: 'The costs of achieving a 20 percent reduction in CO_2 emissions (in the U.S.) relative to today's level range from 0.9 percent to 1.7 percent of U.S. GDP in 2010' (Gaskins and Weyant 1993: 320).

However, these results showing costs were generated by returning the carbon tax revenues to households on a lump-sum basis, rather than by reducing distortionary taxes. It is clear that such a procedure is suboptimal.

For example, Jorgenson and Wilcoxen argue: '[Lump-sum recycling] is probably not the most likely use of the revenue. . . . Using the revenue to reduce a distortionary tax would lower the net cost of a carbon tax by removing inefficiency elsewhere in the economy' (Jorgenson and Wilcoxen 1993: 20). This is precisely the effect that is obtained in all models that do in fact reduce distortionary taxes to offset a carbon tax. Jorgenson and Wilcoxen (ibid.: 22 (Table 5)) themselves find that a 1.7 per cent GDP loss under lump-sum redistribution is converted to a 0.69 per cent loss and a 1.1 per cent gain by reducing labour and capital taxes respectively.

This effect has also been shown in the work of Nordhaus. Nordhaus (1991a), on the basis of an abatement-cost curve derived from his survey of extant models in Nordhaus (1991b), and his own calculation of a global warming damage function, arrived at an efficient level of a carbon tax of $7.33 per ton CO_2 equivalent (Nordhaus 1991a: 934). By 1993, using his own DICE model, the optimum carbon tax had fallen to $5.24 per ton CO_2 equivalent. Using a carbon tax of $56 per ton to cut emissions in 1995 by 20 per cent from 1990 levels caused an annualised global GDP loss of $762 billion (Nordhaus 1993b: 315). However, these DICE results came from recycling the carbon tax revenues through lump-sum rebates. When instead carbon taxes are used to reduce other, burdensome taxes, assumed to have a deadweight loss of $0.30 per $ of revenue raised, then the optimal tax rate becomes $59 per ton, emissions go below the 20 per cent cut, and annualised GDP *rises* by $206 billion. Nordhaus notes: 'The importance of revenue recycling is surprising and striking. These findings emphasize the critical nature of designing the instruments and use of revenues in a careful manner. The tail of revenue recycling would seem to wag the dog of climate-change policy' (ibid.: 317).

Barker has consistently argued against lump-sum rebates to offset revenues: 'An alternative treatment would be to find which existing tax creates the largest distortions in the economy and the highest loss of welfare and then to use the carbon tax revenues . . . to reduce the marginal rates of this tax' (Barker 1992: 9). Boero *et al.* agree: 'Economically we should seek to reduce the most distortionary [tax]' (Boero *et al.* 1991: 93). On Jorgenson and Yun's figures this would mean initially offsetting taxes with an MEB of 95c/$. Because of interaction effects between the taxes, it is not possible to argue that, for this tranche of offset, each dollar of carbon tax revenue raised would generate a 95c increase in welfare because of distortionary reductions elsewhere; but it may be noted that this rate of offset is more than three times that used by Nordhaus in his 'tail-wagging' calculation discussed earlier, and could thus be expected to yield a substantially higher optimal tax rate than his $59 per ton CO_2 equivalent.

While they do not report the MEB figure they used, Gaskins and Weyant confirm the importance of this approach to revenue recycling: 'Simulation with four models of the US economy indicate that from 35 per cent to more than 100 per cent of the GDP losses could ultimately be offset by recycling revenues through cuts in existing taxes' (Gaskins and Weyant 1993: 320). Models that do not take account of the possibly beneficial effects of revenue recycling may be expected to overstate the costs of carbon reduction under rational policy making.

Barker *et al.* (1993) have modelled the effects on the UK economy of the proposed EC carbon/energy tax. Their scenarios were tax retention by the government, what Barker *et al.* call the 'depression scenario', EC tax with VAT offset and EC tax with income tax offset. The per centage differences of GDP from base by 2005 were −0.37, 0.17, 0.09. Once again, the recycling of the tax converted a cost into a benefit. Such results suggest that, although the carbon tax in a tax-reform package might be regarded as an extra economic constraint, its negative effects can be offset by loosening, or even removing, the constraints represented by other taxes. The effect on macroeconomic variables such as output cannot be deduced *a priori* but will depend on the relative elasticities of demand and substitution of the goods and services affected by the package.

In addition to the GDP level, a further macroeconomic indicator which is highly sensitive to the tax offsets to a carbon tax is inflation. Clearly, a carbon tax, by raising the prices of fossil fuels, will raise the general price level; but offsetting it with reductions in VAT or other taxes will tend to reduce the price level. Different offsetting arrangements can vary the overall price effects from being inflationary to being largely inflation-neutral. Reducing VAT tends to offset the carbon tax's inflation more than reducing other taxes. In fact, using VAT the tax 'package' can be designed to be inflation-neutral, to eliminate the effect of inflation on other variables in the model (e.g. wages).

The preservation of broad neutrality with regard to inflation would appear to be an important consideration if negative macroeconomic impacts from a carbon tax are to be avoided. For, example, the study by Yamaji *et al.* (1993: 127) shows output losses in the Japanese economy of 5 per cent in 2005 following the imposition of a carbon tax, even when the tax is offset by reductions in income tax. This is because inflation induced by the increased demand due to higher disposable incomes largely erodes the nominal output gains due to recycling the revenues. It would have been interesting to see results from this model from offsetting the carbon taxation by reducing indirect taxes, which might have been expected to have resulted in lower inflation as well as maintaining demand.

It must be emphasised that these model results do not 'prove' the existence of multiple dividends from environmental taxation. They arise from the specification of the model that is being used, with regard, for example, to the relative distortions introduced by carbon/energy and labour taxes. Furthermore, if these specifications had included the 'interdependency' and 'erosion' effects discussed earlier, then the multiple dividends would not have emerged. Goulder (1995a) believes that the models should include these effects. For example, Goulder dismisses the Nordhaus results presented above on the grounds that 'they do not capture the tax interaction effect because the model did not include pre-existing taxes. Including pre-existing taxes in the benchmark data would likely reverse the Nordhaus results' (Goulder 1995a: 173).

However, even this is far from certain. In a simulation using the Jorgenson-Wilcoxen model, which does contain pre-existing taxes, multiple dividends arise when either labour or capital taxes are replaced by a carbon tax, a result which, as far as the labour tax is concerned, Goulder finds 'difficult to account for' (Goulder 1995a: 172). Simulations from other models reported in Goulder's paper, replacing a personal income tax, do not show multiple dividends. However, insofar as replacing a personal income tax (as opposed to SSCs) does not bring about substitutions in production as well as consumption, one would have expected smaller multiple dividends in this case anyway. INFRAS (1996: 141) considers that its empirical result reported in the previous section 'disproves the theoretical hypothesis of Bovenberg' (and, implicitly, of Goulder) on the importance of the distortions introduced by a carbon tax.

On balance, the conclusion drawn here is that a triple dividend from environmental taxation, with appropriate revenue-recycling, yielding increases in environmental quality, employment and output, is both predicted theoretically and emerges from simulations often enough to be regarded as a likely outcome, with the output dividend being the least certain and the least significant.

8.3 EVIDENCE FROM IMPLEMENTATION

Tax systems, and environmental taxes within them, are complex and subject to restructuring, so that it is no easy matter to compare how the imposition of environmental taxes has changed over time. However, three OECD reports (Opschoor and Vos 1989; OECD 1994b, 1995b) do enable some comparisons of recent experience to be made.

Table 8.2 shows how the percentage of tax in the price of petrol has changed between 1990 and 1994 in a number of OECD countries. The percentage has increased in all the countries shown, in some quite markedly. The US has the lowest tax rate by a large margin.

Between 1990 and 1994 five countries – Denmark, Finland, the Netherlands, Norway and Sweden – introduced carbon or carbon-energy taxes as part of a reconfiguration of their systems of energy taxation according to environmental criteria. Norway also introduced taxes on SO_2 emissions, and Sweden imposed taxes on SO_2 and NO_x. While the changes involved in these reconfigurations are limited (see OECD 1994b, 1995b), they remain important examples of environmental tax reform.

Table 8.2 Total taxes as per cent of end-user price of petrol (households)

Country	1990	1994	1996
Belgium	65.5	74.2	73.9
Canada	42.4	50.0	50.5
France	74.3	80.8	81.3
Germany	63.1	76.9	76.4
Italy	74.9	76.1	74.4
Japan	45.6	48.3	55.9
Netherlands	64.5	75.9	76.4
UK	61.9	73.5	79.4
US	26.7	34.4	29.0

Sources: OECD (1995b: 48 (Table 2)); OECD/IEA (1996)

Table 8.3 gives some examples of the broad range of taxes which have been introduced in OECD countries in recent years, the great majority of them since 1990. Over this period it is generally true to say that tax rates have tended to be increased and some new taxes have been introduced.

If multiple dividends from environmental taxation do not exist, then policy makers should evaluate such taxation purely on the basis of whether its environmental benefits are worth its economic costs. But there is substantial evidence that this is not in fact the way that policy makers are currently assessing environmental taxes; nor are the environmental benefits the only reason for their slowly but steadily increasing introduction.

As an example of the shift in perception on this point, it is striking that, in 1989, the OECD survey of 'economic instruments for environmental protection' (Opshoor and Vos 1989), which include environmental taxes, made no mention at all of possible multiple dividends. Although the study noted increasing interest in economic instruments, it attributed this to a desire for more cost-effective environmental protection, for greater policy integration, both within environmental policy and between it and other policy areas, and for a more preventive rather than curative approach. Yet by 1993 the European Commission's White Paper *Growth, Competitiveness, Employment* was making the employment dividend a core *raison d'être* for environmental taxes: 'If the double challenge of unemployment/environmental pollution is to be addressed, a swap can be envisaged between reducing labour costs through increased pollution charges' (EC 1993: 150). This idea was explicitly endorsed by the UK Chancellor of the Exchequer in his 1994 Budget, when he stated: 'Taxes can play an important role in protecting the environment. . . . But I am determined not to impose additional costs on business overall. . . . In brief, I want to raise tax on polluters to make further cuts in the tax on jobs' (Clarke 1994: 35).

This position was more or less reaffirmed by the new UK Government in 1997, which issued with its first Budget a Statement of Intent on Environmental Taxation which included the commitment:

Table 8.3 Some environmental taxes in some OECD countries

Target of tax	Type of tax	Country(ies) of implementation
Pollution		
Air	Emission charges	F
	CO_2 tax	DK, N, NL ,S, SK
	NO_x tax	S
Water	Waste water charges	D, DK, F, NL
Soil	Surplus manure tax	B, NL
Waste	Waste/landfill tax	DK, NL, UK
Noise	Aircraft tax	B, F, D, NL, N, P, S, CH
Products		
Pesticides/fertilisers	Product tax	B, N, S
Batteries	Product tax	B, I, P, S
Various disposables	Product tax	B
Uranium	Product tax	NL
CFCs	Product tax	USA
Minerals	Product tax	C, DK
Fuels	Product tax	All European countries
Depletion		
Water	Groundwater depletion	NL
Space	Congestion charge	I, N
Minerals	Minerals tax	C, DK

Sources: Opschoor and Vos (1989), OECD (1995b)

Note:

B	Belgium	C	Canada	CH	Switzerland
D	Germany	DK	Denmark	F	France
I	Italy	N	Norway	NL	Netherlands
P	Portugal	S	Sweden	SK	Finland
UK	United Kingdom	USA	United States of America		

Over time the Government will aim to reform the tax system to increase incentives to reduce environmental damage. That will shift the burden of tax from 'goods' to 'bads'; encourage innovation in meeting higher environmental standards; and deliver a more dynamic economy and a cleaner environment, to the benefit of everyone.

(HM Treasury 1997)

An OECD (1997) evaluation of environmental taxes confirmed: 'Environmental tax policies are increasingly being implemented as part of an integrated approach to tax reform, in which revenues from environmental taxes are used to permit reductions in labour taxes and/or other existing taxes' (OECD 1997: 19). Another study by the OECD, of the Swedish implementation of environmental taxes, makes clear that the desire to use revenues from environmental taxes in this way is not an unimportant motivation for their introduction, concluding: 'It seems fair to say that, without the opportunity offered by the need felt to reduce income taxes, while keeping the total volume intact, environmental taxes would not have been introduced to the extent that now is the case' (OECD 1994b: 57). In other words the environmental dividend from environmental taxation was perceived as of no greater importance than the benefits of reducing distortionary taxes elsewhere.

8.4 CONCLUSION

Of course, the fact that policy makers seem to have been converted to the idea of the possibility of multiple dividends from environmental taxation does not necessarily mean that such dividends either exist or will be achieved in practice. This chapter has sought to show that there are sound theoretical reasons for believing that the systematic shift of the tax burden from labour and capital to the use of environmental resources can improve environmental quality, increase employment, thereby reducing unemployment, and, at the least, have no significant effect on output, though this last result depends, as has been seen, on perceptions of the importance of tax interaction effects and of the effects of shifting the tax burden from a broad to a relatively narrow base.

Modelling of environmental taxes with appropriate revenue-recycling suggests, though with exceptions, that multiple dividends exist. However, the output dividend is likely to be small. The chief significance that it exists at all lies in the fact that it suggests that environmental tax reform may be a way of improving environmental quality without negatively affecting the economy, fear of which has tended to militate against action for environmental improvement. The employment dividend may be more substantial than the output dividend. While it certainly will not 'solve' unemployment on its own, it seems likely that it could make a useful contribution towards reducing it. There are not many macropolicies for reducing unemployment. Environmental tax reform is not a policy that those committed to such reduction can afford to ignore.

But the principal dividend of environmental taxation remains the environmental dividend. Those who have questioned the existence of multiple dividends have performed an important service in re-emphasising 'the critical importance of attending to the environmental benefits' (Goulder 1995a: 176). It is not likely to result in optimal policy to allow the introduction of environmental taxation to be driven by the perception that income, or other distortionary or unpopular, taxes are too high. The principal purpose of environmental taxation is, and should remain, the improvement of environmental quality through the internalisation of environmental costs. But what this analysis of other possible dividends does suggest is that this process is not likely to involve the economic costs that have often been attributed to environmental improvement in the past. Rather it may yield net non-environmental economic benefits. This should make environmental tax reform attractive even to policy makers who are more sensitive to economic performance than to environmental damage. The evidence suggests that, despite the political difficulties of introducing environmental taxes (discussed in Hanley *et al.* 1990 and, more briefly, OECD 1994b: 43–5, but outside the scope of this chapter), this is proving to be the case.

9 Decision making and the costs related to climate change

9.1 INTRODUCTION

The issue of possible climate change induced by global warming due to the anthropogenically enhanced greenhouse effect has become the most studied environmental problem, generating a huge economic, as well as natural scientific, literature, to which this chapter can do scant justice. Yet it is a particularly important issue for this investigation of the limits, or lack of limits, to economic growth, because both sides of the damage equation (damage costs from climate change and economic damage costs of seeking to mitigate it) are routinely expressed as percentages of global economic product forgone. In other words it is explicitly recognised that climate change, as well as attempts to abate it, may act as a constraint on economic growth. While this is, of course, the case for negative environmental impacts apart from climate change, with climate change the possible scale of the effects throws both sets of constraints, those from environmental damage as well as those from trying to do something about it, into sharp relief.

The climate change issue therefore raises two questions which are central to this book. First, how should the costs of climate change be evaluated? Are the various economic techniques of environmental valuation discussed in Chapter 2 able to provide credible monetary estimates of impacts from an effect of this kind? If so, and assuming that the costs of mitigating climate change can similarly be evaluated, then the standard economic approach of optimisation through cost–benefit analysis (CBA) would be appropriate. If not, then some other approach, such as the sustainability approach developed in Chapter 4, may need to be employed.

Second, whichever approach is used, if some mitigation of climate change is found to be desirable or necessary, the question arises as to what effects mitigation will have on economic growth. In the terms of Chapter 6, will the measures of mitigation fall in sectors A, B or C of Figure 6.1?

Faced with the possible damages and the related uncertainties of human-induced climate change, there are three possible choices of decision:

1   Inaction, which involves acceptance of the damages.
2   Adaptation, which involves acceptance of climate change but action to reduce the damage that it inflicts (e.g. by building dikes against sea-level rise, increasing air-conditioning to reduce heat stress, or changing agricultural practices in response to different climatic conditions).
3   Mitigation, which involves action to reduce the amount of climate change that takes place, by either reducing the emission of greenhouse gases (GG), or increasing global sinks of such gases, or deflecting solar radiation from the earth.

It is likely that a practical decision-making strategy will contain elements of all three kinds of decision: some damages will be accepted, and some measures of both adaptation and mitigation will be taken. All three kinds of decision may entail costs. The crucial decision-making question obviously concerns the balance to be struck between inaction, adaptation and mitigation, once the prior question has been addressed as to how decision making on this issue should be approached.

There are therefore three interdependent kinds of costs associated with climate change: damage costs (C_D), adaptation costs (C_A) and prevention costs (C_P). The damage costs will depend on the extent of warming and, therefore, on emissions (e), and on the extent of adaptation measures adopted (a). Adaptation costs depend only on (a). The costs of prevention or abatement are a (negative) function of emissions. The greater the reduction in emissions from the baseline, the higher the abatement cost.

The total cost (C_T) can therefore be written:

$$C_T(e,a) = C_D(e,a) + C_A(a) + C_P(e)$$

where $\partial C_T/\partial e$, $\partial C_T/\partial a$, $\partial C_D/\partial e$, $\partial C_A/\partial a > 0$, $\partial C_D/\partial a$, $\partial C_P/\partial e < 0$.

Each of the individual components of the total cost needs to be calculated net of all benefits other than their reduction of other components in the equation, which will be taken into account directly. Thus C_P will be the cost of reducing CO_2 emissions *net* of any secondary benefits this reduction may bring about, such as the reduction of air pollutants apart from CO_2. Its benefit in reducing climate change, in contrast, will be reflected in reductions in C_D and, through the reduced amount of adaptation that is likely to be called for, C_A.

It is the purpose of optimal policy with regard to the emissions of greenhouse gases to reduce C_T to a minimum by calculating the optimal trade-off between C_D, C_A and C_P. The next section of this chapter explores C_D and C_A, both descriptively and through some of the monetary estimates of these costs that have been made. The adequacy of these monetary estimates for economic decision making is assessed. Section 9.3 examines the possible costs of mitigation as they have been modelled, presenting a range of results that have been derived. The section notes several factors that suggest that some of these models may have overestimated the net costs of mitigation. Finally, the chapter draws some conclusions.

9.2 THE COSTS OF CLIMATE CHANGE

As noted in Chapter 1, the most recent IPCC conclusion on climate change is that 'the balance of evidence suggests that there is a discernible human influence on climate change' (Houghton *et al.* 1995: 39–40). While even this is not undisputed in the scientific literature, the effects of any climate change from global warming are far more uncertain than the warming itself. On the one hand, as Schelling says: 'We will be moving into a climate regime that has never been experienced in the inter-glacial period' (Schelling 1992: 3). On the other, as Schelling also notes, the absolute temperature differences seem quite small and rather less than migrants in previous ages, and travellers today, have been and are able to adjust to quite comfortably.

However, a relatively modest average warming of the Earth's surface is likely to include larger individual variations at local level which have important effects on the environment and humanity. Three economists who have made a detailed study of the science of the greenhouse effect have come to the following conclusions. Schelling says: 'Natural ecosystems will be destroyed; plant and animal species will become extinct; places of natural beauty will be degraded. Valuable chemistries of plant and animal life will be lost before we learn their genetic secrets' (Schelling 1992: 7–8). Cline's assessment of the economic impacts is as follows:

> Global warming could cause agricultural losses in many regions. The level of the seas would rise, imposing costs of barrier protection of coastal cities and the loss of land area (including valuable wetlands). There would be increased electricity needs for air conditioning, potentially serious declines in the availability of water to agriculture and cities, increased urban pollution, increased intensity and frequency of hurricanes, increased mortality from heat waves, and losses in leisure activities associated with winter sports.
>
> (Cline 1992: 30–1)

Like Schelling, Broome also accepts that 'the strains on natural ecologies are likely to be very great' (Broome 1992: 13) and, like Cline, identified substantial costs associated with global warming:

> Without increased sea defences low-lying areas will become more susceptible to flooding. The danger will be amplified if storms become more frequent or more severe. . . . Regions threatened by flooding

include densely populated areas. Eight to ten million people live within one metre of high tide in each of the unprotected river deltas of Bangladesh, Egypt and Vietnam. A flood in Bangladesh, caused by a tropical storm in 1970, killed 300,000 people. Rising sea levels, then, must be expected to kill very large numbers of people. This is an enormous and easily predictable harm that will be caused by global warming. Moreover, sea levels will continue to rise for centuries. This must cause large migrations of population and it is difficult to see where the people can move to. There seems to be inevitable harm in this too: the forced migration of many million people is inevitably a disaster. Another class of bad effects is also quite easily predictable. As the world warms, more people will become subject to tropical diseases. This, too, will shorten many people's lives.

(ibid.: 14)

Similar impacts have been suggested by recent modelling by the UK Hadley Centre (1998), the 'Key Findings' (1998: 2) of which include:

- The global mean surface temperature in 1998 is likely to be the highest on record.
- In the middle of the next century, the Amazon rainforests will die back in many places, and terrestrial biomass will become a substantial net source of carbon dioxide, instead of acting as a substantial sink.
- Due to climate change an extra 66 million people will live in countries with water stress, and by 2050 an extra 20 million people each year will be at risk from flooding because of sea-level rise.

Of course, CO_2 pollution is not the only negative environmental effect of the use of fossil fuels. Barker (1993: 4) has calculated that, in the UK, 99 per cent of SO_2 and NO_x, 97 per cent of CO and 91 per cent of particulate matter, as well as substantial contributions to methane (48 per cent) and volatile organic compounds (38 per cent), all come from this source. The damages from these emissions are substantial, as will be discussed later.

A. Solow (1991: 25) points out that the estimates of damage from climate change have been moving away from 'apocalyptic scenarios'. For example, likely sea-level rise over the next 100 years is put at less than 1 metre now, as opposed to 3 metres or more a few years ago. Climate change could also have some beneficial effects. An atmosphere richer in CO_2 may enhance photosynthesis and raise productivity in agriculture and forestry. More northern latitudes, becoming warmer, may become more agriculturally productive. Warming may also lead to greater comfort in such latitudes. Warmer climates in some places may benefit industries as diverse as tourism and construction.

The analysis of Broome and Schelling, and of other major contributors in this field such as Nordhaus (1991a), focus exclusively on climate change and its likely effects in the next century. Yet, as Cline emphasises, without significant policy changes, the atmospheric concentration of greenhouse gases, and concomitant global warming, are likely to increase by considerably more than the factor of two (measured in CO_2-equivalents), that is the conventional benchmark for studies of impacts from global warming. Cline (1992: 36) considers, and the political difficulty of abating carbon emissions makes it a not unreasonable conclusion, that it is unlikely that global warming resulting from a doubling of CO_2-equivalents can or will be prevented. The IPCC's central estimate of this warming is 2.5°C, and it is likely to be realised by 2050 under business-as-usual, or 70–80 years later under IPCC's scenario of 'accelerated policies' to mitigate it (ibid.: 36). Therefore the Earth appears already committed to a likely warming of 2.5°C. Cline has calculated, using the IPCC climate parameters, that business-as-usual projections of greenhouse emissions to 2275 would result in global warming of 6–18°C, with a central value of 10°C (ibid.: 57). This much larger temperature change would amplify global warming's negative effects and reduce its benefits. Cline warns:

> It is important to recognize from the outset, however, that as a general rule one would expect the economic size of damage from global warming to rise more than linearly with the magnitude of warming. The costs of 10°C warming in the very long term could thus be far more than four times the costs of the 2.5°C benchmark warming for a doubling of carbon dioxide equivalent.
>
> (ibid.: 72)

This greater warming would increase the possibility of some catastrophic climate reaction to higher average temperatures. Even within the 100-year time-frame and with the relatively low temperature increase, Broome observed: 'Human-induced global warming, then, could possibly start a chain of events that could lead to the extinction of civilization or even of humanity. This is a remote possibility, but it exists' (Broome 1992: 16).

The balance of evidence from studies of impacts from global warming suggests that four statements concerning the impacts of any appreciable global warming and associated climate change may be made with some confidence. First, the impacts will be felt in many different ways. Second, the net impacts will be negative from the human point of view across the world as a whole. Third, the impacts will be different in different regions of the world. In general, the physical impacts will be greater in tropical regions. Given the present global distribution of wealth, this means that, in general, poorer countries will be harder hit physically, and in terms of relative economic costs, than richer ones. Fourth, the size of the impacts and their incidence in either time or place is still subject to great uncertainty.

Using the IPCC's estimate of 2.5°C warming due to a doubling of CO_2-equivalents, Nordhaus (1991a: 933), Cline (1992: 131), Fankhauser (1995: 55 (Table 3.15)) and Tol (1995: 355) estimate the damage caused by this level of warming at 1–2 per cent of US or world GDP. On the basis that CO_2-doubling will produce a warming of 4°C rather than 2.5°C, Titus (1992) estimates the damage to be 2.5 per cent of GDP. These were the estimates that formed the basis of the IPCC's assessment (largely by the same authors, Pearce *et al.* 1996) of the damage costs of climate change. Subsequently Fankhauser and Tol (1996) noted the emergence of some changes in emphasis, which did little to alter the main thrust of their calculations, which have been subject to not inconsiderable, and ongoing, criticism (see, for example, Demeritt and Rothman 1999; Ekins 1999). An independent estimate of the damage costs from climate change, that is more cautious in its conclusions than the IPCC, is provided by Eyre *et al.* (1997), as part of the European Commission's ExternE project that is seeking to estimate all the external costs of energy use.

Table 9.1 reproduces Fankhauser, Cline and Eyre *et al.*'s damage costs for doubling CO_2-equivalents, and Cline's estimates for much higher long-term warming, his central estimate of which is 10°C. From these figures it is clear that several of the Fankhauser and Cline entries (e.g. construction of dikes, electricity requirements and migration) actually represent the costs of adapting to climate change, rather than of the damages associated with it. This distinction is important because the costs of damage and adaptation are not independent. In particular, incurring costs of adaptation may reduce the costs of damage. Indeed it should do so by more than the cost of adaptation, if adaptation is economically rational. Dikes are built to protect land from sea-level rise. Air-conditioning in hot climates may reduce death and morbidity from heat stress (a significant item in Cline's damage costs). With the exception of the figures on sea-level rise, it is not clear in any of the estimates how far it has been possible to take these trade-offs into account.

From Table 9.1 it can be seen that there is relatively close agreement between the overall totals of damage costs (1.3 and 1.1 per cent of GDP), and these totals also agree quite closely with the other overall levels of damage in the literature, so that the damage costs of $2 \times CO_2$ global warming (the warming caused by the doubling of the concentration of CO_2 equivalents of greenhouse gases in the atmosphere) are quite often quoted as 1–2 per cent of GNP.

However, it can be seen from Table 9.1 that the agreement between the totals comes about despite entries in individual categories that vary substantially. Many of the entries differ by more than a factor of two. The differences between Fankhauser and Cline come about for three reasons, illustrating the uncertainties involved in calculating the damage costs of climate change:

Table 9.1 Estimates of annual damage and adaptation costs from global warming incurred by the US economy (Fankhauser and Cline) and the global economy (Eyre *et al.*) at 1990 scale (billions of 1990 dollars)

	Fankhauser[a]	Cline (2 × CO$_2$ warming)	Eyre et al.	Cline (long term)
Agriculture	8.4	17.5	−31.2	95.0
Forest loss	0.7	3.3		7.0
Species/ecosystem loss	8.4	4.0+[b]	0	16.0+
Sea level rise			3.4	35.0
• Coastal defences	0.2	1.2		
• Wetlands loss	6.4	4.1		
• Drylands loss	2.4	1.7		
Electricity requirements	—	11.2		64.1
Non-electric heating	—	−1.3		−4.0
Human amenity[c]	7.7	+		+
Human life	11.4	5.8	233.9	33.0
Human morbidity	+	+		+
Migration	0.6	0.5		2.8
Hurricanes	0.2	0.8	9.2[d]	6.4
Tourism	—	1.7		4.0
Water supply	15.6	7.0		56.0
Urban infrastructure	—	0.1		0.6
Air pollution	7.3			
• Tropospheric ozone		3.5		19.8
• Other		+		+
Total (billion $1990)	69.3	61.6	215.3	335.7
Total (% GNP)	1.3	1.1	1.1	6.0

Sources: Cline (1992: 131 (Table 3.4)); Fankhauser (1995: 55 (Table 3.15)); Eyre *et al.* (1997: 27 (Table 5.1.1))

Notes:
a In the source the figures given are in $1988. They have been scaled up in the column below by the ratio of 1990 to 1988 GDP
b + means that the source indicates (further) unquantified costs
c This entry in Fankhauser corresponds to the previous two rows in Cline. Cline indicates further unquantified costs under this heading as shown
d Includes hurricanes, winter storms, river floods

1   Use of different scientific predictions of the likely physical impact of climate change (e.g. for forestry Cline uses a source that suggests a loss of 40 per cent of US forests, whereas Fankhauser's source leads him to a figure of 16 per cent).
2   Different interpretations of the same scientific prediction of the likely physical impact of climate change (e.g. Fankhauser derives 6,642 increased deaths per year from heat stress, while Cline's figure using the same source is 9,800).
3   Different valuations of a given impact (e.g. Cline values his loss of life in 2 above at $0.6 million per life, while Fankhauser uses a figure of $1.5 million).

The estimates by Eyre *et al.* are dominated by valuations of the loss of human life and omit a number of the categories covered by Fankhauser and Cline. Agriculture, on these estimates, actually benefits from climate change, as northern latitudes become more productive, while the value of species and ecosystem loss is not given. However, unlike Fankhauser and Cline, Eyre *et al.* (1997: 30) explicitly state that these results should not be seen as 'best estimates', because alternative assumptions to those on which their calculations are based would produce quite different results, and yet are just as plausible.

In addition to the above uncertainties, climate change also entails a risk, as noted above, which is incalculable and may be small but cannot be ruled out, of a major disruption to the biosphere or to human ways of life or both, which could amount to catastrophe. The issues of valuation and risk are discussed further below.

Table 9.2 gives an estimate as to how the costs of global warming may be distributed. It can be seen that low income countries (China, Rest of the World) have substantially higher proportional costs (Fankhauser and Tol 1996: 665 quote these as up to 9 per cent of GDP for some developing countries).

For any approach to decision making on climate change the costs and benefits of its impacts and of responses to it are of major importance and will need to be carefully considered in order to inform the trade-offs that are likely to be necessary. However, seeking to undertake an optimisation through CBA involves more than careful consideration. It requires that all the relevant costs and benefits can not only be identified and quantified, but also that they can be expressed in monetary form. Where this is possible, i.e. where costs and benefits are well defined, and the valuation of them is widely agreed, CBA clearly has much to recommend it, and its outputs, the benefit–cost ratio or the revealed optimal course of action, give powerful guidance to decision makers.

Table 9.2 Damage due to doubling of atmospheric CO_2 equivalents for different regions (present scale economy)

Region	% GNP (1988)
European Union	1.4
United States	1.3
Other OECD	1.4
Former USSR	0.7
China	4.7
Rest of the world	2.0
OECD	1.3
Non-OECD	1.6
World	1.4

Source: Fankhauser (1995: 55 (Table 3.16))

However, where benefits and costs are uncertain within a wide range or cannot have probabilities attached to them, or where the basis for valuing non-market effects is difficult or disputed, then it is not clear that CBA is helpful to decision making. A benefit–cost ratio of less than one, that is subject to the qualification that certain substantial benefits were omitted from the analysis because they could not be adequately identified, quantified or monetised, cannot be used for decision making because there is always the possibility that, had the benefits been able to be included, the ratio would become greater than one, thereby reversing the recommendation for decision making. There is also the danger that the existence of the numerical ratio causes the qualification to be overlooked or ignored, so that the ratio is given more weight than is justified.

Even more problematic are situations where the basis for valuation itself is disputed, because the use of the disputed valuation methodology in such situations runs the risk of obscuring important issues rather than illuminating them, and heightening controversy rather than resolving it. These issues can be clearly illustrated through the problems that arise in seeking to derive a CBA for climate change.

9.2.1 Problems of valuation

Grubb considers that the estimates of damages exemplified in Table 9.1

> suffer from five important limitations because they: do not reflect the probable dynamics of climate change; make invalid extrapolations from industrialized to developing countries; require largely subjective valuations of non-market impacts; neglect important issues raised by long-term and extreme atmospheric changes; and ignore the possibility of major and costly surprises arising from the sheer complexity of the global system.
>
> (Grubb 1993: 153)

It is perhaps easiest to illustrate these problems that arise with the valuation of impacts from climate change by considering the examples of land-loss, migration, agriculture and human mortality.

The principal estimate in the literature of the damage costs from sea-level rise from climate change (Fankhauser 1994) is only of the costs related to the loss of land values. Because these are relatively high in OECD countries, a substantial level of protection against sea-level rise in these countries is found to be warranted (nearly 100 per cent for cities and harbours, 75–80 per cent for open coasts and 50–60 per cent for beaches) (ibid.: 27). But Fankhauser acknowledges that:

> the value of land is only an imperfect indicator of the true welfare loss to consumers, and for many people their home land may be worth

more than just its market value. Further, the resettlement of people
from abandoned areas may not take place without friction and may
be subject to considerable adjustment costs.

(ibid.: 32)

Yet these 'adjustment costs' are simply left out of Fankhauser's figures.
Such considerations are likely to be even more important, and make the
exclusive use of land values for such calculations even more problematic,
with regard to developing countries, where land values are much lower.

Similarly, Hope *et al.*'s (1993) advocacy of 'an aggressive package of
adaptation measures' (rather than the mitigation of warming through the
abatement of emissions, Hope *et al.* 1993: 334) is based on an analysis of
'economic impacts' that does not include the loss of biodiversity or sites
of particular social, natural or educational value, a lower quality of life
through environmental degradation and health effects, the loss of human
life, or the implications of large-scale migration (ibid.: 335).

Both Fankhauser (1995) and Cline (1992) have put a value on the migration costs. However, as Fankhauser admits: 'To these costs would have to
be added the costs of hardship and stress suffered by migrants', which
Cline recognises are so substantial that 'peoples have often fought wars to
avoid being forced to leave their homelands against their will' (Cline 1992:
119). Fankhauser accepts that 'it is therefore quite likely that these costs
exceed the pure economic losses. Unfortunately it seems almost impossible to assess them properly' (Fankhauser 1995: 51). So these costs are
omitted altogether. Any CBA which used these estimates would therefore
be excluding a major category of costs that may exceed those that are
included.

With regard to agriculture, Cline estimates that agricultural losses would
be $40 billion for $2 \times CO_2$ warming, which is 7 per cent of world agri-
cultural output. Regionally, the effects could be much more severe. For
example, Rosenzweig *et al.* (1993: 15 (Table 9)) put Egypt's aggregate losses
in wheat yields from $2 \times CO_2$ warming at 25–50 per cent. In the very
long term, Cline puts world agricultural losses at $212 billion, which is
35 per cent of world agricultural output (Cline 1992: 99, 101).

Food is a basic human need, with a value that rises very fast at a level
of supply that is below a basic level of sufficiency. At present there is
enough food for the human population, but its distribution is such that in
1990–2 20 per cent of people in developing countries, 841 million people,
did not have access to enough food for healthy living, with malnutrition
in 1990 contributing to 12 per cent of all deaths (WRI 1998: 16). Moreover,
by 2050 on current trends population is likely to have doubled and there
are some doubts whether, even without climate change, the global food
supply will be able to expand enough to meet this new level of need (see,
for example, Brown *et al.* 1993: 11–14). Furthermore, to avoid disruption
it is not enough for average supply levels to be broadly maintained. Extreme

weather events that destroy particular crops in particular places in particular periods could have an impact quite out of proportion to their effect on such averages.

Cline's long term loss of \$212 billion is only about 1.1 per cent of world GDP, which illustrates the limitation of GDP figures in such situations. As Cline notes: 'If world agricultural production fell to zero, so would world population. The economic loss would equal the entirety of GDP, not just the ex ante share attributable to agriculture' (Cline 1992: 87 (note 9)). The loss of 35 per cent of world agricultural output in a world with a fast-growing population would be unlikely to be felt as the loss of just 1 per cent of total output. Yet it is not clear, in the absence of global demand curves under such circumstances, how else, in a global CBA, it could be valued.

But the greatest difficulty in the global cost–benefit approach to climate change is in the valuation of the associated loss of human life. Fankhauser (1995: 47 (Table 3.11)) estimates that 137,727 lives are likely to be lost worldwide each year due to $2 \times CO_2$ global warming (of which 22,923 are in OECD countries, 7,722 in the former USSR, and the rest in the so-called developing world), which Cline (1992: 36) regards as 'almost inevitable'. As already noted, Fankhauser chooses a valuation of \$1.5 million per life for deaths in industrial countries. He reports the range of such values from the literature as \$200,000 to over \$16 million, with an average of around \$3 million, and so regards his figure of \$1.5 million as 'fairly conservative' (Fankhauser 1995: 47).

For middle and low income countries Fankhauser chooses 'arbitrary' values of \$300,000 and \$100,000 respectively. He claims:

> This, of course, does *not* mean that the life of, say, a Chinese is worth less than that of a European. It merely reflects the fact that the *willingness to pay* for increased safety (a lower mortality risk) is higher in developed countries.
>
> (Fankhauser 1995: 47, original emphasis)

This may be true, but the fact is that, irrespective of their mode of derivation, the purpose of these figures is to inform benefit–cost analyses as to whether investments in the prevention of climate change are economically desirable. If the figures are high enough, more investments may be seen as justified and lives may be saved. In this sense, the figures are indications of the 'worth' of the lives concerned.

The correct way from a welfare-theoretic point of view to seek to take equity considerations into account, where prevailing income distributions are not perceived to be just, is to multiply the basic valuations (derived from willingness-to-pay, WTP, estimates, see Chapter 2, p. 30) by a weight that reflects the marginal utility of income and the assumed social welfare function (Fankhauser *et al.* 1997: 254). Unfortunately neither of these variables can be determined empirically with any precision, so the decision on the weights to be used, or whether to use them at all, remains a matter of largely subjective judgement or, as Fankhauser *et al.* (ibid.: 263) put it, 'a political question that cannot be addressed here'.

Yet the plausible range of weights can make a very significant difference to the aggregate valuation of the lives lost. Thus, although Fankhauser *et al.* (1997: 263) claim that their method, using weights, 'has the advantage of being firmly based on the principles of welfare economics', the 'main strengths' of which 'are its consistency and rigour', in fact the utilisation of the method depends first and foremost on subjective political judgements. The vaunted 'consistency and rigour' of the method, together with its highly technical exposition, actually serve to obscure this essential fact.

It is argued below that considerations of justice could cause all lives that might be lost as a result of climate change to be given developed-country valuations. If this is done, then Fankhauser's estimated loss of life is valued at $206 billion (instead of $49 billion in Fankhauser's own calculation), increasing the total costs of climate change by nearly 60 per cent. Even in this calculation, as in Fankhauser's, the distress and mental health effects suffered by survivors remain uncounted.

Yet even this may greatly underestimate the impact of climate change on human mortality. For example, Hohmeyer and Gärtner (1992) calculate that an extra 900 million deaths from hunger could be caused in the period 2010–30, due to climate change damage to agriculture. Such an estimate for hunger-related deaths alone is two orders of magnitude higher than the Fankhauser figures for all climate change induced fatality, and obviously makes the optimal policy even more dependent on how these lives should be valued.

9.2.2 Accounting for risk and uncertainty

The uncertainties relating to the impacts of climate change and their valuation mean that ranges of damage costs are typically derived for each impact, which then yield best estimates. However, the best estimate should only be used in the CBA if it is assumed that society is indifferent to risk. If, on the other hand, the more common assumption is made that society is risk-averse (i.e. it is relatively more desirous to avoid heavier than average costs than to secure lighter than average costs) then the best estimate should be appropriately weighted to reflect this risk aversion.

The incorporation of risk aversion into a CBA in this way can make a substantial difference to its outcome. In Cline's study of global warming, one of his scenarios is of 'aggressive abatement action', which involves cutting CO_2 emissions by 82 per cent from the baseline projection by 2100 to 4 GtC (gigatonnes of carbon) annually, which is only about 60 per cent of emissions in 1990. With no adjustment for risk aversion, the central estimate's benefit–cost ratio for this scenario is 0.74, i.e. the aggressive abatement is not economically justified. When Cline applies risk-aversion weights of 0.125 to his low damage estimate, 0.5 to his central damage estimate and 0.375 to his high damage estimate, the benefit–cost ratio changes to 1.26, thus economically justifying aggressive abatement action (Cline 1992: 300).

There is, however, no way of knowing whether these weights are 'right' or 'appropriate' or not so that the issue of risk aversion actually does little more than introduce another element of uncertainty and potential controversy into the calculation.

Of course, risk aversion is only one consideration in the treatment of the huge uncertainties that characterise climate change, the attendant risks of which Chichilnisky and Heal (1993: 67) describe as 'poorly understood, endogenous, collective and irreversible'. They stress the possible importance of the option value of controlling emissions given the irreversibilities attendant on climate change, pointing out that the analyses of both Cline (1992) and Manne and Richels (1992) fail to consider option values and consequently may underestimate the benefits of mitigating climate change:

> As the value of an option generally increases with increasing uncertainty about the future, and as uncertainty looms large in any projections regarding global warming, the extent of the underestimate could be important. It could, for example, be decisive in the endorsement of a global carbon tax.
>
> (Chichilnisky and Heal 1993: 81)

More generally, Nordhaus (1994: 188) concurs as to the importance of uncertainty to the calculation in his model of an optimal carbon tax: 'Roughly speaking, the optimal carbon tax doubles when uncertainty is taken into account, and the optimal control rate increases by slightly less than half.'

9.2.3 The use of time-discounting

The various costs of damage from, adaptation to, and mitigation of climate change will arise in different periods of time. In order to compare such costs the normal treatment is to convert them to present values by the use of a discount rate, whereby a positive discount rate involves giving a lower present value to a given cost the further into the future it is expected to fall. Because the damage costs are projected to occur further into the future than the costs of mitigation, the higher the discount rate used the lower will be the present value of the damage costs and the lower will be the amount of mitigation that appears to be justified.

Unfortunately there is no consensus among economists or anyone else about the discount rate that should be used in such circumstances. The recent IPCC report concluded: 'How best to choose a discount rate is, and will likely remain, an unresolved question in economics' (Bruce *et al.* 1996: 8). The debate is complex, technical and controversial, and suffice it to say here that a wide range of discount rates has been advocated and used in climate change calculations, with substantial implications for the optimal policy indicated. After a lengthy review, Broome concludes that only 'pure discounting' (as opposed to using the consumer or producer interest rates) is appropriate theoretically for the climate change issue, and further finds no reason to adopt a discount rate different from zero (Broome 1992: 108). Cline notes that Mishan, too, advocated a zero discount rate for intergenerational comparisons (Cline 1992: 239). Cline, however, advocates the conversion of quantities to 'consumption equivalents', which are then discounted at the social rate of time preference (SRTP). Setting the 'pure impatience' component of SRTP equal to zero, Cline arrives at his preferred SRTP, related to the diminishing marginal utility of income on the assumption that societies will be richer in the future than at present, of 1.5 per cent. Eyre *et al.* (1997: 11) use discount rates of 1 per cent and 3 per cent 'on the grounds that these are closest to the long term per capita growth rate'.

Cline also performs benefit–cost analyses with SRTPs of 3 per cent and 5 per cent. The effect of varying this parameter is shown by the different benefit–cost ratios obtained for Cline's programme of 'aggressive abatement action'. With high damage assumptions, this ratio is 2.60 for an SRTP of 1.5 per cent, 1.09 for an SRTP of 3 per cent and 0.56 for an SRTP of 5 per cent. The central estimate of Nordhaus (1991: 934) uses an SRTP of 1 per cent, while Nordhaus (1992b: 15, 18) and (1993c: 37) uses an SRTP of 3 per cent higher. Birdsall and Steer suggest an SRTP, based on the methodology advocated by Cline, of 8 per cent (Birdsall and Steer 1993: 8). Rotmans and Dowlatabadi (1998: 347) note that present-day investment decisions suggest a discount rate of 3–5 per cent, but also that some public policy on the environment (e.g. related to the preservation of wilderness) implies a zero discount rate. They make no suggestion as to what the appropriate rate within this range for climate change might be.

These examples show the kind of variations in discount rate that arise on this issue and the difference they make to assessments of optimal policy.

9.2.4 The question of equity

In any issue involving the distribution of costs and benefits, the question of equity – fairness or justice – inevitably arises. Climate change is no exception.

Consideration of equity relating to climate change involves raising the following questions:

• Who is primarily responsible for the GG emissions that seem likely to bring it about?

- Who has primarily benefited from those emissions?
- How will this situation change in the future?
- Who will suffer most from climate change?
- Who is best able to undertake mitigation of climate change?

Fortunately this is one set of questions to which categoric and quantitative answers can be given relatively easily, at least with regard to CO_2 from fossil fuel use which is still the major contributor to global warming. From 1860–1949 this source released 187 billion metric tons of CO_2; from 1950–89 the figure was 559 billion metric tons, of which industrial countries were responsible for around 80 per cent (WRI 1992: 206, Figure 13.1). Historic emissions are relevant because CO_2 may remain in the atmosphere for a century or more. Industrial countries now account for about 60 per cent of CO_2 emissions from fossil fuel use and this proportion will continue to fall as industrialisation in Asia and elsewhere gathers pace. Per capita these emissions in the US related to other regions are as follows: Africa, 19 times; Asia, 9 times; Europe, 2.4 times; former USSR, 1.6 times (WRI 1994: 363 (Table 23.1)).

The already industrialised countries have therefore been responsible for the great majority of fossil fuel use to date, and may be presumed to have derived the lion's share of the benefits associated with this. Other countries will increase their emissions to reduce this share in the future. Per capita, the already industrialised regions are expected to dominate for the foreseeable future.

On the other hand, as already discussed, the physical damage from climate change is expected to be greater in non-industrial countries. Even when this damage is valued using lower valuations (e.g. for the loss of a life) than are used for industrial country damages, the costs of damage in non-industrial countries are likely to be relatively greater than in industrial countries, as Table 9.2 showed.

Finally, it is clear that insofar as mitigation of climate change will require the commitment of financial resources, the richer countries are better able to undertake this. For all these reasons the Framework Convention on Climate Change agreed at the Rio Summit looked to the industrial world to make the first moves on mitigating climate change. The currently relevant political question is how much mitigation of climate change industrial-country decision makers who care about equity should seek to achieve. Their decision on this matter is obviously dependent on how much they value lives in developing countries that might be saved thereby.

In contrast to the valuations of Fankhauser (1995), Lockwood (1992: 70 (note 3)) considers that 'in the interests of intercountry equity, it is desirable to cost statistical lives in different countries equally, but it is not sensible to use valuation of statistical life for a high-income country such as the U.K.'. Instead he divides his valuation for the UK (£2 million, or about $3 million) by the ratio of UK GDP to world GDP, arriving at a uniform valuation of statistical life of £540,000 in both industrial and developing countries. But, assuming that the full UK valuation is used in other cases in which only UK lives are affected, such a procedure means that the loss of a UK life is worth less in situations where people in developing countries are to be killed as well.

The Eyre *et al.* valuations of human life given in Table 9.1 also take a common per unit value of life, of about £700,000. However, this is less than a third of the valuations of European lives used elsewhere in the ExternE project, leading to the curious result that one European life lost due to local air pollution is worth the same as three European lives lost due to climate change. There would seem to be little logical justification for such results.

Such tortuous inconsistencies may be avoided by changing the basis of the perception of climate change as principally an *economic* issue. In fact, climate change is a complex and multidimensional issue, to analyse which a range of possible social science approaches could be used. Equally clearly the problem has an economic *dimension*. However, this is very different from identifying it even mainly as an economic problem, which was the obvious presumption behind the damage assessment which IPCC produced. Having made this presumption, the only way to proceed is to use techniques of economic valuation of the environment.

Economic valuation is based on utilitarianism, entailing the quantification and aggregation of costs or benefits as experienced by individuals. Once economics had been identified as the relevant discipline, and climate change damages were cast as 'economic costs' pure and simple, the IPCC authors had little choice but to proceed as they did. Within this frame of reference Pearce *et al.* were right to use 'valuations of statistical life' (VOSLs) that give higher values to rich-country lives than to poor, and they were right to resist calls for VOSL equalisation at rich-country levels. They were, however, disingenuous in the extreme in trying to maintain a distinction between a VOSL and 'the value of human life', for the whole economic purpose of giving a monetary value to the damage costs is to give insights into the 'rational' (on cost–benefit grounds) amount of climate change mitigation, and therefore into how many lives should be saved. Moreover, differential VOSLs have the unequivocal implication that, when it comes to saving lives, rich-country lives should be saved first, because they are more valuable. Those who reject this conclusion are, in effect, saying that they do not believe the economic dimension of climate change damages to be the most important one.

With regard to the valuation of ecosystem services in general, which certainly include climate regulation, Goulder and Kennedy (1997: 23–4) have written that there is an inescapable 'philosophical element' that 'seeks to identify the ethical or philosophical basis of value, that is, articulate what constitutes the source of value'. The problems of trying to value lives lost due to anthropogenic climate change arise from the presumption that utilitarianism provides the appropriate philosophical framework for assessing such values in such a situation.

Alternative philosophical approaches to valuing ecosystem services have been suggested by de Groot (1992: 1), and include:

- *sentimentalism*, 'stressing the need to achieve a certain harmony between man and nature';
- *ethical argument*, 'based on the perception that all living beings have an equal right to exist';
- *educative argument*, based on the view that nature is necessary to humans' discovery of their identity and their place in the universe;
- *survival argument*, 'that the continued functioning of natural processes is essential to human existence on earth'.

The ethical argument may be extended to the formulation, common in definitions of sustainable development, that no group of people has the right, in their provision for themselves, to degrade the environment such that the capacities of other people, in the present or future, to make similar provision are reduced. It may be noted that of the four arguments above only the second is not anthropocentric (i.e. not oriented towards human well-being) but all go beyond the utilitarian focus on individual preferences and none are amenable to techniques of economic valuation.

Goulder and Kennedy (1997: 27) accept that alternative philosophical approaches to valuing ecosystem services exist, but make the mistake, especially common among economists, of presuming that only utilitarianism is 'practical'. In fact, there are numerous examples of human institutions that uphold values on a basis other than utilitarianism. Perhaps most obvious among these are systems of justice, which are not based on cost–benefit analysis. The robber is not exonerated of theft however much he may show that he can put wealth to greater social advantage than his victim. This is simply not a relevant consideration with regard to justice, and it may well be argued, given the likely distribution of climate change damages, that justice is a better analytical framework within which to decide mitigation imperatives than economic rationality.

In deciding the extent of climate-change mitigation, developed country decision makers are likely to apply developed country valuations to the lives of their citizens. It could be argued that justice (if not welfare economics) should cause them to apply the same valuation to the lives of citizens in poorer countries. The very fact that such a valuation is based explicitly on normative arguments is a strength in such a situation. By contrast, seeking to perform a cost–benefit analysis (CBA) for issues of this kind simply engenders mistrust, because its claims of rationality and rigour are belied by the subjective judgements that are required in the choice of discount rates, and weights to take account of risk aversion and income distribution, and which can be used to justify practically any desired CBA result.

Cost–benefit analysis is intended to facilitate decision making by giving values to different effects using a common metric (money) so that the values may be more easily compared and the aggregate outcome more easily appreciated. According to a standard text on the subject, cost–benefit analysis has 'a fundamental attraction of reducing a complex problem to something less complex and more manageable' (D. Pearce 1983: 21). But it can only fulfil this function if the basis of valuation commands a wide consensus.

Where this is not the case, and the methodology of valuation itself becomes disputed ground, especially if the dispute centres on concerns with justice or morality, then the use of cost–benefit analysis is likely to inflame an issue rather than illuminate it. This can be easily seen by refer-ring again to Fankhauser's numbers of deaths from climate change. His first-stage calculation, that the number of deaths in OECD countries and the rest of the world could be 22,923 and 114,804 respectively is informative and meaningful. It gives clear insight into the scale and distri-bution of the problem. His second-stage calculation that, on the basis of values differing by factors of ten or fifteen, these lives are 'worth' $34.4 billion and $14.8 billion respectively, cannot but cause rage and a deep sense of injustice in those who believe developing country lives to be as valuable as industrial country lives. Certainly such calculations do not make climate change 'more manageable'. They arouse passions, and will make it very diffi lt to forge the global consensus that will be required if climate change is to be controlled and some at least of the lives in question are to be saved.

In summary, while a cost–benefit analysis of climate change may initially appear the reasonable way to proceed to approach the issue in order to gain guidance for decision making, it transpires that it is actually very problematic. The valuation of the damage costs, the treatment of risk aver-sion, the choice of discount rate and the need for fairness all introduce complications and uncertainties before which the seeming rigour of the methodology dissolves. As Fankhauser himself has noted: '[T]hrough the choice of appropriate parameter values almost any abatement policy can be justified' (Fankhauser 1993: 22).

The attempted use of such a methodology in these circumstances would seem guaranteed to intensify controversy rather than resolve it, and so indeed it proved, both at the Conference of the Parties at Berlin in 1994 and in response to the work of the Working Group of the IPCC that was concerned with climate change's socio-economic impacts (Pearce *et al.* 1996). Another methodology would seem to be required and it is suggested below that an approach based on an explicit commitment to justice and environmental sustainability may be suitable. However, it is first necessary to give some attention to the other side of the climate change cost–benefit equation, namely the costs of mitigation.

9.3 COSTS OF MITIGATING CLIMATE CHANGE

As already noted, climate change can be reduced by reducing GG emissions, by increasing GG global sinks or by deflecting solar radiation away from the Earth. The National Academy of Sciences (NAS 1991) lists some 'geoengineering' possibilities of large-scale deflection or sink-creation. The ICAM-1 model of Dowlatabadi and Morgan (1993) has some consideration of these, and in his DICE model Nordhaus (1994) finds them to be the optimal response to climate change, but they are not considered at all by the IPCC and will not be further discussed here.

The increase in carbon sink capacity through reforestation has been investigated in detail (see Bruce *et al.* 1996: 345ff. for the IPCC assessment), as has the reduction of GG emissions. Because CO_2 has contributed about 60 per cent of the 'radiative forcing' from the increase in the greenhouse effect over the past 200 years, and is expected to continue to provide approximately this share in the future (Cline 1991: 906), and because any serious attempt to mitigate climate change will require substantial reductions in CO_2 emissions, whatever other measures are adopted, among the GGs the abatement of CO_2 has attracted the most attention, and will be the focus of discussion here.

9.3.1 Modelling CO_2 abatement

The costs of CO_2 abatement have been estimated in three principal ways: through the use of global models; through the use of single country models (the results of which then may or may not be generalised to the world level); and through detailed calculations of the cost and environmental performance of different carbon-saving technologies. The models may be either general equilibrium (GE) models, macromodels or technology-based models. Whole economy modelling is sometimes referred to as a 'top–down' approach; modelling based on detailed technological analysis is sometimes called 'bottom–up'.

There have been several reviews in varying amounts of detail of the studies reporting results of various CO_2-abatement modelling exercises: Boero *et al.* (1991); Hoeller *et al.* (1991); Nordhaus (1991b); Cline (1992: Chapter 4); Dean and Hoeller (1992); Bruce *et al.* (1996); Repetto and Austin (1997). Boero *et al.* divide the CO_2-abatement models into two broad classes, while emphasising that many of the models contain characteristics from each class. There are the general equilibrium (GE) models, concentrating on long-term equilibrium resource allocations and relative prices; and there are the macroeconomic models focusing more on short-term adjustments and disequilibrium. The intention here is not to repeat or extend the earlier surveys, but rather to concentrate on a few issues that have been important in influencing the results obtained.

9.3.2 Increasing the price of energy

For energy-related CO_2 emissions to be reduced, so must the consumption of fossil fuels, and this is typically achieved in models by raising the price of such fuels, often through the imposition of a carbon tax – a tax related to the carbon content of the fuel in question (coal, oil, gas have different carbon contents per unit of energy, in descending order of magnitude). Increasing the price of energy according to its carbon content can be expected to result in the following effects (over different time-scales):

- reduction in demand for carbon-based fuels;
- substitution between more and less carbon-intensive fuels;
- substitution between carbon-based and non-carbon fuels;
- substitution between energy and other factors of production;
- substitution between more and less carbon-intensive products and processes;
- improvements in the efficiency of fuel use in delivering a particular energy service;
- development of new, less carbon-intensive technologies, products and processes.

Whether the reduction in demand for carbon-based fuels induced by energy price increases results in reduced output (GDP) depends in the first instance on possibilities for substitution, efficiency improvements and technological development, so that the 'costs' of CO_2-abatement will depend very largely on how these factors are modelled.

9.3.3 Prices and substitution

Much general equilibrium greenhouse modelling is based on a production function approach (including Nordhaus and Yohe 1983; Manne and Richels 1991; Whalley and Wigle 1991; Burniaux *et al.* 1992a; Nordhaus 1992b), such that:

$$X = F(C,E)$$

where X is output, E is energy, C is all other factors, F(.) is the production function.

The model first establishes a 'base run', incorporating assumptions about future supplies, demands and prices of all production factors and such parameters as the elasticities of energy demand and substitution and 'autonomous energy efficiency improvement' (see p. 270). This base run proceeds on the assumption that there are no unemployed resources. When a carbon tax is introduced, this raises the price of energy and, through the model's demand system, inevitably reduces the demand for it. Because the other factors are in unchanged supply, a lower demand for energy will convert, through the production function, into a lower output. This is what causes GDP losses from the imposition of a carbon tax. In the nine studies surveyed by Boero *et al.* (1991: S19 (Figure S1)), GDP losses ranged from 1 per cent by 2050 for a 40 per cent emission reduction from base, to 7.5 per cent by 2075 for a 65 per cent emissions reduction. The range of GDP losses from the slightly different set of global studies reviewed by Bruce *et al.* (1996: 336 (Figure 9.22)) is 0.1 per cent for a 14 per cent reduction from base in 2025, to 5.7 per cent for an 88 per cent reduction in 2095.

The fairly large spread of costs reported above from the different modelling exercises comes about due to both the different structure of the models, and differences in input assumptions (e.g. population and economic growth rates, energy prices). The Stanford Energy Modeling Forum (EMF), some of the results of which were quoted in Chapter 8, has sought to reduce this variance by standardising the input assumptions in the fourteen different models that took part in EMF. Figure 9.1 shows the average losses of all the models for the three EMF scenarios: stabilisation of emissions at their 1990 level by 2000; a 20 per cent reduction below this by 2010; and a 50 per cent reduction below 1990 levels by 2050. It can be seen that the average loss in the third scenario is more than 3 per cent of GDP, when the average carbon tax is about \$400 per tonne. While Figure 9.1 shows the losses still rising beyond 2050, it may be noted that the EMF exercise did not include any backstop technologies yielding effectively unlimited energy at constant marginal cost (which is an assumption

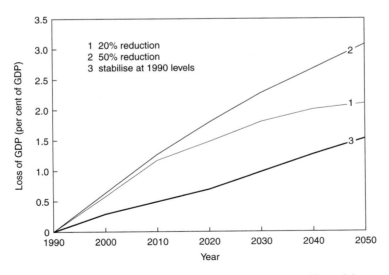

Figure 9.1 US GDP loss projections, average of all EMF models
Source: Bruce *et al.* (1996: 307 (Figure 9.5))

used in some other studies). It is at least plausible that renewable energy sources would in fact have developed sufficiently by 2050 to play such a role at a cost below the cost of fossil fuels including a $400 per tonne carbon tax, in which case this would ensure that the GDP losses stabilised at their 2050 level.

Models that use the production function approach use energy elasticities that are derived from past experiences of energy price changes. But as Barker *et al.* (1995: 311–14) make clear, there are a number of reasons why such elasticities are unlikely to provide a reliable projection of the economy's response to carbon taxes. These reasons are partly structural and methodological, such as the different carbon intensities of different fuels, the relationship of energy intensity and capital intensity and the length of time-scale that is relevant to climate change policy. More importantly, perhaps, the reasons concern the differences between price changes induced by carbon taxes and those of the 1970s. With carbon taxes the price changes would be gradual (over decades) and anticipated, with revenues available to counteract both recessionary and inflationary effects, and to address market failures in the energy or energy efficiency markets, while the OPEC price rises were sudden, unexpected, and extracted large sums of money from industrial economies, causing both recession and inflation. Gradual, anticipated price changes would be likely to lead to easier adjustments than sudden shocks, with lower associated costs in terms of reduced output. Therefore although Jorgenson (1990: 85), for example, found that the increase in energy prices in the 1970s was a major cause of the reduction in US GDP growth in the 1970s and 1980s, this is likely to be of limited relevance to the outcome of a well-introduced carbon tax in the future.

The explicit negative linkage in the models between higher energy prices and GDP is therefore of doubtful relevance to the long-term impact of a carbon tax. However, even if such a linkage does exist, there are a number of countervailing considerations which might offset this effect. These include the issues of existing distortions and the possible existence of unemployed resources in the economy, and the effects of different modes of revenue-recycling, which have been explored in Chapter 8 and will not be further discussed here. They also include considerations of:

- *Competitiveness:* If a carbon tax is introduced in a single country, it is sometimes feared that this will lead to a loss of competitiveness in that country.
- *Investment and technical change:* One would expect changes in relative prices, implying changes in both production costs and patterns of demand, to change the relative attractiveness of investment options. They might also be expected to affect the rate and direction of technical change and, through the technical bias of energy use, perhaps also the rate of productivity growth.

9.3.4 **Competitiveness**

At the corporate level competitiveness simply refers to the ability of a business to sell its products in an open market. Because the imposition of a carbon tax will change relative prices, it can be expected to have an effect on the international competitiveness of any given product. This effect will be determined by a number of influences, including:

- the size of the carbon tax and the nature and extent of the offsets;
- the carbon intensity of the product;
- the trade intensity of the product (ratio of exports plus imports to production).

Because the second two of these influences differ between countries, even the imposition of an identical tax-offset arrangement in all countries would differentially affect their competitiveness.

The evidence reviewed in Chapter 6 did not indicate substantial losses in competitiveness from past environmental taxes and regulation. According to the OECD (1996: 45): 'The trade and investment impacts which have been measured empirically are almost negligible.' However, this is possibly because the environmental regulations applied so far have been relatively modest compared to those sometimes considered necessary to move towards environmental sustainability, and they have not predominantly been in the form of green taxes. These may impose higher costs on seriously affected sectors because the firms concerned will need to pay for abatement (up to the efficient level) *and* for residual emissions (although these payments should be regarded as transfers through the tax system rather than macroeconomic costs as such). However, it is therefore important to note that the overall effects on business competitiveness from the tax will depend on how the tax revenues are recycled through the economy: while environmentally intensive sectors may end up worse off, clean businesses are likely actually to benefit from it. The mechanism at work is clearly shown in Pezzey (1991), who simulated the introduction of a carbon tax in the UK.

In Table 9.3, Row 1 is the relative production of the different sectors of UK industry compared to the total production of all those sectors in seven industrial countries. It can be seen that, in terms of absolute value, the UK's most important industrial sectors are machinery and food, followed by chemicals, transport equipment, paper and iron and steel. Row 2 shows the relative contribution of each UK sector relative to the seven countries' total output in that sector. Overall the UK produces 7.2 per cent of the seven countries' output in these sectors, but a greater share than this of their iron and steel (11.3 per cent), chemicals (9.4 per cent), non-metallic minerals and food (8.8 per cent), paper (8.6 per cent) and cloth etc. (7.6 per cent). Row 3 gives the UK's trade intensity in these

Table 9.3 Sectoral competitiveness effects for a carbon and energy tax

UK	AI	IS	CH	NFM	NMM	TE	M	F	P	W	CL
1 RP	72	6	9	1	3	7	19	14	7	2	5
2 SP	72	113	94	45	88	49	64	88	86	67	76
3 TI	59	25	62	124	28	108	77	30	29	43	83
4 ICc	1.6	4.0	3.8	4.5	4.4	0.8	0.6	0.7	0.8	0.1	0.8
5 ICco	0.0	2.4	2.1	2.9	2.8	−0.7	−1.0	−0.8	−0.7	−1.4	−0.7
6 SCco	0.0	−0.6	−1.3	−3.5	−0.8	0.8	0.7	0.2	0.2	0.6	0.6
7 SCeo	0.0	−0.5	−1.7	−4.2	−0.9	0.9	0.8	0.3	0.2	0.7	0.7

Source: Pezzey (1991)

Tables	6.3		6.5		6.8		6.9		6.11		6.16
Pages	106			107		110		111		113	115

Key: AI – All industry; IS – Iron and steel; CH – Chemicals; NFM – Non-ferrous metals; NMM – Non-metallic minerals; TE – Transportation equipment; M – Machinery; F – Food etc.; P – Paper; W – Wood; CL – Cloth etc.

Notes:
1 Value of UK production by sector relative to value of total output of tradeable manufactures in seven countries (US, Japan, Germany, France, UK, Italy, Spain) in 1985 ($\times$ 1,000)
2 Value of sectoral production of UK relative to value to total output in that sector of seven countries ($\times$ 1,000)
3 Trade intensity: percentages of exports plus imports to domestic production
4 Impact cost of a tax of $100 per ton of carbon with no offset: percentage of sectoral value of production
5 Impact cost of a tax of $100 per ton of carbon with offset (uniform subsidies per unit value of production): percentage of sectoral value of production'
6 Sectoral competitiveness (trade intensity $\times$ [−]impact cost) under carbon tax with offset: relative impact on output, arbitrary scale
7 Sectoral competitiveness (trade intensity $\times$ [−]impact cost) under energy tax ($100/toe) with offset: relative impact on output, arbitrary scale

sectors, defined as the percentage ratio of exports plus imports to production in that sector. It can be seen that the highest trade intensities are in non-ferrous metals, transport equipment, cloth and machinery. Row 4 indicates the cost impacts on the different sectors of a carbon tax of $100 per ton of carbon levied on fuel inputs, with no tax offsets. It therefore indicates relative sectoral carbon intensities. It is clear that iron and steel, chemicals, non-ferrous metals and non-metallic minerals are the most carbon-intensive sectors. Row 5 shows the sectoral impact cost of the carbon tax when revenues are rebated as uniform subsidies per unit value of industrial production. All entries with a negative sign indicate that these sectors have experienced a cost-improvement due to the carbon tax plus offset. These are the sectors of below average carbon intensity. Row 6 translates these cost (and therefore price) effects into relative effects on output by using the trade intensity as a proxy for price elasticity (based on the intuition that the higher the ratio of traded products in a sector, the more domestic price changes will affect that trade). This is clearly a crude approximation and can only be used to give indicative effects.

Row 7 is as Row 6, except for an energy tax, rather then a carbon tax, plus offset. Differences are due to differential consumption by sector of non-carbon energy (e.g. nuclear electricity).

There are many reasons why these results should be treated as rough approximations, not least in that they only take account of immediate, first-round effects of the relative price changes, rather than eventual adjustments to equilibrium. But the main mechanisms through which imposing environmental taxes influences sectoral competitiveness are clear.

First, as in Row 4, the imposition of a broad-based environmental tax, such as a carbon or energy tax, will increase the costs of all sectors, with a greater impact on those sectors that make the greatest use of the environmental good in question (in this case the carbon-intensive sectors IS, CH, NFM, NMM). Row 5 then shows that these costs can be completely offset in all but these four sectors by recycling the revenues from the tax back to the sectors that paid them. In this example this is done on the basis of sectoral output, so that any sector that is less than averagely carbon-intensive will end up better off. The recycling could just as easily be done by reducing employers' labour taxes (e.g. employers' National Insurance Contributions in the UK), in which case the sectors that end up better off will be those whose labour intensity is more above average than their carbon intensity. The actual extent to which Table 9.3's changes in price-competitiveness will result in more or less output by sector will depend on price elasticities, rather than the trade intensities here computed. But there is no *a priori* reason for assuming that the price elasticities for carbon-intensive sectors will be greater than those for non-carbon-intensive sectors (which would lead to proportionately greater output loss in the former than output gain in the latter). The reverse could just as easily be true, in which case competitiveness effects would be positive for the country concerned. Resolving this issue empirically is made very difficult by the wide range of elasticities which tends to emerge from studies (as compared, for example, in Barker *et al.* 1995).

The principal point is that as long as the revenues are returned to industry, losses of price-competitiveness in the carbon-intensive sectors will be counterbalanced by gains in the non-carbon intensive sectors. Moreover, the carbon-intensive sectors will only lose competitiveness to the extent that they do not reduce their carbon intensity, for example by increasing their energy efficiency, at a rate equal to the tax being applied. This point is discussed further below. Another critical issue associated with changes in competitiveness from the imposition of a carbon tax is the degree and speed of change of relative prices and, therefore, the economy's potential adjustment costs to reach a new equilibrium. Clearly the more gradually a tax can be introduced, and the more anticipated it is, the less costly will be this adjustment. This condition for minimising the adjustment costs relating to shifts in competitiveness is the same as that discussed on p. 270 pertaining to minimising capital adjustment costs by gradual phasing in of the tax so that adjustment may be made as part of normal investment cycles.

International competitiveness depends not only on cost increases but also on the trade intensity of the affected products. Relative price rises of untraded goods may affect demand for those goods in domestic markets, but they will not affect international trade. Row 6 shows that the low trade intensity of IS and NMM (both sectors comprising heavy, bulky goods including iron and cement) substantially reduces the trade impacts that these sectors will suffer from the carbon tax. Indeed, the trade impacts on CH are also reduced by the medium trade intensity of this sector, leaving NFM as the only sector in which a high trade intensity and high cost increase from the tax may cause significant trade effects from the tax. Against this it may be noted that 57 per cent of UK exports in 1995 were to EU countries, so that if the carbon tax were imposed on an EU-wide basis (as was the proposal from the European Commission in 1991), all the trade effects for these sectors would be much attenuated.

Table 9.3 clearly shows the difference between the impacts from environmental taxes on sectoral and national competitiveness. The cost increases in the four most affected sectors will impair their position in domestic markets with respect to the products of other sectors. The six sectors whose costs are decreased by the revenue-recycling will be particular beneficiaries from the shift in relative prices. For the country as a whole, however, there is no reason for thinking that its competitiveness will be affected at all by the shift.

Table 9.4 shows the export share of the sectors identified in Table 9.3, plus some others, aggregating the sectors in the UK Input–Output Tables of 1989 to get as close as possible to Pezzey's classification. The four sectors relatively disadvantaged by the tax-plus-rebate account for 16 per cent of UK exports. On the other hand, 30.4 per cent of UK exports are in the six relatively advantaged sectors. In addition, three other sectors have been identified (FS, AE, OM, see Table 9.4 for the code) which have a similar energy intensity to some of the relatively advantaged sectors, and so might also be expected to benefit from the tax-plus-rebate. Adding in their export share takes the proportion that might be expected to benefit

Table 9.4 Export share of various UK sectors as a percentage of total UK exports in 1989

IS	CH	NFM	NMM	TE	M	F	P	W	CL	FS	AE	OM
2.2	11.3	2.1	0.5	13	8	4.7	2.1	0.4	2.2	12.5	6.8	4.9

Source: Hayes and Hughes (1992: 118 (Table 3))

Notes:

Sectors as in Table 9.3 plus:

FS – Financial and other non-transport services; AE – Aerospace equipment manufacturing and repairing; OM – Office machinery and computer equipment to around 55 per cent of UK exports. On these figures it may well be that the UK's international trading position would be improved by the tax-plus-rebate arrangement.

This conclusion would appear to be borne out by the experience of Denmark, which has a small, open economy, and which has been a pioneer in the area of environmental taxation. According to its Ministry of Economic Affairs: 'Danish experience through many years is that we have not damaged our competitiveness because of green taxes. In addition, we have developed new exports in the environmental area' (Kristensen 1996: 126). The study of the Norwegian Green Tax Commission has also endorsed this essential conclusion:

> Reduced competitiveness of an individual industry is not necessarily a problem for the economy as a whole. . . . It is hardly possible to avoid loss of competitiveness and trade effects in individual sectors as a result of policy measures if a country has a more ambitious environmental policy than other countries or wishes to be an instigator in environmental policy. On the other hand, competitiveness and profitability will improve in other industries as a result of a revenue neutral tax reform.
>
> (Norwegian Green Tax Commission 1996: 90)

However, a loss of competitiveness in key sectors at the corporate level (say iron and steel and chemicals in the UK, see Table 9.3) may result in effects at the national level, at least while the economy adjusts, such as increased unemployment, relocation of industries and currency devaluation, all of which are of political concern. This is why considerations of competitiveness are one of the major constraints on the introduction of carbon taxes at the national level and why even the European Commission, in its proposal for a European carbon-energy tax, made its implementation conditional on a similar tax being imposed in other major OECD countries. It also proposed that energy-intensive sectors should be exempted from the tax, and in fact most countries that have already introduced carbon/energy taxes, such as Denmark, Sweden and Norway, grant energy-intensive industries a lower tax rate than, for example, households. Thus Swedish manufacturing industries are completely exempt from the energy tax on mineral fuels and are eligible for a 25 per cent reduction of the carbon tax on mineral fuels.

While these exemptions are understandable, they can be economically costly, and seem unlikely even to benefit the sectors to which they apply. A study by Oliveira-Martins *et al.* (1992) showed that, for a given emission-reduction target, the tax exemption of energy-intensive industries in the EU does not affect the output level of these industries. This outcome arises because the exemptions result in higher tax rates for the rest of the economy, so that the costs of the other sectors are higher and total output falls. A similar result has been reported by Böhringer and Rutherford (1997) in their analysis of the consequences of exempting energy-intensive sectors from a carbon tax. They find that wage subsidies to export- and energy-intensive sectors, rather than tax exemptions, retain more jobs and are less costly. The study's general conclusions are:

> Welfare losses associated with exemptions can be substantial even when the share of exempted sectors in overall economic activity and carbon emissions is small. Holding emissions constant, exemptions for some sectors imply increased tax rates for others and higher costs for the economy as a whole.
>
> (Böhringer and Rutherford 1997: 201)

Rather than exempting energy-intensive sectors from a carbon tax, it would seem preferable either to return the revenues from the tax to the sectors, on some other basis than carbon, or to allow the tax payments to be set against investments in energy efficiency. Both of these measures would cushion the tax's effects while maintaining its incentive for carbon-reduction.

9.3.5 Investment, efficiency and technological change

Implementing a carbon tax will increase the relative price of fossil energy compared to other inputs, an effect which may be enhanced by reducing taxes on these other inputs (e.g. labour, capital). As has been seen, modelling suggests that choosing the offsetting taxes carefully can cause both employment and GDP to rise in an inflation-neutral way. But the change in relative prices could affect economic development in a number of other ways.

Increased scrapping

A change in relative prices caused by the imposition of a carbon tax might affect economic development by making existing capital equipment uneconomic, thereby bringing forward its scrapping date. This could be a major potential source of adjustment costs related to the tax.

Using a vintage model of the UK manufacturing sector, which allows firms to change their machines' energy–output ratio, according to relative factor prices, both between different machine vintages and with existing machines, Ingham and Ulph (1991) found that there is a significant increase in the tax rate required to meet, and the associated cost of meeting, a given target if the target date is brought closer or if action is delayed, or if the target entails cutting existing emissions rather than preventing future growth. As Ingham and Ulph (1991: 143) say: 'It is much more expensive to undo the effects of emissions-generating plant already installed, than it is to offset the effects of emissions-generating plant yet to be installed.'

Thus, one would expect that the least disruptive imposition of a carbon tax would be one introduced initially at a low level, with modest annual increases over a substantial, pre-announced period of time. This would allow responses to the tax to be synchronised with normal investment schedules, and argues for early action to mitigate climate change, rather than delay, as discussed below. As noted earlier, if a carbon tax were introduced in this gradual, expected way, it is unlikely that experience gained in response to the energy price shocks of the 1970s would provide a reliable guide to the economy's response. Elasticities derived from these responses should, therefore, be treated with caution when applied to this different situation.

Improvements in energy efficiency

Several of the global models (see the review in Dean and Hoeller 1992: 26–7) employ a parameter called AEEI (Autonomous Energy Efficiency Improvement) to capture a perceived economic tendency to move towards greater energy efficiency independently of relative price changes (i.e. of substitution effects, which Manne and Richels 1991, for example, model through a separate parameter, ESUB, the elasticity of price-induced substitution).

In another application of the model mentioned in the previous section, Ingham *et al.* (1992: 128–9) identify, for UK manufacturing, the separate contribution to the decline in the energy–output ratio of relative factor prices, output and an exogenous component of technical progress. They conclude that in the period 1971–80 'changes in energy prices have explained all the improvements in energy efficiency' (ibid.: 129), as expressed in the UK manufacturing sector's energy–output ratio (this is clearly different from reductions in energy intensity due to changes in the structure of production of industry as a whole, which was not considered in the model). Although Ingham *et al.* stress the tentative nature of their result, at the least it suggests what might have been expected from theory, namely that technical change in the achievement of energy efficiency would increase with the price of fossil energy. This casts doubt on other models' treatment of energy efficiency as autonomous and unaffected by the imposition of a carbon tax.

The values of AEEI vary in the models between 0.25 per cent and 1.0 per cent. Even this range does not encompass the uncertainty associated with AEEI. Williams (1990), for example, considers that a 1 per cent value is too low, on the basis of historical decreases in energy intensity from 1973–86. Hogan and Jorgenson (1991), on the other hand, find on the basis of econometric estimates using US data, that AEEI is effectively negative, in other words that, without substitutions between factors induced by relative price changes, the energy–GDP ratio would increase. This is because their results indicate a positive technical bias for energy, which would mean that increasing the price of energy, for example, through a carbon tax, could reduce the growth of total factor productivity and thereby bring about a reduction in the growth rate. Their initial calculations suggest that the effect of this on output could be of the same order of magnitude as the reduction in output due directly to energy's higher price.

The value chosen for AEEI makes a substantial difference to the baseline CO_2 generated. Manne and Richels (1990b) and Burniaux *et al.* (1992b) have performed some sensitivity analysis with different values of the AEEI coefficient, and found that it considerably changes the welfare effects of a carbon tax. Manne and Richels (1990b: 74) calculate that the discounted cost to the US economy of reducing emissions by 20 per cent is reduced from just less that $1 trillion to a negligible level by increasing the AEEI from 0.5 to 1.5 per cent per annum (which latter figure they doubt is sustainable over the long term). Dean and Hoeller, in their comparative study of the six main global models, note:

> A difference of 0.5 per cent in this parameter (autonomous energy efficiency improvement), given compounding, can lead to an outcome in 2100 which is as much as 20 billion tons (of carbon emissions) different. . . . Uncertainty about the size of this parameter is likely to remain large as it depends on future technical progress.
>
> (Dean and Hoeller 1992: 19, 26 (Table 3))

Obviously differences in baseline emissions of this magnitude would greatly affect the cost of reducing these emissions to any particular level.

Whether or not investment and improvements in energy efficiency will accelerate with a carbon tax, many analysts have argued that market failures are preventing the implementation of some cost-efficient energy-conservation measures now (e.g. Jackson and Jacobs 1991; Lovins and Lovins 1991; Jackson 1995). It is possible that complementary government initiatives to encourage energy conservation and efficiency, and investment in clean energy technologies, would cost relatively little and significantly increase the energy elasticities on the basis of which the costs of a carbon tax are calculated, thereby reducing the cost of achieving any given CO_2 reduction target. Jackson (1991) provides evidence that the energy market is far from perfect, finding that out of seventeen technological possibilities for the reduction of CO_2 emissions, eight could have been implemented at negative cost on the basis of then-current prices, saving a total of 165 million tonnes of CO_2 per year by 2005, or 24 per cent of UK 1991 emissions. On this analysis the UK could exceed the Toronto target for CO_2 emissions (20 per cent reduction from 1988 levels by 2005) *and* save money.

Such results are not uncontroversial. It is quite possible that the non-implementation of seemingly profitable energy-efficiency technologies is not due to market failures, but to information or transaction costs that are higher than the economic gains from the technologies, or to consumer preferences for particular qualities associated with relatively energy-inefficient options, the loss of which would represent a cost to them.

Weyant and Yanigisawa (1998: 221ff.) have analysed the differences between various possible social choices related to energy: the economic optimum, the social optimum, the least-cost energy option and the maximum energy-efficiency option. Figure 9.2 plots a society's energy efficiency against its economic efficiency, with its current position, the baseline, at the origin. If there are market failures, either from the immediate point of view of the individual consumer, or institutional failures in energy markets, then appropriate public policy can move the economy along A towards the economic optimum, increasing both its economic and energy efficiency. This corresponds to the win–win opportunities of Sectors A and B in Figure 6.1, in which it is possible both to improve the environment and increase economic growth.

If energy use is associated with negative externalities, then appropriate public policy can increase the economy's energy and economic efficiency still further by internalising these costs, moving along path B to the social optimum. While some of the associated measures may still be located in Sector B in Figure 6.1, some are also likely to be in Sector C, in which net financial investments are required to yield non-market improvements in social welfare, which increase welfare overall.

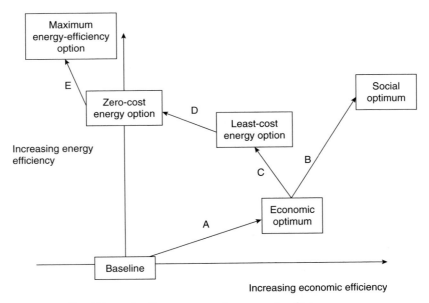

Figure 9.2 Possible paths for energy and economic efficiency
Source: Adapted from Weyant and Yanigisawa (1998: 222)

It may be that the economic optimum does not correspond to the least-cost delivery of energy services, calculated from technological considerations alone, because of high information and transaction costs or particular consumer preferences. If so, achieving the least-cost energy option along path C will increase energy efficiency but reduce economic efficiency relative to the economic optimum (the corresponding path from the social optimum would be parallel but starting from the social optimum box). The zero-cost energy option (zero-cost relative to the baseline) can be achieved along path D by further investment in energy efficiency that is not cost-effective even in terms of delivering energy services. At this point the economic gains achieved along path A have been given up for the sake of increased energy efficiency along paths C and D. Both paths C and D fall into Sector D of Figure 6.1. Path E represents the gain of even more energy efficiency, up to the maximum energy efficiency possible with current technologies, but the additional costs cause this option to represent an economic efficiency loss compared to the baseline, the costs associated with which may be substantial.

The actual positions of the various boxes in Figure 9.2, and therefore the extent of possible costless carbon reductions, are still a matter of contention. However, after reviewing this issue, Cline (1992: 227) decides that a reasonable estimate is that the first 22 per cent of carbon emissions from base can be cut back at zero cost. The IPCC survey of this literature (Bruce *et al.* 1996: 310, 318) finds that zero cost emission reductions by 2025/2030 estimated by various studies ranged from > 61–82 per cent (for the US) and from > 45–60 per cent for other OECD countries. The incorporation of such costless cuts in the cost-generating models would obviously reduce their negative outcomes from a carbon tax.

There is no guarantee that, by itself, the implementation of these efficiency measures would reduce energy consumption. On the contrary, the income effect of increased efficiency (lower costs) may increase the overall demand for energy. The generally increased energy efficiency in OECD countries during the last two decades, has led to a fall in the energy intensities of GDP, but not in absolute energy demand. For the latter to occur, which is required if CO_2 emissions are to be reduced, the efficiency increases would have to be accompanied by rising energy prices. For CO_2 abatement, energy efficiency is not a substitute for a carbon tax, but a complement to it. Clearly, too, a rising energy price would increase the number of cost-effective efficiency measures and the probability that they would be implemented.

Changed investment opportunities

A changing relative price of energy would change patterns of investment and demand. There are opposite tendencies at work here. One tendency is the possible complementarity between energy and capital, a still unresolved issue (J. Solow 1987). If energy and capital are complements, then increasing the price of energy will reduce the demand in production for both energy and capital, thereby reducing both investment and growth. A related tendency working in the same direction is the possible energy-using bias of technical change, already mentioned in the context of energy efficiency (Hogan and Jorgenson 1991). The results of Jorgenson's empirical work in this area have showed that productivity growth had an energy-using bias in thirty-two out of thirty-five sectors studied (Jorgenson 1990: 83), which would mean that, in these sectors, increasing the price of energy would reduce productivity growth.

A third negative effect on investment of an energy price increase is the obvious one that certain investments involving energy-intensive capital goods or processes would become uneconomic and would not, therefore, be made. However, working in the opposite direction to all these growth-reducing tendencies is the stimulus that the relative price change would give to energy-saving investment. If it is true that many presently economic opportunities for energy-saving remain unimplemented because of market failures, then it might be expected that a continuously increasing energy price, by providing a continuously increasing incentive to correct such failures, would result in substantial investments in energy efficiency and further innovation in this area. If energy efficiency could be increased at the same rate as the price of energy, then the negative effect of the rising price on investment plans would be cancelled out. There would also be a positive stimulus with regard to the development of non-fossil energy technologies. Such technical change would be what Grubb (1995: 305) calls 'induced technology development', which he speculates may be a cause of asymmetrical elasticities of energy demand, for which there is now substantial evidence (in general falls in energy prices have not increased energy demand by as much as the preceding energy price increases reduced it). Grubb's conclusion is directly relevant to the theme of this chapter:

> If price rises stimulate technical development and in addition governments take further associated action to encourage energy saving, long-term solutions may emerge at relatively lower cost as a result of the accumulation of technical change in the direction of lower CO_2-emitting technologies, infrastructure and behaviour.
>
> (ibid.: 309)

As for the issues of energy–capital complementarity and technical bias, it is possible that all the empirical results showing energy–capital complementarity or the loss of productivity induced by energy price rises owe more to the inflationary and recessionary effects of the 1970s and the *kind* of energy price rises then experienced, than to the fact of the price rise itself (see Barker *et al.* 1995: 11–12). Furthermore, in addition to the uncertainties involved in the empirical estimates, the whole methodology by which the estimates are derived has been called into question by Scott, using reasoning which 'effectively knocks out the production function and the measurement of total factor productivity as they are currently used' (Scott 1992: 622). Conventional growth theory based on a production function relates output to the size of the capital stock and growth of output to net investment (i.e. gross investment less depreciation). Scott's basic argument, in contrast, is that it is *gross investment* that plays the dominant role in the growth process. Defining investment as 'the cost (in terms of consumption forgone) of changing, hopefully, of improving, economic arrangements' (ibid.: 625), he writes:

> Investment is a much more important proximate cause of growth than conventional theory, backed up by many growth-accounting studies, would have us believe. Furthermore, raising the investment ratio raises the rate of growth indefinitely, and not by an amount which diminishes asymptotically to zero. Finally, there is a large externality of investment, due mainly to the learning effect whereby investment by one firm creates and reveals investment opportunities for other firms. These are all conclusions from my study which, if accepted, point to the need for policies to promote investment. There is, on these grounds, a rather strong case for reducing taxes on savings and replacing them by other taxes, for example on consumers' expenditures, or, better still, taxes designed to protect the environment and reduce traffic congestion.
>
> (ibid.: 629)

Scott's views cannot be explored in detail here but, if they are correct, and if the stimulus to energy efficiency and innovation from a rising energy price is greater than its dampening effect, then this conclusion is a striking echo of the earlier one which advocated the substitution of environmental taxes for those on capital and labour in order to reduce economic distortions. In that case, a carbon tax was perceived as yielding a double dividend by internalising an externality *and* reducing other distortionary taxes. A conclusion of Scott's view of the relation between investment and growth would seem to be that a carbon tax can yield a double dividend here too, both by creating investment opportunities directly related to the changes in energy's relative price (always assuming that these are greater than the investment opportunities lost) *and* by removing taxation disincentives to investment elsewhere. On this view, a carbon tax could act as a spur to growth.

The timing of abatement

It is clear from the forgoing that the costs of CO_2 abatement are dependent not only on the ultimate emission levels and atmospheric concentrations to be achieved, but also on the timing of emission reduction.

Wigley *et al.* (1996: 242) have suggested four reasons why, for any given stabilisation target, it may be desirable to delay abatement:

- The present value of delayed costs of abatement will be lower.
- The present carbon-intensive capital stock will not need to be prematurely scrapped.
- Technical change will make future abatement less costly than it is now.
- Delayed abatement allows more carbon to be emitted (because its longer residence in the atmosphere allows for greater absorption).

Grubb (1996) has pointed out that there are countervailing considerations to each of these reasons:

- Delayed abatement will lead to earlier damage from climate change, which will also have a higher present value.
- The capital stock turns over all the time. Delayed abatement will mean that carbon-inefficient stock continues to be installed. The higher rates of abatement, for a given stabilisation target, that are necessary with delayed abatement will impose higher costs through the premature scrapping of this stock.
- Carbon-abating technical change will be best stimulated by implementing the abating technologies that currently exist.
- Higher overall emissions of carbon mean higher rates of climate change, and higher associated costs, before stabilisation.

It is the technological issues that are of interest here. At root the differences between these two views derive from differences in perception about how technical change takes place. For Wigley *et al.* it is exogenous: new technologies come on stream at future dates and lower costs, and it is worth waiting for them. This is the way much of the modelling of carbon abatement has been carried out. For Grubb technology choice happens all the time and is continually evolving. Today's choices influence the pace and direction of technical change and therefore tomorrow's technologies.

There can be little doubt as to which portrayal of technical change is more realistic. Technologies do not emerge from on high. They evolve in response to pressures, which may be the competitive forces of the market, or the demands of public policy. Grubb *et al.* (1995: 420) point out that the no-regrets potential for increased energy efficiency in the UK in 1980 was identified as about 20 per cent. In 1990 it was again identified as about 20 per cent, despite the fact that the earlier 20 per cent had largely been realised. They comment:

> It seems a curious feature of energy efficiency studies that they seem regularly to identify cost-effective potentials of around 20–30% of current demand, almost irrespective of the potential already exploited. . . . The persistence of such results suggests that investing in greater energy efficiency helps itself to stimulate and identify options previously overlooked.
>
> (Grubb *et al.* 1995: 420)

Then there is the issue of the uncertainty of the eventual stabilisation concentration that will need to be achieved. If a target is selected now, and later evidence of high likely damage requires it to be reduced, then a delayed abatement strategy could prove particularly costly. The 'putty-clay' nature of much investment, as portrayed in the Ingham and Ulph model discussed earlier, means that policy should ensure that all new capital investment is carbon efficient, and therefore carbon abating as against business-as-usual, to minimise the possibilities of its premature obsolescence. Given that there are so many opportunities for low- or no-cost energy efficient investment, this is hardly likely to be a high-cost strategy, but it calls for positive risk-averse preventive action, rather than a wait-and-see approach.

9.3.6 Presentation of the costs of CO_2 abatement

Many of those who have studied the cost of abating CO_2 emissions have concluded that significant abatement will be costly. Thus Nordhaus (1991c: 49) has concluded: 'First, the cost of reducing CO_2 emissions is low for small curbs ... The second conclusion is that the cost of reducing CO_2 emissions grows rapidly and becomes extreme for substantial reductions.' Pezzey (1991: 25), in his study of the implications of CO_2 abatement for UK competitiveness, starts from the position that: 'The costs of achieving enough control of GHG emissions to reduce global warming significantly will be very large.' Similar opinions can be found in Beckerman (1991) and Hampson (1993). Hogan (1990: 75), reviewing the estimates in Manne and Richels (1990a), describes them as 'a huge cost on the same scale as recent defense budgets that have been a drain for the United States'. The US Council of Economic Advisers also used the Manne-Richels study in its 1990 Report to the President in support of its conclusion that 'the costs of policies to stabilize or reduce carbon dioxide emissions from fossil fuel combustion would be high' (CEA 1990: 214). It would be surprising if such perceptions did not contribute to the 'no targets' negotiating position adopted by the US in the preparation of the Framework Convention on Climate Change (FCCC) for the 1992 Rio Summit. Indeed Cline (1992: 312) specifically states that Nordhaus' early results had 'great policy influence, especially in the United States'. The US continues to resist significant cuts in its carbon emissions under the FCCC largely because of its perception of the costs involved.

As has already been seen, the costs of abating climate change can be, and are, presented in different ways. While these ways are mathematically equivalent (if correctly computed), they can give a significantly different impression of the costs of abatement as the following examples from the literature show.

The most common presentation of the results is as a percentage loss of GDP due to abatement, with figures of 1–3 per cent often quoted. Although in money terms this may seem a heavy cost to bear, Schelling has pointed out that 'subtracting 2 per cent from GNP in perpetuity lowers the GNP curve by not much more than the thickness of a line drawn with a number two pencil . . . it postpones the GNP of 2050 until 2051' (Schelling 1992: 8).

Apart from expressing the costs as a percentage of GNP, there are two principal ways of giving them in monetary terms. One is to compute them as an annualised money loss. This is how Nordhaus quotes the results of his DICE model: 'The environmentally correct policy of a 20-percent cut would impose significant net global costs of $762 billion in annualized terms' (Nordhaus 1993b: 315). Another way is to calculate them as a present value, as in the key statement of abatement costs in the influential Manne and Richels paper mentioned earlier:

> By 2030 roughly 5% of total annual macroeconomic consumption is lost as a consequence of the carbon constraint. This percentage remains relatively constant for the remainder of the time horizon. Adding all the years from 1990 through 2100, the present value of these losses would be $3.6 trillions, discounting to 1990 at 5% per year.
>
> (Manne and Richels 1990a: 68)

It was the $3.6 trillion loss to the US economy, equal to two thirds of 1990 US GDP, that was quoted by the Council of Economic Advisers, in support of its conclusion quoted above.

Barker (1991) has shown that the Manne and Richels figure can be recalculated in two different ways: it is equivalent either to a once-and-for-all loss of 2.47 per cent of 1990 US consumption (1.48 per cent of 1990 GNP); or to a 0.074 per cent reduction in the growth rate, which in the study is 3 per cent per annum from 2000 to 2050, falling to 1 per cent per annum by 2100). Expressed like this it is not at all clear that the Manne and Richels costs of abatement are so 'huge'. The growth rate reduction is well below the margin of forecasting error for growth rates; and *ex post* it would be impossible to detect that such a reduction had in fact taken place. The effect of abating CO_2 emissions would, on these figures, be all but imperceptible.

This is also very much the way that Gaskins and Weyant (1993) express the preliminary results of the models comparison project being carried out by the Energy Modeling Forum at the University of Stanford:

> [T]he cost of achieving a 20-per cent reduction in CO_2 emissions relative to today's level range from 0.9 per cent to 1.7 per cent of U.S. GDP in 2010. Although 1.7 per cent of U.S. GDP in 2010 amounts to about $130 billion 1990 dollars, the implied reduction in the GDP growth rate would only be from about 2.3 per cent per year to 2.25 per cent per year. *Thus it is possible to reduce emissions significantly from their noncontrolled level without significantly reducing the growth of the economy.*
>
> (Gaskins and Weyant 1993: 320, emphasis added)

This is a very different story indeed from the quotations from Nordhaus and others which opened this section.

9.4 CONCLUSIONS: SUSTAINABILITY AND CLIMATE CHANGE

The sustainability approach to climate change accepts that climate stability should be maintained. In line with the argument in Chapter 6, an unstable climate is a possible source of 'immoderate costs' (for example, Nordhaus 1994: 97 specifically acknowledges that 'the potential for rapid or catastrophic change' cannot be ruled out). Sustainability, based on a safe minimum standard, therefore clearly demands that CO_2 emissions be abated to the necessary level to maintain a stable climate, unless there is a risk that doing so would also involve 'immoderate', in the same sense of potentially catastrophic, costs.

The IPCC 1995 report (Houghton *et al.* 1996: 80) reported: 'For stabilisation at 450 ppmv (parts per million by volume) in the 1994 calculations fossil emissions had to be returned to about a third of today's levels (i.e. to about 2 GtC/year) by the year 2200.' Pre-industrial CO_2 concentrations were about 280 ppmv (ibid.: 14–15), so 450 ppmv represents a substantial rise. The 1994 concentration was 358 ppmv, to maintain which the IPCC 1990 report calculated that CO_2 emissions would have to fall by 60–80 per cent almost immediately (the IPCC 1995 report did not include the scenario of stabilisation of CO_2 concentrations at 350 ppmv). It may be that 450 ppmv is, in fact, not consistent with climate stability. Certainly it is right at the upper end of any range that might be said to be based on a safe minimum standard. At the very least, then, for sustainability CO_2 emissions should be cut by 70 per cent from 1990 levels. Are the costs of achieving this likely to prove 'immoderate', so as to call the desirability of achieving sustainability into question?

In a multi-model comparative study, Repetto and Austin (1997) used econometric regression on a sample of 162 different predictions from sixteen of the most reputable and widely used economic models, which show a very wide variation in the costs of carbon reduction. They found that changing eight assumptions explained 80 per cent of the differences in the modelling outcomes. The five assumptions which had the most effect were: the eventual availability of non-carbon energy sources, efficient adjustment of the economy in the long term, greater substitution possibilities, joint implementation (i.e. possibilities for industrial countries with relatively high abatement costs to achieve carbon reduction by investing in countries with relatively low abatement costs) and recycling tax revenues to reduce other, distortionary, taxes. With unfavourable assumptions across these dimensions, a 50 per cent reduction in US baseline emissions by 2020 was projected to cost about 6 per cent of GDP. With favourable assumptions there would be a modest positive impact on GDP relative to the baseline. The evident and growing opportunities for renewables and energy efficiency, and the obvious potential for joint implementation and a tax shift, suggest that the more favourable assumptions are the more realistic ones.

For another estimate, the EMF modelling exercise, the average results of which were illustrated in Figure 9.1, showed that the average GDP loss from a 50 per cent emissions cut by 2050 was about 3 per cent of GDP. This can hardly be classed as immoderate, but even this does not take account of the factors reviewed in this and the previous chapter which could substantially reduce this cost: the 35 – 100+ per cent that can be offset by recycling the revenues in such a way that distorting taxes are reduced; the > 45 per cent (minimum) reduction in emissions (by 2025/2030) by implementing energy-efficient technologies. In addition, 4–18 per cent of global CO_2 emissions could be cut with increases in output by phasing out fossil fuel subsidies (Bruce *et al.* 1996: 73). It is now well established that the secondary benefits of CO_2 abatement (the reduction in air pollutants apart from CO_2) substantially reduce the gross costs of such abatement. Ekins (1996a) has calculated that, even if only the secondary benefits from SO_2-reduction are considered, and calculations are performed taking into account the abatement of SO_2 emissions in accordance with the Second Sulphur Protocol (see Chapter 10, p. 302), these suggest secondary benefits such that 25–50 per cent of the CO_2 abatement brought about by a \$100/tC carbon tax would be achieved at negative net cost. Combining these offsets and no-regrets options makes it seem unlikely that the EMF 50 per cent reduction will cost anything at all.

Looking beyond 2050, whether further reductions in emissions will incur more costs depends most importantly on whether backstop energy technologies will have been developed which are competitive with the by then substantially depleted fossil fuels. Nordhaus, in his DICE model, rather pessimistically assumes that they will not, and projects several scenarios with rising costs of abatement through to the next century. Figure 9.3 illustrates these scenarios, from which it can be seen that, by 2100, the climate stabilisation scenario (which restricts the global average temperature rise to 1.5°C above the level in 1900) would cost about 8 per cent of per capita consumption, reducing it from about \$9,500 in the no-controls case to \$8,750. This scenario involves substantially earlier stabilisation than the IPCC 450ppmv case (which was by 2200), and therefore much more ambitious emission reduction in the next century – Nordhaus (1994: 87 (Figure 5.2)) has CO_2-equivalent emissions falling practically to zero by 2035 and staying below about 1.5 GtC (compared to current levels of about 7 GtC) per annum thereafter. This would therefore be a more ambitious sustainability target. Are its associated costs immoderate?

In a world in which per capita consumption is four times its present level, sacrificing 8 per cent of it for climate stability may not seem excessive,

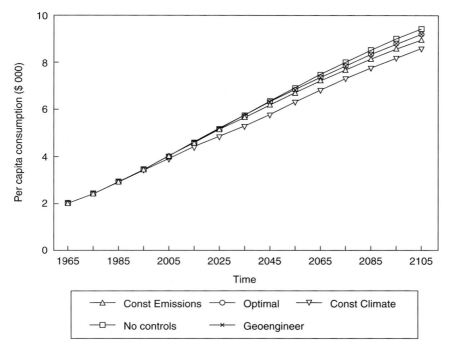

Figure 9.3 Consumption per capita under a base scenario and four scenarios of
control of global warming: no controls, control through geoengineering,
optimal CO_2 abatement, constant emissions, constant climate
Source: Nordhaus (1994: 92 (Figure 5.5))

yet this number too does not contain the offsets from revenue-recycling,
energy efficiency or removing subsidies. Add in secondary benefits, risk
aversion and any kind of distributional consideration, and the possibility
of stimulating the development of a backstop technology, such as solar
power, and the Nordhaus stabilisation scenario begins to look not only
feasible but desirable.

It is not 'optimal', of course. Figure 9.3 makes that clear. Nordhaus' estimates of damage costs for CO_2-doubling, at 1.0 per cent of GNP, are less
than both Fankhauser and Cline's, and seem to warrant little abatement.
But for those who believe that the techniques for arriving at such damage
figures, especially with regard to such effects discussed earlier as land loss,
migration, damage to agriculture and loss of human of life, are unable effectively to capture the costs involved, the sustainability approach offers an
alternative basis for emission control.

This chapter has shown that, to the middle of the next century at least,
a cost-effective strategy to stabilise the climate is feasible and will cost little
if anything. Thereafter much depends on technological development in

the interim, but even without any breakthroughs, further costs incurred by stabilisation seem modest and supportable. The proviso is that the process of change starts sooner rather than later. Unless the signals from energy prices and efficiency regulations start transforming the energy performance of new investment and the priorities for energy research development, there will be little prospect of realising the win–win opportunities that are clearly apparent in the economics of global warming, climate stability will become an ever more expensive goal and humanity will effectively have embarked on an irreversible experiment with a change in climate that is outside all prior human experience.

10 Sustainability and sulphur emissions: the case of the UK, 1970–2010

10.1 INTRODUCTION

SO_2 is a major pollutant which has been linked to substantial damage to human health and to the natural and built environment. As a result, far-reaching international measures for its control have been adopted, dating in Europe from 1979. While it cannot be argued that the regulation of SO_2 is typical, because different pollutants have their own characteristics, the study of the evolution of SO_2 emissions, with and without emission controls, can give insights into how pollution can be addressed and the associated costs. This in turn sheds light on whether a substantial diminution of environmental impacts, leading to the achievement of environmental sustainability, will necessarily entail a reduction in economic growth rates, and perhaps a cessation in economic growth altogether, the question which is at the centre of this book, and which has been a major strand in the debate over the negative effects of economic activity on the environment since the early 1970s, as has been seen.

In the second section of the chapter, UK SO_2 emissions from 1970–95 are analysed and various reasons are adduced for their reduction. In section 10.3, estimates of the damage from SO_2 emissions are presented and the legal framework for their control is described. Estimates are presented of the costs that have been projected for that control. Section 10.4 discusses future UK SO_2 emissions and, in particular, how the electricity supply industry (ESI) may be able to meet the sulphur limits that have been imposed. Section 10.5 concludes.

10.2 PAST UK EMISSIONS OF SO_2

Figure 10.1 shows total UK SO_2 emissions from 1970 to 1995, and shows a fall of 63 per cent over that period. The periods of steepest decline were 1979–83 and 1992–5. Figure 10.2 shows the emissions by fuel use. Coal and coke account for easily the largest proportion (61 per cent in 1970, 71 per cent in 1995), followed by fuel oil (34 per cent in 1970, 19 per cent in 1995).

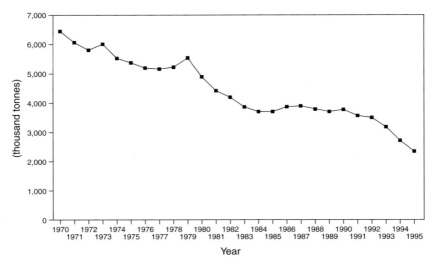

Figure 10.1 UK SO$_2$ emissions, 1970–95 (thousand tonnes)
Source: Cambridge Econometrics

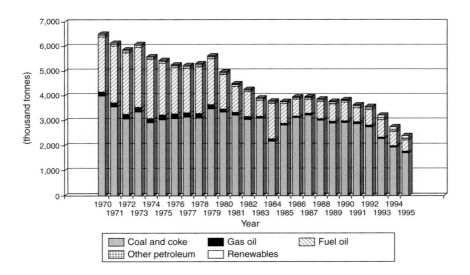

Figure 10.2 SO$_2$ emissions by fuel use, 1970–95 (thousand tonnes)
Source: Cambridge Econometrics

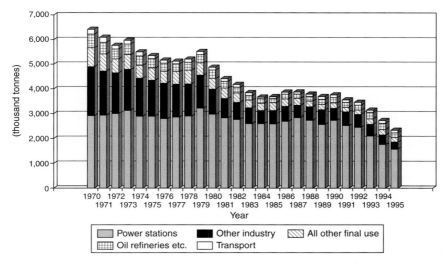

Figure 10.3 SO$_2$ emissions by fuel user, 1970–95 (thousand tonnes)
Source: Cambridge Econometrics

The reduction in emissions is due to two main factors: the decline in the use of fuel oil in both power generation and industry generally throughout the period, and the switch in power generation from coal to natural gas, which began to have a major effect from 1992. Thus SO$_2$ emissions from fuel oil show the largest fall over the period to 1992 (72 per cent), whereas those from coal and coke only fell by 31 per cent. However, from 1992 to 1995 emissions from coal and coke fell by 38 per cent.

Figure 10.3 shows SO$_2$ emissions by fuel user. Power stations are easily the largest emitters (45 per cent in 1970, 67 per cent in 1995). Their emissions from 1970 to 1992 only fell by 17 per cent over the period, but then fell by 35 per cent from 1992 to 1995. In contrast, emissions from Other Industry (excluding also the own use of energy by energy industries, such as in oil refineries) fell by 81 per cent from 1970 to 1995, and its share of emissions fell from 31 per cent in 1970 to 13 per cent in 1995. Though less important in absolute terms, a sharp drop in emissions (83 per cent) was also experienced over this period by the sectors in Other Final Use (within which domestic sector emissions, the largest component, fell by 87 per cent).

10.2.1 Methods of reducing SO$_2$ emissions

SO$_2$ emissions result from various factors arising from the nature and use of energy sources, which can be expressed as a sequence of ratios (where S stands for sulphur):

$$SO_2 = \frac{SO_2 \text{ output}}{S \text{ input}} \cdot \frac{S \text{ input}}{\text{energy input}} \cdot \frac{\text{energy input}}{Y} \, Y$$

or $SO_2 = S_A \cdot S_I \cdot E_I \cdot Y$ \hfill (10.1)

or $SO_2 = S_F \cdot E_I \cdot Y$

where S_A indicates the extent of abatement (for full abatement, $S_A = 0$); S_I indicates the sulphur intensity of fuel use; S_F is the SO_2 emissions intensity ($= S_A \cdot S_I$); E_I is the energy intensity of the economy; and Y is output.

Thus SO_2 emissions can be reduced by increasing abatement (reducing S_A), switching to the use of low or non-sulphur fuels (reducing S_I), reducing the economy's energy intensity (E_I) or reducing output.

A second sequence of ratios can link energy (En) input to the energy services (E_s) which actually deliver welfare:

$$En \text{ service} = \frac{En \text{ service}}{En \text{ delivered}} \cdot \frac{En \text{ delivered}}{En \text{ available}} \cdot \frac{En \text{ available}}{En \text{ input}} \cdot En \text{ input}$$

or $E_s \qquad = e_u \cdot e_d \cdot e_c \cdot E$ \hfill (10.2)

where e_u is the end-use efficiency of appliances or buildings or the energy efficiency of a production process; e_d is the distribution or transmission efficiency; e_c is the efficiency of energy conversion or generation; and E is the energy input. Increasing any of these efficiencies allows energy users to achieve the same level of energy service (and therefore the same level of welfare) from a lower consumption of energy.

From (10.1) and (10.2):

$$SO_2 \quad = \frac{S_A \cdot S_I}{e_u \cdot e_d \cdot e_c} \frac{E_s}{Y} \cdot Y$$ \hfill (10.3)

Equation (10.3) shows that SO_2 emissions can be reduced by increasing abatement or reducing the sulphur intensity of fuels, by increasing any of the efficiencies defined in equation (10.2), by reducing the needs or preferences of consumers for energy services per unit of output or by reducing output itself. Examples of the kinds of measures involved are as follows:

- improving appliance efficiency or thermal insulation will increase e_u;
- installing combined heat and power will increase e_d;
- improving conversion or generation efficiencies will increase e_c;
- switching to less energy-intensive processes will reduce E, and therefore E_I. e_u may increase (signifying that the same energy service can be provided by a lower quantity of delivered energy) or E_s (and therefore E_s/Y) will fall;

- switching from combustion (especially fossil) fuels to non-combustion fuels (e.g. wind, hydro, nuclear), or from high to low sulphur combustion fuels (e.g. from coal to gas or from high to low sulphur coals) will reduce S_I;
- cleaning sulphur from fuel inputs (e.g. in the oil refining process) will reduce S_I;
- using technologies that leave more of the input sulphur in post-combustion solid residues will reduce S_A;
- cleaning sulphur from exhaust gases (e.g. through flue-gas desulphurisation) will reduce S_A.

10.2.2 Explaining past UK emissions

The (pre-abatement) emission factors of different fuels differ substantially. In 1990, those of fuel oil and refinery input oils, the highest, were around 50kg SO_2/tonne, with that of coal around 30kg/tonne, of other solid fuels and gas oil for shipping around 20kg/tonne and of other petroleum products ranging from 5kg/tonne to negligible (Gillham *et al.* 1992: Tables B1–B3).

In the MDM model of the UK economy (see Barker and Peterson 1987 for a detailed description) SO_2 (and other) emissions are disaggregated by twelve fuel users and ten fuel types. Data from the model shows that changes in fuel use by sector contributed to the changing patterns of emissions of Figures 10.2 and 10.3. For example, 8 per cent more coal was burnt in power stations in 1992 than in 1970, but their use of fuel oil fell by 53 per cent over this period. This meant that although overall their use of sulphur-emitting (SE) fuels (coal and fuel oil) only fell by 7 per cent, the switch away from fuel oil to less sulphur-intensive coal caused the 17 per cent drop in sulphur emissions from this sector (between 1970 and 1992). By 1995 coal use in power generation had fallen 22 per cent from the 1992 level, with non-SE natural gas replacing it. Also, from 1993 the flue-gas desulphurisation (FGD) plant on 6GW of generating capacity had begun to come on stream. These factors, together with a further fall in fuel oil use in power generation from 1992–5, resulted in the sector's 35 per cent reduction in SO_2 emissions over this period shown in Figure 10.3.

Other shifts between 1970 and 1995 included:

- A 74 per cent drop in the use of SE fuels by Other Industry (this comprises all the industry sectors in MDM except power generation and refining, i.e. iron and steel, mineral products, chemicals and other industry), but its use of sulphur-intensive fuel oil fell by 82 per cent. In addition, the average sulphur intensity of fuel oil used fell by 20 per cent between 1970 and 1995, and that of coal use fell by 13 per cent. All these factors contributed to these sectors' 84 per cent decline in sulphur emissions from 1970–95 (Figure 10.3).

- An 84 per cent drop in SE fuel use in the sectors of Other Final Use (domestic emissions and the MDM sector other final use), with sulphur emissions falling by about the same amount (Figure 10.3).
- A 73 per cent drop in SE fuel use in energy industries' own use of energy (e.g. oil refineries), including an 85 per cent reduction in their use of coal. However, the use of relatively sulphur-intensive fuel oil only fell by 18 per cent, so that SO_2 emissions only fell by 63 per cent (Figure 10.3).
- Considerable increase in the use of gas by all sectors except transport. This included increases of 214 per cent in the domestic sector, 125 per cent in energy industries' own use of energy, 171 per cent in Other Industry and 395 per cent in the MDM sector other final use (mainly commerce and public administration). In power generation, gas demand between 1990 and 1995 rose from 86 to 5,100 million therms, a fifty-eight-fold increase.

With MDM's twelve fuel users and ten fuel types, sectoral SO_2 emissions are given by the following equation:

$$SO_{2i} = \sum_{j=1}^{10} S_{A,i,j} \cdot S_{I,i,j} \cdot E_j \qquad (10.4)$$

$$\text{and} \quad \text{Total } SO_2 = \sum_{i=1}^{12} SO_{2i}$$

where i refers to the fuel user or sector, and j refers to the fuel. Both the innate sulphur content of the fuel (S_I) and the abatement factor (S_A) can vary according to the fuel use. For example, gas oil for shipping has a far higher emission factor than gas oil for other uses, while flue gas desulphurisation of coal exhausts is appropriate for large-scale industrial emissions but not for those from the domestic sector use of coal.

As in equation (10.1), sectoral sulphur output can also be expressed in terms of the following product:

$$SO_{2i} = \frac{SO_{2i}}{E_i} \cdot \frac{E_i}{Y_i} \cdot Y_i$$

$$\Rightarrow SO_{2i} = S_{F,i} \cdot E_{I,i} \cdot Y_i \qquad (10.1a)$$

$$\text{or} \quad SO_{2i} = \frac{SO_{2i}}{Y_i} \cdot \frac{Y_i}{Y} \cdot Y$$

$$\Rightarrow SO_{2i} = S_{V,i} \cdot S_{Y,i} \cdot Y \qquad (10.1b)$$

where $S_{V,i}$ is the sectoral sulphur intensity of value-added, and $S_{Y,i}$ is the sectoral share of value-added.

Table 10.1 gives for 1970, 1990, 1992 and 1995 the various ratios in equations (10.1a) and (10.1b). Between 1970 and 1990, value-added in production grew by 62 per cent, while consumers' expenditure grew by 76 per cent. In contrast, energy use in production fell by 7 per cent and in the domestic sector only grew by 11 per cent. The result is that the energy intensities of production and consumers' expenditure fell by 43 per cent and 37 per cent respectively. Not only did the energy intensity of the economy fall remarkably, but so too did the sulphur intensity of the energy used: by 33 per cent across productive sectors as a whole and by 80 per cent for domestic final use. (Note that sulphur emissions from power generation are allocated to that sector rather than to the electricity user. Thus falling sectoral sulphur intensities are consistent with, and may be reinforced by, rising electricity consumption.) The combination of reductions in both the energy intensity of value-added and the sulphur intensity of energy use (the first two terms of equation (10.1a)) means that the sulphur intensity of value-added (the product of these two terms) shows an even greater proportionate fall: 62 per cent for the productive sectors and 87 per cent for consumers' expenditure.

The only sectors not to show falling energy intensity of value-added are road and water transport. Power generation has easily the highest sulphur intensity of value-added, followed by water transport. The decrease in the sulphur intensity of energy use of power generation and road transport is only about 20 per cent, substantially less than for other productive sectors (apart from air transport). The combination of these effects means that power generation and the transport sectors have reduced their sulphur intensity of value-added by less than other sectors.

Equations (10.1a) and (10.1b) can be used to express the proportionate reduction in sulphur emissions in a period (RSO_2) as the product of various ratios, as follows:

$$SO_{2i}^1 = S_{F,i}^1 . E_{I,i}^1 . Y_i^1 \text{ and}$$
$$SO_{2i}^2 = S_{F,i}^2 . E_{I,i}^2 . Y_i^2$$

where the superscripts ^{1} and ^{2} refer to different periods of time.

$$\frac{SO_{2i}^2 - SO_{2i}^1}{SO_{2i}^1} = \frac{S_{F,i}^2 . E_{I,i}^2 . Y_i^2}{S_{F,i}^1 . E_{I,i}^1 . Y_i^1} - 1$$

$$\Rightarrow RSO_2 = RSF.REI.RYI - 1$$

$$\text{or } RSO_2 = \frac{S_{V,i}^1 . S_{Y,i}^1 . Y^2}{S_{V,i}^2 . S_{Y,i}^2 . Y^1} - 1$$

$$\Rightarrow RSO_2 = RSV.RSY.RY - 1$$

Table 10.1 Sectoral value-added, energy use, SO$_2$ emissions and related intensities

	Sectoral value-added m pounds, Y_i							Share of value-added %, SYI			
	1970	1990	Index 1970 =100	1992	Index 1970 =100	1995	Index 1970 =100	Share 1970 %	Share 1990 %	Share 1992 %	Share 1995 %
1 Power generation	3,363	5,950	177	6,325	188	6,967	207	1.2	1.3	1.4	1.4
2 Own use of energy	8,055	16,161	201	17,412	216	22,473	279	2.8	3.4	3.8	4.4
3 Ind. iron & steel	4,719	3,854	82	3,368	71	4,828	102	1.6	0.8	0.7	1.0
4 Ind. mineral prod.	4,704	5,448	116	4,721	100	4,897	104	1.6	1.1	1.0	1.0
5 Ind. chemicals	6,409	11,510	180	12,066	188	13,215	206	2.2	2.4	2.6	2.6
6 Other industry	73,678	89,752	122	83,259	113	88,299	120	25.2	18.9	18.1	17.5
7 Rail transport	4,355	3,973	91	3,677	84	2,009	46	1.5	0.8	0.8	0.4
8 Road transport	6,635	10,216	154	10,001	151	12,697	191	2.3	2.2	2.2	2.5
9 Water transport	1,582	961	61	1,029	65	978	62	0.5	0.2	0.2	0.2
10 Air transport	962	3,693	384	4,075	424	3,843	399	0.3	0.8	0.9	0.8
12 Other final use	177,874	322,226	181	313,762	176	344,866	194	60.8	68.0	68.3	68.3
Totals	292,336	473,744	162	459,695	157	505,072	173	100.0	100.0	100.0	100.0
11 Consumers' expend.	197,598	347,527	176	339,946	172	364,046	184				

Table 10.1 (continued)

	Sectoral energy use m therms, E_i							Sectoral SO₂ emissions k tonnes, $SO_{2,i}$						
	1970	1990	Index 1970 =100	1992	Index 1970 =100	1995	Index 1970 =100	1970	1990	Index 1970 =100	1992	Index 1970 =100	1995	Index 1970 =100
1 Power generation	25,457	28,366	111	29,604	116	29,891	117	2,913.2	2,722.3	93	2,427	83	1,588	55
2 Own use of energy	12,741	7,679	60	7,589	60	8,637	68	569.6	213.9	38	210.8	37	211	37
3 Ind. iron & steel	7,003	3,042	43	2,859	41	3,064	44	4,34.5	88.3	20	83.2	19	62	14
4 Ind. mineral prod.	2,220	1,520	68	1,231	55	1,221	55	282.2	85.6	30	74.5	26	42	15
5 Ind. chemicals	2,382	2,884	121	2,873	121	2,090	88	232.7	104.4	45	125.8	54	68	29
6 Other industry	11,415	8,139	71	8,066	71	7,936	70	1,018.5	236.6	23	262.8	26	144	14
7 Rail transport	640	445	70	466	73	513	80	25.4	2.6	10	2.7	11	2	8
8 Road transport	8,505	15,409	181	15,545	183	15,690	184	44.4	63.2	142	61.5	139	51	115
9 Water transport	505	541	107	542	107	479	95	109.3	56.7	52	57.7	53	57	52
10 Air transport	1,536	2,911	190	2,952	192	3,389	221	0.8	1.5	188	2.5	313	3	375
12 Other final use	7,435	7,791	105	8,180	110	8,459	114	272.1	89.1	33	88.2	32	69	25
Totals (exc. power generation)	54,382	50,361	93	50,303	92	51,478	95	5,902.7	3,664.2	62	3,396.7	58	2,297	39
11 Domestic final use	14,642	16,261	111	17,438	119	16,943	116	521.9	117.7	23	103.1	20	68	13

Table 10.1 (continued)

| | Sectoral energy intensity therms/pound value-added, E_i/Y_i (= EI_i) | | | | | | |
	1970	1990	Index 1970 = 100	1992	Index 1970 = 100	1995	Index 1970 = 100
1 Power generation	7.570	4.767	63	4.680	62	4.290	57
2 Own use of energy	1.582	0.475	30	0.436	28	0.384	24
3 Ind, iron & steel	1.484	0.789	53	0.849	57	0.635	43
4 Ind, mineral prod.	0.472	0.279	59	0.261	55	0.249	53
5 Ind, chemicals	0.372	0.251	67	0.238	64	0.158	43
6 Other industry	0.155	0.091	59	0.097	63	0.090	58
7 Rail transport	0.147	0.112	76	0.127	86	0.255	174
8 Road transport	1.282	1.508	118	1.554	121	1.236	96
9 Water transport	0.319	0.563	176	0.527	165	0.490	153
10 Air transport	1.597	0.788	49	0.724	45	0.882	55
12 Other final use	0.042	0.024	58	0.026	62	0.025	59
Total economy	0.186	0.106	57	0.109	59	0.102	55
11 Dom.fin.use/Con.exp.	0.074	0.047	63	0.051	69	0.047	63

Table 10.1 (continued)

Sectoral sulphur emission intensities

	of value-added g SO$_2$/pound v.a., SO$_{2i}$/Y$_i$ (= SV$_i$)							of energy use g SO$_2$/therm, SO$_{2i}$/E$_i$ (= SF$_i$)						
	1970	1990	Index 1970 =100	1992	Index 1970 =100	1995	Index 1970 =100	1970	1990	Index 1970 =100	1992	Index 1970 =100	1995	Index 1970 =100
1 Power generation	866.25	457.53	53	383.72	44	227.93	26	114.44	95.97	84	81.98	72	53.13	46
2 Own use of energy	70.71	13.24	19	12.11	17	9.39	13	44.71	27.86	62	27.78	62	24.43	55
3 Ind, iron & steel	92.07	22.91	25	24.70	27	12.84	14	62.04	29.03	47	29.10	47	20.23	33
4 Ind, mineral prod.	59.99	15.71	26	15.78	26	8.58	14	127.12	56.32	44	60.52	48	34.40	27
5 Ind, chemicals	36.31	9.07	25	10.43	29	5.15	14	97.69	36.20	37	43.79	45	32.54	33
6 Other industry	13.82	2.64	19	3.16	23	1.63	12	89.22	29.07	33	32.58	37	18.15	20
7 Rail transport	5.83	0.65	11	0.73	13	1.00	17	39.69	5.84	15	5.79	15	3.90	10
8 Road transport	6.69	6.19	92	6.15	92	4.02	60	5.22	4.10	79	3.96	76	3.25	62
9 Water transport	69.09	59.00	85	56.07	81	58.28	84	216.44	104.81	48	106.46	49	119.00	55
10 Air transport	0.83	0.41	49	0.61	74	0.78	94	0.52	0.52	99	0.85	163	0.89	170
12 Other final use	1.53	0.28	18	0.28	18	0.20	13	36.60	11.44	31	10.78	29	8.16	22
Total economy	20.19	7.73	38	7.39	37	4.55	23	108.54	72.76	67	67.52	62	44.62	41
11 Dom.fin.use/ Con.exp.	2.64	0.34	13	0.30	11	0.19	7	35.64	7.24	20	5.91	17	4.01	11

Source: Cambridge Econometrics

where RSF, REI, RYI, RSV, RSY, RY are the ratios respectively of the sulphur emission factors, the energy intensity, sectoral value-added, the sulphur intensity of value-added, the sectoral share of value-added and the total value-added in the two periods. Table 10.2 uses the data from Table 10.1 to present these ratios for the different fuel users and for the economy as a whole for the periods 1970–90, 1970–92 and 1970–95. In the UK 1991 and 1992 were years of recession, so comparison of the first two periods should yield some insights into how these ratios move both in the long term, for an economy like the UK's, and during recession. After 1992 the recession came to an end, and power generation began to use large quantities of gas, so that the extended period 1970–95 should pick up the effects of those changes.

For the 1970–90 period, Table 10.2 shows that for the production sectors of the economy as a whole reductions in the overall sulphur emission factor (RSF, 33 per cent) and in energy intensity (REI, 43 per cent) both played a role in both counteracting the 62 per cent growth in value-added (RY) and reducing SO_2 emissions by 38 per cent (RSO_2) Reduced sulphur intensities were more important in all sectors except power generation, own use of energy and air transport. Only road and water transport became more energy intensive over the period; no sector became more sulphur intensive. Only road and air transport increased their emissions (though the former is small and the latter is negligible in absolute size, see Table 10.1). The greatest falls in sulphur intensities are in the sectors that have made substantial substitutions towards natural gas, to a lesser extent electricity or, for the power sector, nuclear generation. In some respects it would be desirable to allocate the SO_2 emissions from power generation to electricity users. But this is only a particular (though the most important) example of the desirability in further analysis to use input–output techniques to allocate the emissions from intermediate goods to their final users. This is beyond the scope of this chapter which seeks in any case to concentrate in what follows on the power generation sector itself.

Table 10.2 also shows the effect of structural change between 1970 and 1990, 1992 and 1995. Using equation (10.1b) the sulphur emissions for 1990, 1992 and 1995 are projected by multiplying the product of the sectoral sulphur intensities of value-added and total value-added for those years by the sectoral shares for 1970. These projections give the SO_2 emissions which would have resulted had the economy not changed its structure during the period, which can then be compared with the actual SO_2 emissions. It can be seen from Tables 10.1 and 10.3 that the two fuel-using sectors with the highest shares of value-added, Other Final Use and Other Industry (61 per cent and 25 per cent value-added in 1970 respectively) had very different sulphur intensities of value-added (1.5 and 13.8 g $SO_2/\pounds$ respectively). Both these intensities decreased dramatically in the years to 1990, but they remained in about a 1:10 ratio. However, the sectoral share of the large, low sulphur Other Final Use sector grew by 12 per cent from

Table 10.2 Factors contributing to SO$_2$ reductions

1970–90	1 RSF	2 REI	3 RYI	1 * 2 * 3	1 * 2 * 3 – 1 RSO2	1 * 2 RSV	4 RSY	1 * 2 * 4 * RY – 1 RSO2
1 Power generation	0.839	0.630	1.769	0.934	−0.066	0.528	1.092	−0.066
2 Own use of energy	0.623	0.300	2.006	0.376	−0.624	0.187	1.238	−0.624
3 Ind, iron and steel	0.468	0.532	0.817	0.203	−0.797	0.249	0.504	−0.797
4 Ind, mineral prod.	0.443	0.591	1.158	0.303	−0.697	0.262	0.715	−0.697
5 Ind, chemicals	0.371	0.674	1.796	0.449	−0.551	0.250	1.108	−0.551
6 Other industry	0.326	0.585	1.218	0.232	−0.768	0.191	0.752	−0.768
7 Rail transport	0.147	0.762	0.912	0.102	−0.898	0.112	0.563	−0.898
8 Road transport	0.786	1.177	1.540	1.423	0.423	0.924	0.950	0.423
9 Water transport	0.484	1.764	0.607	0.519	−0.481	0.854	0.375	−0.481
10 Air transport	0.989	0.494	3.839	1.875	0.875	0.488	2.369	0.875
12 Other final use	0.312	0.578	1.812	0.327	−0.673	0.181	1.118	−0.673
Total economy	0.670	0.571	1.621 (= RY)	0.621	−0.379	0.383	1.000	−0.379
11 Dom.fin.use/Con.exp.	0.203	0.631	1.759	0.226	−0.774	0.128		

1970–92	1 RSF	2 REI	3 RYI	1 * 2 * 3	1 * 2 * 3 – 1 RSO$_2$	1 * 2 RSV	4 RSY	1 * 2 * 4 * RY – 1 RSO$_2$
1 Power generation	0.716	0.618	1.881	0.833	−0.167	0.443	1.196	−0.167
2 Own use of energy	0.621	0.276	2.162	0.370	−0.630	0.171	1.375	−0.630
3 Ind, iron and steel	0.469	0.572	0.714	0.191	−0.809	0.268	0.454	−0.809
4 Ind, mineral prod.	0.476	0.553	1.004	0.264	−0.736	0.263	0.638	−0.736
5 Ind, chemicals	0.448	0.641	1.883	0.541	−0.459	0.287	1.197	−0.459
6 Other industry	0.365	0.625	1.130	0.258	−0.742	0.228	0.719	−0.742
7 Rail transport	0.146	0.862	0.844	0.106	−0.894	0.126	0.537	−0.894
8 Road transport	0.758	1.213	1.507	1.385	0.385	0.919	0.959	0.385
9 Water transport	0.492	1.650	0.650	0.528	−0.472	0.812	0.414	−0.472
10 Air transport	1.626	0.454	4.236	3.125	2.125	0.738	2.694	2.125
12 Other final use	0.295	0.624	1.764	0.324	−0.676	0.184	1.122	−0.676
Total economy	0.622	0.588	1.572 (= RY)	0.575	−0.425	0.366	1.000	−0.425
11 Dom.fin.use/Con.exp.	0.166	0.692	1.720	0.198	−0.802	0.115		

Table 10.2 (continued)

1970–95	1	2	3	1*2*3	1*2*3 – 1	1*2	4	1*2*4*RY – 1
	RSF	REI	RYT		RSO_2	RSV	RSY	RSO_2
1 Power generation	0.464	0.567	2.072	0.545	-0.455	0.263	1.199	-0.455
2 Own use of energy	0.546	0.243	2.790	0.370	-0.630	0.133	1.615	-0.630
3 Ind, iron and steel	0.326	0.428	1.023	0.143	-0.857	0.139	0.592	-0.857
4 Ind, mineral prod.	0.271	0.528	1.041	0.149	-0.851	0.143	0.603	-0.851
5 Ind, chemicals	0.333	0.426	2.062	0.292	-0.708	0.142	1.193	-0.708
6 Other industry	0.203	0.580	1.198	0.141	-0.859	0.118	0.694	-0.859
7 Rail transport	0.098	1.738	0.461	0.079	-0.921	0.171	0.267	-0.921
8 Road transport	0.623	0.964	1.914	1.149	0.149	0.600	1.108	0.149
9 Water transport	0.550	1.534	0.618	0.522	-0.478	0.844	0.358	-0.478
10 Air transport	1.700	0.552	3.995	3.750	2.750	0.939	2.312	2.750
12 Other final use	0.223	0.587	1.939	0.254	-0.746	0.131	1.122	-0.746
Total economy	0.411	0.548	1.728 (= **RY**)	0.389	-0.611	0.225	1.000	-0.611
11 Dom.fin.use/Con.exp.	0.113	0.628	1.842	0.130	-0.870	0.071		

Source: Cambridge Econometrics

61 per cent to 68 per cent of value-added, while that of Other Industry fell by 28 per cent from 25 per cent to 19 per cent of value-added. This structural change was beneficial for the environment: actual emissions from Other Industry in 1990 were substantially less than they would have been without structural change (237 rather than 315kt SO_2, see Table 10.3, a decrease which was hardly offset at all by the increase in the very low sulphur Other Final Use sector (from 80 to 89kt).

However, this effect, and that from the reduced shares of other relatively sulphur-intensive sectors (e.g. iron and steel, mineral products), were largely counteracted by an increase in the share of the most sulphur intensive sector of all, power generation (increases of 9 per cent, from 1.2 per cent to 1.3 per cent, from 1970 to 1990 and nearly 20 per cent, from 1.2 per cent to 1.4 per cent, from 1970 to 1992). This results in actual emissions from power generation being 9 per cent (nearly 230kt) higher in 1990 than their projected level on the basis of the 1970s' economic structure. By 1992, with further strong growth in power generation's share of value-added, this effect has become dominant, so that total actual SO_2 emissions from production, at 3397kt, are 155kt, or nearly 5 per cent, higher than they would have been without structural change. The effect would have been even greater had power generation not reduced its sulphur intensity of value-added by 16 per cent (from 458 to 384 g $SO_2/£$) between 1990 and 1992. In contrast, the sulphur intensity of value-added for iron and steel, mineral products, chemicals and Other Industry actually increased over this period. By 1995 the overall picture is little changed, with total actual emissions from production (2297kt) still higher than those projected without structural change (2170kt), because of power generation's increased share of value-added, although the sulphur-emission intensities of the four non-energy manufacturing sectors fell substantially between 1992 and 1995.

Comparing the 1970–92 part of Table 10.2 with that for 1970–90, and also the 1990 and 1992 figures from Table 10.1, gives some interesting insights into the effect of recession. From 1990 value-added fell in all the sectors shown except power generation, other energy industries, chemicals, water and air transport. The largest sectors – Other Industry and Other Final Use – both showed substantial falls in value-added, so that the economy as a whole was 3 per cent smaller in 1992 than in 1990. However, energy use hardly changed over these two years, so that the economy's energy intensity increased from 57 per cent to 59 per cent of 1970's figure. The domestic use of energy also rose substantially between 1990 and 1992, despite consumer expenditure falling. The fact that sulphur emissions continued to fall despite increased fuel use reflects a substantial drop in 1990–2 of the sulphur intensity of fuel used. By 1995 RSF (reduction in sulphur intensity of fuel) had become a significantly more important contributor to lower sulphur emissions than REI (reduction in energy intensity), whereas in 1990 the reverse was true. The drop in sulphur emissions from 1990–5 was very largely due to reductions in the power

Table 10.3 The effect of structural change on SO₂ reductions

	SO_{2i}/Y_i g SO_2/£ 1990	SYI % 1970	Y mill. £ 1990	Projected SO_2 kt 1990	Actual SO_2 kt 1990	SO_{2i}/Y_i g SO_2/£ 1992	Y mill. £ 1992	Projected SO_2 kt 1992	Actual SO_2 kt 1992
1 Power generation	457.53	1.2	473,744	2,493.5	2,722.3	383.72	459,695	2,029.2	2,427
2 Own use of energy	13.24	2.8	473,744	172.8	213.9	12.11	459,695	153.3	210.8
3 Ind, iron & steel	22.91	1.6	473,744	175.2	88.3	24.70	459,695	183.3	83.2
4 Ind, mineral prod.	15.71	1.6	473,744	119.8	85.6	15.78	459,695	116.7	74.5
5 Ind, chemicals	9.07	2.2	473,744	94.2	104.4	10.43	459,695	105.1	125.8
6 Other industry	2.64	25.2	473,744	314.8	236.6	3.16	459,695	365.7	262.8
7 Rail transport	0.65	1.5	473,744	4.6	2.6	0.73	459,695	5.0	2.7
8 Road transport	6.19	2.3	473,744	66.5	63.2	6.15	459,695	64.2	61.5
9 Water transport	59.00	0.5	473,744	151.3	56.7	56.07	459,695	139.5	57.7
Air transport	0.41	0.3	473,744	0.6	1.5	0.61	459,695	0.9	2.5
12 Other final use	0.28	60.8	473,744	79.7	89.1	0.28	459,695	78.6	88.2
Total economy	7.73	100.0	473,744	3,672.9	3,664.2	7.39	459,695	3,241.6	3,396.7

	SO_{2i}/Y_i g SO_2/£ 1995	SYI % 1970	Y mill. £ 1995	Projected SO_2 kt 1995	Actual SO_2 kt 1995
1 Power generation	227.93	1.2	505,072	1,324.3	1,588
2 Own use of energy	9.39	2.8	505,072	130.7	211
3 Ind, iron & steel	12.84	1.6	505,072	104.7	62
4 Ind, mineral prod.	8.58	1.6	505,072	69.7	42
5 Ind, chemicals	5.15	2.2	505,072	57.0	68
6 Other industry	1.63	25.2	505,072	207.6	144
7 Rail transport	1.00	1.5	505,072	7.5	2
8 Road transport	4.02	2.3	505,072	46.0	51
9 Water transport	58.28	0.5	505,072	159.3	57
10 Air transport	0.78	0.3	505,072	1.3	3
12 Other final use	0.20	60.8	505,072	61.5	69
Total economy	4.55	100.0	505,072	2,169.6	2,297

Source: Cambridge Econometrics

generation sector, due in turn to the decrease in its sulphur intensity of value-added as noted above, as the first sizeable generation from natural gas began to substitute for that from coal and fuel oil (a development that has continued strongly into the present, and is projected to continue into the future, as will be seen).

In this case, therefore, recession does not seem to have brought environmental benefit. Energy use barely changed and the only gains in SO_2 reduction came from power generation, which was not in recession (i.e. it increased its output), some of which reductions were offset by increases in emissions from Other Industry, which was in recession. From 1990–2 both the two largest economic sectors (Other Industry and Other Final Use) were in recession, but Other Final Use used more energy, and Other Industry increased its SO_2 emissions. In addition to the increases in sulphur intensities noted above, the energy intensities of Other Industry, iron and steel and of production generally also increased markedly over these two years. This is a counter-intuitive outcome of some relevance to the growth-environment debate. When the recession ended, although total energy use increased slightly, the energy intensity of the economy resumed its downward trend.

10.3 THE RATIONALE AND LEGAL FRAMEWORK FOR SO₂ ABATEMENT

10.3.1 Damages caused by SO₂

SO_2 emitted into the atmosphere returns to Earth as either dry or wet deposition and contributes to acidification, with deleterious effects on lakes and other water bodies, soil, forests, crops and buildings. In addition, SO_2 emissions impair visibility and have adverse effects on human health.

Emissions of SO_2 may be transported over large distances and different places have very different propensities for sustaining damage from sulphur deposition. The Emissions Monitoring and Evaluating Programme (EMEP), set up by the Convention on Long-Range Transboundary Air Pollution (see p. 302) has created a grid structure across the European continent, with each grid about 150km square, within which emissions and their corresponding depositions can be mapped. The EMEP emission/deposition budget shows that the UK is a significant net exporter of airborne sulphur. In 1991 its net exports were 68 per cent of its emissions (Sandnes 1993: 12 (Table 1), Table C7).

Different localities with different ecosystems have different sensitivities to the deposition of sulphur (or other pollutants). The concept that has come to differentiate these sensitivities is the 'critical load', defined as follows: 'a quantitative estimate of an exposure to one or more pollutants below which significant harmful effects on specified sensitive elements of the environment do not occur according to present knowledge' (Nilsson and Grennfelt 1988, quoted in Amann 1989: 3–4). Thus the critical load concept indicates the threshold below which emissions cause no damage to the relevant ecosystems. This is the sustainability principle that was formulated for pollution of ecosystems in Chapter 4. Emissions of SO_2 that do not exceed critical loads for ecosystems are also unlikely to have adverse effects on human health, so that for SO_2 it is the sustainability standard for ecosystem critical loads that is likely to prove binding, rather than a standard for impacts on human health.

Damages from SO_2, whether to ecosystems, human health or buildings will be dependent on local factors, such as ambient concentrations or weather conditions. Values quoted for such damages should therefore be regarded as overall and very approximate averages, rather than damages that would be expected in specific situations. Table 10.4 gives estimates of such values for a number of different countries, based on different studies.

There is no space here to list the many caveats which the above studies include concerning the likely accuracy of their figures, so that the wide range of damage cost estimates is not wholly surprising. The fact that 74 per cent of the UK costs from D. Pearce (1992) are thought to derive from damage to buildings, while over 80 per cent of damages in some of the other studies is contributed by health effects, indicates the uncertainties involved. ECOTEC (1994: 10) concludes: 'The range in benefit estimates derives largely from the uncertainty surrounding the possible health effects', as can be seen from the way the share of health costs changes from the lower to upper bound estimates. This also happens in the Hohmeyer (1988) estimates. ECOTEC's central estimate gives substantial weight to health effects. It must be stressed that the ECOTEC (1994) calculations of the benefits from UK SO_2 reduction *only* include the benefits in the UK from reduced UK emissions. With nearly three-quarters of that reduction being felt elsewhere, because of the export of that proportion of UK emissions, the total benefits of UK SO_2 reduction would be substantially greater.

It is immediately evident that the ExternE (1998) estimates, which are the most recent, are substantially greater than the others. These derive from a model called EcoSense, which takes account of impacts on health, crops, building materials, forests and ecosystems. However, the damages are dominated by the health costs, so the main reason for the variations in the cost estimates between countries are differences in the populations affected by emissions (dense, populous countries will tend to have higher damage costs).

Overall, the figures give a broad indication of the level of damage costs, which should, with the exception of Alfsen *et al.* (1992), be regarded as average rather than marginal costs. These damage costs can be compared with sulphur abatement costs (see p. 303ff.) to give some indication of the desired level of abatement. As the most recent and extensive project estimating damage costs of pollutants, it is possible that the ExternE results should be given most credence. If they are, then current sulphur abatement efforts make very good economic sense, as will be seen.

Table 10.4 Some estimates of damage costs from sulphur emissions

Study	Country	Damage cost US$(1990)/ tonne S emitted	Comment
Pearce (1992)[a]	UK	4,661	74% building costs
ECOTEC (1992)	UK[b]	861–5,191	21–87% health costs
	Germany[c]	3,959–4,368	77–85% health costs
ECOTEC (1994)[d]	UK1	L: 107–272	78% buildings, 21% health
		C: 796–2,011	15% buildings, 81% health
		H: 989–2,499	16% buildings, 65% health
	UK2	L: 98–267	62% buildings, 38% health
		C: 1,221–3,080	7% buildings, 90% health
		H: 1,351–3,402	8% buildings, 81% health
Alfsen *et al.* (1992)[e]	Norway	500–8,960	80–90% health costs
Hohmeyer (1988)[f]	Germany	1,589–8,533	L: 61% plant life, 16% health
	(West)		H: 17% plant life, 76% health
ExternE (1998)[g]	Austria	18,000	Mainly health costs throughout
	Belgium	22,776–24,282	
	Denmark	5,980–8,432	
	Finland	2,054–2,972	
	France	15,000–30,600	
	Germany	3,600–27,376	
	Greece	3,956–15,664	
	Ireland	5,600–10,600	
	Italy	11,400–24,000	
	The Netherlands	12,410–15,162	
	Portugal	9,920–10,848	
	Spain	8,438–19,166	
	Sweden	4,714–5,620	
	United Kingdom	12,054–20,050	

Notes:

a Table 5: 14, derived from Pearce *et al.* (1992), with £1 = $1.5

b Figure calculated from ECOTEC (1992: 9 (Table 1.2)), which uses a 1981 OECD range of UK SO_2 damage costs of £1,407–8,478 million p.a., using the following figures: total 1980 UK SO_2 emissions were 4,900kt, 2t SO_2 contains 1t S and £1 = $1.5

c Figure calculated from ECOTEC (1992: 9 (Table 1.2)), which uses a 1991 range of SO_2 damage costs, from the German Federal Ministry of the Environment, of £6,335–6,989 million p.a., using the following figures: total German 1989 SO_2 emissions contained 2,400kt sulphur (Sandnes 1993: Table C5), £1 = $1.5

d Derived from ECOTEC (1994: 3 (Figure 1), 5, 6 (Tables 1, 2)). UK1 and UK2 are different scenarios in the study. L, C, H are the low, central and high estimates respectively

e Calculated from pp. 11, 12 (Tables 3, 4) and personal communication

f Page 40 (Table 3.5), gives the range of damages (excl. climate costs) from several pollutants as 9,970–53,530 million 1982 DM. Of these, 21.6% are due to SO_2 (p. 33 (Table 3.4)), giving the range 2,153–11,562 mil. DM_{82}. 1985 West German SO_2 emissions were 979kt S (Sandnes 1993: Table C2). Also the deflator from DM_{82} to DM_{90} is 1.156 and the exchange rate was DM_{90} 1 = $0.625 (IMF 1991: 387, 385)

g Table on p. 10. These damages are quoted in the source as Ecu per tonne of pollutant emitted, where the pollutant in the source is given as SO_2. The damage costs have therefore been doubled to convert to damage/tonne S, and $1 = 1 Ecu has been used as the exchange rate. No date of the money value is given, but presumably it is somewhat later than the 1990 date which applies to the other figures in the Table

10.3.2 Legislation on sulphur emissions

In the 1970s and 1980s the Industrial Air Pollution Inspectorate (formerly the Alkali Inspectorate) in England and Wales, and the Industrial Pollution Inspectorate in Scotland ensured that sulphur emissions from 'scheduled' processes were controlled using 'best practicable means'. Emissions from unscheduled processes (e.g. domestic coal burning) were largely controlled as a by-product of the Clean Air Act (1956, amended in 1968), which directly controls the emission of smoke, grit and dust from combustion processes and which accelerated the shift away from sulphur-intensive fuels which was in any case underway.

In 1979 the UK was a signatory to the Convention on Long-Range Transboundary Air Pollution (Geneva Convention), which was drawn up under the auspices of the United Nations Economic Commission for Europe (UNECE) and came into force in 1983. It provides for exchange of information, research and monitoring, and development of policies to combat the discharge of air pollutants. In 1986 a Protocol, to which the UK is a Party, was agreed concerning the funding of the Emissions Monitoring and Evaluation Programme (EMEP). Another Protocol, signed in Helsinki in 1985, required Parties to reduce their emissions from 1980 levels by 30 per cent by 1993 ('the 30 per cent Club'). The UK was not a signatory to this Protocol, although in the event it complied with it (1993 emissions were down 35 per cent from 1980 levels, DOE 1995: 12). A new Protocol, the Second Sulphur Protocol (SSP) setting new targets was agreed with the UK as a Party in June 1994 (see p. 308).

The European Commission has issued four Directives on sulphur emissions, two of which reduced the maximum permitted sulphur content of gas oil, while a third set air quality limit values and guide values for sulphur dioxide and suspended particulates. The fourth and most important Directive, introduced in 1988, covers large combustion plants (greater than 50MW thermal inputs), mandating that new plant must meet emission limits for SO_2 based on BATNEEC (best available technology not entailing excessive cost), while existing plants must reduce their emissions by amounts that would result in an EU-wide SO_2 emissions reduction of 58 per cent by 2003, based on 1980 levels. The required British reductions are 20, 40 and 60 per cent by 1993, 1998 and 2003 respectively. By 1993, emissions from large combustion plants were down 40 per cent from 1980 levels (DOE 1995: 12 (Table 2.2)), so the first limit of the Directive was comfortably met.

10.3.3 The costs of SO_2 abatement

A major factor in the degree of SO_2 reduction that is undertaken is the level of cost involved. Cost was, for example, the most important consideration in the UK Government's decision not to sign up to the 30 per cent SO_2 reduction mandated by the 1985 Helsinki Protocol discussed earlier (see Kula 1992: 191).

There are two quite distinct kinds of costs associated with pollution control. The first kind concerns the actual expenditures made in order to reduce pollution. The second comprises the overall macroeconomic costs, the effects that the expenditures have on the economy as a whole. The first kind of costs are always 'costs' in the sense that they entail the allocation of resources that cannot then be used for other purposes. While the costs of the second kind are likely also to be 'costs', in the slightly different sense that overall marketable output has been reduced, this need not always be the case, as will be seen, because of the stimulus which new investments, including pollution control investments, can give to economic activity.

Expenditures for controlling SO_2 emissions

As has been seen (equation (10.3)), SO_2 emissions can be reduced by increasing the efficiencies of energy conversion, transmission and end-use, by switching to fuels of lower sulphur content, by removing sulphur from fuels or exhaust gases or retaining it in ash, by reducing the energy intensity of output, or by reducing output. It is generally difficult to compute the costs of increasing the various efficiencies, or of developing low-sulphur or fuel-substitution technologies or, at least, arriving at that portion of the costs of such development which is to be attributed to sulphur abatement. The process of developing new products and technologies is a complex and integrated one that seeks to meet a number of different objectives and is associated with benefits as well as costs. Some low-sulphur technologies (e.g. combined cycle gas turbines, CCGTs) may even be cheaper than the high-sulphur technologies they replace, because they are able to take advantage of new cheap fuel sources or because they are more energy efficient.

Typically, therefore, the cost calculations for SO_2 that have been made do not include the costs of technological development, but focus exclusively on the deployment of technologies that modify the existing capital stock or the fuels burned by it (see, for example, Klaassen and Nentjes 1991: 350; Klaassen 1992: 9, 11; Halkos 1993: 14, 22 (Note 9)). These studies incorporate into their baselines their authors' estimated reductions in SO_2 emissions from these other reduction options, but do not compute the associated costs or benefits, which would have to be added to the studies' cost estimates to arrive at total pollution control costs.

Different abatement technologies have different marginal costs (per tonne of sulphur removed) and different operating and performance characteristics. Halkos (1993: 2) classifies the technologies into three categories: pre-combustion (physical coal washing and oil desulphurisation), during combustion (sorbent injection and fluidised bed combustion), and post-combustion (FGD). He presents detailed cost estimates for a range of these technologies, building up a total cost curve for the UK (ibid.: 24

(Figure 2)). This cost curve yields the total costs of different levels of abatement. Unabated emissions in 2000 are projected to be 1,844kt sulphur. The costs of 30 per cent and 60 per cent abatement are found to be $\$_{85}285$ and $\$_{85}887$ million respectively (ibid.: 28 (Table 5)). This implies an average cost of abatement of $\$_{90}625$ and $\$_{90}973$ per tonne S respectively (where $\$_{85}1 = \$_{90}1.214$, IMF 1991: 753).

The same method of determining cost-efficient technological abatement is used in the RAINS model (described in Alcamo *et al.* 1990), developed by the International Institute for Applied Systems Analysis. Using this model, Klaassen (1992: 19, 20 (Tables 8, 9)) calculated the marginal and average costs of abatement of UK SO_2 emissions from 1980 levels to be as in Table 10.5.

Comparing the Halkos and Klaassen 60 per cent abatement figures, it should be noted that Halkos is abating from a year 2000 SO_2 level of 3504kt, while Klaassen is abating from a 1980 SO_2 level of 4,842kt. So Halkos is abating 2,102kt to arrive at an emissions level of 1,404kt, while Klaassen abates 2,905kt to a level of 1,937kt. In general one would expect abatement to be more expensive the less sulphur there was to be removed from economic activity (i.e. the more abatement that has already taken place). Halkos' average cost of abatement ($973) being higher than Klaassen's ($920) accords with this intuition.

Comparing these numbers with Table 10.4's SO_2 damage cost estimates suggests that for all but the lowest estimates, this level of abatement is economically rational, even taking into account that it is marginal rather than average costs which should be equated in such a comparison. Klaassen's MC of 60 per cent abatement in 2000 is only $926. The average damage costs in Table 10.4 are likely to be higher than the marginal damage costs once substantial abatement has taken place, but the central UK2 estimates, which compute extra benefit after substantial abatement,

Table 10.5 Marginal and average costs of SO_2 abatement from 1980 levels $\$_{90}$/tonne S abated[a]

Abatement in 1990				Abatement in 2000[b]			
60%		80%		60%		80%	
MC[c]	AC	MC	AC	MC	AC	MC	AC
1,611	949	2,624	1,390	926	920	2,624	1,335

Source: Klaassen (1992: 19, 20 (Tables 8, 9))

Notes:

a Multiplication factors used: 1.9 tonne SO_2 contain 1 tonne S; $DM_{85}1 = DM_{90}1.07$ (IMF 1991: 387), $DM_{90}1 = \$0.625$ (IMF 1991: 385)

b This is lower than in 1990 because baseline sulphur emissions were lower, i.e. they were assumed to decline from 1990–2000 even in the absence of abatement. Klaassen's unabated emissions in 2000 are 171kt SO_2 lower than those of Halkos

c MC, AC stand for marginal cost and average cost respectively suggest that this difference may not be too great. In any case, all the pre-SSP (i.e. not ECOTEC 1994) estimates, and all but the low end of the UK1 ECOTEC (1994) figures, suggest that if the health costs are given some weight, the average costs of SO_2 damage are substantially greater than $1,000 per tonne. In some European countries, according to the ExternE estimates in Table 10.4, even the low estimates of the damages are many times this.

It would be interesting to compare these modelling estimates with figures of actual expenditures on pollution abatement. Unfortunately it is not possible to do this with any precision for two reasons. First, data for expenditure specifically on sulphur abatement in the 1980s do not exist. Second, it is not known what the path of sulphur emissions through the 1980s without abatement would have been. However, Klaassen (1992: 18 (Table 7)) suggests that even with no abatement 1990 emissions would only have been 80 per cent of their 1980 level. In fact, 1990 emissions (3,782kt) were 77 per cent of their 1980's level (4,899kt), the extra 3 per cent amounting to 127kt SO_2 (67kt S). Assuming that all of this was due to abatement, and valuing it at $950 per tonne S (between the Klaassen and Halkos figures), this would have cost $63.7 million. Assuming that this was evenly spread across the decade, with more investment in the early years and more operating costs later on, this would be $_{90}6.4 million per annum, or £$_{86}$2.8 million (£$_{90}$1 = $1.78, £$_{86}$1 = £$_{90}$1.29, IMF 1991: 749).

Of course it is possible that the various abatement technologies examined by Halkos and Klaassen were more expensive in the 1980s. But even if this increases the cost figure by a factor of four to, say, £11 million per annum, this seems rather a small contribution for control of a major pollutant to have made to overall expenditures on air pollution control in 1985–6 estimated at £$_{86}$1,160 million (Department of Environment, reported in ECOTEC 1989: 17 (Table 3.2)). It seems to confirm the earlier analysis that the 1980s reduction in SO_2 emissions was predominantly due to fuel-switching to less sulphur-intensive fuels rather than abatement. Cost figures for such switching are not available, but much of it was undoubtedly due to market considerations rather than policy constraints (see DEn 1992: 176 for an acknowledgement of this), confirming that the direct expenditure costs of SO_2 control up to 1990 are likely to have been low.

However, it must be stressed that the analysis above and its conclusion is for the UK and may not apply to other countries. Some European countries invested heavily in FGD during the 1980s and will have incurred costs for their sulphur abatement substantially higher than the UK. For example, by 1990 W. Germany had fitted 159 FGD units to 38GW of power generating capacity, thereby reducing SO_2 emissions from the power sector by 88 per cent from their 1983 level (Mez 1993: 2), but at an investment cost of DM22 billion and annual running costs from 1989 of DM5 billion (ibid.: 9). Moreover, the costs of abatement vary widely between countries. The marginal costs of a ᴜ0 per cent cut in 1980 SO_2 levels by

2000 vary between DM712 (E. Germany) and DM5817 (Switzerland) per tonne SO_2 removed (Klaassen 1992: 20 (Table 9)), with the UK very close to the bottom of the range at DM729. Further evidence contrary to the UK experience comes from a study of the impact of sulphur emission limits on electric power utilities in the US:

> The principal conclusion is that sulfur dioxide emissions regulations have resulted in both significantly higher generating costs and markedly lower rates of productivity growth. . . . This cost impact arises primarily from regulation-induced input bias, particularly from increased reliance on expensive, low-sulfur fuels.
>
> (Gollop and Roberts 1983: 672)

Care must therefore be taken not to apply the above conclusions for the UK to countries in different situations.

Macroeconomic costs of SO_2 abatement expenditures

The small costs of SO_2 control in the UK up to 1990 noted in the previous section will certainly have had an imperceptible macroeconomic impact. However, this may not be true for major investments such as that of Germany in FGD described above, or for a major piece of environmental policy such as the EC's Large Combustion Plant Directive (LCPD), introduced in 1988. Klaassen and Nentjes (1991: 349 (Table 1)) estimated that, in its original form, compliance costs could have entailed investments across the then European Community of 15 billion Ecu and annual costs of 3.4 billion Ecu. For the UK the respective figures are 3,145 million Ecu and 656 million Ecu (in 1991 £1 was approximately 1.4 Ecu, IMF 1992: 713). These figures will be assessed later in the light of sulphur projections that will be made, but certainly it cannot be assumed *a priori* that such expenditures are of negligible macroeconomic importance.

As Klaassen and Nentjes note (1991: 355), similarly to the OECD (1985) study quoted in Chapter 6, environmental expenditures in general have two macroeconomic characteristics. The investments in pollution control raise aggregate demand but do not increase the capacity to produce marketable output, and both the investments in and operation of pollution control equipment raise total production costs and the costs per unit of output. These characteristics can have ambiguous economic effects, which were modelled using the OECD's INTERLINK model, which confirmed that in the investment period output and employment were indeed higher than in the base run, but subsequently fell below their base levels. For the period and EC as a whole, GDP, employment and government balances were above base, but consumer prices were higher and the trade balance was more negative. But the effects are small: for the UK the GDP and employment changes are less than ±0.1 per cent, and this analysis does not take into account the economic benefit of removing coal subsidies. If these are included, it may be that the UK would achieve the LCPD limits at a net benefit. For the European countries as a whole, it appears that:

> the long-run opportunity costs of environmental protection, expressed in forgone consumption, were about 5% of the annual pollution control costs. The macroeconomic costs of the EC directive are considerably less of a burden than a partial analysis of the investment and costs would suggest.
>
> (Klaassen and Nentjes 1991: 361)

So if the expenditures themselves were economically rational because of the benefits (damage forgone) they yield, as the previous section suggests, then this is even more true for the lower macroeconomic costs.

10.4 ESTIMATING FUTURE UK EMISSIONS

10.4.1 Complying with LCPD and SSP

As noted above, the first major control on UK sulphur emissions was mandated by the Large Combustion Plant Directive (LCPD) of the European Commission in 1988, which required sulphur reduction from large UK combustion plants of 20, 40 and 60 per cent from 1980 levels by 1993, 1998 and 2003 respectively.

LCPs include power stations, refineries and a number of plants in other sectors. Table 10.6 sets out UK large combustion plant sulphur emissions by sector, together with the LCPD limits. It can be seen from the Table that the 1993 limit was very comfortably met, and that in fact the 1993 LCP emissions had very nearly reduced to the 1998 LCPD limit. It can also be seen that the majority of this reduction occurred between 1990

Table 10.6 SO$_2$ emissions from large combustion plants and the LCPD limits

	1980	1985	1990	1993	1994	1998	2003
Power stations	3,007	2,627	2,722	2,089	1,759	1,013	637
Refineries	237	96	108	155	138		
Other LCP	623	320	344	85	72		
Total LCP	*3,867*	*3,043*	*3,174*	*2,329*	*1,969*		
R80^a, %	0	21	18	40	50		
LCPD limit				3,094		2,320	1,547
LCPD R80, %				20		40	60

Sources: 1980–94   DOE (1996b: 23 (Annex B))
          1998 onwards   CE (1998: 113)

Note:
a R80 signifies the percentage reduction from 1980

and 1993, largely due to the fact that the use of coal in power stations fell by 20 per cent over this period. It can be seen further that the forecast by Cambridge Econometrics (CE) for power station emissions in 2003 projects a further substantial reduction so that the final LCPD limit looks set to be achieved by a wide margin.

In 1994 the UK was a party to the UNECE's Second Sulphur Protocol (SSP), which set new limits for overall emissions, entailing for the UK a reduction from 1980 levels of 50, 70 and 80 per cent by 2000, 2005 and 2010 respectively.

The targets set by the SSP emerged from a complex and innovative approach to environmental policy based on the critical loads concept discussed earlier. The original objective of the protocol was to bring sulphur depositions in Europe everywhere within the calculated critical loads. However, modelling showed that, because of high sensitivities to acidity in some parts of Europe, and natural sources of emissions and sources outside the EMEP area, critical loads could be either impossible or very expensive to achieve (Amann 1989: 7–8; Amann *et al.* 1992: 13). Abatement strategies have therefore tended to concentrate on *target loads*, where it is envisaged that these will be progressively reduced to critical loads. The target agreed was to reduce by at least 60 per cent the excess depositions of 1990 depositions relative to critical loads, while modelling was used to allocate reductions to countries that would achieve this target in the most cost-effective way.

Table 10.7 sets out total emissions, starting from 1980, for selected years to 1995. It also gives forecasts of SO_2 emissions to 2010 by both Cambridge Econometrics (CE 1998: 29) and the Department of Trade and Industry's Energy Paper 65 (EP65) (DTI 1995: 141 (CL Scenario, Table E3)), together with the SSP limits.

It can be seen that the SPP limit for 2000 was reached by 1995, and that for 2005 is forecast by CE (but not EP65) to be reached by 2000. As already noted, SO_2 reduction through the 1990s has been very largely due to the substitution of gas for coal in power generation. Power station coal

Table 10.7 Total SO_2 emissions and the SSP limits

	1980	1990	1995	2000	2005	2010
Total SO_2 emissions	4,903	3,752	2,365	EP65:1,660	1,470	980
				CE:1,423	1,200	1,062
R80[a], %	0	23	52	CE:71	76	78
SSP limit				2,451	1,471	981
R80, %				50	70	80

Sources: 1980–94   DOE (1996b: 23 (Annex B))
      1995 onwards   CE (1998: 29) and EP65, DTI (199b: 141 (Table E3))

Note:
a R80 signifies the percentage reduction from 1980

use in 2000 is forecast by CE to be only 37 per cent of its level in 1990, and a substantial part of that use will be in stations with FGD fitted during the 1990s. After 2000 the CE forecast shows the reduction in sulphur emissions slowing substantially, such that by 2010 the emissions are in excess of the SSP limit, albeit only slightly. The EP65 forecast shows SO_2 emission reduction picking up again from 2005–10, such that the SSP 2010 limit is just achieved.

10.4.2 Further regulatory limits on the ESI

The LCPD and SSP limits provide the SO_2 emission reduction framework to which the UK is committed, and it has always been clear that the predominance of power generation in the emission of SO_2 meant that the bulk of the emission reduction to meet the SSP had to come from the power stations of the electricity supply industry (ESI). However, this has been accentuated by the detailed regulation of SO_2 emissions which has been applied to the ESI under the Environmental Protection Act of 1990 (EPA90), first by Her Majesty's Inspectorate of Pollution (HMIP) and then, from 1996, by the Environment Agency.

EPA90 prescribes the application in emissions regulation of the principle of BATNEEC (Best Available Technology Not Entailing Excessive Cost), whereby regulated plant is expected to deploy, or move towards the deployment, of such technology. Applying BATNEEC to the ESI in England and Wales (E&W), HMIP's review of sulphur authorisations 'builds on changes in fuel use and on current FGD commitment' (DOE 1996: 1) and established a maximum schedule of emissions for these power stations as set out in Table 10.8. The Table shows that achieving the HMIP limits after 2000 is likely to require substantial extra measures from power generators in E&W. Although the CE model does not forecast E&W emissions separately, in 1994 non-E&W UK SO_2 emissions were only 136kt, and it is unlikely that they will be any higher in 2001. To meet the HMIP limits, the E&W generators will probably need to cut their emissions by 100kt by 2001 and 150kt by 2005, over and above the reductions already in the CE forecast.

Table 10.8 SO_2 emissions from power stations and the HMIP limits

	1980	*1990*	*1994*	*1998*	*2000*	*2001*	*2003*	*2005*	*2010*
UK power stations	3,007	2,722	1,759	1,013	769	713	637	584	484
of which E&W			1,623						
HMIP limit on E&W					1,500	1,100	500	500	365

Sources: 1980–94   DOE 1996b: 23 (Annex B), 17 (Table 1))
       1998 onwards   CE (1998: 112–13 (Table A8))
       HMIP limits   HMIP (1996a: Annex A)

In 1998 the Environment Agency again reviewed this issue and proposed to bring the 365kt limit forward from 2005 to 2001 (EA 1998: 3), which would increase the required extra cut in SO_2 emissions by that date to 235kt. To explain the thinking behind this tightening of the limit, the EA described the analytical process originally undertaken by HMIP:

> HMIP undertook a separate assessment of critical loads impacts for SO_2 from each station in order to determine the proposed limits. It considered each station in the context of the overall levels of SO_2 releases from UK and European industry and from natural sources, since the critical loads impact of any particular station will depend on such releases. A 'dose-response' curve was produced for the power stations to show the effects of different SO_2 emission levels on areas sensitive to acid deposition. ... This indicated that the level of critical loads impacts on the environment decreases as SO_2 releases from the coal- and oil-fired power stations decrease from the [1991 level of] approximately 2 million tonnes to 200–300 kilotonnes (kt). Beyond 200–300kt, there appeared to be little environmental improvement consequent on reduction in SO_2 emissions from the power stations.
>
> (EA 1998: 11)

To use the terms employed in this book, HMIP decided that the ecosystem 'sustainability standard' for SO_2 emissions from power stations in E&W was 200–300kt, implying approximately a factor ten reduction from the 1991 level. In accordance with its requirement to regulate in accordance with BATNEEC, it judged that the economics of emission reduction would permit the limit schedule set out in Table 10.8. However, in its 1998 review, the Environment Agency considered that BATNEEC would permit a faster reduction of emissions as described above.

The latest EA proposed limits are still out for consultation and have yet to be definitely imposed, but the process involved in setting them is a striking example of the concept of sustainability, as defined in this book, being used in public policy making. The key question to be explored next is whether this approach to sustainability in sulphur emissions is likely to have a negative impact on economic growth.

10.4.3 The costs of sulphur abatement in the ESI to 2005

To gain insights into the economic implications of attaining the HMIP/EA ESI emission limits, it is necessary to explore in some detail the various ways in which SO_2 emission reduction from power generation can be achieved. There are three broadly available options:

1   continue to burn high-sulphur coal and oil but install flue-gas desulphurisation (FGD) equipment to extract the SO_2 emissions from the flue gases;

2   switch to burning low-sulphur coal and oil in unmodified existing power stations;

3   build new power stations burning gas, with no sulphur emissions, to drive combined cycle gas turbines (CCGTs).

The options can be used singly or in combination as the emission limits require.

The economics of these options is extremely complex, depending on the price and performance of the FGD equipment; the performance of the CCGTs; the present and future prices of the fuels; the relative sulphur content of high and low sulphur coal and oil; and the structure of the ESI and the regulatory and political context within which it operates.

In a series of papers Newbery (1990, 1993, 1994a, 1994b) has subjected this economics to detailed analysis. It is clear that sulphur reduction to date has been driven by option 3 above. CCGTs have been the only kind of new generating capacity ordered during the 1990s (apart from a small quantity of renewables), and by 1996 13GW had been installed (DOE 1996b: 8). The relative prices of coal and gas generation given in Newbery (1993, 1994b) show that these new contracts were entirely valid on financial grounds irrespective of the sulphur limits as far as competition with British coal was concerned, given that the first CCGT stations would be competing against high cost coal plant. In addition they would give the main generators flexibility, reducing their dependence on coal; while for the RECs they represent, as Newbery (1994b: 26–7) makes clear, a highly desirable emancipation from an actual or potential predatory pricing policy of the main generators' market power.

The EC Large Combustion Plant Directive (LCPD) was agreed in 1988, two years before the dash for gas. Gas was then still considered a 'premium' fuel and was not permitted to be used in power generation. In consequence the installation of FGD seemed the only way to meet the LCPD's emission limits and 8GW (later reduced to 6GW) of FGD were incorporated into the UK Plan to meet the Directive. In the event the dash for gas has meant that this plant has not so far been needed to meet the sulphur limits, and has been relatively little used because of its higher running costs. This situation will change as the sulphur limits tighten.

The Seven Year Statement of the National Grid Company (NGC) projects that new gas build will continue, rising to 24GW by 2001 (HMIP 1996: 25 (Table 3)) and the CE forecast above incorporates this projection. Furthermore the CE model assumptions about the development of relative fuel prices from 2000–10 results in a further gas build of 16GW, taking the 2010 gas generating capacity to 40GW, a very similar outcome to that of EP65. A difference between the EP65 and CE (1998) forecasts is that the former assumed a further 4GW of FGD retrofitted to coal power stations, and this is one reason its SO_2 emissions were lower than CE's by 2010. However, by 1996 it was clear that the economics of generation was now convincingly against retrofitting FGD on existing coal plants (ibid.: 71).

It is not yet clear how these projections will be affected by the moratorium on planning consents for new CCGTs that was announced by the UK Government in October 1998 (DTI 1998: 12). Up to 2001 the effect will be minimal, because substantial planned new CCGT capacity already has the necessary consents. Furthermore, CCGTs which incorporate Combined Heat and Power (CHP) are exempted from the moratorium. It is assumed that the CE (1998) forecast for CCGT capacity and SO_2 reduction up to 2005 are broadly unaffected by the moratorium. This SO_2 reduction is not assumed to entail net costs, because the forecast is based on cost-efficient generation, so it is only the extra reductions required to meet the limits that need to be calculated. As was seen above, these extra reductions below the CE forecast are 100kt by 2001 and 150kt by 2005 for the HMIP limits, or 235kt by 2001 for the EA limits.

One way of achieving these extra reductions is to substitute even more CCGTs for coal plant, or substitute low-sulphur imported coal for high-sulphur UK coal. Detailed calculations in Ekins (1996b: 363) but not reproduced here show that 1GW of CCGT running on base load would displace 2.6mt of high-sulphur UK coal and reduce SO_2 emissions by 75kt. Furthermore, imports may be assumed to emit half of high-sulphur UK coal's emissions of 30kg SO_2/t, so that SO_2 emissions may be reduced by about 15kt for every 1mt of imported coal that substitutes for UK coal.

The required 100kt reduction to meet the HMIP limit for 2001 could therefore be achieved by building an extra 1GW CCGT and importing an extra 5mt of low-sulphur coal. An extra 2GW of CCGT by 2005 would save the 150mt required to meet the HMIP limit by that date. The EA reduction of 235mt by 2001 would require an extra 2GW of CCGT plus an extra 6mt of low-sulphur imports.

The cost implications of substituting 2GW of new CCGTs for ageing coal plant, or of substituting imports for UK coal, are not likely to be great, as the EA must have perceived when it considered that such measures qualified as BATNEEC and justified bringing the limits forward to 2001. Indeed, both substitutions may actually be cost-reducing for the generators. The conclusion must be that for the ESI to burn more gas and imported coal to meet the new EA limits, which are, as was seen, close to a calculated sustainability standard, the extra costs to the economy as a whole will be minimal, if not negative.

Another way of meeting the EA limits would be to install more FGD. It may be noted in this connection that, despite the extra costs of this option, the major UK generator Eastern Group has announced its intention to install FGD on one of its 2GW plants, and the UK Government has said that it expects all major generators to have, and use intensively, at least one large FGD station (DTI 1998: 15). If 5 million tonnes of UK coal were burned in a 2GW FGD, rather than non-FGD, plant, annual SO_2 emissions would be reduced by about 135kt. Installing 2GW FGD by 2001 and 3GW by 2005 would therefore enable the HMIP limits to be met. Meeting the EA limits would require 4GW FGD to be installed by 2001.

HMIP (1996b: 82) gives the capital cost of FGD as £180/kW, and operating costs as 0.5–0.6p/kWh. Assuming that 10GW of FGD operating on base load generates 65TWh of electricity per year, this gives a total cost of the UK FGD programme (6GW already installed, plus 4GW new FGD to come), when in full operation, as £1.8 billion in capital costs, and £390 million in operating costs. This would therefore be the cost of meeting the EA limits using FGD and UK coal rather than gas and coal imports.

It was noted earlier that Klaassen and Nentjes (1991: 349 (Table 1)) estimated that meeting the LCPD limits could cost the UK 3,145 million Ecu (£2.25 billion) in investments and 656 million Ecu (£469 million) in operating costs. It was also seen earlier that these costs had only a small macroeconomic impact. Clearly that of the 10GW FGD installation envisaged above will be even smaller. But the really startling insight to emerge from this analysis is that the availability of a low-sulphur fuel (natural gas) and appropriate technologies (CCGTs) to burn it cost-effectively, would enable the tough new EA targets, entailing an 82 per cent reduction in SO_2 emissions from the ESI in only ten years, to be met at essentially no net macroeconomic cost at all.

10.5 CONCLUSIONS

This chapter has explored in detail the trajectory, and the reasons behind it, of UK SO_2 emissions from 1970 to 1995. Up to 1990 there was little if any explicit end-of-pipe abatement of emissions. The reductions came almost equally from reductions in the energy intensity of value-added and in the sulphur intensity of fuel use. This position changed strikingly when the period was extended to 1992, with the sulphur intensity of fuel use becoming more important, while the energy intensity of the economy increased over the 1990 level. Contrary to expectation, the recession years actually resulted in higher overall energy use. Structural change in the economy increased SO_2 emissions over what they would have been without it. This is because the net reduction in emissions due to an overall shift from industry to services was more than outweighed by an increase in the value-added share of power generation, easily the most sulphur-intensive sector. A further conclusion about this period is that the sulphur reductions were achieved at very little cost and, if the benefits of removing coal subsidies are taken into account, perhaps at a net benefit.

The programme of emissions control that was adopted under the Second Sulphur Protocol, and which was then tightened by the limits applied to the ESI by HMIP and the Environment Agency, is worthy of special note as an example of the sustainability approach that was outlined in Chapter 4. The environmental objective of the Protocol – eventually to bring sulphur depositions in Europe within the critical loads of receiving eco-systems – relates closely to the fifth of the sustainability principles in that chapter (see p. 96). The speed of approach to this objective was to be determined by many factors, including the costs and benefits involved, but the objective itself was the outcome of applying environmental criteria rather than economic optimisation techniques.

The subsequent application of BATNEEC to the ESI by HMIP led to the time-scale of emission reduction for that sector being substantially fore-shortened. Again HMIP used the critical load concept to arrive at the desired environmental objective, while the use of BATNEEC ensured that the cost of approaching a limit that was then close to the sustainability standard was not excessive. On the basis of the same methodology, the EA is seeking to foreshorten the time-scale again.

This case study gives important insights into the economic implications of moving towards a sustainability standard for a major pollutant. The emission reduction required was of the order of a factor of ten, as was estimated likely to be the case in Chapter 6. Initial perceptions were that this would be unacceptably costly, which is why the UK refused to join the 30 per cent Club during the 1980s. But the removal of government subsidies from the UK coal industry, and the emergence of a cost-effective low-sulphur fuel and technology (natural gas and CCGTs) changed the cost situation, such that the sustainability standard is attainable with essentially no negative impact on economic growth at all. In this case, economic growth and sustainability in sulphur emissions have proved to be quite compatible.

Of course, this has only resolved part of the sustainability problem of power generation. Gas is also a fossil fuel, with a forecast depletion timespan of relatively few decades, and with substantial carbon emissions, albeit less than the coal it has replaced. Unless another non-sulphur fuel is developed to replace it, coal and its attendant environmental problems (though no doubt ameliorated by technological advance in this area too) will be back once gas reserves decline.

But this case study has illustrated two important facts in the growth/sustainability issue. First, that meeting sustainability standards from current levels of environmental impact without constraining economic growth requires whole new resources and technologies to be developed and deployed in a way that substitues for existing practices at no net cost. Second, that once these resources and technologies become available, and especially if they are driven by a cost advantage, they can substitute for polluting or otherwise unsustainable technologies quite quickly, even in a sector like power generation, in which the capital stock is relatively long-lived.

The challenge for sustainable development is to repeat this experience, with genuinely sustainable resource and technology substitutes, across all sectors which are currently environmentally unsustainable.

11 Conclusions

The functions of the natural environment play a fundamental role in processes of production (particularly the resource and waste-disposal functions), in contributing to human welfare (both through production and directly) and in maintaining the conditions of life on Earth which have shaped human evolution and culture and to which human physiology and current ways of life are best adapted.

Many of the environmental functions that contribute to the economy or directly to human welfare are unpriced or underpriced, are provided by open-access resources or are otherwise difficult to accommodate within normal processes of economic and other decision making. Concerning many of the functions of ecosystems and fundamental processes of life on Earth there remains profound uncertainty coupled with the knowledge that loss of these functions, or changes in the processes, may be irreversible. Yet it is clear that, over the last fifty years, the combination of exponential population growth, exponential increases in economic activity and the development of technologies that are at best foreign to, and at worst destructive of, normal ecological cycles, is resulting in the loss of environmental functions, the loss or degradation of ecosystems and the generation of global environmental change on an unprecedented scale. Barring catastrophe there is much more population growth to come. The appetite for economic growth in both North and South continues undiminished. This book has sought to answer the question: what prospects are there that the demographic momentum will be able to work itself out without disaster and that the aspirations of both rich and poor societies for environmentally sustainable economic growth can be fulfilled?

This question immediately raises the issue of priorities. If, under current systems of production and consumption, environmental sustainability is in conflict with population growth and economic growth, what trade-offs should be permitted between these three 'goods'? The conventional economic answer, as between sustainability and economic growth at least, is that this trade-off should be determined through optimisation – the maximisation of the present value of consumption. This study has found such an approach to the question of growth/environment compatibility to be inadequate for the most serious environmental problems, because:

a   it proceeds from too narrow a perception of human welfare;
b   it requires impacts on the environment and on humans to be given monetary valuations which are very controversial and uncertain;
c   it relies on the use of discount rates which are essentially arbitrary within a certain range;
d   it cannot take account of either the full range of environmental complexities or of uncertainties and the possibility of irreversible outcomes with catastrophic impacts, associated with environmental damage.

The same is essentially true even when the optimisation is constrained to produce sustainable consumption, because it begs the whole question of whether 'environmental consumption' is entirely commensurable with and substitutable for other forms of consumption.

This study has therefore not sought to determine how much economic growth and consequent environmental damage are optimal. Rather it has explored whether, if the sustainable use of environmental functions is adopted as a prime objective of public policy, this would exert a substantial constraint on economic growth. The optimality and sustainability approaches to these issues are quite different. The former has as its objective function the maximisation of the present value of consumption, taking account of ecological damage. The latter has as its objective function the maximisation of human welfare, subject to the sustainable use of important environmental functions, which are taken to be so fundamental to the maintenance of welfare, and yet so difficult to assign value to, that they are taken out of the normal calculus of economic trade-off. In opting for the sustainability approach, this study has sought to determine whether the constraint of environmentally sustainable use is binding on economic growth and, if so, to what extent.

The first conclusion to emerge is that the sacrifice of the environment to economic growth, which has unquestionably been a feature of economic development at least since the birth of industrialism, is not ineluctable. It is not like the normal economic choice between two goods under a budget constraint, where the constraint permits so much of this or so much of that, but not the same amounts of both. Environmental destruction is not something that is desired in and of itself. It is goods and services that are desired; the environmental destruction arises as the unintended by-product of their production or consumption or both. Yet there are many goods and services which do not entail environmental destruction in their production or consumption. If consumer preferences were to shift towards these goods and services, or if processes of production and consumption could be changed to reduce the environmental impacts associated with currently destructive goods and services, there is no theoretical reason why increasing incomes, and increasing real consumer expenditures, should not be associated with greatly reduced environmental impacts such that important environmental functions are sustained. Environmentally sustainable economic growth is not an oxymoron.

However, the fact that environmentally sustainable economic growth is not an oxymoron does not mean that environmentally sustainable economic growth has ever existed in practice (it has not, certainly since the industrial revolution) or that it ever will do so. There are many states of the world which could exist but which do not exist and may never exist. Just because a shift in consumer preferences away from environmentally intensive goods and services could improve the environment without loss of income does not mean either that such a shift will take place spontaneously, even under severe environmental pressure, or that it will be possible to legislate for its occurrence. Consumer preferences derive from powerful social and cultural perceptions. The fact, for example, that many people continue to smoke despite the well-established negative impact of smoking on health, mandatory advertising of this impact and substantial taxation of tobacco, indicates the resilience of some aspects of human behaviour. Such resilience may well also be characteristic of some environmentally intensive consumption.

The conditions for bringing about sustainable economic growth, starting from the current state of the world, are readily identified from the Commoner-Ehrlich equation, $I = P.C.T.$ If P is to double over fifty years, and C is to quadruple over the same period, as is the almost universal aspiration, then T will have to be reduced by 90 per cent if I is to be reduced to half its present level, the level here identified as broadly sustainable. Thereafter T will have to go on decreasing at a rate that is equal to the sum of the rates of population and consumption growth for I to be maintained at the sustainable level.

Reductions in T of this order of magnitude will not, on past evidence, be achieved without determined policy over a long time-period. Such policy may be expected to exert a constraint on economic growth, unless one of two conditions holds:

1   The environmental policy can, in addition to improving the environment, reduce economic distortions such that economic allocative efficiency is increased.
2   The environmental policy induces technical change which both contributes to environmental sustainability and increases labour productivity at least to the same extent as would have occurred without the policy.

Somewhat surprisingly, there is substantial evidence that there is a range of possibilities over which the first condition may hold. There are technologies which can improve both economic and environmental performance which have not yet been introduced. The deployment of environmental management systems which reduce environmental impacts can improve economic

management as well. Many government policies are economically inefficient as well as environmentally destructive. The taxation system is a source
of inefficiency which may be reduced by the implementation of environmental taxes or the removal of environmentally destructive subsidies.

Just as, with regard to growth/environment compatibility, its logical
possibility says nothing about whether it will be possible to achieve it, so
there is no guarantee that, just because these inefficiencies exist, it will be
possible to remove them. Often these inefficiencies exist for a good reason:
they may benefit powerful economic or social interests which would stand
to lose from their removal, even though society overall would gain; they
may be justified on grounds of equity, or fairness; or there may be institutional, informational or transactional obstacles to their removal. One of
the unanswered political questions about environmental sustainability is
whether, by making it a prime objective of public policy, it becomes
possible to enact policies which are a socio-economic improvement on the
status quo irrespective of their environmental benefits, but which before the
rise of environmental concern were politically unfeasible. Conversely it
may be the case that the pursuit of traditional socio-economic improvements, or social sustainability in the current generation, may marginalise
the importance, or jeopardise the achievement, of environmental goals
which are necessary to achieve environmental sustainability in the future.

Inefficiencies can only be removed once, and the opportunities for
win–win gains must diminish with their realisation, leaving the second
condition, induced technical change, as the possible source of environmental gain as well as undiminished growth. It is impossible to predict *a
priori*, and very little less difficult to assess *ex post*, whether environmentally
conserving technical change is as economically productive as what would
have taken place had there been no environmental considerations for such
change to take into account. The new generation of resource-conserving,
low-pollution technologies is typically more economically productive than
its more environmentally intensive predecessor. Such technologies provide
evidence that economic and environmental gains can be simultaneously
achieved, but it is a moot point whether the short-term economic gains
are as great as they might have been had environmental performance been
of no concern. No less uncertain is whether the technologies will prove
socially and culturally acceptable. Technical *change*, as opposed to technical *possibility*, depends not only on new production processes and
equipment becoming available, but on the right fit of skills, institutions
and social attitudes to enable them to be effectively deployed. The absence
or imperfect fulfilment of these social requirements for the successful introduction of new technology may add greatly to the normal delay in
technological diffusion due to time lags in investment, which, it may be
recalled from Chapter 6, even a technological optimist like Anderson recognises may lead to much environmental destruction before the benefits of
new technologies can be realised.

Just as there are limits to the economic efficiencies which may be achieved in practice, so there are thermodynamic limits to the efficiencies of resource and energy use that may be attained. Beyond these limits, there is the need to reduce entropy. Global sustainability, the globally sustainable use of environmental functions, is incompatible with globally increasing entropy. The second law of thermodynamics states that a closed system is always characterised by increasing entropy. The Earth and its atmosphere is effectively a closed system, with the exception of incoming solar energy. It is through the use of ambient solar energy that evolution has resulted in ever more complex and highly structured systems (i.e. brought about a reduction in global entropy in the biosphere). It is the use of fossil and nuclear energy sources that is one of the main sources of the current global increase in entropy that is a characteristic of unsustainability. Another is the reduction in the Earth's own capacity to process solar energy, through soil degradation, deforestation and other reductions in the stock of biomass. A third is the production of substances which, because of their nature or volume, cannot be easily assimilated in or by solar-driven natural processes, or which disrupt these processes. A fourth is the simplification of complex ecosystems, through the destruction of biodiversity, which are the product of the process of de-entropification which also produced humans. There is no guarantee that these simplified ecosystems will be able to sustain the kind of ambient conditions that are congenial to human life and to which humans have adapted. Across all these dimensions, the imperative for sustainability is that human ways of life come increasingly to rely on entropy-reducing activities and technologies, because they either use solar energy themselves or reinforce other processes which do. A range of solar technologies has made remarkable technical and economic progress in the last two decades, but it remains too early to say whether they can be developed at the speed and to the extent necessary to substitute for fossil and nuclear fuels at the much higher levels of energy use that continuing economic growth in the next century seems likely to demand (the 'fossil-free energy future' scenario of SEI/G (1993) is a projection that considers such an energy transition to be possible).

If the UK achieves the SSP sulphur targets within the broad cost framework identified in Chapter 10, this will provide an example of the kind of T trajectory (but based on renewable resources rather than a substitute fossil fuel), at very little if any cost, that will be required across all important environmental issues if sustainability is to be achieved. The Netherlands National Environmental Policy Plan (NEPP) (MOHPPE 1988, 1994) envisages a similar T trajectory to 2010 across a range of issues, but even NEPP does not project substantial reductions in carbon emissions in this timeframe. The factors that have contributed so far to the UK sulphur trajectory have been many, but most important have been the opportunity for fuel-switching between high-sulphur coal and zero-sulphur natural gas and nuclear power. Similar results could have been achieved by sulphur abatement through FGD, as in Germany, but at significantly greater cost (although there is no evidence that this has affected Germany's overall economic performance). It must also be recognised that, while replacing coal with gas yields significant environmental benefits, gas is also a non-renewable fossil fuel which produces CO_2 emissions (although relatively less than coal). This experience therefore underlines the importance of developing renewable energy sources at a competitive price to fossil and nuclear power if issues of CO_2 emissions and depletion related to the former, and of radiation hazards related to the latter, are to be effectively addressed.

To gain insights from the Commoner-Ehrlich equation requires, at least, a distinction to be drawn between North and South. In the South, policies that would stop human populations from more than doubling (e.g. mass sterilisation) over the next fifty years are not generally regarded as ethically acceptable or practically feasible, nor would most people question the need and right of southern countries to expand their economies four-fold over the same period (as noted in Chapter 6, their average per capita income would then only be one-sixth of that of rich countries in 1990). Moreover, demographic transition theory suggests that quadrupling southern incomes, and ensuring that women get a substantial part of the benefit of this, is likely to be the best way of stabilising southern population growth.

In the $I = PCT$ framework, then, in addition to the necessary reduction in I, one may take the future increase in southern P and C as given. The variables of interest then become northern P and C, and T globally. If C, P, T were independent then it would be desirable (cost minimising) to constrain the growth of each such that the marginal cost of each constraint was equal. Are there interdependencies between northern P,C,T that might argue against northern C being reduced?

Certainly there is no evidence of a $P = P(C)$ ($dP/dC < 0$) relationship in the North to parallel the demographic transition theory for the South. Sometimes it is said that the North must grow in order to provide the investment to bring T down. Yet northern growth is not required for this. An increase in the northern saving rate would do just as well. Moreover, much T reduction can be achieved without any investment at all, simply by changing patterns of consumption. For example, a shift from private to public transport, foreign to domestic holidays or conventional to organic foods, does not require an increase in net investment, but such shifts could reduce T substantially if widely adopted. These are issues of consumer preference not required investment, although, as noted earlier, there is no guarantee that the shifts will be easy to bring about. With some such shifts, both T and C might decrease, giving a double benefit to I. Finally there is the argument that northern growth is required to promote southern growth, but this effect could be achieved with far less increase in I by northern countries investing directly in the South to produce goods for consumption there. In a number of Asian countries at least foreign direct investment is already an important engine of southern growth.

Of course, northern growth may be necessary for sustainability in the broad sense that, in a context of rising labour productivity, it provides necessary employment or that it fulfils fundamental consumer expectations of wider consumer choice. But there is no reason strictly for environmental sustainability why northern countries should grow economically, contrary to the 'growth is good for the environment' conclusions which sometimes emerge from a loose reading of the EKC literature reviewed in Chapter 7. And, as Chapter 6 showed, no growth, or even a reduction, in northern C makes the required reduction in global T considerably less demanding.

Such considerations suggest a menu of possible ways in which northern countries could approach sustainability:

- they could be prepared to forgo economic growth if necessary in order to constrain the operation of the sectors with the highest T;
- they could be prepared to change their lifestyles from more to less environmentally intensive ways of living;
- they could be prepared to see a steady rise, through the taxation system, in the price of all environmentally intensive goods and services;
- they could be prepared to invest substantial sums to flatten the EKCs in southern countries by reducing the T associated with growth there;
- they could be prepared to accord the kind of priority to such environmentally necessary technical change as the development of solar technologies as has hitherto been reserved for social projects like defence, space exploration or nuclear power.

Such changes as these might well not result in a reduction in the level, or even in the growth, of real average incomes, and they might even increase employment, as relative prices increasingly favoured the use of labour as opposed to energy or materials. But, because of this change in relative price, the composition of a bundle of produced goods and services that could be bought by a given income would be very different from today's.

It is not yet clear how much choice there will be between the various items on the menu above, if sustainability is to be approached. Duchin and Lange's (1994) study throws some light on this. Using a global input–output economic model of fifty interacting sectors in each of sixteen geographic regions, they incorporated various assumptions across a whole range of issues about possible environmentally conserving technical changes, which they considered reflected the recommendations of the Brundtland Report (WCED 1987). This they termed the OCF scenario. The model also included three air emissions (CO_2, SO_2, NO_x). The model was run without the technological changes to generate the Reference scenario, which showed that from 1990 to 2020 all the air emissions 'would increase nearly two and a half times' (Duchin and Lange 1994: 34). (Elsewhere it is clear that this means a 150 per cent increase.) In the OCF scenario the increases are 60 per cent for CO_2, 16 per cent for SO_2 and

63 per cent for NO_x, indicating substantial reductions from the Reference scenario. Both scenarios project a 2.8 per cent world GDP growth rate, which is within the range of the simulations in Chapter 6. The results suggest that, with such an impetus to growth in the world economy, existing technologies can make a significant positive difference to the environmental outcome. However, the difference is nowhere near the −50 per cent that is here considered necessary to reach sustainability. Even in another of Duchin and Lange's scenarios, with a larger share of hydro and nuclear power, and a rapid modernisation (i.e. increase in efficiency) in China and India, as the most populous fast developing economies, the increases in emissions were only reduced to 43 per cent (CO_2), 0 per cent (SO_2) and 44 per cent (NO_x) above base (ibid.: 40 (Table 3.8)). The principal economic result from the OCF scenario is that its realisation requires a significant increase in investment in southern countries, largely accompanied by an increase in net imports and indebtedness.

Duchin and Lange draw two conclusions from their OCF scenario which are relevant for this study. First:

> It is unlikely that these (developing) countries will be inclined to under-take the path to sustainable development described in that scenario, or that they would be able to obtain the credits if they wanted to, in the absence of economic assistance of a magnitude that dwarfs even optimistic assumptions about the proportion of GDP that donor nations are inclined to devote to economic aid.

Second:

> It is clear that the scenarios based on our interpretation of the prescriptions in the Brundtland Report are not adequate to arrest the growth in global emissions of the pollutants that were examined. On the basis of this analysis, we believe that far more strenuous actions need to be taken that – unlike the assumptions of the OCF scenario – may be politically difficult or may require technological breakthroughs.
>
> (Duchin and Lange 1994: 27)

The OCF scenario is far from being business as usual. It embodies pretty well all the substantial technical change related to dematerialisation, increased efficiency and increased recycling that seems likely to be available over the next twenty-five years. This is not enough, if global economic growth is 2.8 per cent per annum, even to stabilise atmospheric emissions at their present unsustainable levels. Much more is required for sustainability.

The OCF scenario assumes North American and West European rates of growth in the first three decades of the next century of around 2.8 per cent. Such growth would intensify the environmental challenge, as has been seen, but it would permit the challenge to be met from a situation of generally increasing output. Glyn (1995) considers that there are good reasons deriving from demographic and structural change in northern economies why northern growth in the middle of the next century could decline from present levels, perhaps to zero. This might reduce the growth in northern environmental pressures, but it might also diminish the will of northern publics to address existing pressures and any increase in them that might result from economic growth in the South. The political response to periods of slow growth in the North does not instil confidence that environmental policy which was perceived further to constrain it would be resolutely pursued, and other problems associated with slow growth, such as unemployment or financing the welfare state, could well undermine environmental commitments and concern. Glyn makes the point that, under these circumstances:

> a quite different attitude to consumption, and in particular to matters of distribution, would be the only way to circumvent the social conflicts which seem inevitably to result at present from economic slow-down. Such new attitudes would then have the additional, very important benefit of facilitating acceptance of the measures necessary to combat environmental degradation.
>
> (Glyn 1995: 66)

This echoes Duchin and Lange's point above, made in a North–South context, that successfully addressing environmental problems would require a level of aid and mutual commitment which was currently the exception rather than the rule in international relations.

In conclusion, then, the path to environmental sustainability may require three possible types of change to current patterns of production and consumption:

1   satisfying present wants with technologies of vastly improved environmental performance;
2   changing present wants so that the overall package of desired goods and services is far less environmentally damaging than at present;
3   constraining present wants where they relate to environmentally damaging goods and services, the production or consumption of which are not amenable to environmental improvement.

The first type of change may be termed the technical fix – the 'ecological modernisation' of industrial society whereby the productive system is transformed but the human aspirations that drive it are not. As has been seen in this book, not only are economic growth and environmental sustainability theoretically compatible, but there is also a good chance that the technologies required simultaneously to increase value-added and reduce environmental impacts could, over the next five decades, become available and economically viable. In the meantime there are market and government failures, a distortionary tax system and unexploited technologies which provide opportunities for both economic and environmental gains. But developing and deploying the new technologies, and enacting the necessary policies, will require large-scale, long-term public commitment and international cooperation in the North; and a process of profound social change in the South. In both North and South realising the win–win opportunities will require institutional creativity, political will and social stamina. These are the scarce resources on the adequate supply of which a successful, technology-led route to environmental sustainability ultimately depends.

The second type of change requires a transformation in consumer preferences. There is a certain amount of rhetoric, in the North at least, as to the desirability of such a transformation (see, for example, Miljøverndepartementet 1994). But, it has to be said, there is little practical evidence of consumers in the North dramatically shifting the pattern of their desires. There is, for example, no sign of a rejection of, or even satiation with, the motor car, even in those countries which have most of them. In the South the trend is still dramatically towards more consumerism as the allure of western consumer lifestyles penetrates the furthest corners of the as yet unindustrialised world. There is some resistance, notably from some Islamic societies, but the paradigm of modernity, progress and desirable living remains that depicted in the American soap operas that now find their way into the remotest villages in the least accessible places.

The third type of change is that envisaged by those who believe that meeting the challenge of environmental sustainability will inevitably entail placing limits on economic growth. Whatever the theoretical possibilities that a combination of technical fixes, the removal of inefficiencies and distortions and changed consumer preferences will permit incomes to continue growing indefinitely, this view does not accept that such a situation can be realised in practice, that GDP can, in Daly's term already quoted in Chapter 3, be sufficiently 'angelized'.

A pragmatic response to the continuing uncertainty as to the contribution of each of the three types of changes to moves towards, and the eventual achievement of, environmental sustainability might be to advocate each type of change in appropriate situations: to try to stimulate technical change and remedy market and government failures where possible, and to seek to change consumer aspirations, while not hesitating to demand reduced environmental impacts from environmentally intensive sectors even at the cost of reducing their economic activity. This is actually the approach adopted, with varying degrees of commitment, by those countries which are taking seriously their undertakings at Rio and elsewhere to make their future development sustainable. If the modern desire for economic growth, in both North and South, is too strong to be gainsaid, or if the results of failing to achieve it are too traumatic, then this opportunistic pragmatism is perhaps the most rigorous response to environmental unsustainability that can be expected. However, it remains open to the charge that, by failing to challenge head on the whole urge for indefinite economic growth and the fundamental aspirational foundations of western consumer society, such pragmatism is ducking the only issue that really matters. The problem, in turn, with this reaction is that a resolute message of 'no economic growth' in order to save the environment may either fail to convince a public that desires growth, as is currently broadly the case, and so fail to make any kind of headway in terms of practical public policy; or, if it were to be politically successful, it may so inhibit the dynamism and innovation that are the peculiar characteristics of growing market economies that new environmentally superior technologies are not developed or deployed. In other words, in terms of the Commoner-Ehrlich equation, reducing the growth of C may also reduce the reduction in T.

This continuing debate between the advocates of sustainable growth, on the one hand, and limits to growth, on the other, will be resolved, if at all, only over time and through experience. This book has shown that it is not the case that environmentally sustainable economic growth is a contradiction in terms, as is sometimes claimed. It has also highlighted the enormity of the technological challenge, with inevitably profound social and cultural implications, posed by a commitment to both environmental sustainability and indefinite economic growth. If a combination of technical change and efficient public policy begins to deliver both economic growth and improvements in environmental performance such that the disturbing environmental trends outlined in the Introduction become less threatening, then the faith of such documents as the Brundtland Report in the possibility of a synergy between growth and environment that goes beyond mere compatibility will have been vindicated. If not, then those who continue to insist that the environment will impose its own, perhaps catastrophic, limits to economic growth if humans do not learn to live without it first may well be proved right. At present societies seem more inclined to try to realise growth-environment synergy than accept overall limits to growth. It can only be hoped that, if time proves the former to be little more than wishful thinking, humanity will find ways of dispensing with the need for economic growth while the environment is still capable of supporting large-scale human civilisation.

Bibliography

Aaheim, A. and Nyborg, K. 1993 '"Green National Product": Good Intentions, Poor Device?', Discussion Paper No. 103, Statistics Norway Research Department, Oslo.

Adger, N. 1992 'Sustainable National Income and Natural Resource Degradation: Initial Results for Zimbabwe', CSERGE GEC Working Paper 92–32, University of East Anglia, Norwich.

Adriaanse, A. 1993 *Environmental Policy Performance Indicators*, SDU, The Hague.

Agarwal, A. 1985 'The State of the Environment and the Resulting State of the "Last Person"', The Fifth Annual World Conservation Lecture, 8 October, World Wildlife Fund, WWF UK, Godalming.

Alcamo, J., Shaw, R. and Hordijk, L. Eds 1990 *The RAINS Model of Acidification: Science and Strategies in Europe*, Kluwer Academic Publishers, Dordrecht, Netherlands.

Alfsen, K.H., Brendemoen, A. and Glomsrød, S. 1992 'Benefits of Climate Policies: Some Tentative Calculations', Discussion Paper No. 69, March, Central Bureau of Statistics: B. 8131, Dep.0033, Oslo 1.

Alfsen, K., Bye, T. and Lorentsen, L. 1987 *Natural Resource Accounting and Analysis: the Norwegian Experience 1978–1986*, Central Bureau of Statistics of Norway, Oslo.

Amalric, F. 1995 'Population Growth and the Enviornmental Crisis: Beyond the "Obvious"' in Bhaskar, V. and Glyn, A. Eds *The North, the South and the Environment*, Earthscan, London, pp. 85–101.

Amann, M. 1989 'Using Critical Loads as the Basis for Abatement Strategies in Europe', Working Paper submitted to the UN-ECE Task Force Meeting on Integrated Assessment Modelling, October, International Institute for Applied Systems Analysis (IIASA), Laxenburg, Austria.

Amann, M., Bertok, I., Cofala, J., Klaassen, G. and Schöpp, W. 1992 'Strategies for Reducing Sulphur Dioxide Emissions in Europe', IIASA, Laxenburg, Austria.

Anderson, D. 1992 'Economic Growth and the Environment', Background Paper for the *World Development Report 1992*, World Bank, Washington, DC.

Arrow, K.J. 1962 'The Economic Implications of Learning by Doing', *Review of Economic Studies*, Vol. 29, pp. 155–73.

Atkins, L.V. and Wilson, D.G. 1984 'Origins and Implications of Tax-Plus-Rebate Policies', *Journal of Resource Management and Technology*, Vol. 13 No. 3 (November), pp. 163–9).

Atkinson, G. 1995 'Measuring Sustainable Economic Welfare: a Critique of the UK Index of Sustainable Economic Welfare (ISEW)', CSERGE Working Paper GEC 95–08, University of East Anglia, Norwich.

Ayres, R. and Walter, J. 1991 'The Greenhouse Effect: Damages, Costs and Abatement', *Environmental and Resource Economics*, Vol. 1, pp. 237–70.

Baldwin, R. 1995 'Does Sustainability Require Growth?' in Goldin, I. and Winters, A. Eds *The Economics of Sustainable Development*, Cambridge University Press, Cambridge, pp. 51–78.

Ballard, C.L., Shoven, J.-B. and Whalley, J. 1985 'General Equilibrium Computations of the Marginal Welfare Costs of Taxes in the United States', *American Economic Review*, Vol. 75 No. 1 (March), pp. 128–38.

Baranzini, A. and Bourguignon, F. 1995 'Is Sustainable Growth Optimal?', *International Tax and Public Finance*, Vol. 2, pp. 341–56.

Barbier, E.B. 1987 'The Concept of Sustainable Economic Development', *Environmental Conservation*, Vol. 14 No. 2, pp. 101–10.

Barbier, E.B. 1989 *Economics, Natural Resource Scarcity and Development: Conventional and Alternative Views*, Earthscan, London.

Barbier, E.B., Burgess, J. and Folke, C. 1994 *Paradise Lost? The Ecological Economics of Biodiversity*, Earthscan, London.

Barker, T. 1991 'Measuring Economic Costs of CO_2 Emission Limits', *Energy*, Vol. 16 No. 3, pp. 611–14.

Barker, T. 1992 'The Carbon Tax: Economic and Policy Issues', Energy-Environment-Economy Modelling Discussion Paper No. 3, Department of Applied Economics, University of Cambridge, Cambridge, also published in Carraro, C. and Siniscalco, D. Eds 1993 *The European Carbon Tax: an Economic Assessment*, Kluwer, Dordrecht, pp. 239–54.

Barker, T. 1993 'Secondary Benefits of Greenhouse Gas Abatement: the Effects of a UK Carbon-Energy Tax on Air Pollution', Energy-Environment-Economy Modelling Discussion Paper No. 4, Department of Applied Economics, University of Cambridge, Cambridge.

Barker, T. 1994 'Taxing Pollution instead of Employment: Greenhouse Gas Abatement through Fiscal Policy in the UK', Energy-Environment-Economy Discussion Paper No. 9, June, Department of Applied Economics, University of Cambridge, Cambridge.

Barker, T. 1996 *Space-Time Economics*, Cambridge Econometrics, Cambridge.

Barker, T. and Johnstone, N. 1993 'Equity and Efficiency in Policies to Reduce Carbon Emissions in the Domestic Sector', *Energy and Environment*, Vol. 4 No. 4, pp. 335–61.

Barker, T. and Lewney, R. 1991 'A Green Scenario for the UK Economy' in Barker, T. Ed. *Green Futures for Economic Growth: Britain in 2010*, Cambridge Econometrics, Cambridge, pp. 11–38.

Barker, T. and Peterson, A. Eds 1987 *The Cambridge Multisectoral Dynamic Model of the British Economy*, Cambridge University Press, Cambridge.

Barker, T., Baylis, S. and Madsen, P. 1993 'A UK Carbon-Energy Tax: the Macroeconomic Effects', *Energy Policy*, Vol. 21 No. 3 (March), pp. 296–308.

Barker, T., Ekins, P. and Johnstone, N. Eds 1995 *Global Warming and Energy Demand*, Routledge, London/New York.

Barnett, H. 1979 'Scarcity and Growth Revisited' in Smith, V. Ed. *Scarcity and Growth Reconsidered*, Johns Hopkins University Press, Baltimore, MD, pp. 163–217.

Barnett, H. and Morse, C. 1963 *Scarcity and Economic Growth: the Economics of Natural Resource Availability*, Johns Hopkins University Press, Baltimore, MD.

Bartelmus, P. and Tardos, A. 1993 'Integrated Environmental and Economic Accounting – Methods and Applications', *Journal of Official Statistics*, Vol. 9 No. 1, pp. 179–88.

Bartelmus, P. Lutz, E. and Schweinfest, S. 1993 'Integrated Environmental and Economic Accounting: a Case Study for Papua New Guinea' in Lutz, E. Ed. *Toward Improved Accounting for the Environment*, World Bank, Washington, DC, pp. 108–43.

Bartelmus, P. Stahmer, C. and Van Tongeren, J. 1993 'Integrated Environmental and Economic Accounting – a Framework for an SNA Satellite System' in Lutz, E. Ed. *Toward Improved Accounting for the Environment*, World Bank, Washington, DC, pp. 45–65.

Becker, G. 1964 *Human Capital: a Theoretical and Empirical Analysis, with Special Reference to Education*, National Bureau of Economic Research and Columbia University, New York.

Beckerman, W. 1968 *An Introduction to National Income Analysis*, Weidenfeld & Nicolson, London.

Beckerman, W. 1974 *In Defence of Economic Growth*, Jonathan Cape, London.

Beckerman, W. 1991 'Global Warming: a Sceptical Economic Assessment' in Helm, D. Ed. *Economic Policy Towards the Environment*, Blackwell, Oxford, pp. 52–85.

Beckerman, W. 1992 'Economic Growth and the Environment: Whose Growth? Whose Environment?', *World Development*, Vol. 20 No. 4, pp. 481–96.

Bellis, A. and Barron, J. 1997 'Material Inputs into the UK Economy Arising from Trade in Unprocessed and Semi-Processed Goods', Draft Report to EUROSTAT Directorate B6, Office for National Statistics, London.

Beltratti, A., Chichilnisky, G. and Heal, G. 1995 'Sustainable Growth and the Green Golden Rule' in Goldin, I. and Winters, A. Eds *The Economics of Sustainable Development*, Cambridge University Press, Cambridge, pp. 147–66.

Bernstam, M. 1991 *The Wealth of Nations and the Environment*, Institute for Economic Affairs, London.

Birdsall, N. 1994 'Government, Population and Poverty: a Win–Win Tale' in Kiessling, K. and Landberg, H. Eds *Population, Economic Development and the Environment*, Oxford University Press, Oxford, pp. 173–98.

Birdsall, N. and Steer, A. 1993 'Act Now on Global Warming – But Don't Cook the Books', *Finance and Development*, March: 6–8, International Monetary Fund, Washington, DC.

Bishop, R. 1978 'Endangered Secies and Uncertainty: the Economics of a Safe Minimum Standard', *American Journal of Agricultural Economics*, Vol. 60 (February), pp. 10–18.

Bishop, R. 1993 'Economic Efficiency, Sustainability and Biodiversity', *Ambio*, Vol. 22 No. 2–3 (May), pp. 69–73.

Boero, G., Clarke, R. and Winters, L. 1991 *The Macroeconomic Consequences of Controlling Greenhouse Gases: a Survey*, Department of the Environment, HMSO, London.

Böhringer, C. and Rutherford, T.F. 1997 'Carbon Taxes with Exemptions in an Open Economy: a General Equilibrium Analysis of the German Tax Initiative', *Journal of Environmental Economics and Management*, Vol. 32, pp. 189–203.

Bojö, J., Mäler, K.-G. and Unemo, L. 1992 *Environment and Development: an Economic Approach*, Kluwer, Dordrecht.

Bosch, P. and Ensing, B. 1995 'Imports and the Environment: Sustainability Costs of Imported Products', paper presented to the Second Meeting of the London Group on Natural Resource and Environmental Accounting, March, Washington, DC.

Bovenberg, A.L. and de Mooij, R.A. 1994 'Environmental Levies and Distortionary Taxation', *American Economic Review*, Vol. 94 No. 4 (September), pp. 1085–9.

BP (The British Petroleum Company plc) 1997 *BP Statistical Review of World Energy 1997*, BP, London.

Braverman, H. 1974 *Labour and Monopoly Capital: the Degradation of Work in the 20th Century*, Monthly Review Press, New York/London.

Brekke, K.A. 1997 *Economic Growth and the Environment: on the Measurement of Income and Welfare*, Edward Elgar, Cheltenham.

Broad, R. 1994 'The Poor and the Environment: Friends or Foes?', *World Development*, Vol. 22 No. 6, pp. 811–22.

Broad, R. and Cavanagh, J. 1993 *Plundering Paradise: the Struggle for the Environment in the Philippines*, University of California Press, Berkeley/Los Angeles/Oxford.

Broome, J. 1992 *Counting the Cost of Global Warming*, White Horse Press, Cambridge.

Brouwer, R. and Leipert, C. 1998 'The Role of Environmental Protection Expenditures in a System of Integrated Economic and Environmental Accounting: Theory, Practice and Future Prospects', CSERGE Working Paper GEC 98–01, University of East Anglia, Norwich.

Brown, G.M. and Field, B. 1979 'The Adequacy of Measures for Signalling the Scarcity of Natural Resources' in Smith, V. Ed. *Scarcity and Growth Reconsidered*, Johns Hopkins University Press, Baltimore, MD, pp.218–48.

Brown, L.R., Flavin, C. and Kane, H. 1996 *Vital Signs 1996–1997*, Earthscan, London.

Brown, L.R., Lenssen, H. and Kane, H. 1995 *Vital Signs 1995–1996*, Earthscan, London.

Brown, L.R., Abramowitz, J., Bright, C., Flavin, C., Gardner, G., Kane, H., Platt, A., Postel, S., Roodman, D., Sachs, A. and Starke, L. 1996 *State of the World 1996*, Earthscan, London.

Brown, L.R., Brough, H., Durning, A., Flavin, C., French, H., Jacobson, J., Lenssen, N., Lowe, M., Postel, S., Renner, M., Ryan, J., Starke, L. and Young, J. 1992 *State of the World 1992*, Earthscan, London.

Brown, L.R., Durning, A., Flavin, C., French, H., Jacobson, J., Lenssen, N., Lowe, M., Postel, S., Renner, M., Ryan, J., Starke, L. and Young, J. 1991 *State of the World 1991*, Earthscan, London.

Brown, L.R., Durning, A., Flavin, C., French, H., Jacobson, J., Lenssen, N., Lowe, M., Postel, S., Renner, M., Starke, L., Weber, P. and Young, J. 1993 *State of the World 1993*, Earthscan, London.

Bruce, J., Lee, H. and Haites, E. Eds 1996 *Climate Change 1995: Economic and Social Dimensions of Climate Change*, contribution of Working Group III to the Second Assessment Report of the Intergovernmental Panel on Climate Change (IPCC), Cambridge University Press, Cambridge.

Bryant, C. and Cook, P. 1992 'Environmental Issues and the National Accounts', *Economic Trends*, No. 469 (November), pp.99–122, HMSO, London.

Buitenkamp, M., Venner, H. and Wams, T. Eds 1993 *Action Plan Sustainable Netherlands*, Vereniging Milieudefensie (Friends of the Earth Netherlands), Amsterdam.

Burniaux, J.-M., Nicoletti, G. and Oliveira-Martins, J. 1992a 'GREEN: a Global Model for Quantifying the Costs of Policies to Curb CO_2 Emissions', *OECD Economic Studies*, No. 19, winter, pp. 49–92.

Burniaux, J.-M., Martin, J.P., Nicoletti, G. and Oliveira-Martins, J. 1992b 'The Costs of Reducing CO_2 Emissions: Evidence from GREEN', OECD Economics Department Working Paper No. 115, May, OECD, Paris.

Business International 1990 *Managing the Environment: the Greening of European Business*, Business International, London.

CE (Cambridge Econometrics) 1998 *UK Energy and the Environment: Analysis and Forecasts to 2010*, January, Cambridge Econometrics, Cambridge.

CEA (Council of Economic Advisers) 1990 *1990 Report to the President*, CEA, Washington, DC.

CEC (Commission of the European Communities) 1992a Proposal for a Resolution of the Council of the European Communities, *Towards Sustainability: a European Community Programme of Policy and Action in Relation to the Environment and Sustainable Development*, Vol. 1, Commission of the European Communities, Brussels.

CEC (Commission of the European Communities) 1992b Executive Summary, *Towards Sustainability: a European Community Programme of Policy and Action in Relation to the Environment and Sustainable Development*, Vol. 2, Commission of the European Communities, Brussels.

CEC (Commission of the European Communities) 1992c *The State of the Environment in the European Community: Overview*, COM(92) 23 – Vol. III, March, CEC, Brussels.

CEC (Commission of the European Communities) 1994 'Directions for the EU on Environmental Indicators and Green National Accounting', COM(94) 670 final, CEC, Brussels.

CEST (Centre for the Exploitation of Science and Technology) 1991 *Industry and the Environment: a Strategic Overview*, CEST, London.

CEST (Centre for the Exploitation of Science and Technology) 1994 *Waste Minimisation: a Route to Profit and Cleaner Production*, CEST, London.

Chambers, R. 1992 'Sustainable Livelihoods: the Poors' Reconciliation of Environment and Development' in Ekins, P. and Max-Neef, M. Eds *Real-Life Economics: Understanding Wealth Creation*, Routledge, London, pp. 214–29.

Chichilnisky, G. and Heal, G. 1993 'Global Environmental Risks', *Journal of Economic Perspectives*, Vol. 7 No. 4, pp.65–86.

Christainsen, G. and Tietenberg, T. 1985 'Distributional and Macroeconomic Aspects of Environmental Policy' in Kneese, A. and Sweeney, J. Eds *Handbook of Natural Resource and Energy Economics*, Vol. 1, Elsevier Science Publishers, Amsterdam, pp. 345–93.

Ciriacy-Wantrup, S.V. 1952 *Resource Conservation: Economics and Policies*, University of California Press, Berkeley, CA.

Clark, C. 1990 *Mathematical Bioeconomics: the Optimal Management of Renewable Resources* (2nd edn), John Wiley, New York.

Clarke, K. 1994 'The Chancellor's Speech', Budget 1994, *Financial Times*, 30 November, pp.33–5.

Cleveland, C. 1991 'Natural Resource Scarcity and Economic Growth Revisited: Economic and Biophysical Perspectives' in Costanza, R. Ed. *Ecological Economics: the Science and Management of Sustainability*, Columbia University Press, New York: 289–317.

Cleveland, C. 1993 'An Exploration of Alternative Measures of Natural Resource Scarcity: the Case of Petroleum Resources in the U.S.', *Ecological Economics*, Vol. 7, pp. 123–57.

Cline, W.R. 1991 'Scientific Basis for the Greenhouse Effect', *Economic Journal*, No. 101 (July), pp. 904–19.

Cline, W.R. 1992 *The Economics of Global Warming*, Institute for International Economics, Washington, DC.

Cline, W.R. 1993 'Give Greenhouse Abatement a Fair Chance', *Finance & Development* (March), pp.3–5, International Monetary Fund, Washington, DC.

Coase, R.H. 1960 'The Problem of Social Cost', *Journal of Law and Economics*, Vol. 3: 1–44.

Cobb, C.W. and Cobb, J.B. 1994 *The Green National Product*, University Press of America, Lanham, MD.

Cole, H.S.D., Freeman, C., Jahoda, M. and Pavitt, K.L.R. Eds 1973 *Thinking about the Future: a Critique of the Limits to Growth*, Chatto & Windus for Sussex University Press, London.

Common, M.S. 1995 *Sustainability and Policy: Limits to Economics*, Cambridge University Press, Cambridge.

Commoner, B. 1971a *The Closing Circle: Confronting the Environmental Crisis*, Jonathan Cape, London.

Commoner, B. 1971b 'The Environmental Cost of Economic Growth' in Schurr, S. Ed. *Energy, Economic Growth and the Environment*, Johns Hopkins University Press, Baltimore/London: 30–65.

Conroy, C. and Litvinoff, M. Eds 1988 *The Greening of Aid*, Earthscan, London.

Cropper, M. and Griffiths, C. 1994 'The Interaction of Population Growth and Environmental Quality', *American Economic Review Papers and Proceedings*, Vol. 84 No. 2 (May), pp. 250–4.

Cropper, M. and Oates, W. 1992 'Environmental Economics: a Survey', *Journal of Economic Literature*, Vol. 30 (June), pp.673–740.

Daly, H.E. 1977 *Steady-State Economics*, W.H. Freeman, San Francisco, CA.

Daly, H.E. 1990 'Toward Some Operational Principles of Sustainable Development', *Ecological Economics*, Vol. 2, pp.1–6.

Daly, H.E. 1991 'Elements of Environmental Macroeconomics' in Costanza, R. Ed. *Ecological Economics: the Science and Management of Sustainability*, Columbia University Press, New York, pp. 32–46.

Daly, H.E. 1992 'From Empty World to Full World Economics' in Goodland, R., Daly, H.E. and Serafy, S. El Eds *Population, Technology and Lifestyle: the Transition to Sustainability*, Island Press, Washington, DC, pp.23–37.

Daly, H.E. 1995 'On Wilfrid Beckerman's Critique of Sustainable Development', *Environmental Values*, Vol. 4, pp.49–55.

Daly, H.E. 1996 *Beyond Growth: the Economics of Sustainable Development*, Beacon Press, Boston, MA.

Daly, H.E. and Cobb, J. 1989 *For the Common Good: Redirecting the Economy Towards Community, the Environment and a Sustainable Future*, Beacon Press, Boston, MD (UK edition 1990 Green Print, Merlin Press, London).

Dasgupta, P. 1995 'Optimal Development and the Idea of Net National Product' in Goldin, I. and Winters, A. Eds *The Economics of Sustainable Development*, Cambridge University Press, Cambridge, pp. 111–43.

Dasgupta, P. and Heal, G. 1974 'The Optimal Depletion of Exhaustible Resources', *Review of Economic Studies*, Symposium on the Economics of Exhaustible Resources, pp. 3–28.

Dasgupta, P. and Heal, G. 1979 *Economic Theory and Exhaustible Resources*, Cambridge University Press, Cambridge.

Dasgupta, P., Kriström, B. and Mäler, K.-G. 1994 'Current Issues in Resource Accounting', Beijer Discussion Paper Series No. 47, Beijer International Institute of Ecological Economics, Stockholm.

Davis, S. 1992 'Indigenous Views of Land and the Environment', Background Paper for *World Development Report 1992*, World Bank, Washington, DC.

Dean, A. and Hoeller, P. 1992 'Costs of Reducing CO_2 Emissions: Evidence from Six Global Models', *OECD Economic Studies*, No. 19, winter, pp. 16–47.

Dean, J. 1992 'Trade and the Environment: a Survey of the Literature' in Low, P. Ed. *International Trade and the Environment*, World Bank Discussion Paper No. 159, World Bank, Washington, DC, pp.15–28.

De Boer, B., De Haan, M. and Voogt, M. 1994 'What Would Net Domestic Product Have Been in a Sustainable Economy: Preliminary Views and Results', *National Accounts and the Environment*, Papers and Proceedings from a Conference, London, March, Statistics Canada, Ottawa.

De Bruyn, S.M. and Opschoor, J.B. 1997 'Developments in the Throughput–Income Relationship: Theoretical and Empirical Observations', *Ecological Economics*, Vol. 20, pp. 255–68.

De Groot, R.S., 1992 *Functions of Nature*, Wolters–Noordhoff, Groningen, Netherlands.

De Haan, M., Keuning, S. and Bosch, P. 1993 'Integrating Indicators in a National Accounting Matrix including Environmental Accounts (NAMEA)', National Accounts Occasional Paper Nr. NA–060, Central Bureau of Statistics, Voorburg.

Demeritt, D. and Rothman, D. 1999 'Figuring the Costs of Climate Change: an Assessment and Critique', *Environment & Planning A*, Vol. 31 No. 3, pp.389–408.

DEn (Department of Energy) 1992 *Digest of UK Energy Statistics 1992*, DEn, HMSO, London.

DETR (Department of the Environment, Transport and the Regions) 1997 *Digest of Environmental Statistics*, No. 19, The Stationery Office, London.

DETR (Department of the Environment, Transport and the Regions) 1998 *Sustainability Counts: Consultation Paper on a Set of 'Headline' Indicators of Sustainable Development*, DETR, London.

Diamond, P.A. and Hausman, J.A. 1994 'Contingent Valuation: Is Some Number Better Than No Number?', *Journal of Economic Perspectives*, Vol. 8 No. 4 (fall): 45–64.

Diamond, P. and Mirrlees, J. 1971 'Optimal Taxation and Public Production, I: Production Efficiency and II: Tax Rules', *American Economic Review*, Vol. 61, pp.8–27, 261–78.

DOE (Department of the Environment) 1994 *Digest of Environmental Protection and Water Statistics 1994*, DOE/HMSO, London.

DOE (Department of the Environment) 1995 *Digest of Environmental Protection and Water Statistics 1995*, DOE/HMSO, London.

DOE (Department of the Environment) 1996a *Indicators of Sustainable Development for the UK*, DOE/HMSO, London.

DOE (Department of the Environment) 1996b *Reducing National Emissions of Sulphur Dioxide: a Strategy for the United Kingdom*, DOE, London.

DOH (Department of Health) 1998 *The Quantification of the Effects of Air Pollution on Health in the United Kingdom*, Report of the Committee on the Medical Effects of Air Pollutants (COMEAP), HMSO, London.

Douthwaite, R. 1992 *The Growth Illusion*, Green Books, Devon, UK.

Dowlatabadi, H. and Morgan, M.G. 1993 'A Model Framework for Integrated Studies of the Climate Problem', *Energy Policy*, Vol. 21 (March), pp.209–21.

DRI 1994 *Potential Benefits of Integration of Environmental and Economic Policies: an Incentive-Based Approach to Policy Integration*, report prepared for the European Commission, Graham & Trotman, London/Kluwer, New York.

DTI (Department of Trade and Industry) 1994 *Digest of UK Energy Statistics 1994*, DTI/HMSO, London.

DTI (Department of Trade and Industry) 1995 *Energy Projections for the UK, EP65*, (March), DTI/HMSO, London.

DTI (Department of Trade and Industry) 1998 *Conclusions of the Review of Energy Sources for Power Generation*, October, The Stationery Office, London.

Duchin, F. and Lange, G.-M. 1994 *The Future of the Environment and Technical Change*, Oxford University Press, Oxford/New York.

EA (Environment Agency) 1998 'Proposals for Reducing Emissions of Polluting Substances from Existing Coal- and Oil-Fired Power Stations', Consultation Paper, February, EA, London.

Eagan, V. 1987 'The Optimal Depletion of the Theory of Exhaustible Resources', *Journal of Post Keynesian Economics*, Vol. IX No. 4 (summer), pp.565–71.

Earth Summit '92, Regency Press, London.

EC (European Commission) 1993 *Growth, Competitiveness, Employment: the Challenges and Ways Forward into the 21st Century*, White Paper, Bulletin of the European Communities Supplement 6/93, European Commission, Brussels.

EC (European Commission) 1994 'Taxation, Employment and Environment: Fiscal Reform for Reducing Unemployment', Study No. 3, *European Economy*, No. 56: 137–77, Directorate-General for Economic and Financial Affairs, European Commission, Brussels.

ECDGXII (European Commission Directorate General XII) 1997 'Methodological Problems in the Calculation of Environmentally Adjusted National Income Figures: Final Summary Report', Report for ECDGXII on contract number EVSV–CT94–0363, July, Brussels.

ECG (Environmental Challenge Group) 1994 *Environmental Measures: Indicators for the UK Environment*, available from World Wide Fund for Nature, Godalming, Surrey.

ECOTEC 1989 *Industry Costs of Pollution Control*, Final Report to the Department of the Environment, ECOTEC Research and Consulting Ltd, Birmingham.

ECOTEC 1992 'A Cost–Benefit Analysis of Reduced Acid Deposition: UK Natural and Semi-Natural Ecosystems – An Assessment Framework for Evaluating the Benefits of Reduced Acid Deposition', Working Paper One for the Department of the Environment, April, ECOTEC Research and Consulting Ltd, Birmingham.

ECOTEC 1993 *A Review of UK Environmental Expenditure: a Final Report to the Department of the Environment*, HMSO, London.

ECOTEC 1994 *An Evaluation of the Benefits of Reduced Sulphur Dioxide Emissions: a Summary Report for the Department of the Environment*, ECOTEC Research and Consulting Ltd, Birmingham.

EEA (European Environment Agency) 1995 *Europe's Environment: the Dobris Assessment*, EEA, Copenhagen.

Ehrlich, P. and Ehrlich, A. 1990 *The Population Explosion*, Hutchinson, London.

Ehrlich, P. and Holdren, J. 1971 'Impact of Population Growth', *Science*, Vol. 171 (26 March), pp.1212–17.

Ehrlich, P., Ehrlich, A. and Holdren, J. 1977 *Ecoscience: Population, Resources, Environment*, W.H. Freeman, San Francisco, CA.

Eisner, R. 1988 'Extended Accounts for National Income and Product', *Journal of Economic Literature*, Vol. 26 (December): 1611–84.

Ekins, P. 1990 'An Indicator Framework for Economic Progress', *Development*, 1990:3/4, pp.92–8.

Ekins, P. 1992 'A Four-Capital Model of Wealth Creation' in Ekins, P. and Max-Neef, M. Eds *Real-Life Economics: Understanding Wealth Creation*, Routledge, London/New York, pp.147–55.

Ekins, P. 1996a 'How Large a Carbon Tax is Justified by the Secondary Benefits of CO_2 Abatement?', *Resource & Energy Economics*, Vol. 18 No. 2, pp.161–87.

Ekins, P. 1996b 'The Relationship Between Economic Growth, Human Welfare and Environmental Sustainability', Ph.D. Thesis, Birkbeck College, London.

Ekins, P. 1997 'On the Dividends from Environmental Taxation' in O'Riordan, T. Ed. *Ecotaxation*, Earthscan, London, pp.125–62.

Ekins, P. 1999 'Figuring the Costs of Climate Change: a Comment', *Environment & Planning A*, Vol. 31 No. 3, pp.413–15.

Ekins, P. and Max-Neef, M. Eds 1992 *Real-Life Economics: Understanding Wealth-Creation*, Routledge, London.

Ekins, P. and Simon, S. 1998 'Determining the Sustainability Gap: National Accounting for Environmental Sustainability' in Vaze, P. Ed. *UK Environmental Accounts: Theory, Data and Application*, Office for National Statistics, London, pp.147–67.

El Serafy, S. 1989 'The Proper Calculation of Income from Depletable Natural Resources' in Ahmad, Y., El Serafy, S. and Lutz, E. Eds *Environmental Accounting for Sustainable Development*, World Bank, Washington, DC, pp.10–18.

El Serafy, S. 1993 'The Environment as Capital' in Lutz, E. Ed. *Toward Improved Accounting for the Environment*, World Bank, Washington, DC, pp.17–21.

ESEF (European Science and Environment Foundation) 1996 *The Global Warming Debate: the Report of the European Science and Environment Forum*, ESEF, London.

EUROSTAT 1994 *SERIEE*, EUROSTAT, Luxembourg.

EUROSTAT 1997 'Environmental Accounts: Present State and Future Developments', September, EUROSTAT, Luxembourg.

ExternE 1998 'Assessment of Impacts from Air Pollution', *ExternE – The Newsletter of the EC Study on the Externalities of Energy*, No. 6 (March), pp.9–11.

Eyre, N., Dowring, T., Hoekstra, R. and Rennings, K. 1997 'Global Warming Damages', Final Report to the European Commission on Contract JO53–CT95–0002, November, European Commission, Brussels.

Faber, M. and Proops, J. 1991 'National Accounting, Time and the Environment: a Neo-Austrian Approach' in Costanza, R. Ed. *Ecological Economics: the Science and Management of Sustainability*, Columbia University Press, New York, pp.215–33.

Faber, M. and Proops, J. 1993 *Evolution, Time, Production and the Environment* (1st edn 1990), Springer Verlag, Heidelberg.

Faber, M., Manstetten, R. and Proops, J. 1995 'On the Conceptual Foundations of Ecological Economics: a Teleological Approach', *Ecological Economics*, Vol. 12 No. 1 (January), pp.41–54.

Fankhauser, S. 1993 'Global Warming Economics: Issues and State of the Art', CSERGE Working Paper GEC 93–28, CSERGE, University College London, London.

Fankhauser, S. 1994 'Protection vs. Retreat: Estimating the Costs of Sea-Level Rise', CSERGE Working Paper GEC 94–02, University College London, London.

Fankhauser, S. 1995 *Valuing Climate Change: the Economics of the Greenhouse*, Earthscan, London.

Fankhauser, S. and Tol, R. 1996 'Climate Change Costs: Recent Advancements in the Economic Assessment', *Energy Policy*, Vol. 24 No. 7, pp.665–73.

Fankhauser, S., Tol, R. and Pearce, D. 1997 'The Aggregation of Climate Change Damages: a Welfare-Theoretic Approach', *Environmental and Resource Economics*, Vol. 10, pp.249–66.

Farrow, S. 1985 'Testing the Efficiency of Extraction from a Stock of Resources', *Journal of Political Economy*, Vol. 93 No. 3, pp.452–87.

Faucheux, S., O'Connor, M. and Van den Hove, S. 1998 'Towards a Sustainable National Income?' in Faucheux, S. and O'Connor, M. Eds *Valuation for Sustainable Development: Methods and Policy Indicators*, Edward Elgar, Cheltenham.

Fisher, A. 1979 'Measures of Natural Resource Scarcity' in Smith, V. Ed. *Scarcity and Growth Reconsidered*, Johns Hopkins University Press, Baltimore, MD, pp.249–75.

FOE (Friends of the Earth) 1995 *Towards Sustainable Europe*, FOE, London.

Folke, C., Holling, C.S. and Perrings, C. 1994 'Biodiversity, Ecosystems and Human Welfare', Beijer Discussion Paper Series No. 49, Beijer International Institute of Ecological Economics, Stockholm.

Gaskins, D.W. and Weyant, J.P. 1993 'Model Comparisons of the Costs of Reducing CO_2 Emissions', *American Economic Review (AEA Papers and Proceedings)*, Vol. 83 No. 2 (May), pp.318–23.

Georgescu-Roegen, N. 1971 *The Entropy Law and the Economic Process*, Harvard University Press, Cambridge, MA.

Georgescu-Roegen, N. 1975 'Energy and Economic Myths', *Southern Economic Journal*, Vol. 41 No. 3, pp.347–81.

Gillham, C.A., Leech, P.K. and Eggleston, H.S. 1992 *UK Emissions of Air Pollutants, 1970–1990*, Warren Spring Laboratory, Department of Trade and Industry, London.

Glyn, A. 1995 'Northern Growth and Environmental Constraints' in Bhaskar, V. and Glyn, A. Eds *The North, the South and the Environment*, Earthscan, London, pp.47–67.

Goldin, I. and Winters, A. 1995 'Economic Policies for Sustainable Development' in Goldin, I. and Winters, A. Eds *The Economics of Sustainable Development*, Cambridge University Press, Cambridge, pp.1–15.

Goldschmidt-Clermont, L. 1992 'Measuring Households' Non-Monetary Production' in Ekins, P. and Max-Neef, M. Eds *Real-Life Economics: Understanding Wealth Creation*, Routledge, London, pp.265–82.

Goldschmidt-Clermont, L. 1993 'Monetary Valuation of Non-Market Productive Time: Methodological Considerations', *Review of Income and Wealth*, Vol. 39 No. 4 (December), pp.419–33.

Gollop, F. and Roberts, M. 1983 'Environmental Regulations and Productivity Growth: the Case of Fossil-Fueled Electric Power Generation', *Journal of Political Economy*, Vol. 91, pp.654–74.

Goodland, R. and Daly, H.E. 1992 'Ten Reasons Why Northern Income Growth is not the Solution to Southern Poverty' in Goodland, R., Daly, H.E. and Serafy, S. El Eds *Population, Technology and Lifestyle: the Transition to Sustainability*, Island Press, Washington, DC, pp.128–45.

Goulder, L.H. 1995a 'Environmental Taxation and the Double Dividend: a Reader's Guide', *International Tax and Public Finance*, Vol. 2, pp.157–83.

Goulder, L.H. 1995b 'Effects of Carbon Taxes in an Economy with Prior Tax Distortions: an Intertemporal General Equilibrium Analysis', *Journal of Environmental Economics and Management*, Vol. 29, pp.271–97.

Goulder, L. and Kennedy, D. 1997 'Valuing Ecosystem Services: Philosophical Bases and Empirical Methods' in Daily, G. Ed. *Nature's Services: Societal Dependence on Natural Ecosystems*, Island Press, Washington, DC, pp.23–47.

Graaff, J. de V. 1967 *Theoretical Welfare Economics* (1st edn 1957), Spottiswoode, Ballantyne & Co., London.

Gray, W. and Shadbegian, R. 1993 'Environmental Regulation and Manufacturing Productivity at the Plant Level', National Bureau of Economic Research (NBER) Working Paper No. 4321, NBER, Cambridge, MA.

Grossman, G. 1993 'Pollution and Growth: What Do We Know?', CEPR Discussion Paper No. 848, October, Centre for Economic Policy Research, London.

Grossman, G. and Krueger, A. 1991 'Environmental Impacts of a North American Free Trade Agreement', NBER Working Paper No. 3914, November, National Bureau of Economic Research, Cambridge, MA.

Grossman, G. and Krueger, A. 1993 'Environmental Impacts of a North American Free Trade Agreement' in Garber, P. Ed. *The US-Mexico Free Trade Agreement*, MIT Press, Cambridge, MA.

Grossman, G. and Krueger, A. 1994 'Economic Growth and the Environment', NBER Working Paper No. 4634, February, National Bureau of Economic Research, Cambridge, MA.

Grubb, M. 1993 'The Costs of Climate Change: Critical Elements' in Kaya, Y., Nakicenovic, N., Nordhaus, W. and Toth, F. Eds *Costs, Impacts and Benefits of CO_2 Mitigation*, CP–93–2, June, Proceedings of a Workshop held on 28–30 September 1992, International Institute for Applied Systems Analysis (IIASA), Laxenburg, Austria, pp.153–66.

Grubb, M. 1995 'Asymmetrical Price Elasticities of Energy Demand' in Barker, T., Ekins, P. and Johnstone, N. Eds *Global Warming and Energy Demand*, Routledge, London/New York, pp.305–10.

Grubb, M. 1996 'Technologies, Energy Systems and the Timing of CO_2 Emissions Abatement: an Overview of the Economic Issues', paper presented to workshop on 'Incorporating Technology Issues into the Consideration of Policy Responses to Human Induced Climate Change', February, mimeo, Energy and Environmental Programme, Royal Institute for International Affairs, London.

Grubb, M., Chapuis, T. and Ha Duong, M. 1995 'The Economics of Changing Course: Implications of Adaptability and Inertia for Optimal Climate Policy', *Energy Policy*, Vol. 23 No. 4/5, pp.417–32.

Hadley Centre 1998 *Climate Change and its Impacts*, UK Meteorological Office, Bracknell.

Haigh, N. 1990 *EEC Environmental Policy and Britain*, 2nd revised edn, Longman, Harlow, Essex.

Halkos, G. 1993 'An Evaluation of the Direct Cost of Abatement under the Main Desulphurization Technologies', Discussion Paper No. 9305, Dept. of Environmental Economics and Environmental Management, University of York, York.

Hall, D. and Hall, J. 1984 'Concepts and Measures of Natural Resource Scarcity, with a Summary of Recent Trends', *Journal of Environmental Economics and Management*, Vol. 10 (December), pp.363–79.

Hamilton, K. 1994 'Green Adjustments to GDP', *Resources Policy*, Vol. 20 No. 3, pp.155–68.

Hamilton, K. and Atkinson, G. 1996 'Air Pollution and Green Accounts', *Energy Policy*, Vol. 24 No. 7, pp.675–84.

Hammond, A., Adriaanse, A., Rodenburg, E., Bryant, D and Woodward, R. 1995 *Environmental Indicators*, World Resource Institute, Washington, DC.

Hampson, C. 1993 'CO_2 Emission Policy and Industry' in Vellinga, P. and Grubb, M. Eds *Climate Change Policy in the European Continent*, Royal Institute for International Affairs, London, pp.48–54.

Hanemann, W.M. 1994 'Valuing the Environment Through Contingent Valuation', *Journal of Economic Perspectives*, Vol. 8 No. 4 (fall), pp.19–43.

Hanley, N., Hallett, S. and Moffatt, I. 1990 'Why is More Notice Not Taken of Economists' Prescriptions for the Control of Pollution?', *Environment and Planning A*, Vol. 22, pp.1421–39.

Hardoy, J., Mitlin, D. and Satterthwaite, D. 1993 *Environmental Problems in Third World Cities*, Earthscan, London.

Harrison, A. 1993 'National Assets and National Accounting' in Lutz, E. Ed. *Toward Improved Accounting for the Environment*, World Bank, Washington, DC, pp.22–45.

Harrison, P. 1987 *The Greening of Africa*, Paladin, London.

Hartwick, J. 1977 'Intergenerational Equity and the Investing of Rents from Exhaustible Resources', *American Economic Review*, Vol. 67 No. 5, pp.972–4.

Hartwick, J. 1990 'Natural Resources, National Accounting and Economic Depreciation', *Journal of Public Economics*, Vol. 43, pp.291–304.

Hayes, K. and Hughes, D. 1992 'Input–Output Balance for the United Kingdom 1989', *Economic Trends*, No. 467 (September), pp.101–29.

Heal, G. and Barrow, M. 1980 'The Relationship Between Interest Rates and Metal Price Movements', *Review of Economic Studies*, Vol. 47, pp.161–81.

Heintz, R.J. and De Bruyn, S.M. 1997 'The Environmental Kuznets Curve: More than a Hypothesis?', mimeo, Free University, Amsterdam, April, forthcoming in Van den Bergh, J. Ed. 1998 *Handbook of Environmental and Resource Economics*, Edward Elgar, Cheltenham.

Herfindahl, O. and Kneese, A. 1973 'Measuring Social and Economic Change: Benefits and Costs of Environmental Pollution' in Moss, M. Ed. *The Measurement of Economic and Social Performance*, National Bureau of Economic Research/Columbia University, New York, pp.441–508.

Hettige, H., Lucas, R. and Wheeler, D. 1992 'The Toxic Intensity of Industrial Production: Global Patterns, Trends and Trade Policy', *American Economic Review Papers and Proceedings*, Vol. 82 No. 2 (May), pp.478–81.

Hicks, J. 1946 *Value and Capital* (2nd edn), Oxford University Press, Oxford.

Hirsch, F. 1976 *Social Limits to Growth*, Harvard University Press, Cambridge, MA.

HMG (Her Majesty's Government) 1990 *This Common Inheritance: Britain's Environmental Strategy*, Cm1200, HMSO, London.

HMIP (Her Majesty's Inspectorate of Pollution) 1996a 'ESI Review by HMIP: Background Brief', HMIP, London.

HMIP (Her Majesty's Inspectorate of Pollution) 1996b *Power Generation: a Review of the Way Forward*, DOE Report No. DOE/HMIP/RR/95/016, DOE/HMIP, London.

HMSO (Her Majesty's Stationery Office) 1985 *United Kingdom National Accounts: Sources and Methods*, HMSO, London.

HM Treasury 1997 'Statement of Intent on Environmental Taxation', Budget Statement, July, HM Treasury, London.

Hoeller, P., Dean, A. and Nicolaisen, J. 1991 'Macroeconomic Implications of Reducing Greenhouse Gas Emissions: a Survey of Empirical Studies', *OECD Economic Studies*, No. 16 (Spring), pp.45–78.

Hogan, W.W. 1990 'Comments on Manne and Richels: "CO_2 Emission Limits: an Economic Analysis for the USA"', *Energy Journal*, Vol. 12 No. 2, pp. 75–85.

Hogan, W.W. and Jorgenson, D.W. 1991 'Productivity Trends and the Cost of Reducing CO_2 Emissions', *Energy Journal*, Vol. 12 No. 1, pp.67–86.

Hohmeyer, O. 1988 *Social Costs of Energy Consumption*, Springer-Verlag, Berlin.

Hohmeyer, O. and Gärtner, M. 1992 *The Costs of Climate Change*, Report to the Commission of the European Communities, Fraunhofer Institut für Systemtechnik und Innovations-Forschung, Karlsruhe, Germany.

Holdren, J. and Ehrlich, P. 1974 'Human Population and the Global Environment', *American Scientist*, Vol. 62 (May–June), pp.282–92.

Holmberg, J. and Karlsson, S. 1995 'On Deriving Socio-Ecological Indicators' in Holmberg, J. *Socio-Ecological Principles and Indicators for Sustainability*, Institute for Physical Resource Theory, Göteborg, Sweden.

Holmberg, J. and Sandbrook, R. 1992 'Sustainable Development: What is to be Done?', Holmberg, J. Ed. *Policies for a Small Planet*, Earthscan, London.

Holtz-Eakin, D. and Selden, T. 1992 'Stoking the Fires? CO_2 Emissions and Economic Growth', NBER Working Paper No. 4248, December, National Bureau of Economic Research, Cambridge, MA.

Hope, C., Anderson, J. and Wenman, P. 1993 'Policy Analysis of the Greenhouse Effect: an Application of the PAGE Model', *Energy Policy*, Vol. 21 No. 3 (March), pp.327–38.

Horvath, R.J. 1997 'Energy Consumption and the Environmental Kuznets Curve Debate', Department of Geography, University of Sydney, Sydney, NSW.

Hotelling, H. 1931 'The Economics of Exhaustible Resources', *Journal of Political Economy*, Vol. 39 No. 2, pp.137–75.

Houghton, J., Jenkins, G. and Ephraums, J. Eds 1990 *Climate Change: the IPCC Scientific Assessment*, Cambridge University Press (for the IPCC Intergovernmental Panel on Climate Change), Cambridge.

Houghton, J., Meira Filho, L., Callander, B., Harris, N., Kattenburg, A. and Maskell, K. Eds 1996 *Climate Change 1995: the Science of Climate Change*, contribution of Working Group I to the Second Assessment Report of the Intergovernmental Panel on Climate Change (IPCC), Cambridge University Press, Cambridge.

Hueting, R. 1980 *New Scarcity and Economic Growth*, North-Holland, Amsterdam (Dutch edition first published 1974).

Hueting, R. 1986 'An Economic Scenario for a Conserver Economy' in Ekins, P. Ed. *The Living Economy: a New Economics in the Making*, Routledge & Kegan Paul, London, pp.242–56.

Hueting, R. 1992 'The Economic Functions of the Environment' in Ekins, P. and Max-Neef, M. Eds *Real-Life Economics: Understanding Wealth Creation*, Routledge, London/New York, pp.61–9.

Hueting, R., Bosch, P. and de Boer, B. 1992 *Methodology for the Calculation of Sustainable National Income*, Statistical Essay M44, Netherlands Central Bureau of Statistics, Voorburg/Heerlen.

IIED (International Institute for Environment and Development) 1995 *Citizen Action to Lighten Britain's Ecological Footprints*, report for the UK Department of the Environment, February, IIED, London.

IIED (International Institute for Environment and Development) 1997 *Unlocking Trade Opportunities: Case Studies of Export Success from Developing Countries*, report for the UN Department of Policy Co-ordination and Sustainable Development (UNDPCSD), IIED, London/UNDPCSD, New York.

IMF (International Monetary Fund) 1991 *International Financial Statistics Yearbook 1991*, IMF, Washington, DC.

IMF (International Monetary Fund) 1992 *International Financial Statistics Yearbook 1992*, IMF, Washington, DC.

INFRAS 1996 *Economic Impact Analysis of Ecotax Proposals: Comparative Analysis of Modelling Results*, Final Report of a project conducted in co-operation with the 3rd Framework Programme of DGXII of the European Commission, INFRAS, Zurich.

Ingham, A. and Ulph, A. 1991 'Market-Based Instruments for Reducing CO_2 Emissions: the Case of UK Manufacturing', *Energy Policy*, Vol. 19 No. 3 (March), pp.138–48.

Ingham, A., Maw, J. and Ulph, A. 1992 'Energy Conservation in UK Manufacturing: a Vintage Model Approach' in Hawdon, D. Ed. *Energy Demand: Evidence and Expectations*, Surrey University Press, Guildford, pp.115–41.

Irvine, S. 1990 'No Growth in a Finite World', *New Statesman and Society*, 23 November, pp.16–18.

Jackson, T. 1991 'Least-Cost Greenhouse Planning', *Energy Policy*, January–February, pp.35–46.

Jackson, T. 1995 'Price Elasticity and Market Structure – Overcoming Obstacles to Ensure Energy Efficiency' in Barker, T., Ekins, P. and Johnstone, N. Eds *Global Warming and Energy Elasticities*, Routledge, London, pp.254–66.

Jackson, T. and Jacobs, M. 1991 'Carbon Taxes and the Assumptions of Environmental Economics' in Barker, T. Ed. *Green Futures for Economic Growth*, Cambridge Econometrics, Cambridge, pp.49–67.

Jackson, T. and Marks, N. 1994 *Measuring Sustainable Economic Welfare – a Pilot Index: 1950–1990*, Stockholm Environment Institute, Stockholm.

Jacobs, M. 1991 *The Green Economy*, Pluto Press, London.

Jaeger, W.K. 1995 'Is Sustainability Optimal? Examining the Differences Between Economists and Environmentalists', *Ecological Economics*, Vol. 15 No. 1, pp.43–57.

Jaffe, A., Peterson, S., Portney, P. and Stavins, R. 1995 'Environmental Regulation and the Competitiveness of US Manufacturing: What Does the Evidence Tell Us?', *Journal of Economic Literature*, Vol. XXXIII (March), pp.132–63.

Jänicke, M., Monch, H., Ranneberg, Th. and Simonis, U. 1989 'Economic Structure and Environmental Impacts: East–West Comparisons', *The Environmentalist*, Vol. 19, pp.171–82.

Jänicke, M., Monch, H., Ranneberg, Th. and Simonis, U. 1993 'Ecological Aspects of Structural Change', *Inter Economics*, Vol. 28, pp.159–69.

Jaszi, G. 1973 'Comment on Juster 1973' in Moss, M. Ed. *The Measurement of Economic and Social Performance*, National Bureau of Economic Research/ Columbia University, New York, pp.84–99.

Jenkins, T. 1990 *Future Harvests*, Council for the Protection of Rural England, London and World Wide Fund for Nature, Godalming, Surrey.

Jevons, W. 1965 *The Coal Question: an Inquiry Concerning the Progress of the Nation and the Probable Exhaustion of Our Coal Mines* (3rd edn, 1st edn 1865), Augustus M. Kelley, New York.

Jorgenson, D. 1990 'Productivity and Economic Growth' in Berndt, E.R. and Triplett, J.E. Eds *Fifty Years of Measurement: the Jubilee of the Conference on Research in Income and Wealth*, University of Chicago Press, Chicago, IL, pp.19–118.

Jorgenson, D. and Wilcoxen, P. 1990 'Environmental Regulation and US Economic Growth', *RAND Journal of Economics*, Vol. 21 No. 2 (summer), pp.314–40.

Jorgenson, D. and Wilcoxen, P. 1992 'Energy, the Environment and Economic Growth', Harvard Institute for Economic Research Discussion Paper No. 1604, in Kneese, A.V. and Sweeney, J.L. Eds 1993 *Handbook of Natural Resource and Energy Economics*, Vol. 3, North-Holland, Amsterdam, pp.1267–349.

Jorgenson, D. and Wilcoxen, P. 1993a 'Reducing US Carbon Emissions: an Econometric General Equilibrium Assessment', *Resource and Energy Economics*, Vol. 15 No. 1 (March), pp.7–25.

Jorgenson, D. and Wilcoxen, P. 1993b 'Reducing US Carbon Dioxide Emissions: an Assessment of Different Instruments', *Journal of Policy Modeling*, Vol. 15 Nos. 5&6, pp.491–520.

Jorgenson, D. and Yun, K.-Y. 1990 'The Excess Burden of Taxation in the US', Harvard Institute of Economic Research Discussion Paper No. 1528, November, Harvard University, Cambridge, MA.

Juster, F.T. 1973 'A Framework for the Measurement of Economic and Social Performance' in Moss, M. Ed. *The Measurement of Economic and Social Performance*, National Bureau of Economic Research/Columbia University, New York, pp.25–84.

Kapp, K.W. 1950 *The Social Costs of Private Enterprise*, Harvard University Press, Cambridge, MA.

Karadeloglou, P. 1992 'Carbon Tax vs. Energy Tax: a Quantitative Analysis' in Laroui, F. and Velthuijsen, J. *The Economic Consequences of an Energy Tax in Europe: an Application with HERMES*, SEO Foundation for Economic Research, University of Amsterdam, Amsterdam, pp.177–201.

Keuning, S. 1996 'The NAMEA Experience: an Interim Evaluation of the Netherlands' Integrated Accounts and Indicators for the Environment and the Economy', paper presented to the International Symposium on Integrated Environmental and Economic Accounting in Theory and Practice, Tokyo, March 5–8, mimeo, Statistics Netherlands, National Accounts Department, Voorburg.

Klaassen, G. 1992 'Marginal and Average Costs of Reducing Nitrogen and Sulphur Dioxide Emissions in Europe', WP–92–050, July, IIASA, Laxenburg, Austria.

Klaassen, G. and Nentjes, A. 1991 'Macroeconomic Impacts of an EEC Policy to Control Air Pollution', *Journal of Policy Modeling*, Vol. 13 No. 3, pp.347–66.

Klaassen, G., Kee, P., Nentjes, A., Hafkamp, W. and Olsthoorn, A.A. 1988 *The Macroeconomic Impacts of the EC Large Combustion Plants Directive Proposal*, Vols 1 & 2, Commission of the European Communities, Luxemburg.

Kosmo, M. 1987 *Money to Burn? The High Cost of Energy Subsidies*, World Resources Institute, Washington, DC.

Kristensen, J.P. 1996 'Environmental Taxes, Tax Reform and the Internal Market – some Danish Experiences and Possible Community Initiatives' in *Environmental Taxes and Charges: National Experiences and Plans*, European Foundation for the Improvement of Living and Working Conditions, Dublin, and Office for Official Publications of the European Communities, Luxemburg, pp.121–36.

Kula, E. 1992 *Economics of Natural Resources and the Environment*, Chapman & Hall, London.

Kuznets, S. 1955 'Economic Growth and Income Inequality', *American Economic Review*, Vol. 49 (March), pp.1–28.

Kuznets, S. 1973 'Concluding Remarks' in Moss, M. Ed. *The Measurement of Economic and Social Performance*, National Bureau of Economic Research/Columbia University, New York, pp.579–92.

Lecomber, R. 1975 *Economic Growth Versus the Environment*, Macmillan, London.

Leggett, J. Ed. 1990 *Global Warming: the Greenpeace Report*, Oxford University Press, Oxford/New York.

Leipert, C. 1989a 'National Income and Economic Growth: the Conceptual Side of Defensive Expenditures', *Journal of Economic Issues*, Vol. XXIII No. 3 (September), pp.843–56.

Leipert, C. 1989b 'Social Costs of the Economic Process and National Accounts: the Example of Defensive Expenditures', *The Journal of Interdisciplinary Economics*, Vol. 3 No. 1, pp.27–46.

Lélé, S. 1991 'Sustainable Development: a Critical Review', *World Development*, Vol. 19 No. 6, pp.607–21.

Lockwood, B. 1992 'The Social Costs of Electricity Generation', CSERGE Discussion Paper GEC 92–09, University of East Anglia, Norwich.

Lone, Ø. 1992 'Environmental and Resource Accounting' in Ekins, P. and Max-Neef, M. Eds 1992 *Real-Life Economics: Understanding Wealth Creation*, Routledge, London, pp.239–53.

Long, B.L. 1994 'Managing Change: the Challenge of Sustainable Consumption' in *Symposium: Sustainable Consumption*, report of a Symposium on 19–20 January, Ministry of the Environment, Oslo, Norway.

Lovins, A.B. and Lovins, H.L. 1991 'Least Cost Climatic Stabilization', *Annual Review of Energy and Environment*, Vol. 16, pp.433–531.

Low, P. and Yeats, A. 1992 'Do "Dirty" Industries Migrate?' in Low, P. Ed. *International Trade and the Environment*, World Bank Discussion Paper No. 159, World Bank, Washington, DC, pp.89–103.

Lucas, R., Wheeler, D. and Hettige, H. 1992 'Economic Development, Environmental Regulation and the International Migration of Toxic Industrial Pollution: 1960–88' in Low, P. Ed. *International Trade and the Environment*, World Bank Discussion Paper No. 159, World Bank, Washington, DC, pp.67–86.

Lutz, E. 1993 'Toward Improved Accounting for the Environment: an Overview' in Lutz, E. Ed. *Toward Improved Accounting for the Environment*, World Bank, Washington, DC, pp.1–14.

McCormick, J. 1989 *Acid Earth*, Earthscan, London.

MacGillivray, A. 1993 *A Green League of Nations: Relative Environmental Performance in OECD Countries*, New Economics Foundation, London.

MacKenzie, D. 1992 'Cod Crisis Forces Canada to Curb Fishing', *New Scientist*, 7 March, p.8.

McLaren, D., Bullock, S. and Yousuf, N. 1998 *Tomorrow's World: Britain's Share in a Sustainable Future*, Earthscan, London.

Maddison, D., Pearce, D., Adger, N. and McLeod, H. 1997 'Environmentally Damaging Subsidies in the United Kingdom', *European Environment*, Vol. 7, pp.110–17.

Majocchi, A. 1996 'Green Fiscal Reform and Employment: a Survey', *Environmental and Resource Economics*, Vol. 8, pp.375–97.

Mäler, K.-G. 1991 'National Accounts and Environmental Resources', *Environmental and Resource Economics*, Vol. 1, pp.1–15.

Malthus, T. 1970 *An Essay on the Principle of Population* (1st edn, first published 1798), Penguin, Harmondsworth.

Malthus, T. 1974 *Principles of Political Economy: Considered with a View to their Practical Application* (2nd edn, first published 1836), Augustus M. Kelley, Clifton, NJ.

Manne, A.S. and Richels, R.G. 1990a 'CO_2 Emissions Limits: an Economic Cost Analysis for the USA', *The Energy Journal*, Vol. 11 No. 2, pp.51–74.

Manne, A.S. and Richels, R.G. 1990b 'The Costs of Reducing US CO_2 Emission: Further Sensitivity Analyses', *Energy Journal*, Vol. 11 No. 4, pp.69–78.

Manne, A.S. and Richels, R.G. 1991 'Global CO_2 Emission Reductions – the Impacts of Rising Energy Costs', *The Energy Journal*, Vol. 12 No. 1, pp.87–107.

Manne, A.S. and Richels, R.G. 1992 *Buying Greenhouse Insurance*, MIT Press, Cambridge, MA.

Markandya, A. and Milborrow, I. 1998 'Green Accounting Research Project' in Vaze, P. Ed. *UK Environmental Accounts: Theory, Data and Application*, Office for National Statistics, London, pp.169–89.

Marshall, A. 1959 *Principles of Economics* (8th edn, 1st edn 1890), Macmillan, London.

Max-Neef, M. 1991 *Human Scale Development: Conception, Application and Further Reflection*, Apex Press, New York.

Meadows, D.H. 1995 'Who Causes Environmental Pollution?', *ISEE Newsletter*, Vol. 6 No. 3 (July), pp.1, 8, International Society for Ecological Economics, University of Maryland.

Meadows, D.H., Meadows, D.L. and Randers, J. 1992 *Beyond the Limits: Global Collapse or a Sustainable Future*, Earthscan, London.

Meadows, D.H., Meadows, D.L., Randers, J. and Behrens, W. 1974 *The Limits to Growth*, Pan Books, London/Sydney.

Meyer, B. and Ewerhart, G. 1998 'Multisectoral Policy Modelling for Environmental Analysis' in Uno, K. and Bartelmus, P. Eds *Environmental Accounting in Theory and Practice*, Kluwer, Dordrecht, pp.396–406.

Mez, L. 1993 'Successful Environmental Policy in Germany: the Reduction of Exhaust Gases at Large Combustion Plants', FFU report 93–5, Freie Universität, Berlin.

Miles, I. 1992 'Social Indicators for Real-Life Economics' in Ekins, P. and Max-Neef, M. Eds *Real-Life Economics: Understanding Wealth Creation*, Routledge, London, pp.283–97.

Miljøverndepartementet 1994 *Symposium: Sustainable Consumption*, Ministry of Environment, Oslo, Norway.

Mill, J.S. 1904 *Principles of Political Economy With Some of their Applications to Social Philosophy* (6th edn, 1st edn 1848), Longmans, Green & Co., London.

Mishan, E.J. 1967 *The Costs of Economic Growth*, Staples Press, London.

Mishan, E.J. 1977 *The Economic Growth Debate: an Assessment*, George Allen & Unwin, London.

MOHPPE (Ministry of Housing, Physical Planning and Environment) 1988 *To Choose or to Lose: National Environmental Policy Plan*, MOHPPE, The Hague.

MOHPPE (Ministry of Housing, Physical Planning and Environment) 1994 *The Netherlands National Environmental Policy Plan 2*, MOHPPE, The Hague.

Munasinghe, M. and Shearer, W. Eds 1995 *Defining and Measuring Sustainability: the Biogeophysical Foundations*, the United Nations University and World Bank, World Bank, Washington, DC.

Myers, N. 1986 'Tackling Mass Extinction of Species: a Great Creative Challenge', XXVIth Horace M. Albright Lecture in Conservation, University of California, Berkeley, CA.

Myers, N. 1998 'Lifting the Veil on Perverse Subsidies', *Nature*, Vol. 392 (26 March), pp.327–8.

NAS (National Academy of Sciences) 1991 *Policy Implications of Greenhouse Warming*, NAS, Washington, DC.

National Power 1994 *National Power Environmental Performance Review '94*, National Power, Swindon.

Newbery, D. 1990 'Acid Rain', *Economic Policy*, October, pp.297–346.

Newbery, D. 1993 'The Impact of EC Environmental Policy on British Coal', *Oxford Review of Economic Policy*, Vol. 9 No. 4, pp.66–95.

Newbery, D. 1994a 'UK Energy Policy Versus EU Environmental Policy', paper presented at the 17th Annual Energy Economics Conference at Stavanger, Norway, 25–27 May, mimeo, Department of Applied Economics, University of Cambridge.

Newbery, D. 1994b 'The Impact of Sulfur Limits on Fuel Demand and Electricity Prices in Britain', *The Energy Journal*, Vol. 15 No. 3, pp.19–41.

New Scientist 1992 'Reprieve for Cod', *New Scientist*, 11 July, p.11.

Nilsson, J. and Grennfelt, P. Eds 1988 *Critical Loads for Sulphur and Nitrogen*, Nordic Council Report NORD, p.15.

Nordhaus, W.D. 1973 'World Dynamics: Measurement Without Data', *Economic Journal*, Vol. 83 (December), pp.1156–83.

Nordhaus, W.D. 1991a 'To Slow or Not to Slow: the Economics of the Greenhouse Effect', *Economic Journal*, Vol. 101 (July), pp.920–37.

Nordhaus, W.D. 1991b 'The Cost of Slowing Climate Change: a Survey', *The Energy Journal*, Vol. 12 No. 1, pp.37–65.

Nordhaus, W.D. 1991c 'Economic Approaches to Global Warming' in Dornbusch, R. and Poterba, J. Eds *Global Warming: Economic Policy Responses*, MIT Press, Cambridge, MA, pp.33–69.

Nordhaus, W.D. 1992a 'Is Growth Sustainable? Reflections of [sic] the Concept of Sustainable Economic Growth', paper for International Economic Association meeting, Varenna, mimeo, Yale University, New Haven, CT.

Nordhaus, W.D. 1992b 'The "DICE" Model: Background and Structure of a *D*ynamic *I*ntegrated *C*limate-*E*nergy Model of the Economics of Global Warming', Cowles Foundation Discussion Paper No. 1009, February, Yale University, New Haven, CT.

Nordhaus, W.D. 1993a 'Lethal Model 2: the Limits to Growth Revisited', Cowles Foundation Paper No. 831, Yale University, New Haven, CT.

Nordhaus, W.D. 1993b 'Optimal Greenhouse Gas Reductions and Tax Policy in the "DICE" Model', *American Economic Review* (AEA Papers and Proceedings), Vol. 83 No. 2 (May), pp.313–17.

Nordhaus, W.D. 1993c 'Rolling the "DICE": an Optimal Transition Path for Controlling Greenhouse Gases', *Resource and Energy Economics*, Vol. 15 No. 1 (March), pp.27–50.

Nordhaus, W.D. 1994 *Managing the Global Commons: the Economics of Climate Change*, MIT Press, Cambridge, MA.

Nordhaus, W.D. and Tobin, J. 1973 'Is Growth Obsolete?' in Moss, M. Ed. *The Measurement of Economic and Social Performance*, National Bureau of Economic Research/Columbia University, New York, pp.509–32.

Nordhaus, W.D. and Yohe, G. 1983 'Future Carbon Dioxide Emissions from Fossil Fuels' in National Research Council/National Academy of Sciences *Changing Climate*, National Academy Press, Washington, DC, pp.87–153.

Norwegian Green Tax Commission 1996 *Policies for a Better Environment and High Employment*, Oslo.

OECD (Organisation for Economic Cooperation and Development) 1985 *The Macroeconomic Impact of Environmental Expenditure*, OECD, Paris.

OECD (Organisation for Economic Cooperation and Development) 1991a *The State of the Environment*, OECD, Paris.

OECD (Organisation for Economic Cooperation and Development) 1991b *Environmental Indicators: a Preliminary Set*, OECD, Paris.

OECD (Organisation for Economic Cooperation and Development) 1994a *Environmental Indicators: OECD Core Set*, OECD, Paris.

OECD (Organisation for Economic Cooperation and Development) 1994b *Environment and Taxation: the Cases of the Netherlands, Sweden and the United States*, OECD, Paris.

OECD (Organisation for Economic Cooperation and Development) 1995a *OECD Environmental Data: Compendium 1995*, OECD, Paris.

OECD (Organisation for Economic Cooperation and Development) 1995b *Environmental Taxes in OECD Countries*, OECD, Paris.

OECD (Organisation for Economic Cooperation and Development) 1996 *Implementation Strategies for Environmental Taxes*, OECD, Paris.

OECD (Organisation for Economic Cooperation and Development) 1997 *Evaluating Economic Instruments for Environmental Policy*, OECD, Paris.

OECD/IEA (Organisation for Economic Cooperation and Development/ International Energy Agency) 1996 *Energy Prices and Taxes: First Quarter 1996*, OECD/IEA, Paris.

Oliveira-Martins, J., Burniaux, J.-M. and Martin, J.P. 1992 'Trade and Effectiveness of Unilateral CO_2-Abatement Policies: Evidence from Green', *OECD Economic Studies*, No. 19, Paris.

Opschoor, J.B. and Vos, H.B. 1989 *Economic Instruments for Environmental Protection*, Organisation for Economic Cooperation and Development, Paris.

Opschoor, J.B. and Weterings, R. 1994/5 'Environmental Utilisation Space: an Introduction', *Milieu: Tijdschrift voor Milieukunde* (Netherlands Journal of Environmental Sciences), Vol. 9, pp.198–205.

O'Riordan, T. 1993 'Interpreting the Precautionary Principle', CSERGE Working Paper PA 93–01, University of East Anglia, Norwich.

Palmer, K., Oates, W. and Portney, P. 1995 'Tightening Environmental Standards: the Benefit–Cost or the No-Cost Paradigm?', *Journal of Economic Perspectives*, Vol. 9 No. 4 (fall), pp.119–32.

Panayotou, T. 1993 'Empirical Tests and Policy Analysis of Environmental Degradation at Different Stages of Economic Development', World Employment Programme Research Working Paper WEP 2–22/WP 238, January, International Labour Office, Geneva.

Pangare, G. and Pangare, V. 1992 *From Poverty to Plenty: the Story of Rahegan Siddhi*, Indian National Trust for Art and Cultural Heritage, New Delhi.

Parris, B. 1997 'Development in Wonderland: the Social and Ecological Sustainability of Economic Growth', Issues in Global Development No. 9, February, World Vision Australia, Melbourne.

Parry, I. 1995 'Pollution Taxes and Revenue Recycling', *Journal of Environmental Economics and Management*, Vol. 29, pp.S64–S77.

Pearce, D. 1983 *Cost–Benefit Analysis* (2nd edn, 1st edn 1971), Macmillan, London.

Pearce, D. 1991 'The Role of Carbon Taxes in Adjusting to Global Warming', *Economic Journal*, Vol. 101, pp.938–48.

Pearce, D. 1992 'The Secondary Benefits of Greenhouse Gas Control', CSERGE Working Paper 92–12, University College London, London.

Pearce, D. 1993 *Economic Values and the Natural World*, Earthscan, London.

Pearce, D. and Atkinson, G. 1992 'Are National Economies Sustainable?: Measuring Sustainable Development', CSERGE Discussion Paper GEC 92–11, University College London, London.

Pearce, D. and Atkinson, G. 1993 'Capital Theory and the Measurement of Sustainable Development: an Indicator of Weak Sustainability', *Ecological Economics*, Vol. 8, pp.103–8.

Pearce, D. and Moran, D. 1994 *The Economic Value of Biodiversity*, Earthscan, London.

Pearce, D. and Turner, R.K. 1990 *Economics of Natural Resources and the Environment*, Harvester Wheatsheaf, Hemel Hempstead, Herts, UK.

Pearce, D., Bann, C. and Georgiou, S. 1992 *The Social Cost of Fuel Cycles*, report to the UK Department of Trade and Industry, CSERGE, University College London, London.

Pearce, D., Markandya, A. and Barbier, E. 1989 *Blueprint for a Green Economy*, Earthscan, London.

Pearce, D., Barbier, E. and Markandya, A. 1990 *Sustainable Development: Economics and Environment in the Third World*, Edward Elgar, Aldershot.

Pearce, D., Cline, W., Achanta, A., Fankhauser, S., Pachauri, R., Tol, R. and Vellinga, P. 1996 'The Social Costs of Climate Change: Greenhouse Damage and the Benefits of Control' in Bruce, J., Lee, H. and Haites, E. Eds *Climate Change 1995: Economic and Social Dimensions of Climate Change*, contribution of Working Group III to the Second Assessment Report of the Intergovernmental Panel on Climate Change (IPCC), Cambridge University Press, Cambridge, chap. 6.

Pearce, F. 1996 'After the Falklands Bonanza', *New Scientist*, 17 February, pp.32–5.

Pearson, M. and Smith, S. 1991 'The European Carbon Tax: an Assessment of the EC's Proposals', Institute of Fiscal Studies, London.

Perrings, C., Turner, R.K and Folke, C. 1995 'Ecological Economics: the Study of Interdependent Economic and Ecological Systems', Beijer Discussion Paper Series No. 55, Beijer International Institute of Ecological Economics, Stockholm.

Pethig, R. 1996 'Ecological Tax Reform and Efficiency of Taxation: a Public Good Perspective', Diskussionsbeitrag Nr.57–96, Universität-Gesamthichschule Siegen, Siegen, Germany.

Pezzey, J. 1991 *Impacts of Greenhouse Gas Control Strategies on UK Competitiveness*, Department of Trade and Industry, HMSO, London.

Pezzey, J. 1992a 'Sustainability: an Interdisciplinary Guide', *Environmental Values*, Vol. 1 No. 4, pp.321–62.

Pezzey, J. 1992b *Sustainable Development Concepts: an Economic Analysis*, World Bank Environment Paper No. 2, World Bank, Washington, DC.

Pezzey, J. 1994 'The Optimal Sustainable Depletion of Renewable Resources', paper presented to the Fifth Annual Conference of the European Association of Environmental and Resource Economists, June, mimeo, University College London, London.

Pigou, A.C. 1932 *The Economics of Welfare* (4th edn, 1st edn 1920), Macmillan, London.

Pimm, S. 1995 'Seeds of Our Own Destruction', *New Scientist*, 8 April, pp.31–5.

Porter, M. 1990 *The Competitive Advantage of Nations*, Free Press, New York.

Porter, M. and Van Der Linde, C. 1995 'Toward a New Conception of the Environment–Competitiveness Relationship', *Journal of Economic Perspectives*, Vol. 9 No. 4 (fall), pp.97–118.

Portney, P.R. 1994 'The Contingent Valuation Debate: Why Economists Should Care', *Journal of Economic Perspectives*, Vol. 8 No. 4 (fall), pp.3–17.

Proops, J., Faber, M. and Wagenhals, G. 1993 *Reducing CO_2 Emissions: a Comparative Input–Output Study for Germany and the UK*, Springer Verlag, Berlin.

Proops, J., Schlotheim, B. von and Simon, S. 1996 'Measuring Sustainability in Europe when there is International Trade' in *The Measurement and Achievement of Sustainable Development*, Main Report to DGXII of the European Commission on Contract No.CT940367, chap. 16, pp.249–74.

Radetzki, M. 1992 'Economic Growth and Environment' in Low, P. Ed. *International Trade and the Environment*, World Bank Discussion Paper No. 159, World Bank, Washington, DC, pp.121–36.

Repetto, R. 1985 *Paying the Price: Pesticide Subsidies in Developing Countries*, World Resources Institute, Washington, DC.

Repetto, R. 1986 *Skimming the Water: Rent-Seeking and the Performance of Public Irrigation Systems*, World Resources Institute, Washington, DC.

Repetto, R. 1988 *The Forest for the Trees? Government Policies and the Misuse of Forest Resources*, World Resources Institute, Washington, DC.

Repetto, R. and Austin, D. 1997 *The Costs of Climate Protection: a Guide for the Perplexed*, World Resources Institute, Washington, DC.

Repetto, R., Magrath, W., Wells, M., Beer, C. and Rossini, F. 1989 *Wasting Assets: Natural Resources in the National Accounts*, World Resources Institute, Washington, DC.

Repetto, R., Rothman, D., Faeth, P. and Austin, D. 1996 *Has Environmental Protection Really Reduced Productivity Growth?*, World Resources Institute, Washington, DC.

Ricardo, D. 1973 *The Principles of Political Economy and Taxation* (1st edn 1817), J.M. Dent & Sons, London.

Rosenzweig, C., Parry, M., Frohberg, K. and Fisher, G. 1993 *Climate Change and World Food Supply*, Environmental Change Unit, Oxford.

Rotmans, J. and Dowlatabadi, H. 1998 'Integrated Assessment Modelling' in Rayner, S. and Malone, E. Eds *Human Choice and Climate Change*, Vol. 3 (Tools for Policy Analysis), Battelle Press, Columbus, OH, pp.292–377.

RS & NAS (Royal Society and National Academy of Sciences) 1992 *Population Growth, Resource Consumption and a Sustainable World*, Royal Society, London, and National Academy of Sciences, New York.

Ruggles, R. 1983 'The United States National Income Accounts, 1947–1977: Their Conceptual Basis and Evolution' in Foss, M.F. Ed. *The U.S. National Income and Product Accounts*, University of Chicago Press, Chicago, IL.

Ruijgrok, E. and Oosterhuis, F. 1997 *Energy Subsidies in Western Europe*, Greenpeace International, Amsterdam.

Sachs, W., Loske, R., Linz, M., Behrensmeier, R., Bierter, W., Bleischwitz, R., Böge, S., Bringezu, S., Burdick, B., Fischedick, M., Hinterberger, F., Jung, W., Kristof, K. and Schütz, H. 1998 *Greening the North: a Post-Industrial Blueprint for Ecology and Equity*, Zed Books, London.

Sadik, N. 1991 *The State of the World Population 1991*, UNFPA (UN Fund for Population Activities), New York.

Sandnes, H. 1993 *Calculated Budgets for Airborne Acidifying Components in Europe*, EMEP (Emissions Monitoring and Evaluation Programme), Norwegian Meteorological Institute, PO Box 43, Blindern, N–0313, Oslo.

Schäfer, D. and Stahmer, C. 1989 'Input–Output Model for the Analysis of Environmental Protection Activities', *Economic Systems Research*, Vol. 1 No. 2, pp.203–28.

Schelling, T. 1992 'Some Economics of Global Warming', *American Economic Review*, Vol. 82 No. 1 (March), pp.1–14.

Schmidheiny, S. (with the Business Council for Sustainable Development) 1992 *Changing Course: a Global Business Perspective on Development and the Environment*, MIT Press, Cambridge, MA.

Scott, M. 1992 'Policy Implications of "A New View of Economic Growth"', *The Economic Journal*, Vol. 102 (May), pp.622–32.

SEI/G (Stockholm Environment Institute/Greenpeace) 1993 *Towards a Fossil Free Energy Future: the Next Energy Transition*, a technical analysis for Greenpeace International, Tellus Institute, Boston, MA.

Selden, T. and Song, D. 1994 'Environmental Quality and Development: Is There a Kuznets Curve for Air Pollution Emissions?', *Journal of Environmental Economics and Management*, Vol. 21, pp.147–62.

Sen, A. 1983 'Development: Which Way Now?', *Economic Journal*, Vol. 93, pp.745–62.

Serageldin, I. and Steer, A. 1994 'Epilogue: Expanding the Capital Stock' in Serageldin, I. and Steer, A. Eds *Making Development Sustainable: From Concepts to Action*, Environmentally Sustainable Development Occasional Paper Series No. 2, World Bank, Washington, DC, pp.30–2.

Shafik, S. 1994 'Economic Development and Environmental Quality: an Econometric Analysis', *Oxford Economic Papers*, Vol. 46, pp.757–73.

Shafik, N. and Bandyopadhyay, S. 1992 'Economic Growth and Environmental Quality: Time Series and Cross-Country Evidence', Background Paper for the *World Development Report 1992*, World Bank, Washington, DC.

Simon, J. 1981 *The Ultimate Resource*, Martin Robertson, Oxford.

Simon, J. and Kahn, H. 1984 *The Resourceful Earth: a Response to Global 2000*, Basil Blackwell, Oxford.

Sips, H., Brinkman, R., Lok, M. and Oosterhuis, L. 1994/5 'Environmental Utilisation Space and Dutch Environmental Policy', *Milieu: Tijdschrift voor Milieukunde* (Netherlands Journal of Environmental Sciences), Vol. 9, pp.206–12.

Slade, M. 1982 'Trends in Natural-Resource Commodity Prices: an Analysis of the Time Domain', *Journal of Environmental Economics and Management*, Vol. 9, pp.122–37.

Slade, M. 1991 'Market Structure, Marketing Method and Price Instability', *The Quarterly Journal of Economics*, November, pp.1309–40.

Slade, M. 1992 'Do Markets Underprice Natural-Resource Commodities?', Background Paper for the *World Development Report 1992*, WPS 962, World Bank, Washington, DC.

Smith, S. 1992 'Taxation and the Environment: a Survey', *Fiscal Studies*, Vol. 13 No. 4, pp.21–57.

Smith, V.K. 1981 'The Empirical Relevance of Hotelling's Model for Natural Resources', *Resources and Energy*, Vol. 3, pp.105–18.

Smith, V.K. and Krutilla, J.V. 1979 'The Economics of Natural Resource Scarcity' in Smith, V. Ed. 1979 *Scarcity and Growth Reconsidered*, Johns Hopkins University Press, Baltimore, MD.

Smith, V.L. 1977 'Control Theory Applied to Natural and Environmental Resources', *Journal of Environmental Economics and Management*, Vol. 4, pp.1–14.

Solórzano, R., De Camino, R., Woodward, R., Tosi, J., Watson, V., Vásquez, A., Villalobos, C., Jimenénez, J., Repetto, R. and Cruz, W. 1991 *Accounts Overdue: Natural Resource Depreciation in Costa Rica*, World Resources Institute, Washington, DC.

Solow, A. 1991 'Is There a Global Warming Problem?' in Dornbusch, R. and Poterba, J. Eds *Global Warming: Economic Policy Responses*, MIT Press, Cambridge, MA, pp.7–28.

Solow, J. 1987 'The Capital-Energy Complementarity Debate Revisited', *American Economic Review*, Vol. 77 No. 4 (September), pp.605–14.

Solow, R. 1991 'Growth Theory' in Greenaway, D., Bleaney, M. and Stewart, I.M.T. Eds *Companion to Contemporary Economic Thought*, Routledge, London, pp.393–415.

Sondheimer, J. 1991 'Macroeconomic Effects of a Carbon Tax' in Barker, T. Ed. *Green Futures for Economic Growth*, Cambridge Econometrics, Cambridge, pp.39–47.

South Commission 1990 *The Challenge to the South: the Report of the South Commission*, Oxford University Press, Oxford/New York.

Standaert, S. 1992 'Simulating an Energy Tax (with HERMES-Link)' in Laroui, F. and Velthuijsen, J. *The Economic Consequences of an Energy Tax in Europe: an Application with HERMES*, SEO Foundation for Economic Research, University of Amsterdam, Amsterdam, pp.1–37.

Stern, D. 1997 'Review of the Environmental Kuznets Curve', mimeo, Centre for Resource and Environmental Studies, Australian National University, Canberra, October, forthcoming in Cleveland, C.J., Costanza, R. and Stern, D. *The Nature of Economics and the Economics of Nature*, Edward Elgar, Cheltenham.

Stern, D., Common, M.S. and Barbier, E.B. 1994 'Economic Growth and Environmental Degradation: a Critique of the Environmental Kuznets Curve', Discussion Papers in Environmental Economics and Management No. 9409, August, Department of Environmental Economics and Management, University of York, York.

Stern, D., Common, M.S. and Barbier, E.B. 1996 'Economic Growth and Environmental Degradation: the Environmental Kuznets Curve and Sustainable Development', *World Development*, Vol. 24, pp.1151–60.

Stiglitz, J. and Dasgupta, P. 1971 'Differential Taxation, Public Goods, and Economic Efficiency', *Review of Economic Studies*, Vol. 38 No. 2, pp.151–74.

Summers, R. and Heston, A. 1991 'The Penn World Table (Mark 5): an Expanded Set of International Comparisons, 1950–1988', *The Quarterly Journal of Economics*, Vol. 106 No. 2 (May), pp.327–68.

Tinbergen, J. and Hueting, R. 1992 'GNP and Market Prices' in Goodland, R., Daly, H.E. and Serafy, S. El Eds *Population, Technology and Lifestyle: the Transition to Sustainability*, Island Press, Washington, DC, pp.52–62.

Titus, J.G. 1992 'The Cost of Climate Change to the United States' in Majumdar, S.K., Kalkstein, L.S., Yarnal, B., Miller, E.W. and Rosenfeld, L.M. Eds *Global Climate Change: Implications, Challenges and Mitigation Measures*, Pennsylvania Academy of Science, Pennsylvania, PA.

Tol, R.S.J. 1995 'The Damage Costs of Climate Change: Toward More Comprehensive Calculations', *Environmental and Resource Economics*, Vol. 5, pp.353–74.

Tomer, J. 1973 'Management consulting for private enterprise: a theoretical and empirical analysis of the contribution of management consultants to economic growth in the United States', unpublished Ph.D. thesis, Rutgers University, New Brunswick, NJ.

Tomer, J. 1987 *Organizational Capital: the Path to Higher Productivity and Well-Being*, Praeger, Westport, CT.

Turner, R.K. 1992 'Speculations on Weak and Strong Sustainability', CSERGE Working Paper GEC 92–26, University of East Anglia, Norwich.

Turner, R.K. 1993 'Sustainability: Principles and Practice' in Turner, R.K. Ed. *Sustainable Environmental Economics and Management: Principles and Practice*, Belhaven Press, New York/London, pp.3–36.

UKG (UK Government) 1990 *The United Kingdom's Programme and National Plan for Reducing Emissions of Sulphur Dioxide (SO₂) and Oxides of Nitrogen (NOₓ) from Existing Large Combustion Plants*, Department of the Environment, London, 20 December.

UKG (UK Government) 1994 *Sustainable Development: the UK Strategy*, HMSO, London.

UKGER (UK Global Environmental Research Office) 1993 *Global Environmental Change: the UK Research Framework*, September, UKGER, Swindon.

UNDP (United Nations Development Programme) 1992 *Human Development Report 1992*, Oxford University Press, Oxford/New York.

UNDP (United Nations Development Programme) 1995 *Human Development Report 1995*, Oxford University Press, Oxford/New York.

UNECE (UN Economic Commission for Europe) 1994 'Draft Protocol to the 1979 Convention on Long-Range Transboundary Air Pollution on Further Reduction of Sulphur Emissions', GE 94–30904, Economic Commission for Europe, Geneva.

UNSD (United Nations Statistical Division) 1993 *Integrated Environmental and Economic Accounting: Handbook of National Accounting*, Studies in Methods, Series F, No. 61, Interim Version, UN Statistical Division, New York.

Van Dieren, W. 1995 *Taking Nature into Account: a Report to the Club of Rome*, Copernicus/Springer Verlag, New York.

Van Tongeren, J., Schweinfest, S., Lutz, E., Luna, M.G. and Martin, G. 1993 'Integrated Environmental and Economic Accounting: a Case Study for Mexico' in Lutz, E. Ed. *Toward Improved Accounting for the Environment*, World Bank, Washington, DC, pp.85–107.

Vaze, P. 1998 'Valuing the Depletion of Oil and Gas Reserves' in Vaze, P. Ed. *UK Environmental Accounts: Theory, Data and Application*, Office for National Statistics, London, pp.61–73, reprinted from *Economic Trends*, Issue 510, August 1996, The Stationery Office, London.

Vaze, P., Schweisguth, D. and Barron, J. 1998 'Environmental Accounts – Analysis of the Flow of Material Resources Between the UK and Other Countries' in Vaze, P. Ed. *UK Environmental Accounts: Theory, Data and Application*, Office for National Statistics, The Stationery Office, London, pp.99–124.

Victor, P.A. 1991 'Indicators of Sustainable Development: Some Lessons from Capital Theory', *Ecological Economics*, Vol. 4, pp.191–213.

Victor, P., Hanna, E. and Kubursi, A. 1995 'How Strong is Weak Sustainability?' in Faucheux, S., O'Connor, M. and Van der Straaten, J. Eds *Sustainable Development: Analysis and Public Policy*, Kluwer, Dordrecht, pp.195–210.

Vines, G. 1994 'No Respite for Pacific Mackerel as Stocks Dwindle', *New Scientist*, 26 March, p.14.

Vitousek, P., Ehrlich, P., Ehrlich, A. and Matson, P. 1986 'Human Appropriation of the Products of Photosynthesis', *BioScience*, Vol. 36, pp.368–73.

Wackernagel, M. and Rees, W. 1996 *Our Ecological Footprint: Reducing Human Impact on the Earth*, New Society Publishers, Gabriola Island BC/Philadelphia, PA.

WBGU (German Advisory Council on Global Change) 1995 'Scenario for the Derivation of Global CO_2 Reduction Targets and Implementation Strategies', WBGU, Bremershaven.

WCED (World Commission on Environment and Development) 1987 *Our Common Future* (The Brundtland Report), Oxford University Press, Oxford/New York.

WEC (World Energy Council) 1993 *Energy for Tomorrow's World*, St. Martin's Press, New York/Kogan Page, London.

Weizsäcker, E. von and Jesinghaus, J. 1992 *Ecological Tax Reform*, Zed Books, London.

Weizsäcker, E. von, Lovins, A. and Lovins, H. 1997 *Factor Four: Doubling Wealth, Halving Resource Use*, Earthscan, London.

Weyant, J. and Yanigisawa, Y. 1998 'Energy and Industry' in Rayner, S. and Malone, E. Eds *Human Choice and Climate Change*, Vol. 2 (Resources and Technology), Battelle Press, Columbus, OH, pp.203–89.

Whalley, J. and Wigle, R. 1991 'Cutting CO_2 Emissions: the Effects of Alternative Policy Approaches', *The Energy Journal*, Vol. 12 No. 1, pp.109–24.

Wigley, T., Richels, R. and Edmonds, J. 1996 'Economic and Environmental Choices in the Stabilisation of Atmospheric CO_2 Concentrations', *Nature*, Vol. 379 (18 January), pp.240–3.

Williams, J. 1990 'Will Constraining Fossil Fuel Carbon Dioxide Emissions Cost So Much?', mimeo, Center for Energy and Environmental Studies, Princeton University, Princeton, April.

Wilson, D. 1995, personal communication, DTI, London.

Woodwell, G. 1990 'The Effects of Global Warming' in Leggett, J. Ed. *Global Warming: the Greenpeace Report*, Oxford University Press, Oxford/New York, pp.116–32.

World Bank 1992 *World Development Report 1992*, Oxford University Press, Oxford/New York.

World Bank 1995 *Monitoring Environmental Progress*, World Bank, Washington, DC.

World Bank 1997 *World Development Report 1997*, Oxford University Press, Oxford/New York.

WRI (World Resources Institute) (with UNDP and UNEP) 1990 *World Resources, 1990–91*, Oxford University Press, Oxford/New York.

WRI (World Resources Institute) (with UNDP and UNEP) 1992 *World Resources, 1992–93*, Oxford University Press, Oxford/New York.

WRI (World Resources Institute) (with UNDP and UNEP) 1994 *World Resources, 1994–95*, Oxford University Press, Oxford/New York.

WRI (World Resources Institute) (with UNDP, UNEP and World Bank) 1996 *World Resources, 1996–97*, Oxford University Press, Oxford/New York.

WRI (World Resources Institute) (with UNDP, UNEP and World Bank) 1998 *World Resources, 1998–99*, Oxford University Press, Oxford/New York.

WWF (World Wide Fund for Nature) 1995 *Real Value for Nature: an Overview of Global Efforts to Achieve True Measures of Economic Progress*, WWF, Gland, Switzerland.

Yamaji, K., Matsuhashi, R., Nagata, Y. and Kaya, Y. 1993 'A Study on Economic Measures for CO_2 Reduction in Japan', *Energy Policy*, Vol. 21 No. 2 (February), pp.123–32.

Young, M.D. 1992 *Natural Resource Accounting: Some Australian Experiences and Observations*, Working Document 92/1, February, CSIRO, Canberra.

Index

Page numbers in bold denote tables or figures

Aaheim, A. 140
acidification **7**, 11–13, 17, 21, 70, 143, 299
Adger, N. 116, 125
Adirondack mountains: acidification of
  lakes 12
Adriaanse, A. 112, 152
Africa: deforestation 191; extinction of
  species 16; regeneration of degraded
  land 170
Agarwal, A. 58
Agenda 21 (UNCED) 73, 97
agriculture: beneficial effects of climate
  change 245, 249; economic impacts of
  greenhouse effect 244, 250, 251–2, 281;
  environmentally damaging policies 169;
  erosion of profitability 24; and land
  degradation 16–17, **17**, 191; OEI time
  trends 37; 'perennial polyculture' as
  alternative 173; policies for reducing
  pesticide concentrations 85
aid: need for increase to developing
  countries 323, 324
air: difficulty of valuing as a service 122;
  quality 46, 105, 182, 196
air conditioning 244, 247
air pollution 13–14, 44, 46, 48, 96;
  achievements in reduction programmes
  171, 195; costs as measured by ISEW
  126; from traffic 6; improvements in
  control of 67; reduction in pollutants
  apart from carbon dioxide 280; in
  Third World countries 13
Aire and Calder valley: project for waste-
  reduction 171

Alaska: disappearance of original forests
  16
Alcamo, J. 304
Alfsen, K. 129, 300
algal blooms 19
Algeria 20
allergies 6
Amalric, F. 157, 158
Amann, M. 300, 308
Amazon: effect of climate change on
  rainforests 245
Anderson, D. 166–7, 178–9, 319
animal life: destruction by greenhouse
  effect 244; *see also* species extinction
Antarctica: ozone loss 11; whaling
  38–9
aquatic life: decline due to acidification
  12; *see also* fish; marine phytoplankton
Arrow, K.J. 55
Asia: deforestation 191; foreign direct
  investment 321; industrialisation 256
asthma 6
Atkins, L.V. 219
Atkinson, G. 68, 127
Atlantic *see* South Atlantic
Austin, D. 260, 279
Australia: increase in fecal pollution of
  rivers 191
Autonomous Energy Efficiency
  Improvement (AEEI) 270–1
Ayres, R. 171

Baldwin, R. 158
Ballard, C.L. 224

Bandyopadhyay, S.: research on EKC with Shafik (SB) 182, 186–7, 190, 191, 192–3, 206

Bangkok: lead pollution 14

Bangladesh: effects of flooding of deltas 10, 245; subsidies for irrigation water 168

Baranzini, A. 75

Barbier, E.B. 36, 38, 48–9, 96

Barker, T. 56, 178, 220, 225, 235, 236, 263, 266, 274, 287

Barnett, H. 2, 35

Barron, J. 150

Barrow, M. 32

Bartelmus, P. 52, 116, 124, 124–5, 126, 127, 128, 135, 140–1

Basel Convention 151

BATNEEC (Best Available Technology Not Entailing Excessive Costs) 302, 309, 310, 312, 314

Becker, G. 55

Beckerman, Wilfred 10, 49; defence of economic growth 42, 43, 46, 47; on national accounting 65, 115, 116, 117

beef: low energy 173

Beijing: falling water tables 17–18

Bellis, A. 150

Bernstam, M. 22, 46, 47, 179

Bhopal: disaster 31

biodiversity: loss of 251, 320; maintenance of 95–6, 97

biomass: natural growth 40, 50, 58; reductions in stock 320; regeneration 169–70; targets for changes in production 112

biophysical approaches: scarcity 35–8

Birdsall, N. 157, 255

birth defects 6

Bishop, R. 93

blue whale: near-extinction of 38

Boero, G. 66, 218, 235, 260, 262

Böhringer, C. 269

Bosch, P. 147

bottles: reusing 173

Bourguignon, F. 75

Bovenberg, A.L. 226, 227–8, 228, 229, 230, 231, 237

BP (The British Petroleum Company plc) 20

Braverman, H. 55

Brazil: study of sustainability 127

Britain *see* United Kingdom

Broad, R. 206

Broome, J. 10–11, 244–5, 246, 255

Brouwer, R. 138

Brown, G.M. 35

Brown, L.R. 6, 9, 11, 12, 14, 15, 17, 18, 19, 21, 57, 171, 177–8, 251

Bruce, J. 255, 260, 262, 273, 280

Brundtland Report (WCED, 1987) 5, 45, 48, 72, 322, 323, 326

Bryant, C. 66, 103

buildings: corrosion through acidification 12, 55, 299, 300

Buitenkamp, M. 90, 151

Burkina Faso: regeneration of degraded land 170

Burniaux, J.-M. 261, 271

Business Council for Sustainable Development 5, 170

Business International 171, 173

businesses: programmes to improve environmental quality 163, 170–4

California: investment in industrial water conservation 171

California Paperboard Corporation 171

Cambridge Econometrics (CE): forecasts of sulphur emissions 308–9, 311–12

campaigns: activism for environmental policy 173, 206

Canada: decline of fish stocks 18; destruction of original forests 16; environmental impacts and GDP 202, **202**

cancer 6, 31

capital: as part of production function 51–2; possible complementarity with energy 273–5; and weak sustainability 77

capital stock: in production process **53**, 54, 63, 76, 99; types 52–3, 105–6

carbon 21

carbon cycle 58

carbon dioxide emissions **7**, 8, **9**, **10**, 90, 196, 245; abatement 4, 66, 97, 112, 246, 260, 271, 273, 275–7, 279–81, 320, 321; aggressive abatement action 253–4; costs of abatement 277–81; EKC studies 187–9, 190, 192, 210; and GDP growth 201–2, **202**; input-output study of UK and West Germany 203, 234; IPCC calculations of cuts needed 159; macroeconomic effects of abatement policy 178; OCF model 322–3; per capita in USA 256; and population growth 158; and responsibility 149–50, 256; *see also* global warming; greenhouse effect

carbon tax 178, 218–19, 220, 229–30, 261–2; effect on business competitiveness 263, 264–7, **265**, 268; effect on UK trade and exports 267–9, **267**; effects of implementation 269–77; model of introduction in UK 264–8, **265**; models showing effects on economies 232–7, **233**, 254, 261–8, 269

car-free mobility 173

Carlyle, Thomas: on political economy 24

cars: lead pollution from exhausts 14

Cavanagh, J. 206

Central Europe: environmental damage 168; health hazards through industrialisation 14

Centre for the Exploitation of Science and Technology (CEST): waste-saving projects 171

CFCs (chlorofluorocarbons) **7**, 8, **9**, 11, 21, 171, 196

Chambers, R. 169

chemicals: pollution 15, 168, 191–2

Chernobyl: disaster 31

Chesapeake Bay 19

Chichilnisky, G. 254

China: decrease in grain growing 21; high costs of global warming 249; lead pollution 14; OCF scenario 323; subsidies for electric power production 168

Christainen, G. 174–5, 177

Ciriacy-Wantrup, S.V. 92–3

cities: uglification 44; *see also* urban areas

civil rights and liberties 72–3, 206

Clark, C. 38–9

Clarke, Kenneth 238

classical approaches 2

Clean Air Act (1956/1968) 302

Cleveland, C. 36, 37–8

climate change 8–11, 55, 70; beneficial

effects for agriculture 245, 249; as constraint on economic growth 242; evaluating costs 242, 243–4, 244–50, **248**, 250–9, 277; mitigation and abatement 95, 242, 243, 253–5, 260–9; and species extinction 21; sustainability approach 143, 279–82; *see also* global warming; greenhouse effect

climate regulation: importance of ecosystems 38, 58; stabilisation 111, 279–82

Cline, W.R. 10, 218, 244, 246; carbon dioxide abatement model 247–9, 251, 252, 253–4, 255, 260, 273, 277, 281

Club of Rome 44

coal: decline in use 287, 288, 308; Jevons's underestimation of stocks 34; OEI time trends 38; rate of scarcity 35; removing subsidies from industry 307, 313, 314; substituting low-sulphur burning type 311, 312, 320; sulphur dioxide emissions 283, 285, 287, 302

Coase, R.H. 26

Cobb, C.W. 126

Cobb, J. 57, 67–8, 126

cod fishing: banning of 39

coke: sulphur dioxide emissions 283, 285

Cole, H.S.D. 41, 42

combined cycle gas turbines (CCGTs) 303, 311, 312, 314

combustion plants *see* Large Combustion Plant Directive (LCPD)

Common Agricultural Policy (CAP) 168

Common, M.S. 1, 80–1

Commoner, B. 155, 156–7, 159

Commoner-Ehrlich equation 3, 154–62, 163, 166, 180–1, 318, 321

communities: involvement in land regeration 169–70; sacrifice of traditional ways of life 44

Conroy, C. 170

construction industry: benefits of warmer climates 245

consumer preferences: need for changes 318, 321, 322, 325

consumption: and calculations of optimisation 75–6, 316–17; Commoner-Ehrlich equation 156, 157–8, 180–1; composition effect 202,

203; of consumer societies 74;
environmental impacts 87–9, **88**, 138,
147, 317–18; higher level in the North
160; need for change in attitude 324; as
outcome of production 63, 159; of
resources in OECD countries 15; rising
levels 6, 47, 57, 325; sacrificing for
climate stability 280–1; social impacts
138; used as welfare measure 66
contingent valuation methods (CVM): of
environmental functions 30–1, 134
Convention on International Trade in
Endangered Species 97
Convention on Long-Range
Transboundary Air Pollution 299,
302
Cook, P. 66, 103
corn: rise in prices 21–2
cost-benefit analysis (CBA): approach to
environmental valuation 242, 249–50,
251, 252, 253–4, 258–9
Costa Rica: development of substitute for
asbestos cement by RICALIT 172;
study of national accounting 116, 125;
study of sustainability 127
critical loads: concept 92; for ecosystems
99, 105, 111, 299–300; emissions 96;
sulphur depositions in Europe 308,
310
croplands: degradation through poor
agricultural practices 16–17; reduced
productivity 6
Cropper, M.: research on EKC with
Griffiths (CG) 191, 193
crops: acidification 11–12, 12, 299;
damage by UV-B 21; destruction of by
extreme weather 252
cultural perspectives: consumer
preferences 318; implications of
unsustainability 31; sustainable
development 326
Czech Republic: destruction of forests
through acidification 12

Daly, Herman E. 1, 43, 45, 57, 58–9,
67–8, 76, 95, 160, 325
Dasgupta, P. 35, 65, 75, 124, 229
Davis, S. 206
De Boer, B. 143

De Bruyn, S.M. 200–1, 206, 210
De Groot, R.S. 79–80, 83, 258
De Mooij, R.A. 226, 227–8, 228, 229,
230, 231
De Souza, 81
Dean, J. 203, 260, 269, 271
deaths: due to impacts of greenhouse
effect 245, 248, 250, 259; from hunger
and malnutrition 251, 253
defensive expenditures 3, 138–40, 141,
152
deforestation **7**, 8, 16, 17, 21, 31, 191,
208; *see also* forests; tropical forests
delinking: of biophysical throughput 155,
166, 200
dematerialisation 59–60, 160, 323
Demeritt, D. 247
democracy: and public pressure for
change 206, 207; relationship with
sustainability 73
Denmark: introduction of environmental
taxation 237, 268
Department of Energy (DEn) 305
Department of the Environment (DOE)
112, 305, 311
Department of the Environment,
Transport and the Regions (DETR) 18,
69
Department of Health (DOH) 14
Department of Trade and Industry (DTI):
EP65 forecasts of sulphur emission
308–9, 311–12
desertification 31, 166
developing countries: economic growth
and environmental degradation 210;
malnutrition 251; need for economic
growth 46, 48; OCF scenario on
sustainable development 323; studies of
sustainability 127
development: debate about constitution of
62; indicators 66, 201; and
industrialisation 205; and production
61, 121, 316; as vector of desirable
social objectives 63; and welfare
61–4; *see also* economic development;
industrial development; sustainable
development
Diamond, P. 30–1, 229
diseases *see* tropical diseases

Dobris Assessment see European
  Environmental Agency (EEA)
Douthwaite, R. 57
Dow Chemical Co. (Louisiana) 171
Dowlatabadi, H. 255, 260
DRI: report on environmental taxation
  178, 232, **233**, 234
drought 16–17
Duchin, F. 322–3, 324
Dutch Central Bureau of Statistics 144

Eagan, V. 33
Earth Summit *see* United Nations
  Conference on Environment and
  Development (UNCED)
East Germany: costs of reducing sulphur
  dioxide levels in 1980 306
Eastern Europe: health hazards through
  industrialisation 14; sulphur emissions
  13
Eastern Group 312–13
ecocentrism 73, 106
eco-labelling 149
Ecological Footprint (EF) 89–90, 147, 151
ecological (or natural) capital 52, 53–4,
  55, 57–8, 63, 76, 77, 79, 124, 137, 140;
  elements 78, 105, 122; failure of
  national accounts to assess 115, 123–4;
  manufactured capital as substitute 80;
  overconsumption 143–4; role in
  production and welfare creation 98–9,
  98; satellite account 128–9; studies on
  depletion 125–6, 127
ecological space 151, 160
ecological sustainability 70, 71, 80–1; *see
  also* sustainability
econometric relationships: EKC
  hypothesis 185–95
economic development: scale, technique
  and composition effects on environment
  162, 201, 204; *see also* development
economic distribution: dividend from
  environmental taxation 219–20; equity
  regarding climate change 255–9; need
  for change in attitude 324
economic growth: constraints of climate
  change 242; in developing countries 46,
  48, 210; different kinds 2, 40, 50,
  56–61; enhancement by protecting the

environment 166; as leading to
  improved environmental standards
  183–4; linked with welfare 50, 56,
  56–7, 64; modern desire for 325–6;
  physical limits 44, 242; possible benefits
  of carbon tax 275; projected rates for
  Western Europe and North America
  323–4; as quantitative increase 64;
  relationship with energy use 45–6;
  relationship with environmental
  sustainability 1–3, 4–5, 22, 23, 39, 48,
  71, 79–80, 104, 112, 153, 160, 162,
  178–9, 201, 210, 283, 314, 316–26;
  social costs 43–4; theories of wealth
  creation 51–6
economic sustainability 75–8, 79–80, 82,
  104, 105–6
ecosystems: critical loads 99, 105, 111,
  314; damage through acidification 12,
  299–300; damage through extinction of
  species 15–16, 31, 38, 39; decline and
  resilience 80–1, 95–6, 320; destruction
  of by greenhouse effect 244; and the
  human economy 59; importance of 38;
  impossibility of assigning monetary
  value to 83; ozone loss 11; protection
  95; stable 55; sustainability standard
  310; valuation of services 257–8
ECOTEC 139, 300, 305
Ecuador: mackerel fishing 39
education: expenditures as component of
  human capital creation 121, 127
efficiency: dividend from environmental
  taxation 219, 223–4, 228, 234–7;
  necessity of regulations 282; *see also* use-
  efficiency
Egypt: effects of flooding of deltas 10, 245;
  losses in wheat yields 251
Ehrlich, A. 156
Ehrlich, P. 155–6, 157; *see also*
  Commoner-Ehrlich equation
Eisner, Robert 116, 121, 153
Ekins, P. 52, 68–9, 228, 247, 280, 312
El Serafy, S. 102–3, 114, 135–6, 146,
  153
electricity: conservation projects 172;
  increased needs for air conditioning
  244, 247; rate of scarcity 35; rise in
  consumption 289, 294; subsidies for

production of 168; sulphur emission limits on US utilities 306

electricity supply industry (ESI): meeting sulphur limits 283, 309–13, 314

Emissions Monitoring and Evaluating Programme (EMEP) 299, 302

emphysema 6

employment: dividend from environmental taxation 220–4, 230–1, 232–4, 238, 240, 322; effect of environmental taxation 227–8; and sense of identity 74

Endangered Species Act (USA) 104

energy: backstop technologies to compete with fossil fuels 280, 281; conservation projects 171, 172, 271; efficiency 37, 97, 270–3, **272**, 276, 280, 282, 286–7; environmentally damaging policies 169; non-carbon sources 279; possible complementarity with capital 273–5; price rises 261–2, 263, 269, 273–5; removing subsidies 281; renewable sources 97, 280; sectoral value-added and sulphur dioxide emissions 289–99, **290–3**, 294–9, **295–6, 298**, 313; use and GDP growth 45–6, 202, **202**

energy industries: UK sulphur dioxide emissions 285, 288

energy return on investment (EROI) 35

energy-intensive industries: and environmental taxation 225, 268–9, 274

Ensing, B. 147

entropy: and decrease by solar energy 99, 320; increase of 43, 56–7, 320

Environment Agency (EA): regulation of sulphur emissions 309–10, 313, 314

environmental accounting 128–37; schema for balance sheet **130**

Environmental Challenge Group (ECG) 63

environmental damage: in CEE and former USSR countries 168; continuation of 210–11; costs 82–3, 104, 133–7, 152, 177–8, 281; EKC turning points 208, **209**; failure of national accounts to assess 121–2, 128; from climate change 255; from sulphur emissions 283

environmental degradation: costs of

prevention 127–8, 135, 145; critical zones 92–3; EC countries 196–7; economic ideas 25–31, 122–3; estimating value of ecological capital stock 125; exacerbation by growth of economic activity 48, 121–2, 179, 210; from stresses of production 154; immoderate losses 92–3, 94; implications 5–6, 22; ISEW consideration of 67, 126; prevention expenditures 127–8, 135; relationship with income 182–4; and scarcity of resources 23; types covered by NAMEA 144

environmental distance: valuation 133–7, **133**

environmental functions 29, 79–80, 81, 154, 316; classification 109–10; competition between 79, 84, 86, 94, 98; contribution to human welfare 106, 137; costs 84–5, 137; difficulties in valuing 124, 205, 316; setting sustainable levels 82–4, **83**, 90, 101, 111

environmental goods: contribution to welfare 75–6, 104

environmental growth 57–8

environmental impact coefficient (EIC) 154–6, 165, 166

environmental index: for OECD and COMECON countries 200

Environmental Kuznets Curve (EKC) hypothesis 3–4, 180, 182–4, 322; econometric relationships 185–95; evidence of invalidity 193, 196–7, 200, 210; implications of studies 208–10; income/population distribution **209**; testing against environmental indicators 198–200, 201–8; turning points **209**, 210–11

environmental media: alternative classifications 108–9, **109**

environmental policy: constraints on growth or productivity 174–6, 317; debates 179–80; and gains in productivity 166, 167, 173, 176–7, 178–9; necessity for 207–8, 211, 238, 240–1; as outcome of public pressure 206, 207; towards sustainability 2,

50, 94, 111–12, 163, **164**, 318–19, 325
environmental protection 131, 166; expenditure 137, 139–40, 307; industry 173
Environmental Protection Act (1990) 309
Environmental Protection Expenditure Account (EPEA) 139
environmental quality: approach to estimating impacts of trade 148; econometric relationships with income 185–95, **186**, **188–9**, 211, **211–13**; improving 163, 165, 240; increase in demand for 183, 205, 207; maintenance costs 135, 139, 141–2, 142–3, 240; social costs 124; and welfare 63
environmental regulations: costs of compliance 174–5, 176–7; costs of conforming to in US 172–3, 175; and economic competitiveness 172, 264; first-mover advantages 173
environmental resources 2; categorisation of 108; as contribution to production 52, 53, 56, 63, 115, 137; depletion 67, 84, 122, 123–4, 135–6; depletion accounted for by NAMEA 144, 152; as ecological/natural capital 78, 122; ensured access to 43, 63; exhaustibility and extinction 31–9; failure of national accounts to assess 116, 123, 124, 125–6, 128; Green GNP calculation of costs 152; long-term price trends 47; monetary valuation of 129, 242, 317; per capita use and pollution 151; perceptions of scarcity 23–50; and redefining production boundary of national accounts 123; reducing depletion 41–2, 45; setting minimum life expectancy 100–1, 102; sustainability equation 99–101
environmental services 52, 54, 55, 98, 99
environmental space methodology 90, 159
environmental sustainability *see* sustainability
environmental taxation 4, 26–8, 169, 178, 215–31, 264, 322; with abatement **217**; dividends 232–7, 240–1, 275; economic benefits 240–1; evidence from

implementation 237–40; introduction in OECD countries 237, 238–40, **239**; and investment opportunities 275; simulation models showing dividends 231–7, **233**; without abatement **215**; *see also* carbon tax
environmental themes 108, 109, **109**
environmental utilisation space (EUS) 90, 147; *see also* global environmental space
environmental valuation 28–31, 83
Environmentally Adjusted Domestic Product (EDP) 140, 141, 142
Environmentally Sustainable National Income (ESNI) 137, 142, 143
equity: enhancement of 106, 108; perspectives on climate change 255–9
ethical perspectives: environmental taxation 220; judging unsustainability 94; social and spiritual welfare 106; on sustainability 70, 71, 72–3, 81–2, 104, 106; valuation of ecosystem services 257–8; *see also* morality
Europe: critical load for sulphur depositions 314; depletion of water supplies in some countries 18; disappearance of original forests 16; energy use 46; global environmental space calculations **91**; sulphur deposition and forest damage 12; *see also* Central Europe; Eastern Europe; Western Europe
European Commission: commissioning of DRI report on environmental dividend 232; Communication to the Council and European Parliament 116–17; Directives on sulphur emissions 302, 306, 307–8, 311; ExternE project 247, 257, 300, **301**, 305; lack of support for EKC hypothesis 184, 210; member-countries' progress with environmental problems 195, 196, 202; proposed carbon/energy tax 236, 267; support for environmental taxes and the employment dividend 238
European Commission Directorate General XII (ECDGXII) 143
European Community (EC): approach to indicators of environmental sustainability 108, 109; Fifth Action

Programme 6, 15, 116; high tax
revenues 224
European Environmental Agency (EEA):
Dobris Assessment 8, 11, 16, 17, 18,
196
European Science and Environment
Foundation (ESEF) 10
European System for the Collection of
Economic Information on the
Environment (SERIEE) 139
European System of Integrated Economic
and Environmental Indices 144
European Union (EU): environmental
space methodology calculations for 159;
policy of integrated environmental
economic accounting 151; studies of
economies and effect of environmental
taxation 232, **233**, 268–9
EUROSTAT 117, 139
eutrophication 6, 143
Ewerhart, G. 143
exports: consumption 151–3; effect of
carbon tax on UK sectors 267–9, **267**;
pollutants 147
externalities: and environmental taxes
169, 215, 218, 223, 227, 229, 230; and
failure of resource allocation 42, 174;
negative 63, 138, 215, 218, 272;
Pigouvian description 25–6
ExternE project 247, 257, 300, **301**,
305
Eyre, N. 247, 249, 255, 257

Faber, M. 56, 81, 123–4, 138, 140
'Factor Four' 173–4
factor inputs: substitutions between 41, 52,
155
Fankhauser, S. 247–9, 250–1, 252–3, 256,
259, 281
farmland: loss of 126
Farrow, S. 33
Faucheux, S. 143
fertilisers: nitrogen 202, **202**
Field, B. 35
Finland: introduction of carbon tax 237
fires: pollution from 13
First Conference of the Parties on Climate
Change (Berlin) 97
fish: depletion 12, 18–19, 21; harvesting

levels 96; threatened species 16; toxic
pollution 18–19; UV-B radiation 21
Fisher, A. 35
fisheries: decline and destruction of 6, **7**,
18, 39, 70; environmentally damaging
policies 169; global damage to 63;
Newfoundland 39; OEI time trends 37;
studies on depletion of ecological
capital 125
Flavin, C. 9, 12
flooding: due to sea-level rise 10, 244–5
flue-gas desulphurisation (FGD) 204, 287,
303, 305, 309, 311, 312–13, 321
Folke, C. 95–6
food: danger from industrial waste 15;
need for shift in consumer preferences
321; production of supplies 58;
reducing environmental impacts on
production 166; scarcity 21; unequal
distribution 251
forestry: beneficial effects of climate
change 245; damaging effects of climate
change 248; environmentally damaging
policies 169; OEI time trends 37
forests: acidification 11–12, 21; depletion
70, 125, 248; global damage to 63;
products 35; reduced productivity 6;
replanting 96, 260; studies on
depletion of ecological capital 125;
see also deforestation; tropical
forests
fossil fuels: depletion 19, 31, 70, 280;
emissions 8, **9**, 11, 15, 97, 245, 256,
320; environmentally damaging policies
169; need to reduce consumption 261;
OEI time trends 37–8; photovoltaic
substitution 89–90; switching with non-
combustion fuels 287; *see also* carbon
dioxide emissions; coal; energy
Framework Convention on Climate
Change (FCCC) 256, 277
France: environmental impacts and GDP
202, **202**, 204
Friends of the Earth (FOE) 155; use of
environmental space methodology 90,
159, 160
fuel oil: decline in sulphur dioxide
emissions 283–5, 287, 288
fuels: reducing sulphur intensity 286, 287,

303, 305–6; substitution possibilities 261, 303, 311, 312, 314, 320–1; *see also* fossil fuels

Gabon 20
Gärtner, M. 253
gas: depletion of North Sea reserves 103; forecast depletion timespan 314; as premium fuel 311; rate of scarcity 35; reserves 19, 20; substitution for coal in power generation 287, 288, 294, 299, 308, 312, 320, 321
Gaskins, D.W. 218, 232, 234, 235–6, 278
General Agreement on Tariffs and Trade (GATT) 149
general equilibrium models 231; greenhouse effect 261–2
Georgescu-Roegen, N. 35–6, 43
German Advisory Council on Global Change 97
Germany: benefits of first-mover advantages 173; destruction of trees through acidification 12; environmental protection expenditures 128; global environmental space calculations **91**; *see also* East Germany; West Germany
Global Environmental Monitoring System (GEMS) 193
global environmental space 90–2
global warming 8–11, 244, 246–50; aggressive abatement action 253–4, 255; damage function 235; deforestation as cause 21; estimating costs of damage 27, 31, 244, 246–50, **248**, **249**; IPCC report 159, 244; reducing environmental impacts of 166; uncertainties 247–9, 254; win–win opportunities in economics 282; *see also* climate change; greenhouse effect
globalisation: damage to social community 74–5
Glyn, A. 324
Goldin, I. 1
Goldschmidt-Clermont, L. 120, 129
Gollop, F. 306
Goodland, R. 160
goods and services: economic and environmental 138–9, 317; in national accounts 117–19

Goulder, L.H. 226, 227, 228, 229, 230, 237, 240, 258
governments: commitments to environmental sustainability 84, 111–12; and decision-making 87; economically and environmentally flawed policies 163, 319; failure to protect environment 168–70, 319; UK avoidance of setting sustainability indicators 112, 314; UK headline welfare indicators 69
Graaff, J. de V. 65, 68
grain: depletion of stocks 21
grasslands: reduced productivity 6
Gray, W. 204
Greece: study using net savings rule 127
Green GNP and GDP 142, 143, 146, 147, 152
greenhouse effect **7**, **9**, 244; *see also* climate change; global warming
greenhouse gases (GGs) 21; emissions in OECD countries 15; establishing responsibility for emissions 255–6; and global warming 8, **9**, 246, 247; problems in EC countries 196; reducing 4, 260, 277; stabilisation 4, 8, **9**, 95, 111, 159; *see also* carbon dioxide; CFCs; nitrous oxides
Greenpeace *see* Stockholm Environment Institute/Greenpeace (SEI/G)
Grennfelt, P. 300
Griffiths, C.: research on EKC with Cropper (CG) 191, 195
Gross Domestic Product (GDP) 40, 50, 57, 78, 119; conditions for compatibility with sustainability 78, 155, 165–6, 178; decreases shown in models simulating effects of carbon tax 234–5, 262–3, 277–8, 279–80; and economic aid to developing countries 323; effects of environmental policy 178, 306–7; energy use per unit 45–6; and environmental degradation in poor countries 182; exclusion of non-monetary production in national accounting 119–20; fall in energy intensities 273; growth and environmental impacts 201–3, **202**; improving as indicator of production

140–1; increases shown in models simulating effects of carbon tax 234, 269; as indicator of progress 140; reduction of growth rate in US due to environmental regulation 175; relationship with welfare 57; in study of toxic pollution 192

Gross National Product (GNP) 3, 12, 40, 50, 57, 58, 59–61, 119, 129; decoupling 43, 46, 59; effect of environmental policy measures 162; failure to account for natural resources 116, 122; growth of as principal objective in consumer societies 74; impacts of instruments for sustainability targets 112; inappropriateness as production indicator 69; inappropriateness as welfare indicator 65–6, 66–7, 68, 69; income measured by 64–5; relating environmental accounts to 137–47; relationship with sustainable development 61–2, 163; and resource misallocations 42, 123, 174; and 'sustainability gap' figure 86

Gross Nature Product 58

Grossman, G. 162; research on EKC (G) 185–6, 191–2; research on EKC with Krueger (GK) 182, 185–6, 187, 191–2, 193, 201, 205, 207–8

groundwater: reducing pesticide concentrations 85

'growthmania' 45

Grubb, M. 250, 274, 276

Hadley Centre: modelling of effects of climate change 245

Haiti: regeneration of degraded land 170

Halkos, G. 303–4, 305

Hall, D. 38

Hall, J. 38

Hamilton, K. 124, 127

Hampson, C. 277

Hanemann, W.M. 31

Hanley, N. 241

Hardoy, J. 71

Harihar Polyfibres: implementing of resource efficiency programme 171

Harrison, A. 52, 121, 129, 135

Harrison, P. 170

Hartwick, J. 65, 76, 123, 124, 140

Hausman, J.A. 30–1

HCFCs (hydrochlorofluorocarbons) 21

Heal, G. 32, 35, 254

health: damage from environmental degradation and pollution 13–15, 55, 86, 99, 128, 205, 251; damage from sulphur emissions 283, 300; damage through unsustainability of resources 31, 70; increase in demand for quality 183; maintaining low environmental impacts on 111; as part of human capital 63, 121; protection through environmental regulation 174; and standards of air and water quality 105; *see also* human welfare

Heintz, R.J. 200–1, 206, 210

Helsinki Protocol: on sulphur dioxide emissions 302, 303

Her Majesty's Inspectorate of Pollution (HMIP): regulation of sulphur emissions 309, **309**, 310, 312, 313

Herfindahl, O. 65, 122

Hettige, H. 192

HFCs (hydrofluorocarbons) **9**, 21

Hicks, J. 119, 130

Hirsch, F. 44–5, 74, 207

Hoeller, P. 260, 269, 271

Hogan, W.W. 270–1, 274, 277

Hohmeyer, O. 253, 300

Holdren, J. 155–6, 157

holidays: need for shift in consumer preferences 321

Holmberg, J. 7, 48, 49

Holtz-Eakin, D.: research on EKC with Selden (HES) 183, 187–90, 194

Hon, A. 52

Honduras: regeneration of degraded land 170

Hope, C. 251

Horvath, R.J. 190

Hotelling's Rule 32–3, 34–5

Houghton, J. 10, 11, 244, 279

Hueting, R. 47, 97, 123, 140, 179; on environmental functions 79, 84; method of determining maximum sustainable rate of depletion 100, 101–2, 103, 136; on welfare 57, 64, 68

human capital 52, 53, 76, 105; failure of national accounts to assess 120; indicators 108; and welfare 55, 63
Human Development Index (HDI) 66
human life: loss of due to global warming 251, 252, 281; valuation of loss of 248–9, 252–3, 256–8
human ways of life: environmental sustainability 79–80; unsustainability 70, 81–2, 85–6, 92
human welfare *see* welfare
hunger: deaths from 253; increase in 6
hurricanes: increase due to greenhouse effect 244
hydro power 287, 323
hydrocarbons: NEPP calculations of necessary cuts in emissions 159; *see also* fossil fuels

identity: sense of 74
imports: consumption and environmental impacts 147, 148–51; pollutants 148
income: econometric relationships with environmental indicators 182, 185–95, **186**, **188–9**, **199**, 201–8, 211, **211–13**; and economic welfare 76; effect of rising rates 206–7; in Hicksian sense 119, 122, 137, 146; inequality of distribution in UK 62; limiting inequality 45; link with pollution 180, 208; as measured by GNP or NNP 64–5; and population 208, **209**
Index of Socio-Economic Welfare (ISEW) 67–8, 122, 126, 140
India: implementing of resource efficiency programme by Harihar Polyfibres 171; OCF scenario 323; regeneration of degraded land 169, 170; subsidies for irrigation water 168
individualism: and consumption 74; undermining of morality 45
Indonesia 20; deforestation 16; study of national accounting 116, 125–6
Industrial Air Pollution Inspectorate (England and Wales) 302
industrial development: pollutants 13, 183

Industrial Pollution Inspectorate (Scotland) 302
industrial waste: emissions in OECD countries 15; pollution 166, 167, 203
industrialisation 46, 78, 183, 205, 256
INFRAS: review of studies on effect of carbon tax on economies 229–30, 234, 237
Ingham, A. 269–70, 270, 277
institutional capital 121
institutions: production and wealth creation 55, 63, 121; *see also* social institutions
integrated economic and environmental accounting (IEEA) 52, 117, 124, 132, 137, 151–3; SNA satellite system 129
Intergovernmmental Panel on Climatic Change (IPCC) 10, 159, 244, 246, 247, 254–5, 257, 259, 260, 273, 279
International Energy Agency 46
International Institute for Applied Systems Analysis (IIASA), 304
International Institute for Environment and Development (IIED) 149, 151
International Monetary Fund (IMF) 304
International Whaling Commission 38
investment: and carbon reduction 279; effects of changing relative price of energy 273–5; and implementing environmental taxation 263; and pollution control and abatement 306–7
Iran 20
Iraq 20
Ireland: study using net savings rule 127
irreversibility: in matters of sustainability 90, 97; species extinction 104
Irvine, S. 179
Italy: environmental impacts and GDP **202**

Jackson, T. 63, 68, 271
Jacobs, M. 154, 271
Jaeger, W.K. 75–6
Jänicke, M. 200
Jaffe, A. 176–7, 204
Japan: benefits of first-mover advantages 173; effects of carbon tax on economy 236; environmental impacts and GDP

202, **202**, 204; growth in global
sustainability 150; increase in fecal
pollution of rivers 191; tax system
224
Jaszi, G. 138
Jenkins, T. 168
Jesinghaus, J. 28
Jevons, W.S. 34
jobs *see* employment; unemployment
Johnstone, N. 220
Jorgenson, D. 52, 120, 175, 178, 218,
224, 235, 237, 263, 270–1, 274
Juster, F.T. 122
justice 72–3, 255, 258

Kahn, H. 179
Kane, H. 9, 12
Kapp, K.W. 43
Karlsson, S. 7
Kennedy, D. 258
Keuning, S. 142
Klaassen, G. 303, 304, 305, 306, 307, 313
Kneese, A. 65, 122
Kosmo, M. 169
Kristensen, J.P. 268
Krueger, A. 162; research on EKC with
Grossman (GK) 182, 185–6, 187,
191–2, 193, 201, 205, 207–8
Krutilla, J.V. 52
Kula, E. 303
Kuwait 20
Kuznets, S. 122, 123

labour: as part of human capital 55, 120;
as part of production function 51–2, 55;
productivity 318, 322; subsidies from
environmental taxation 220–1, **221**,
230–1
labour-intensive industries 225
Labrador: decline of fish stocks 18
lakes: acidification 12, 299; carbon
concentrations in North America 21;
sulphur sediments 21
land: changes in use **7**, **9**; degradation **7**,
16–17, **17**, 21, 48, 91, 126, 191; as
ecological capital 54; Ecological
Footprint analysis 89–90; effects of
flooding of deltas 10; loss of due to
climate change 244, 249, 250–1, 281;

as part of production function 51–2;
and population growth 23–4;
regeneration of 169–70; unsustainable
use of 170; *see also* croplands; soils;
wetlands
landscape: effects of agricultural policy 85;
loss of **7**; preservation of 96; reduction
of beauty 55, 244
Lange, G.-M. 322–3, 324
Large Combustion Plant Directive
(LCPD) 302, 306, 307–8, **307**, 311
Latin America: deforestation 191;
extinction of species 16
lead: European progress in reducing
emissions 196; pollution 14, 192
Lecomber, R. 41–2, 60, 154–5, 161,
162–3, 166, 174
Leipert, C. 57, 127–8, 138, 140
Lélé, S. 49
Lewney, R. 178
Libya 20
lifestyles: need for shift in consumer
preferences 322
'limits to growth': ideas and debates 2, 23,
40–5, 45, 47–8, 49–50, 60, 183, 242,
326; Meadows model 40–1; as
sustainable development 40, 325
Litvinoff, M. 170
local communities: and sense of identity
74
Lockwood, B. 256
Lone, Ø. 129
Long, B.L. 195
Lovins, A.B. and H.L. 271
Low, P. 203
Lucas, R. 192, 203
Lutz, E. 116, 124–5, 128, 153

McCormick, J. 12, 13
MacGillivray, A. 156, 197
MacKenzie, D. 39
mackerel fishing: Pacific 39
McLaren, D. 90, 151
macro-economic models 231
macroeconomy: adjusting aggregates for
Green GNP 152; costs and effects of
environmental policy 175–6, 177, 178;
costs of pollution 303; costs of sulphur
dioxide abatement 306–7; effects of

environmental tax 218, 225, 236; impacts of instruments for sustainability targets 112; management by national accounts 116

Maddison, D. 169

Mäler, K.-G. 124, 138

Majocchi, A. 233

malnutrition: deaths from 251

Malthus, T. 2, 23, 23–5, 34

mangroves: pollution and destruction of 18

Manne, A.S. 254, 261, 270, 271, 277, 278

manufactured capital 52, 53, 76, 105, 137; depreciation 140, 142; indicators 108; as substitute for natural capital 78, 80

manufacturing: erosion of profitability 24; model of UK sectors and energy–output ratio 269–70; and pollution 192

marine phytoplankton: damage by UV-B 11, 21

Markandya, A. 134

Marks, N. 63, 68

Marshall, A. 35, 78

Massachusetts Institute of Technology (MIT) 40

Max-Neef, M. 55, 69

Meadows, D.H. 11, 19, 22, 40–1, 44, 46, 47, 158, 179

Meadows, D.L. 40–1

Measure of Economic Welfare (MEW) 66–7, 140

metals: OEI time trends 37

methane 8, **9**, 196

Mexico: environmental protection measures 128, 193; study of national accounting 116, 125, 126–7; subsidies for electric power production 168

Meyer, B. 143

Mez, L. 305

Middle East: depletion of water supplies 18; natural gas reserves 20

migration: problems of resettlement 251; as result of sea-level rises 245, 247, 249, 251

Milborrow, I. 134

Miles, I. 68

Miljøverndepartementet accent 325

Mill, John Stuart 25

minerals: depletion 19, 31; R/P ratios **20**

minimum life expectancy: of resources 100–1, 102, 103, 113

Mirrlees, J. 229

Mishan, E.J. 43–4, 57, 255

Montreal Protocol 11, 97

morality: as basis for environmental concerns 72; undermining of 44–5; *see also* ethics

Moran, D. 30

Morgan, M.G. 260

Morse, C. 2, 35

Multisectoral Dynamic Model: of UK economy 287–9

Munasinghe, M. 81

Myers, Norman 15–16, 169

NAFTA agreement: Salinas and environmental protection 193

National Academy of Sciences (NAS) 6, 260

National Accounting Matrix including Environmental Accounts (NAMEA) 144–5, **145**, 152

national accounts: case for adjusting 115–17, 137, 152–3; causes for concern 119–23; construction 117–19; environmental adjustments 3, 123–37, 140–1, 152–3; failure to assess natural capital 115, 123–4; flows of money **118**; inappropriateness as welfare indicators 65, 66, 112; linking sustainability to 144; as poor measure of production 69, 115; *see also* System of National Accounts (SNA)

National Grid Company: Seven Year Statement 311

national product 117–19, 140; *see also* Net National product (NNP)

natural capital *see* ecological (or natural) capital

Nentjes, A. 303, 306, 307, 313

Nepal: regeneration of degraded land 170

Net National Product (NNP) 119, 129, 152; accounting for environmental assets and costs 130, 141–2, 174; failure to assess ecological/natural capital 122;

income measured by 64–5; used as welfare indicator 65–6, 122, 141
net savings concept 127, 150
Netherlands: global environmental space calculations **91**; introduction of carbon tax 237; NAMEA 152; NEPP 112, 159, 178, 320; *see also* Dutch Central Bureau of Statistics
New England Electric (NEE): energy conservation projects 172
new technologies *see* technological progress; technologies
Newbery, D. 311
Newfoundland: Grand Banks cod fishery 39
Niger: regeneration of degraded land 170
Nigeria 20
Nile, River: problem of sharing water resources 18
Nilsson, J. 299–300
nitrates: land degradation 17; pollution of water 196
nitrogen: damage to European forests 12; pollution of rivers 18–19
nitrogen dioxide emissions 13, 245; EKC studies 187, 192, 194–5, 210; and GDP growth 201–2, **202**; OCF model 322–3; taxation 237
nitrogen oxides: emissions in EC countries 196; emissions in OECD countries 15
nitrous oxide 8, **9**
noise levels: costs of pollution as measured by ISEW 126; as qualitative competition 84; rise in 44; road traffic 85
non-renewable resources: depletion 6–7, 19–20, 31, 70, 96, 113, 114, 122, 126, 145–6; emissions 90; optimal depletion 39; price movements 32, 35; strong sustainability formula 113; sustainable use of 2, 100, 101, 102–3
Nordhaus, William 66–7, 68, 224, 235; on climate change 246, 247, 254, 255, 260, 261, 277, 278, 279, 280–1; limits to growth model 41, 47, 48, 51–2
North America: Ecological Footprint analysis 89–90; interlinkages of damaging environmental effects 21;

projected rates of growth in OCF scenario 323–4
Northern Telecom 171
North–South distinctions 321–2, 324
Norway: destructive effects of acidification 12; introduction of energy taxes 237, 268; physical environmental and resource accounts 129, 132
Norwegian Green Tax Commission 268
Nova Scotia: decline of fish stocks 18
nuclear power 97, 169, 204, 287, 294, 320, 323
nuclear weapons: manufacturing facilities 177
Nyborg, K. 140

Oates, W. 29–30
oceans: pollution 44
OCF scenario 322–4
oil: depletion of North Sea reserves 103; fall in prices 127; low-sulphur burning type 311; OEI time trends 37–8; rate of scarcity 35; reserves 19, 20; studies of depletion of ecological capital 125
Oliveira-Martins, J. 268–9
Oosterhuis, F. 169
OPEC (Organisation of Petroleum-Exporting countries): oil reserves 20, 263
Opschoor, J.B. 90, 200, 201, 237
optimal depletion: private and social 33; unsustainability of resources 39
optimality: compatibility with unsustainability 75, 316–17
Organisation for Economic Cooperation and Development (OECD): approach to indicators of environmental sustainability 108, 109; on environmental regulation 168, 173, 175–6, 177, 264, 306; fall in countries' sulphur emissions 12; INTERLINK model of investments in pollution control 306–7; lack of support for EKC hypothesis 184, 210; member-countries acceding to Polluter Pays Principle 73; member-countries' consumption of resources and resulting pollution 15; member-countries' costs of reducing carbon dioxide emissions 273; member-

countries' need for protection against sea-level rise 250; member-countries' progress with environmental problems 195–6, 202–3; member-countries in study using net savings rule 127; report on taxation of petrol in member-countries 237, **238**; reports on environmental taxation in member-countries 237, 238–40, **239**, 241, 264; study of Swedish implementation of environmental taxes 239–40; survey of economic instruments for environmental protection 238; survey of member-countries' environmental performances 197–200, **198**, **199**

organisational capital *see* social/organisational capital

output: changes in composition 41, 155; of the economic process 54; of total economy-environment system 138

output per energy input (OEI) 35–8

ozone: air pollution 8, 14, 55, 196

ozone depletion **7**, 11, 21, 70, 166; difficulty of establishing costs of environmental damage 27, 31; phasing out substances causing 97; reducing impacts to sustainability levels 143; safeguarding 95

Pacific Ocean: mackerel fishing 39

Palmer, K. 172–3

Panayotou, T.: research on EKC (P) 182–3, 183–4, 186, 187, 192, 193–4, 194–5, 205, 208

Pangare, G. and V. 170

Papua New Guinea: study of national accounting 116

Parris, B. 57, 60

Parry, I. 226, 227, 228, 230

particulates: air pollution 14; EKC studies 187–90, 194–5; European progress in reducing emissions 196, 302

Pearce, D. 49, 53, 83, 127, 247, 257, 259, 300; on development and welfare 63, 64, 68; on environmental taxation 26, 216, 218; on environmental valuation 28, 30, 33–4, 83

Pearce, F. 39

Pearson, M. 220

Perrings, C. 80–1, 81

pesticides 17, 85, 151

Peterson, A. 287

Pethig, R. 228, 230

petrol: taxation in OECD countries 237, **238**

Pezzey, J. 73, 75, 76, 79, 264, 267, 277

Philippines: poverty and environmental activism 206

philosophical perspectives: valuing ecosystem services 258

phosphates: land degradation 17

phosphorus: pollution of rivers 18–19

physical capital 52

Pigou, A.C. 25–6, 120

Pigouvian tax: and external costs of pollution 26–7, **27**, 230

Pimm, S. 38

plants: damage from industrial waste 15; destruction of by greenhouse effect 244; as medicinal source 38

Poland: acidification of trees 12; lead pollution of soils in Katowice 14; subsidies for electric power production 168

political perspectives: environmental sustainability 319; environmental taxation 220

Polluter Pays Principle 73, 89

pollution 7; abatement measures and compliance with regulations 174–5, 178, 203–4; ability to control 41, 176; and adjusting national accounts 123; calculations of costs 126–7, 134–5, 300, 303; critical load 105; domestic emissions 87–9; environmental impacts 87–9, **88**; and environmental taxation 216–18; from industrial development 13, 183; global flows of emissions **209**; health impacts 14–15; increases 56–7, 203; intensities **167**; investment in control measures 174, 176, 306–7; link with income 180, 208; and Pigouvian tax 26–7, **27**; in production process 54–5, 121–2; reducing environmental impacts 166; soil 44, 196; transfrontier flows 148; urban 6, 244; valuation in environmental accounting 134–5; *see also* acidification; air pollution;

Environmental Kuznets Curve (EKC) hypothesis; toxic pollution; water pollution; under pollutants

Pollution Prevention Pays (3P) 171

population: and distribution of world income 208, **209**; and environmental impacts of consumption 155–6, 157–8

population growth 57, 160, 316; and carbon dioxide emissions 158; Commoner-Ehrlich equation 156, 157–8, 180–1; and competition between environmental functions 79; and environmental space calculations 90–2, 159; and global food supply 21, 250–1; limiting 45; Malthus's theory 23–4, 34; Ricardo's theory 23, 34; stabilising 321

Porter, M.: win–win hypothesis 172–3, 176

Portney, P.R. 31

Portugal: study using net savings rule 127

positional goods: increasing demand 44, 207

poverty: alleviation by regeneration of land 169–70; argument for economic growth 43, 48; as cause of environmental degradation 72, 158, 205, 206; and dependency on resources 206–7; economic sustainability 71; and social injustice 74; in the UK 62

power generation sector: high sulphur intensity 289, 313; increased use of gas 287, 288, 294, 299; national limits 4; necessary technological development 314–15

power stations: control of sulphur emissions 307–9, 310–11; substitution of gas for coal 308; UK sulphur dioxide emissions 285, 310

Precautionary Principle 39, 97

primary environmental care (PEC): concept 49

production: capital stocks **53**, 54, 63; composition effect 202, 203, 204, 205; contribution of environmental resources 52, 53, 56, 63, 115, 137, 316; and development 61, 121, 316; energy use 225, 289; environmental impacts 87–9, **88**, 121–2, 128, 138, 147, 154, 317–18,

324–5; growth of 57, 157; increasing value-added 154–5, 324–5; linked with utility 2, 50; in national accounts 69, 115, 117–18; need for changes in current patterns 324; non-monetary 119–20, 121, 129; reductions in sulphur emissions 294; representations of process 51–6; role of ecological capital **98**; social impacts 138

productivity: gains from changing environmental policies 166, 167, 173, 177, 318; labour 318, 322; lower levels due to environmental policy 174–5, 204; *see also* total factor productivity

Proops, J. 56, 123–4, 138, 140, 149–50, 203, 234

public policy 86–7, 111–12, 272–3, 326

Qatar 20

Radetzki, M. 183, 205

rainforests 38, 245

recession 297–9

recycling 41, 96, 101, 166, 202, 323; *see also* revenue-recycling

Rees, W. 89, 151

refineries: control of sulphur emissions 307–8

renewable resources 31, 33–4, 155, 280; depletion 70; harvesting rates 95, 96, 100; natural regeneration of 40; optimal depletion 39; sustainability standard 100

Repetto, R. 116, 125–6, 135, 138, 169, 260, 279

resource economics: concepts and techniques 23–5, 32

revenue-recycling 219–30, 227, 233–4, 234–6, 237, 263, 267, 279, 281

RICALIT: development of substitute for asbestos cement 172

Ricardo, D. 23, 24, 34, 35

rice: rise in price 21–2

Richels, R.G. 254, 261, 270, 271, 277, 278

risk: involved in matters of sustainability 92; judging unsustainability 94

rivers: increase in pollution 18–19, 191; sedimentation 21

Roberts, M. 306
Rosenzweig, C. 251
Rothman, D. 247
Rotmans, J. 255
Royal Society (RS) 6
Ruggles, R. 68
Ruijgrok, E. 169
rural areas: deterioration 196; poverty and dependency on resources 206
Russia: health hazards through industrialisation 14; *see also* Soviet Union
Rutherford, T.F. 269

Sachs, W. 90
Sadik, N. 159
safe minimum standards approach (SMS) 39, 92–4, 97
Salinas de Gortari, Carlos 193
salt marshes: pollution 18
Sandbrook, R. 48, 49
Sandnes, H. 299
Saudi Arabia 20
Schäfer, D. 139
Schelling, T. 218–19, 244, 246, 277–8
Schmidheiny, S. 5, 170, 171, 172
Schweinfest, S. 116, 124–5, 128
Scott, M. 274–5
sea-level: rise of 9–10, 244, 250
Second Sulphur Protocol (SSP) 4, 97, 280, 302, 308–9, **308**, 314, 320
sedimentation: increases 21
Selden, T.: research on EKC with Holtz-Eakin (HES) 183, 187–90, 194; research on EKC with Song (SS) 186, 187, 192, 193, 194–5, 208
self-interest: in concern about unsustainability 82
Sen, A. 43
Serageldin, I. 52, 81
services: industry 183; *see also* environmental services; goods and services
sewage: pollution 13, 18–19
Shadbegian, R. 204
Shafik, N. 191, 193, 201, 207; research on EKC with Bandyopadhyay (SB) 182, 186–7, 190, 191, 192–3, 206
Shearer, W. 81

Simon, J. 179
Sips, H. 90
Slade, M. 33, 35–6
Smith, S. 28, 220
Smith, V.K 32, 52
Smith, V.L. 39
smoking: and human behaviour 318
social cohesion: sustainability 104, 106
social disruption and disintegration 44, 70, 324
social injustice: and poverty 74
social institutions 106, 108
social/organisational capital 52, 55, 105, 106; failure of national accounts to assess 120
social perspectives: choices related to energy efficiency 272–3, **272**; consumer preferences 318; economic growth 43–4; implications of unsustainability 31, 70; question of sustainability 70–1, 73–5, 104, 106, 326
social rate of time preference (SRTP) 255
social welfare 44, 106, 108; *see also* human welfare
societies: and sustainability 81, 104; worldviews 72
soils: acidification 11–12, 17, 299; damage in OECD countries 15, 168; erosion and depletion 17, 70, 125; limiting emissions 96; pollution 44, 196; *see also* land
solar energy 43, 99, 320
solar power and technologies 281, 320, 322
solar radiation 31, 260
Solórzano, R. 116, 125
Solow, A. 10, 245
Solow, J. 273–4
Solow, R. 51
Song, D.: research on EKC with Selden 186, 187, 192, 193, 194–5, 208
South Atlantic: squid fishery 39
South Commission report 158
Soviet Union (former): destruction of original forests 16; environmental damage 168; natural gas reserves 20; subsidies for coal production 168; sulphur emissions 13; *see also* Russia

space: as aspect of environmental capital 56; difficulty of valuing as a service 122

Spain: erosion and land degradation 17

spatial competition 84, 86, 94, 98, 104

species biodiversity 95–6, 97

species extinction **7**, 15–16, 38–9, 70; climate change as cause 21, 244; deforestation as cause 21; unsustainability effect of spatial competition 104

spiritual welfare 106, 108

SPM (suspended particulate matter): EKC studies 194–5; WHO standards 14

squid fishing: South Atlantic 39

Sri Lanka: subsidies for nitrogen fertiliser 168

Stahmer, C. 124, 139, 140–1

Stanford University: Energy Modeling Forum (EMF) 232, 234, 262–3, 278, 280

State of the World (Worldwatch Institute) reports 6, 8

Steer, A. 52, 255

Stern, D. 194, 201, 208, 210

Stiglitz, J. 229

Stockholm Environment Institute/Greenpeace (SEI/G): projection for energy transition 320

subsidies: removing from energy production 168, 280, 307, 313, 314

substitution possibilities 145, 155, 205, 279; for asbestos cement 172; for CFCs 171; fuels and power generation 145, 155, 261, 303, 311, 312, 314, 315, 320; and limits to growth 41; of natural capital 78; photovoltaics 89–90; for polluting practices **167**; technical advance 101; technique effect 202–3, 204

sulphur deposition: critical loads for Europe 314; damage to European forests 12; USSR and Eastern European countries 13

sulphur dioxide emissions 13, 15, 283; abatement 12, 196, 280, 285–7, 294–9, **295–6**, 300, 303, 307–15, 320–1; abatement technologies 303–4; controlling 4, 97, 204, 283, 302, 307–9, **307**, **308**; costs of abatement 283, 300,

301, 302–7, **304**, 310–13; damages caused by 299–300; and deforestation 208; domestic use 285, 288, 302; EKC studies 185–7, 194–5, 208, 210; estimates of damage 283; and GDP growth 201, **202**; legislation 302; monitoring 299; OCF model 322–3; regulatory limits on electricity supply industry 283, 309–13, **309**; secondary benefits from reduction 280; and sectoral value-added 285, 287–99, **290–3**, **295–6**, **298**, 313; taxes on emissions 237; in the UK 14, 245, 283–5, **284**, **285**, 287–99, 307–13

surrogate markets: for environmental functions 29, 134

Sussex University: Science Policy Research Unit 41

sustainability: approach to climate change 279–82; approach to environmental valuation 242; boundaries 86–92; commitments to 84, 116; concepts 64, 69, 106–7; conditions for compatibility with GDP growth 78, 155, 165–6, 323; consideration by NAMEA matrix 144–5, 152; costs 92, 144; definitions and determinants 70–2; economic dimension 75–8, 79–80, 82, 104, 105–6; environmental dimension 104, 106; and environmental policy 2, 50, 94, 111–12, 163, **164**, 177–8, 318–19; ethical dimension 70, 71, 72–3, 81–2, 104, 106; as framework for consideration of environmental costs 31, 165; human ways of life 79–80; incommensurability 108; indicators 104–12, **107**, 112, 144; as maintenance of environmental functions 79–80, 104–5; non-renewable resources 2, 100, 101, 102–3; principles 92–7, 104–5, 111, **111**, 112, 300; qualitative and quantitative constraints 98–103; relationship with democracy 73; relationship with economic growth 1–3, 4–5, 22, 23, 39, 48, 79–80, 106, 153, 160, 162, 178–9, 201, 210, 283, 314, 316–26; safe minimum standards approach 92–4, 97; social dimension 71, 73–5, 104, 106, 326; spatial constraints 104; standards 27, 86, 98–105, 111–12, 137, 142–3, 144; strong 76–7, 78, 101, 103, 113, 145–6; and sulphur emissions in the UK 283–315; targets 112; and trade flows 150; transformations required 324–6; types and their interactions 71–2, **71**, 76–7; UK government avoidance of setting indicators 112; weak 76, 77, 78, 103, 127, 150

Sustainability Gap 3; estimating 86, 137, 143–7, **145**, 152

sustainable development 22, 72; aspiration for 45–50, 316; commitments to producing national strategies 116; concepts and techniques 2, 23, 43, 48–50, 61, 64; developing countries 323; incompatibility of EKC relationships with 184, 211; interaction between biological, economic and social systems 48–9, 50; and 'limits to growth' debate 40–50, 325, 326; and new technologies for power generation 314–15; relationship with GNP growth 61–2

Sweden: acidification of lakes 12; adoption of NAMEA 144; introduction of environmental taxes 237, 239–40, 268

Switzerland: benefits of first-mover advantages 173; costs of reducing sulphur dioxide levels in 1980 306; model of effects of carbon tax 229–30

System of National Accounts (SNA) 128–9, 132, 138

Tardos, A. 52, 135

tax-plus-rebate (TPR) 219–20, 223

taxation: distortionary system 325; interdependency effects 225, 226, 227–8; and investment 275; *see also* environmental taxation

technological progress: as compensation for natural resource loss 80; costs for sulphur abatement 303; danger of inhibiting 326; efficiency-increasing 95, 319; and increasing price of resources 35–6; and limits to growth 41, 47; necessary for climate stabilisation 281–2; necessary for power generation 314–15, 322; physical constraints 43; theories 24–5; towards environmental sustainability 101–2, 155, 318, 324–5, 326

technologies: for avoiding environmental problems 96, 144, 159, 168, 173; backdrop 280, 281; and carbon abatement 276; non-fossil 274; for pollution control 176, 261; productive 157; for reducing sulphur intensity 287, 303–4

teleological perspectives: goals of life 81

temperatures: rise in 9–10, 245

Thailand: deforestation 16

thermodynamics: laws of 43, 56, 57, 58, 320

Third World: pollution in rapidly industrialising countries 13, 14; population growth 159

30 per cent Club 314

3M Corporation 171

throughput: economic limiting by quotas 45; growth of 50, 56–7; and sustainability 112, 154, 166

Tietenberg, T. 174–5, 177

Tinbergen, J. 47, 123, 140, 179

Tobin, J. 51–2, 66–7

Tol, R.S.J. 247

Tomer, J. 55

total economic value (TEV): of environmental systems 28, 93

total factor productivity 204, 275

Total Product 119

tourist industry: benefits of warmer climates 245; effect of environmental degradation through demand 207; and sacrifice of areas of natural beauty 44

toxic pollution 6, **7**, 13–15, 70; and depletion of fish 18–19; of freshwater 21; impossibility of assessing costs 31; OECD countries' success in reducing 195; study of relationship with GDP 192, 203

trade: effect of carbon tax on UK sectors 267–9, **267**; environmental impact 147–51; liberalization 183; material flows 150–1

trade-offs: between economic growth and environmental conservation 48, 173, 174–8, 316, 317
traffic: congestion **7**, 104; noise levels 85; in OECD countries 15; and urban air pollution 6, 44
transport: environmentally damaging policies 169; need for shift in consumer preferences 321, 325; policies to reduce emissions and noise 85
transport sectors: small increases in sulphur emissions 294; sulphur intensity of value-added 289
tropical diseases: increase due to greenhouse effect 245
tropical forests: deforestation 16, 208; and species 15–16; WTP valuations 30
Turner, R.K. 26, 28, 33–4, 53, 76–7, 95, 215

Ulph, A. 269–70, 277
uncertainties: calculating damage costs of climate change 247–9, 254; estimating damages caused by sulphur emissions 300; in matters of sustainability 90, 97, 325; species extinction 104; stabilisation of carbon dioxide emissions 277; valuing environmental functions 124, 249, 317
unemployment: effects 74; increase in UK 62; reduction through environmental taxation and wage subsidy 220–2, **221**, 225, 229, 230–1, 233, 240; structural nature of 71
United Arab Emirates 20
United Kingdom (UK): adoption of NAMEA 144; approach to environmental sustainability indicators 108, 110; carbon dioxide emissions 149–50, 203; decline of fish stocks 18; decline of welfare 62–3; depletion of North Sea oil and gas reserves 103; development over last thirty years **62**; endorsement of idea of environmental taxation 238–9; environment White paper 72; environmental impacts and GDP 202, **202**; Environmental Protection Expenditures (EPE) 139–40; Global Environmental Change research

programme (UKGER) 156; global environmental space calculations **91**; headline welfare indicators 69; models of introduction of carbon tax 236, 264–9, **265**, **267**, 269–70; Office of National Statistics 136; potential for increased energy efficiency 276; sectoral value-added and sulphur dioxide emissions 289–99, **290–3**, **295–6**, 313; study using net savings rule 127, 150; sulphur emissions and reductions 14, 245, 283–5, **284**, **285**, 287–99, 302, 306, 307–15, 320–1; targets for reducing carbon dioxide emissions 112, 178, 271; valuation of statistical lives 256–7
United Nations: population projections 159; recommendation for integrated environmental economic accounting 151; suggested revision of SNA 129; *see also* Intergovernmental Panel on Climate Change (IPCC)
United Nations Conference on Environment and Development (UNCED) (Rio de Janeiro) 5, 40, 84, 116, 159, 325; **Agenda 21** 73, 97; Climate Change Convention 190
United Nations Conference on the Environment (Stockholm, 1972) 5, 40
United Nations Development Programme (UNDP) 8, 64, 194; Human Development Index (HDI) 66
United Nations Economic Commission for Europe 12, 302
United Nations Environment Programme (UNEP) 8; GEMS data on emissions 193
United Nations Statistical Division (UNSD) 116, 124, 128–9, 134, 135, 139, 140–1
United States of America (USA): benefits of first-mover advantages 173; clean-up costs 177–8; costs of conforming to environmental regulations 172–3; costs of reducing carbon dioxide emissions 271, 273, 278, 279–81; Council of Economic Advisers (CEA) 277; decline of fish stocks 18; effects of carbon tax on economy 232, 235–6, 262–3, **262**,

279–80; effects of environmental regulations 175; EKC study of sulphur dioxide emissions 187; Endangered Species Act 104; energy use 45, 46; environmental impacts and GDP **202**; environmental opposition to NAFTA 193; estimates of damage costs from global warming **248**; increase in fecal pollution of rivers 191; low tax rate on petrol 237; OEI time trends for minerals and renewable resources 37–8; sulphur emission limits on utilities 306; tax system 224; *see also* California

unsustainability 5–22, **7**, 31, 84, 122, 320; calculating by environmental space methodology 90; costs 82–4; evidence presented by EKC studies 211; human ways of life 70, 81–2, 90; level of global atmospheric emissions 323; optimal depletion 39; and optimality calculations 75; and problems from competition between environmental functions 94; processes 84–6, **85**, 99

urban areas: pollution 6, 244

use-efficiency 100, 101

USSR (Union of Soviet Socialist Republics) *see* Soviet Union

utilitarianism: as basis for economic valuation 257

utility: and four modes of experience 55; linked with production 2, 50; three-factor model of creation of **51**

UV-B radiation 11, 21

valuations of statistical life (VOSLs) 257

Van der Linde, C. 172

Van Tongeren, J. 116, 124, 125, 126–7, 128, 140–1

Vaze, P. 103, 136, 150

Venezuela 20

Victor, P.A. 77–8

Vietnam: effects of flooding of deltas 245

Vines, G. 39

Vos, H.B. 237

Wackernagel, M. 89, 151

Walter, J. 171

waste disposal: congestion **7**; necessary cuts in emissions 159; rate of 100;

reducing impacts to sustainability levels 143; spatial unsustainability 104

wastes: conversion of energy and material into 154; EKC studies 191–2; emissions 15, 98–9; export of 151; growth in 56–7, 196; municipal 191–2, 202, **202**; natural transformation into resources 99; in production process 53–4, 54–5; reduction programmes 170–1; standards for emissions 95; treatment of hazardous material 166, 177

water: clean-up policy 178; conservation by companies 171; depletion of resources **7**, 13, 17–18, 21, 31, 70, 244; difficulty of valuing as service 122; quality 46, 48, 105, 182, 191; reducing environmental impacts on 166; subsidies for irrigation 168

water cycle 58

water pollution 96; achievements in reduction programmes 171, 195; acidification 11–12, 21; by sewage 13, 191; coastal habitats 18–19; costs as measured by ISEW 126; EKC studies 191; health problems from 86; increase in EC countries 168, 196

wealth creation: contribution to human welfare 106; limiting inequality 45; modelling 51–6; and sustainability 70, 104; three-factor model **51**

Weizsäcker, E. von 28, 173–4

welfare: contribution of environmental functions 106–8, 122, 124, 137, 177, 316; damage from environmental degradation 128; decline in UK 62–3; and development 61–4; and economic growth 50, 56, 56–7, 64; failure of accounting systems to assess 124, 128; growth of in relation to economic growth 2, 40, 50; and human capital 55; measurement of 65–9, 104, 124; narrow perception of 317; relationship with GNP growth 57; role of ecological (or natural) capital 77, **98**; *see also* health; social welfare

well-being 72, 106

West Germany: decline of forests through acidification 12; defensive expenditures

study 140; environmental impacts and
GDP 202, **202**, 204; input-output study
of carbon dioxide emissions 203;
investment in FGD for sulphur
abatement 305, 306, 321; *see also*
Germany
Western Europe: projected rates of growth
in OCF scenario 323–4
Weterings, R. 90
wetlands: pollution and destruction of 18,
128, 244
Weyant, J.P. 218, 232, 234, 235–6, 272,
278
whaling: Antarctica 38–9
Whalley, J. 261
wheat: damage through acidification 12;
rise in prices 21–2
Wigle, R. 261, 275–6
Wilcoxen, P. 52, 175, 178, 218, 235,
237
wildlife: human enjoyment of 38
Williams, J. 270
willingness to pay (WTP): for
environmental goods 29, 252
Wilson, D.G. 219
Wilson, Edward O. 15
wind power 287
winter sports: losses due to greenhouse
effect 244
Winters, A. 1
Woodwell, G. 10
World Bank 19, 22, 52, 155, 159, 166,

168, 170, 194; classification of
environmental themes 109–10, **110**; on
effects of pollution 5–6, 13–14; on
gravity of the environmental situation
48; optimism about environmental
policy and economic growth 178–9,
208
World Biosphere Reserves 97
World Commission on Environment and
Development (WCED) *see* Brundtland
Report
World Conservation Union 16
World Energy Council 20
World Health Organisation (WHO) 14,
193
World Resources Institute (WRI):
classification of environmental functions
109, 110, **110**; on environmental
damage 5, 12, 13, 14, 15, 16, 16–17,
19, 21, 125–6, 256; *World Resources*
reports 8, 48
Worldwatch Institute: *State of the World*
reports 6, 8

Yamaji, K. 236
Yanigisawa, Y. 272
Yeats, A. 203
Yohe, G. 261
Young, M.D. 146
Yun, K.-Y. 224, 235

Zimbabwe: studies 116, 125, 127